Your Browser

You'll probably be using Internet Explorer (shown here) or Netscape Navigator. Both work similarly.

1. Both Explorer and Netscape have shortcut menus, which contain a range of useful commands that pop up when you click your right mouse button.

2. Some pictures are also links. Point to a picture; if the mouse pointer changes to a small hand, it's a link. Click it, and you go to some related information.

3. Text links are generally underlined and colored.

4. Watch the status bar for information about document transfers, links you are pointing at, and menu commands you are about to select.

5. This icon is animated; as long as the browser is transferring data, the animation continues.

6. The Home (or Start Page) button takes you to the page that appears when you open your browser. (You can set the home page to be any page you want—one you created, a search site, or your favorite Web site—using the browser's Preferences or Options dialog box. See Chapter 11.)

7. The Back and Forward buttons move you through the "history" list that contains the names of the Web pages you've seen so far.

8. Stop cancels the current transfer (in case it's taking too long).

9. Reload (or Refresh) grabs from the Web a new copy of the document you're viewing. (Do this to update the information on your screen.)

10. Type a URL (a Web address) and press Enter to go to that page.

11. Most browsers have some kind of bookmark system (in Explorer, it's known as the Favorites). You can mark your favorite Web pages and go back to them by selecting them from a menu.

12. Use these buttons to perform such common tasks as increasing document font size, cutting, copying, and pasting.

Your Web Browser Does Other Things

You can type the following URLs into the Address or Location bar at the top of the Web browser and press Enter.

- Type gopher://*address* to start a Gopher session (see Chapter 14).
- Type ftp://*address* to start an FTP session (see Chapter 12).
- Type news:*newsgroup.name* to open a newsgroup (see Chapters 17 and 18).
- Type telnet://*address* to open your Telnet program (see Chapter 15).
- Type mailto:*e-mail.address* to send e-mail (see Chapter 22).

Important Web Addresses

There are many things to search for on the Internet. The following sections tell you how to locate some important addresses that will help you find what you're looking for.

Searching for Files

- To use Archie (to search for a file) go to http://web.nexor.co.uk/archie.html.
- Find a list of FTP sites at http://hoohoo.ncsa.uiuc.edu/ftp/.

Searching for People

- To search for another Internet user in the Four11 directory, go to http://www.Four11.com/.
- To find more Internet user directories, go to http://www.yahoo.com/ and look in the Reference:White Pages category.
- To find a finger gateway, go to http://www.yahoo.com/Computers_and_Internet/Internet/World_Wide_Web/Gateways/Finger_Gateways/.

Searching for Programs on Computers All Over the World

- To find the HYTELNET directory of Telnet sites, go to http://library.usask.ca/hytelnet/.

Searching for Other Internet Resources

- To find a WAIS site, go to http://wais.wais.com/newhomepages/wais-dbs.html.
- To find a list of Gopher sites, go to gopher://gopher.micro.umn.edu/11/Other%20Gopher%20and%20Information%20Servers.

Searching for Web Pages

- To search the World Wide Web, try http://www.yahoo.com, http://www.jumpcity.com/ or http://www.mcp.com/authors/pkent/chapt25.htm (which lists a variety of search sites).

E-Mail Addresses for Online Services

When you're sending e-mail over the Internet to someone who has an online service, add the following host names to the online service user ID:

America Online	@aol.com
CompuServe	@compuserve.com (replace the comma in the user ID with a period)
GEnie	@genie.geis.com.
MCImail	@mcimail.com
The Microsoft Network	@msn.com
Prodigy	@prodigy.com

The Complete IDIOT'S GUIDE TO the Internet with Windows 95

by Peter Kent

A Division of Macmillan Computer Publishing
201 W. 103rd Street, Indianapolis, IN 46290

To my wife and kids, who complain that I spend more time with my computer than with them. Sorry, just one more book and then I'll slow down.

©1995 Que® Corporation

All rights reserved. No part of this book shall be reproduced, stored in a retrieval system, or transmitted by any means, electronic, mechanical, photocopying, recording, or otherwise, without written permission from the publisher. No patent liability is assumed with respect to the use of the information contained herein. While every precaution has been taken in the preparation of this book, the publisher and author assume no responsibility for errors or omissions. Neither is any liability assumed for damages resulting from the use of the information contained herein. For information, address Que Corporation, 201 W. 103rd Street, Indianapolis, IN 46290. You can reach Que's direct sales line by calling 1-800-428-5331.

International Standard Book Number: 0-7897-0629-6

Library of Congress Catalog Card Number: 95-72553

97 96 95   8 7 6 5 4 3 2 1

Interpretation of the printing code: the rightmost double-digit number is the year of the book's first printing; the rightmost single-digit number is the number of the book's printing. For example, a printing code of 95-1 shows that this copy of the book was printed during the first printing of the book in 1995.

Screen reproductions in this book were created by means of the program Collage Plus from Inner Media, Inc., Hollis, NH.

Printed in the United States of America

Publisher
Roland Elgey

Vice President and Publisher
Marie Butler-Knight

Editorial Services Director
Elizabeth Keaffaber

Publishing Manager
Barry Pruett

Managing Editor
Michael Cunningham

Acquisitions Coordinator
Martha O'Sullivan

Development Editor
Lori Cates

Technical Editor
Martin Wyatt

Production Editor
Audra Gable

Copy Editors
Rebecca Mayfield
San Dee Phillips

Cover Designers
Dan Armstrong
Barbara Kordesh

Book Designer
Kim Scott

Cartoonist
Judd Winick

Indexer
Ginny Bess

Production Team
Jason Carr, Lisa Daugherty, Bryan Flores, Trey Frank, Amy Gornik,
Damon Jordan, Daryl Kessler, Bob LaRoche, Stephanie Layton, Michelle Lee

Contents at a Glance

Part 1: Untangling the Wires and Getting It Running   **1**

  1 Top Ten Things You Need to Know   3
A Top 10 list of the most important Internet facts.

  2 What Is This Thing Called the Internet?   7
An overview of what the Internet is—and isn't.

  3 So Many Ways to Connect   17
The pros and cons of each type of connection.

  4 If You Have to Pay: Picking a Provider   27
Value-shopping for Internet service providers.

  5 Let's Get Physical: What You Need to Get Started   37
Picking your computer, modem, software, and account name/password.

  6 Connecting to the Internet: The Easy Way   47
Using Windows 95 and The Microsoft Network to get connected to the Internet.

  7 The Jumpstart Kit: Connecting to Other Service Providers   61
Using Microsoft tools to set up your connection through an independent service provider.

  8 Internet the Hard Way: Installing from Scratch   75
Getting an independent connection with no help from Microsoft.

Part 2: Working on the Web   **93**

  9 Think Global: The World Wide Web   95
Find out what all the buzz is about.

 10 Let's Surf!: Traveling the World Wide Web   105
Using Microsoft's Internet Explorer browser to see what's out there.

 11 The Web in High Gear   121
Find exactly what you want and learn what to do with it when you get it.

Part 3: Boldly Going Around the Internet   **135**

 12 Grabbing the Goodies—Downloading Files with FTP   137
Finding files and snagging them.

 13 Archie the File Searcher   153
Finding files with Archie (the program, not the cartoon character).

 14 Digging Through the Internet with Gopher   165
Another way to find files on the Internet.

15	Telnet: Inviting Yourself onto Other Systems *See what programs are available on computers throughout the world.*	177
16	Finding Your WAIS Around *Do some heavy-duty research.*	189
17	Newsgroups: The Source of All Wisdom *Newsgroups introduced and briefly explained.*	203
18	Getting Your News *Reading the messages people post to the newsgroups.*	213
19	Yet More Discussion Groups—Mailing Lists *Sign up to have the discussions sent straight to your computer through e-mail.*	233

Part 4: E-Mail Made Easy — **245**

20	Please Mr. Postman: An Intro to E-Mail *A basic primer for sending basic messages.*	247
21	Using Microsoft Exchange *Set up Windows 95's mail program on your computer.*	259
22	Working with E-Mail *Using Microsoft Exchange to send, receive, and organize your messages.*	273
23	Return to Sender, Address Unknown *What to do when your mail comes back, or when you don't know how to reach the person you want to send it to.*	287
A	Creating a Login Script *The techie details, in case your service provider doesn't do this for you.*	299
	Speak Like a Geek: The Complete Archive *A handy compilation of all those semi-useful Internet terms.*	309
	Index	325

Contents

Part 1: Untangling the Wires and Getting It Running   1

1 Top Ten Things You Need to Know   3

    1. Getting onto the Internet: Cheap or Expensive 3
    2. The Four Types of Internet Connections 4
    3. The World Wide Web: Multimedia Internet 4
    4. FTP: The Internet's File Libraries 4
    5. Archie: The Search for Computer Files Is On 4
    6. Gopher: The Great Menu System 4
    7. Telnet: Log On to Other Computers 5
    8. WAIS: Search for Information 5
    9. Newsgroups and Mailing Lists: The Places to
       Meet People Online 5
    10. E-Mail: Free International Communications! 5

2 What Is This Thing Called the Internet?   7

Let's Start with the Basics 8
But That's Not the Internet! 9
It's Like the Phone System… 10
So What's the Catch? 10
    "Sorry, It's Not Our Problem" 12
Who Owns the Internet? 13
    Nobody Owns the Internet… 13
    …And That's the Problem 14
What's in It for YOU? 15
The Least You Need to Know 16

3 So Many Ways to Connect   17

Types of Connections 18
    Permanent Connections 18
    Dial-In Direct Connections 19
    Dial-In Terminal Connections 21
    Mail Connections 21
    What Sort of Connection Do You Have? 22

The Complete Idiot's Guide to the Internet with Windows 95

Let Someone Else Pay	22
Find a Free-Net	23
More Freebies	25
The Least You Need to Know	25

4 If You Have to Pay: Picking a Provider — 27

Where Do I Find Service Providers?	27
What About The Microsoft Network?	28
A Word About Money	29
I Want Another Service Provider!	30
Explaining What You Want	32
The Least You Need to Know	36

5 Let's Get Physical: What You Need to Get Started — 37

Your Computer	38
Your Modem	38
Help! Which Modem Should I Buy?	39
ISDN Modems?	40
I Have a Name	41
The Password Is…	42
Passwords: Pick a Good One	42
Your Domain Name	43
What Are These Domains?	44
Finally, the Software	45
The Least You Need to Know	46

6 Connecting to the Internet: The Easy Way — 47

The Many Faces of Internet Access Through Windows 95	47
If You Go Through The Microsoft Network…	48
If You'd Rather Not…	48
One-Click Internet Access!	49
Bought a New Computer?	49
Joining MSN Without the Microsoft Plus! Software	49
Do You Have the MSN Software?	50
Joining MSN	50
Getting the Internet Software	54
The Internet-Access Numbers	56

Joining MSN with the Microsoft Plus! Software 57
Problems? Surely Not! 57
    Going Back to MSN 57
    Strange Things Are Happening 59
The Least You Need to Know 60

7 The Jumpstart Kit: Connecting to Other Service Providers   61

PPP or SLIP? 62
Gathering Information 63
The Easy Way—Using Microsoft Plus! 65
    Does It Work? 68
    You're Connected, But Is It Working? 69
Still Not Working? 70
I Have to Use SLIP 72
The Least You Need to Know 74

8 Internet the Hard Way: Installing from Scratch   75

Downloading from the Internet and Online Services 76
Bare Bones—Starting from Scratch 77
    Installing Dial-Up Networking 77
    Installing the Networking Components 78
    Setting Up the Connection 80
    Setting Up the Properties 82
    Dial-Up Scripting? 85
Connecting to Your Service Provider 85
Getting the Rest of the Stuff 87
    Some FTP Tips 91
    What Now? 91
The Least You Need to Know 92

Part 2: Working on the Web   93

9 Think Global: The World Wide Web   95

What's the Web? 96
Okay, You've Sold Me—Where's the Browser? 96
    Grabbing the Program 97
    Netscape Envy? 101

The Complete Idiot's Guide to the Internet with Windows 95

A Bit More Web Background 102
   Where Is All This? The Web Server 103
   It's More Than Text 103
The Least You Need to Know 104

10 Let's Surf!: Traveling the World Wide Web   105

Start Your Engines… 106
   Using the Web When You're Not Connected 106
We're Home! 106
Surfing the Web 108
   Moving Around on the Web 109
   Take Me Back 109
   Searching Long Documents 110
   It's Faster When You Come Back 110
   Confused by the Cache? Use Refresh 112
   The Shortest Route Is a Straight Line… 113
Web Pages on Your Hard Disk 114
   Now, Where Was I? Using the History List 114
   Your Very Own Web Directory 116
   Favorites Subcategories 118
The Least You Need to Know 119

11 The Web in High Gear   121

Where's What I Want? 121
I've Gotta Keep It! But How? 123
   Copying the Background 123
   Viewing the Source 124
   Downloading Files from the Web 125
   Downloading .EXE Files 125
   Don't Use Open File! 125
Playing Multimedia Files 126
Adding Viewers 128
   Viewers, Anyone? 128
   I Have the Viewer—Now What? 129
Customizing Internet Explorer 131
   Designating a Home Page 133
   This Could Look Different… 133
There's a Lot More to Learn 134
The Least You Need to Know 134

Part 3: Boldly Going Around the Internet — 135

12 Grabbing the Goodies—Downloading Files with FTP — 137

The Different Flavors of FTP 139
Hitting the FTP Trail 139
   What Is All This? 141
Finding That Pot o' Gold 143
   Look for Clues 143
   Get the File 144
Compressed (Squeezed) Files 145
   EXE's Okay, But What About ZIP? 146
Having Trouble Connecting to a Site? 146
   Try WS_FTP 147
It's Alive! Viruses and Other Nasties 150
   Tips for "Safe Computing" 151
Where to Now? 151
The Least You Need to Know 152

13 Archie the File Searcher — 153

More Client/Server Stuff 154
Getting to Archie 154
Archie on the Web 155
   Searching Archie 155
   Archie's Options 157
      What Are the Search Types? 158
Getting and Using WS_Archie 159
Mail-Order Archie 161
   "Whatis" the Descriptive Index? 162
   More E-Mail Commands 163
The Least You Need to Know 163

14 Digging Through the Internet with Gopher — 165

Let There Be Gopher 166
Enough History. What's Gopher? 167
Let's Gopher It! 167
Archie's Friends: Veronica and Jughead 170
   Jughead 170
      The Boolean Operators 172
      Pick Any Wild Card—As Long As It's * 172

xi

More Boolean Stuff 172
Special Commands—Maybe 173
Veronica 174
Veronica Search Details 174
The Least You Need to Know 176

15 Telnet: Inviting Yourself onto Other Systems — 177

Step 1: Find a Telnet Program 178
Let's Go Telnetting! 179
The HYTELNET Directory: Finding What's
Out There 179
We're In. Now What? 181
Working in a Telnet Session 182
Let's Take a Look at a Site 183
Keeping a Record 185
Starting Telnet Directly 185
Waving Good-Bye to the Telnet Site 186
IBM Mainframe Telnet Sites 186
Telnetting to Your Service Provider 187
The Least You Need to Know 188

16 Finding Your WAIS Around — 189

What Is WAIS? 190
The Different Ways to Run WAIS 190
Web WAIS 191
Pick Your Keywords 192
Let Your Eyes Do the Searching 194
Web—Gopher—WAIS 195
WAIS for Windows—On Your Own Computer 196
Into the Past—Telnetting to a UNIX-Based Client 198
A Good Server Is Hard to Find 199
Reading and Saving the Info 201
The Least You Need to Know 202

17 Newsgroups: The Source of All Wisdom — 203

So What's Out There... 204
Can I Get to It? 205
Gimme a List! 206
Where Do They Come From? 207

Contents

What's in a Name?	207
Reaching the Next Level	209
I'm Ready. How Can I Read These?	210
A Quick Word on Setup	211
The Least You Need to Know	212

18 Getting Your News — 213

Taking a Look	216
A Different Point of View: List and File Views	217
The Messages Are Gone!	217
Marking Your Messages	218
Enlightenment: Reading Your Messages	219
Moving Among the Messages	221
Saving and Printing	221
Your Turn: Sending and Responding	222
Working with the New Message Window	222
What's This Gibberish? ROT13	223
Pictures from Words	224
Practical UUDECODING	226
MSN Is Not Alone…	226
WinVN	227
Free Agent: Partly Free	227
Newsgroups? Mais Oui!	229
A Word of Warning	230
The Least You Need to Know	230

19 Yet More Discussion Groups—Mailing Lists — 233

What's a Mailing List?	234
The Types of Lists	235
Subscribing to Mailing Lists	235
Using a LISTSERV Group	236
The LISTSERV Address	239
Where's the List?	240
Let's Do It—Subscribing	240
Enough Already!—Unsubscribing	241
Getting Fancy with LISTSERV	241
Working with Mailing Lists	242
The Least You Need to Know	243

xiii

The Complete Idiot's Guide to the Internet with Windows 95

Part 4: E-Mail Made Easy — 245

20 Please Mr. Postman: An Intro to E-Mail — 247

Why Use E-Mail? 248
Two E-Mail Caveats 248
   None of That Fancy Stuff… 249
   …And They Can't See Your Face 249
It's Corny, But If It Works for You… 249
   Emoticons Galore 250
   Message Shorthand 252
Now, Where's That Address? 252
E-Mailing to and from CompuServe, AOL,
  MSN, and More 253
   Even More E-Mail Links 254
   And More! 256
Internet Etiquette 256
Which Program Will You Use to Send Mail? 257
The Least You Need to Know 258

21 Using Microsoft Exchange — 259

Setting Up Exchange 260
A Quick Word About Profiles 260
   So What Have I Got? 261
   The Connection Options 263
Getting Personal with Your Folders 265
Address Book Options 267
Taking a Look Inside Exchange 268
   The General Options 268
   The Read Options 270
   The Send Options 271
The Least You Need to Know 272

22 Working with E-Mail — 273

From Me to You—Sending a Message 274
   Now What Can I Write? 275
   Formatting Text 275
   Keeping a Copy of the Message 276
   Sending the Message 276
Sending Computer Files 277

The Microsoft Exchange Window 279
How Do I Get My Messages? 280
Using Remote Mail 280
Working with Messages 282
    Moving Between Messages 283
    There's a File in Here! 283
    Responding to Messages 284
More Things You Can Do 284
An Alternative: Eudora 285
The Least You Need to Know 286

23 Return to Sender, Address Unknown   287

What's Up? 288
    Who Didn't Get It? 288
    So What's the Problem? 289
    Who Ya Gonna Call? 290
The Internet Directory? There Isn't One 290
    Talk to the Postmaster 290
    Ask Someone Else 291
    Finger Him 291
    Register with Four11! 293
    Search for Newsgroup Users 294
    Try Yahoo, and Use the White Pages 295
    Use Netfind 296
The Least You Need to Know 298

Appendix: Creating a Login Script   299

Creating a Login Script 299
    Watching a Login Procedure 300
    You're a Programmer! (Writing the Script) 302
    Assigning the Script File 304
    Let's See If It Works: Testing the Script 305

Speak Like a Geek: The Complete Archive   309

Index   325

Introduction

What have you gotten yourself into? Or what are you about to get yourself into? The Internet is a fantastic service. It provides an e-mail link to almost 30 million people, and that number is rising. It lets you connect to government computers and find information about the most recent research or legislation. It lets you connect to university computers and search thousands of different databases. It lets you "meet" people who can help you with just about anything—from planning a trip to Papua, New Guinea, to designing a scanning tunneling microscope. It lets you "surf" the World Wide Web, where you'll find everyone from the Rolling Stones to Federal Express. The Internet is the electronic highway at work. Forget the popular magazines' projections for the future—the Internet is here today.

When *The Complete Idiot's Guide to the Internet* was published in 1994, I told readers how difficult it was to work with the Internet. I said that if you wanted to create a system that would make its users think they were complete idiots, you couldn't do much better than create the Internet.

But the Internet has changed dramatically since I wrote those words. True, it has a mess of different ways to connect; strange acronyms such as PPP, SLIP, CSLIP, UUCP, and POP; and many different ways to find and get data. To the average user, it's still a tangle of confusion, not something you'll "just pick up." So what has changed? The software you use to access it has improved greatly in the last couple of years.

At the beginning of 1994, the majority of Internet users were working from the *command line* (they faced a black screen on which they typed cryptic commands). They even had to learn a little UNIX to get around properly. Now, however, there's a plethora of new software that makes the Internet much, much easier to use. Most importantly (from this book's point of view), Windows 95 comes with software that lets you connect to the Internet.

Welcome to The Complete Idiot's Guide to the Internet with Windows 95

In *The Complete Idiot's Guide to the Internet with Windows 95*, I explain how to use the software you get with Windows 95 to connect to the Internet. In addition, I'll teach you how to use the software that you get if you become a member of The Microsoft Network (MSN is Microsoft's new online service), and the software from the Microsoft Plus! add-on pack—though you can get by without these things.

I'll explain why you may want to use MSN—and why you may not. If you decide not to, you'll need to read more of the book to find information about how to find another service provider and how to connect Windows 95 to the Internet. Windows 95 doesn't come with every tool you'll need, though, so I'll also explain how to get more software directly from the Internet (including programs that will help you use such systems as WAIS, FTP, e-mail, and so on). I'll explain how to set up a first-class Internet system.

What about the title of this book: *The Complete Idiot's Guide*? Well, I assume that you're no idiot on your own territory. You know how to do your job well, and you know how to do everything you need to do to get by—even thrive—in modern life. But there's one thing you don't know: how to use the Internet.

I also assume that you want to get onto the Internet and get some work done. Perhaps you just want to send e-mail or do a little research on that book you've been planning for years, or perhaps you'd like to find a few "pen pals" on the other side of the world or talk to people who share your passion for orchids. Basically, I take it for granted that you don't really want to know how to use the Internet for its own sake. You want to "get the job done," not become an Internet expert. You don't care about how the Internet Protocol works, for instance (or what it is, for that matter), as long as it gets your messages where they are supposed to go.

Sure, you could learn all there is to know about the Internet, given the time and interest. But do you have enough time? Are you really interested? The answer to at least one of those questions (if not both) is probably No. You don't want to know every geeky little detail about how the Internet works, but you do need to know practical stuff such as:

➤ How to connect your computer to the Internet

➤ How to navigate the World Wide Web

➤ How to transfer files from a computer on the Internet back to your computer

> How to connect to newsgroups and join in discussions on just about any subject you can imagine

> How to do research in government and university computers

> How to address an e-mail message

> How to find e-mail addresses

I do expect a little bit of knowledge on your part, though. I assume you know at least a little about computers: you know what a keyboard is, what a monitor is, and that sort of thing. I also assume that you have Windows 95 installed on your PC and that you know the basics of how to use it: how to move between windows, how to use the Start menu, how to install new programs. If you want really basic beginner's information about using a PC, check out *The Complete Idiot's Guide to PCs* (Joe Kraynak, Que). You might also take a look at *The Complete Idiot's Guide to Windows 95* (Paul McFedries, Que).

How Do You Use This Book?

You don't have to read this book from cover to cover. If you want to find out about e-mail, go to the e-mail chapter; if you want to know how to use Gopher to search the Internet, go to the Gopher chapter. Each chapter is a self-contained unit that has the information you need to use one aspect of the Internet. If you need information that's covered elsewhere in the book, you'll find that I've included plenty of cross-references.

I use a couple of conventions in this book to make it easier to use. For example, when you need to type something, it will appear in bold:

>   Type **this**

Just type what it says. It's as simple as that. If I don't know exactly what you'll have to type—because you have to supply some of the information—I'll put the unknown information in italics. For instance:

>   Type **this** *file name*

I don't know the file name, so you'll have to supply it.

Also, I've used the term "Enter" throughout the book. Your keyboard may have a Return key instead.

Sometimes, I show you longer examples of what you'll see on the Internet. They appear in a special typeface, arranged to mimic what appears on your screen:

Introduction

```
Some of the lines will be in actual English.
Some of the lines will seem to be in a mutant dialect of English.
Some will even show something you type, which appears in bold.
```

Again, don't panic.

If you want to understand more about the subject you are learning, you'll find some background information in boxes. Because this information is in boxes, you can quickly skip over the information if you want to avoid the gory details. These special icons and boxes are used in this book to help you learn just what you need:

Technical Information Skip this background fodder (technical twaddle) unless you're truly interested.

Helpful Information Tips, warnings, cautions, shortcuts, definitions, and that sort of stuff. Don't miss this.

Acknowledgments

I would like to thank a number of people for helping me with this book. I'd like to thank Lori Cates for not complaining when I didn't deliver when I promised I would, and Marty Wyatt for checking the technical details. I'd also like to thank San Dee Phillips and Audra Gable for their editing, and everyone else at Que who sees to the myriad of details involved in moving a book from author to bookstore.

Trademarks

All terms mentioned in this book that are known to be trademarks have been appropriately capitalized. Que Corporation cannot attest to the accuracy of this information. Use of a term in this book should not be regarded as affecting the validity of any trademark or service mark.

Part 1
Untangling the Wires and Getting It Running

The chapters in this section explain what it takes to get started on the Internet. I describe the basics of the Internet, help you select the sort of account you need, and help you get the best price for that account (be warned: prices vary dramatically). I'll tell you what software and hardware you need to connect to the Internet, and how to get up and running. I'll explain the quickest and easiest way to connect Windows 95 to the Internet.

I'll also describe several other connection methods you can use, including one that's guaranteed to give your mouse-click finger a world-class workout. Whether you want to connect to The Microsoft Network, or shun the giants and go with a local service provider, this section of the book tells you all you need to know.

Chapter 1

Top Ten Things You Need to Know

First of all, don't panic! There's nothing difficult in this book. Working with the Internet itself is not difficult per se. You just need to you know a lot of things that you may not already know (such as the different ways to connect your computer to the online world, and a variety of strange acronyms—like FTP, WWW, and PPP). Stick with me, and I promise you'll get out alive.

The Internet has changed tremendously in the last two years. It's still not totally simple—there's a lot to learn. Now, however, with the right software, you have an attractive point-and-click environment in which to work. (A couple of years ago you'd get a UNIX command line and encouragement from your service provider—the company selling you access to the Internet—to sign up for a $200 training course.) Still, before you cruise the Internet with all the other cybergeeks, you've got a lot to learn. Well, you've come to the right place.

Don't try to learn everything at once; that will just give you a headache. For now, breeze through this list of important things you need to know. You'll learn more about each of them later.

1. Getting onto the Internet: Cheap or Expensive

There aren't any fixed prices for services in Internet-land. Providers can charge whatever they want and supply you with whatever services they want. As you might imagine, this leads to some fairly wide variations (in both quality and price) among providers. Prices to get connected range from absolutely free (which is rare) to very expensive, and the prices are not necessarily related to the level of service you receive. Spend some time looking around (see Chapters 3 and 4) before (and after) you choose a service provider.

2. The Four Types of Internet Connections

There are four basic types of Internet accounts: permanent, dial-in direct, dial-in terminal, and mail. To use the fancy software described in this book, you need one of the first two account types (you'll learn more about them in Chapter 3). You have the first type of account if your company or organization has a network connection to the Internet; you simply talk to your system administrator about getting hooked up. If you plan to dial into a service provider, check out Chapters 6 through 8 where I describe exactly how to set up the software.

3. The World Wide Web: Multimedia Internet

The World Wide Web is the current hot spot on the Internet. Mosaic, the first graphical Web "browser" (a program that lets you view Web documents), brought the Web to the masses but has all but disappeared since then. Now other browsers are bringing millions of new users onto the Web. In Chapters 9 through 11, I'll explain how to work on the Web, regardless of which browser you are using. Remember, though, you can get a free browser from Microsoft: Internet Explorer. I'll explain where to get it in Chapter 9.

4. FTP: The Internet's File Libraries

Use FTP to turn the Internet into your own personal computer-file library. Chapter 12 tells how to snag goodies from all over the world. Yes, that includes games.

5. Archie: The Search for Computer Files Is On

Oh, but how do you know where all these computer files are kept? You use a special utility called Archie to find files. With Archie, you can search for a file name (or part of a file name) and end up with a list of FTP sites that contain the file you need. You'll meet Archie in Chapter 13.

6. Gopher: The Great Menu System

Gopher (great name, huh?) was big before the World Wide Web came along and stole some of its thunder. It's still useful, though, as there are thousands of interesting Gopher sites around the world you can explore. Dig around in Chapter 14 for more details.

7. Telnet: Log On to Other Computers

Use Telnet to "get on to" other computer systems to view files and search databases. If you like the idea of reading files and using databases or games on computers on the other side of the world, Telnet's for you. How do you know which Telnet site contains what? Use HYTELNET to search through a list of Telnet sites for a subject that interests you. Chapter 15 explains the wonders of Telnet.

8. WAIS: Search for Information

WAIS provides a way for you to search hundreds of databases on a wide variety of subjects (archaeology, biology, geography, and plenty more). Although relatively few Internet users go near it, by the time you finish Chapter 16, you'll be able to work with WAIS using several different methods.

9. Newsgroups and Mailing Lists: The Places to Meet People Online

The newsgroups let you discuss any subject in the world with people from all over the world. They're similar to what some online services call BBSs or message boards. One person posts a message, another person posts a reply, and so on. You can read anyone else's messages, and even post your own. Your service provider will probably have at least 3,000 different groups for you to work with, and maybe as many as 12,000. Check them out in Chapters 17 and 18. Mailing lists, which are like newsgroups but use e-mail to share messages, provide thousands more discussion groups. Chapter 19 has all the details on those.

10. E-Mail: Free International Communications!

The world is yours with e-mail. E-mail is the most-used service on the Internet. It's convenient and it's easy—once you know how to use it. You can send messages to practically anyone who's connected to the Internet. Windows 95 comes with a built-in messaging system called Microsoft Exchange that can send and receive Internet e-mail. And if you don't like that program, you can try the freeware program Eudora. See Chapters 20 through 22 for more information. And in case you don't know the e-mail address of the person you want to send a message to, there are several directories you can use to find it. See Chapters 23 and 24 for details.

Chapter 2

What Is This Thing Called the Internet?

In This Chapter

- What is a BBS?
- Why the Internet isn't a BBS
- How the Internet began
- Who owns the Internet?
- Why the Internet can be so complicated
- The remarkable resources of the Internet

When I first started working with the Internet, I felt lost. The "documentation" I got from the company that provided my Internet account was a joke. It was badly organized and misleading, and it omitted lots of important stuff. Technical support wasn't much better: phone calls went unanswered, and the help I got wasn't always helpful. I'll bet there's a good chance you feel the same about your Internet account (if you have one).

I shouldn't lay all the blame on a single company, though. One of the problems with the Internet is that of responsibility: who is responsible for which part?

Part 1 ➤ *Untangling the Wires and Getting It Running*

The way in which the Internet was born and has grown has been haphazard, to say the least. It's not like a typical bulletin board system (BBS), where you know who is responsible for the entire system—the owner. With the Internet, it's not always clear who (if anyone) owns what, and who (if anyone) has responsibility for getting you going. In other words, you may be left to your own devices.

It doesn't have to be confusing, though. This book will help you cut through the crud and find the information you need to get to the fantastic resources available on the Internet. This chapter starts you out with an overview of what the Internet is, and how it has come together to become the world's largest network of computer users.

Let's Start with the Basics

Let's start right at the beginning: what is a bulletin board system (BBS), and what is a computer network? A *BBS* is a computer running special software that enables other computers to connect to it through telephone lines. (Actually, a BBS could be several connected computers, but the principle is the same.) A computer user installs a modem in his computer, connects the modem to the phone line, uses communications software to dial the BBS's telephone number, and voilà, he's "connected."

What Does Modem Mean?
The word *modem* is a combination of the words "modulate" and "demodulate." That's what the modem does with the digital signals from your computer when it converts them to the analog signals used by most telephone networks and then back to the digital signals used by computers.

What do you do once you're connected to a BBS? Well, you can read messages left by other BBS users, reply to those messages, leave your own messages, or copy files to and from the BBS. Or you may be able to use other available services. You can play an online game (chess or some kind of arcade game, for instance) with another BBS user; you can "chat" with another user, typing what you want to say and reading the other user's almost-instant response; you can search a database or view photographs and weather maps stored on another computer.

There are thousands of BBSs spread around the world. All it takes to start a BBS is a computer, a phone line, BBS software (which you can find easily and at a low cost), a modem, and the money to pay the electric bill.

You've probably heard the names of a number of the larger BBSs: CompuServe, Prodigy, GEnie, America Online, The Microsoft Network, and even Penthouse Online. These services often don't use the term BBS though. They call themselves online services or information systems, but the principle is the same. They are computers or groups of computers to which other computer users can connect to communicate with others, find computer files, play games, do research, and so on.

But That's Not the Internet!

The Internet is not a BBS. The *Internet* is a network of networks. A computer network is a group of computers that have been connected so they can communicate with each other. They can send messages to each other, and they can share information in the form of computer files. The Internet connects more than 18,000 of these networks, and more are being added all the time. On those networks are millions of computers, computer terminals, and users—several million computers and tens of millions of users according to some estimates. (Personally, I think the numbers have been exaggerated. While 30 million people may have access to a computer that's capable of linking to the Internet, a much smaller number are actually active Internet users.)

The number of computers connected to the Internet is growing extremely rapidly—by more than 1,000 computers a day. It's no wonder the president of ISOC (the Internet Society) recently suggested that the Internet could conceivably reach 1 billion people in the not-too-distant future.

But there's nothing astounding about computer networks per se. I have a small one in my home, connecting my work computer and my kids' "play" computer (which used to be my work computer until technology raced past). Likewise, many small companies have networks that connect anywhere from two or three computers to thousands of them. However, the Internet isn't just a network. It's a network of networks.

The Internet joins lots of different networks to produce the world's largest group of connected computers. Some of the networks are run by government bodies, some by universities, some by businesses, some by local community library systems, and some by schools. And the online services I mentioned (CompuServe, America Online, and so on) are connected, too. Although most of these networks are in the United States, many are overseas, in countries ranging from Australia to Zimbabwe.

As remarkable as all this may seem, if that's all the Internet was, I wouldn't be writing this book. Sure, the Internet might make it possible for you to communicate with all these people on all these computer networks through electronic "mail," but that wouldn't be enough for a book. What makes the Internet so special is the fact that many of the computers on the network are, in effect, BBSs.

Strictly speaking, most computers on the Internet are not set up as BBSs (though a BBS owner would probably complain about my use of terminology here). My point is that these computers enable you to log in and do things, such as grab files, read documents, or use databases (a number of Internet services allow you to grab things without even bothering to log in first). That means that when you connect to the Internet, you have the opportunity to connect to thousands of different systems. Those computers contain government archives, university databases, local-community computing resources, library catalogs, messages about any subject you can imagine, and millions of computer files containing photographs, documents, sound clips, video, and whatever else you can put into digital form.

Check This Out...

Logging In
When you log on or log in to a computer system, you tell the system who you are, and it decides if it wants to let you use its services. A log-on (or login) procedure usually entails providing some kind of account name and a secret password.

The Internet is more like a data highway than it is like a BBS. You dial up a system on the Internet or log on through an institution's terminal, and you're on the road. Then you have to navigate your way through the network to the "city" (computer) that has the data you need. When you dial up a service such as CompuServe, you are connected to a big room with a lot of computers. When you access the Internet, you might find yourself in a government computer in Washington D.C., a university's computer in Seattle, Washington, a community computer system in Elyria, Ohio, or perhaps even the Centre International de Rencontres Mathematiques in Marseilles, France.

It's Like the Phone System...

Perhaps the best way to describe the Internet is to say that it is like a phone system. A phone system has lots of different "switches" that are owned by lots of different companies and are all connected to each other. When someone in Denver tries to call someone in New York, he doesn't need to know how the call gets there (which states and cities the call passes through, for example). A network of telephone companies handles all that for him. These private companies decided among themselves how the mechanics—the electronics—of the process work, and the average caller doesn't care one whit how it's done—as long as his call gets through. The Internet works in much the same way, and just as there is no single telephone company, there is no single Internet company.

So What's the Catch?

The Internet's resources dwarf those of the online systems, but there is a catch. Although it is improving, the Internet is still relatively difficult to use.

By comparison, systems such as CompuServe, Prodigy, and America Online are very easy to use. This is important because they make money each time someone uses their services, and if the service is difficult to learn and use, people will log off and won't come back. So if you have a CompuServe account, for example, you can use a number of different programs called navigators to customize what you see on-screen (aka the *user interface*) and make it simpler for you to get around. Some of these programs are made by CompuServe's own programmers, and some are made by independent companies. If you have an account with America Online, you get an excellent easy-to-use interface to begin with. America Online managed to increase its subscribers from 300,000 to 3 million in a two-year period thanks to its great program.

Until recently, the Internet was very difficult to use. When I wrote *The Complete Idiot's Guide to the Internet*, most users had to work with a very clunky command-line interface and had to remember rather obscure, arcane commands. And even if they could find their way around okay, it was a rather ugly way to do so. A user working with a Macintosh or Windows computer (who was used to working with a colorful graphical user interface) probably felt like he had dropped back to the 1970s when he logged onto the Internet and found himself staring at a monochrome command-line UNIX interface like the one in the following figure.

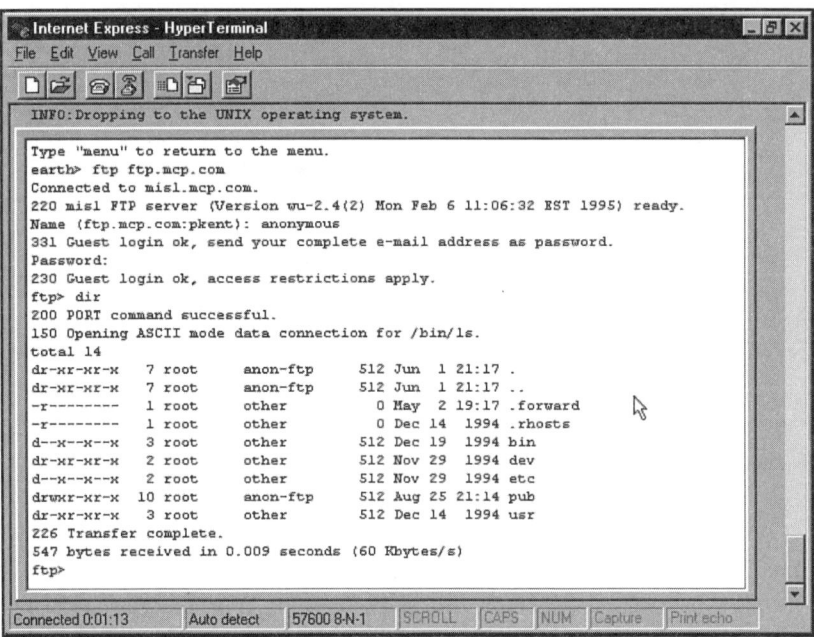

You can dig your way through the Internet with the command-line interface...

Although you can still use the command-line interface if you want, things have changed a lot over the last few years, and most users are now working with graphical user interface software. In a graphical user interface, the screen is filled with pictures and text that make it easy to figure out what you're doing (check out the next figure). In fact, that's why I

11

Part 1 ➤ *Untangling the Wires and Getting It Running*

wrote this book. It's an update to the original *Complete Idiot's Guide to the Internet*, and it's intended to show people how to use the Internet tools that come with Windows 95 to set up a first-rate Internet connection.

...or you can use a point-and-click graphical user interface.

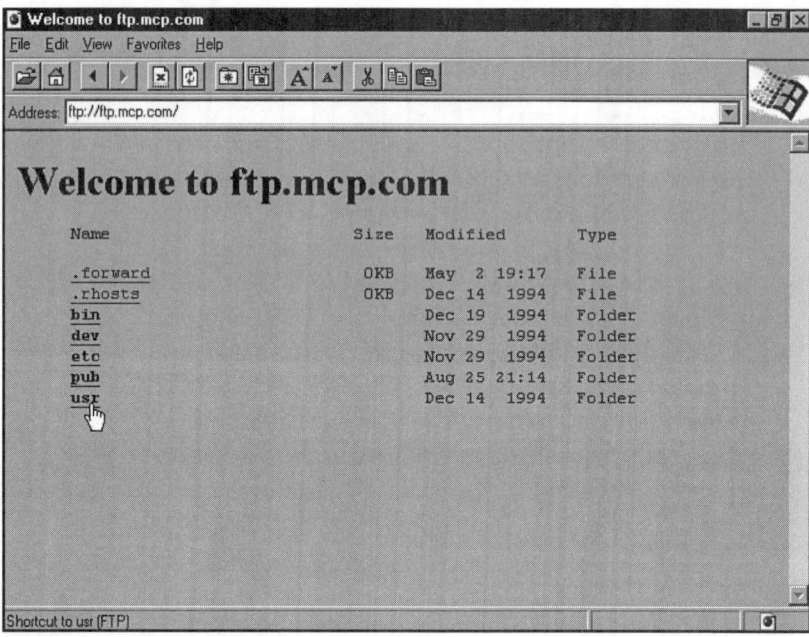

Gopher, Finger, Web...What?
Don't worry if all these names have you baffled. You'll learn how to use these Internet resources later in the book.

Despite the fact that you can now use a graphical user interface, problems still remain. It's often difficult to connect to the Internet (depending on how you try to do so), and once you connect, it's often difficult to find what you need. If you use America Online or CompuServe, for instance, you can get to 90 percent of what the service offers with just a few simple techniques. With the Internet, you have to understand a number of programs and services such as Telnet, FTP, the World Wide Web, WAIS, Gopher, Finger, and more. The Internet is still a vast system, and most users still have a lot to learn.

"Sorry, It's Not Our Problem"

Unfortunately, you may run into cases of "it's not our problem." While most service providers (organizations that can connect you to the Internet) claim to provide great technical support, many of them are small nonprofit organizations or underfunded start-up businesses that have trouble keeping up with the demand. And because the Internet is such an amorphous creature, these organizations can always claim that your problem lies in another area. For instance, if you are having trouble getting your Internet connection working, they may point you in the direction of your software manufacturer.

The Internet has grown so fast in the past year or two that some service providers are providing lousy service. Complaints that it's hard to get a connection and that calls and messages for technical support go unanswered are becoming more common.

Why is the Internet so difficult to use? Mainly it's because of the way the Internet was born, the way it has grown, and the way it is managed.

> **Noncommercial System?**
>
> Because the Internet was originally intended to be a noncommercial system, many service providers are nonprofit organizations. They are often understaffed and underfunded, and they don't have the incentive of the "profit motive." In recent years, the Internet has opened up to commercial service providers, and in general, the result has been easier-to-use software and better service.

Who Owns the Internet?

All BBSs are owned by someone. A company or individual buys a computer, puts it in a room somewhere, and then sells the general public time on the computer. (Or, in many cases, the company lets interested parties onto the BBS for free. Many computer companies have BBSs for their customers so the customers can contact technical support, find the latest program files for their systems, and so on.)

There are literally thousands of such BBSs, from the giants we named earlier to small systems owned and run by one person. If you take a look at a local computer newspaper, you'll see dozens of BBSs. Each one is designed for use by a certain type of person, from Star Trek fans to computer-game nuts to swingers. In each case, though, someone owns the BBS, whether it's H & R Block (who owns CompuServe) or Fred down the street (who owns The Wizard's Secret Games BBS).

Nobody Owns the Internet...

The Internet's not like a BBS in that respect. Nobody "owns" the Internet. As a comparison, consider who owns the nation's—or the world's—telephone network. Nobody does.

13

Sure, each component is owned by somebody, but the network as a whole is not owned by anyone; it's a system that hangs together through mutual interest. The world's telephone companies get together and decide the best way the "network" should function. They decide which country gets which country code, how to bill for international calls, and who pays for transoceanic cables, and they work out the technical details of how one country's lines connect to another. The Internet is very similar.

The origin of the Internet can be traced back to ARPAnet (the Advanced Research Projects Agency network), which was a Department of Defense computer system developed in the '60s. It's an oft-repeated myth that ARPAnet was set up to test methods of keeping computer networks alive under military attack. (Although I admit that I've done my share of repeating this myth, I've recently seen the light.) But Charles Herzfeld, director of ARPA in the 1960s, disputes this claim. Writing recently in *Scientific American*, he stated that ARPAnet's original purpose was to link university computers and researchers so they could conduct basic research on computers and on communication nets, and use these networked computers for basic research. It was only later that efforts were made to use ARPAnet for more direct military research.

Later the NSF (National Science Foundation) gave the Internet a real boost when the Foundation realized it could save money by creating several super-computer centers connected to a network and giving researchers all over the country (in major universities, for example) access to them and the information they stored. In the past decade, all sorts of organizations have got in on the act, each one connecting its own network with its own particular configuration of hardware and software. In this way, the Internet has grown tremendously.

Who Runs the Internet?

So if nobody owns the Internet, who decides how it all hooks together? ISOC, the Internet Society, is a group of interested people (you can join if you want) who elect a "council of elders." This council, known as the Internet Architecture Board (IAB), gets together and decides how the network will function. They are advised by the Internet Engineering Task Force (IETF), another volunteer organization, which studies technical problems.

...And That's the Problem

The problem with the Internet, therefore, lies in the way it has come to be. It's a problem of planning, and it's an inevitable result of the way the network grew. As an example of this theory, compare the cities of Dallas and London. London is a confusing mesh of intertwining roads, while Dallas is laid out on a sensible grid system. London wasn't planned, it just grew. Dallas was planned almost right from the start.

The Internet wasn't developed as a single planned system. It just grew. There is no Internet, Inc.—no single company that decides what the network should look like (which makes it a little confusing when you decide you'd like to use the Internet). Instead, the Internet is governed by consensus, by diverse organizations getting together to figure out the best overall way for it to work.

Going out alone into Internet-land is like venturing on foot across London without a guide or map. It'll be interesting, but you may not find what you're looking for. So take this book along as your guide.

What's in It for YOU?

Why would you want to use the Internet, anyway? There are about 20 or 30 million reasons. That's how many people already have a way to use the Internet, so that's how many people you could send messages to (if you had the time).

Okay, there really aren't that many active users. Most people rarely or never use anything but their own organization's computers and have little idea of what lies out there in the great virtual beyond. When you consider that most Internet users are in the United States, it seems improbable that there are 20–30 million people with even potential access to the Internet (that would be one American in ten). Even though those figures are bandied around a lot, nobody really knows for sure what the numbers are.

But there are plenty of other reasons for using the Internet:

- Are you going on vacation to Costa Rica and want to check out some good scuba locations? Take a look at a scuba newsgroup and find out if anyone's been down there recently. Leave a public message and see if you get any responses (you probably will).

- Would you like to talk with collectors of antiques and vintage articles? How about talking with people who share your interest in high-fidelity audio equipment, interactive multimedia, the tastelessness, *Star Trek*, or importance of romance?

- How about checking out Project Gutenberg (no, it doesn't involve actor Steve Guttenberg), an ambitious attempt to convert works of literature to an electronic form? Go online and select from hundreds of works of copyright-free literature. You could check out the Journalism Periodicals Index at the University of Western Ontario, or Project Hermes, which stores decisions of the U.S. Supreme Court.

- You could research a book or magazine article you are working on using CARL (Denver's online library index search for books or magazine articles) without ever leaving home. Or get onto the World Wide Web and just cruise around looking for neat information: the Rolling Stones' Web site (music and video), various conspiracy sites (information about the Kennedys, the militias, and various dead aliens), online shopping malls, and much more. The Web is so enormous, you can travel around on it for a couple of weeks and only scratch the surface. (And in the time you spend looking around, it will double in size.)

It's difficult to give a good idea of what is on the Internet because there's just so much. The Internet is huge. You will find many sources of information listed in this book, but I can only mention a fraction of what's out there. I'll explain how to find more, though.

➤ Chapters 9 through 11 discuss the World Wide Web and how to navigate that amazing system.

➤ Chapters 12 discusses how to download files from other computers, Chapters 13 and 14 tell you about two important Internet tools (Archie and Gopher), and Chapter 15 explains how to connect to another computer so you can use its files and databases.

➤ Chapter 16 describes WAIS, a special system designed to allow researchers to search hundreds of databases throughout the world.

➤ Chapters 17 and 18 discuss newsgroups, in which you can leave messages for and read messages from people with similar interests. These chapters name a few of the newsgroups and tell you how to find a list of them. And Chapter 19 explains mailing lists, a form of discussion group based on the e-mail system.

The Least You Need to Know

In this chapter, you learned a little background information that will help you understand how the Internet fits together. You don't have to remember the details, but at least remember these things:

➤ The Internet is a network of networks.

➤ Because some of those networks contain what are, in effect, BBSs, the Internet is a pathway to thousands of different sources of information.

➤ Nobody owns the Internet. It's a cooperative venture linking a multitude of companies, government bodies, universities and schools, and community computer networks.

➤ Think of any subject, and you can find information about it somewhere on the Internet.

➤ Okay, so the Internet can be complicated. That's why you need a good guide. Read on.

Chapter 3

So Many Ways to Connect

In This Chapter

- Types of Internet connections
- Advantages and disadvantages
- Why you need a dial-in direct account (SLIP or PPP)
- Finding a Free-Net
- Other forms of free Internet connections
- Why many free connections won't work for you

In this chapter, we're going to look at how to connect to the Internet. Even if you already have an Internet account, you might want to skim through this chapter because it explains the types of accounts and the pros and cons of each. And for those who don't have an Internet account yet, I'll explain how to get one (it's not as straightforward as you might imagine). For most readers, "money's no object" doesn't hold true, so you want to find the cheapest way to connect to the Internet (for nothing, if possible).

Unlike for systems such as CompuServe and Prodigy, there's no set charge for connecting to the Internet. Most BBSs and online information services have a standard set of fees. You might be able to pick one fee schedule from several, but all customers have the same choices. Not so with the Internet. Because there is no single organization running the Internet, what you are buying is access to the network. You need to connect your computer to a computer or network that is already connected to the Internet. You need a *service provider*.

Companies and nonprofit organizations called service providers (or Internet Access Providers) buy computers, connect them to the Internet, and sell connections to anyone who has the money to spare. These service providers set their own rates, and as you'll see in a moment, those rates vary considerably.

Types of Connections

With a few variations, there are four basic ways to connect to the Internet:

- Permanent connection
- Dial-in direct connection
- Dial-in terminal connection
- Mail connection

You won't necessarily hear these terms elsewhere, though. In fact, different service providers use slightly different terms, and the terminology can become blurred. It gets confusing, but the following definitions should clarify things a little.

Permanent Connections

If you have a permanent connection, your computer connects directly to a TCP/IP network that is part of the Internet, or your organization has a large computer connected to the network and you have a terminal connected to that computer. (You may even have a computer that is acting as a terminal, in which case all the work is done by the other computer, and your computer simply passes text to and from your screen.) This type of connection is also known as a *dedicated* or *permanent direct* connection.

> **Check This Out...**
>
> ### TCP/IP
>
> This stands for Transfer Control Protocol/Internet Protocol. A protocol defines how computers should talk to each other; it's like a language. If a group of different people all agree to speak French (or English or Spanish), they can all understand each other. Communication protocols provide a set of rules that define how different modems, computers, and programs communicate.

Permanent or dedicated connections are often used by large organizations such as universities, groups of schools, and corporations. The service provider places a router (a special box that allows him to connect his computer to the Internet) at the organization's office and leases a telephone line that connects the router to the service provider's computer (known as a *host computer*). The details of that process vary though; the service provider might provide the router, or they might tell the organization which router to buy. However, once this is established, the organization can connect its computers and terminals to the Internet. And because the organization has a leased line, it is always connected to the Internet and doesn't have to make a telephone call to reach the service provider's computer. So when a user logs on to the Internet from his terminal, he can transfer files between his organization's computer and other computers on the Internet. What, then, is a service provider? Any organization with a direct connection to the Internet that sells access—sometimes direct connections—to other people and organizations.

This sort of service is very expensive, costing thousands of dollars to set up and thousands of dollars to run. Getting a dedicated line is, of course, way beyond the scope of this book (which is a computer-book writer's euphemism for "let's not get into that"). Of course, if you happen to be an employee or a member of an organization with a direct connection, and you can convince them to let you connect to the Internet through it, you're "in with Flynn," as they say.

Dial-In Direct Connections

A *dial-in direct* connection is often referred to as a SLIP (Serial Line Internet Protocol), CSLIP (Compressed SLIP), or PPP (Point-to-Point Protocol) connection. This is also a TCP/IP connection (like the permanent connection), but it is designed for use over telephone lines instead of a dedicated network.

19

This type of service is the next best thing to the permanent connection. While a permanent connection is out of the price range of most individuals and small companies, a SLIP account can be quite cheap. Prices have dropped considerably in the past year. You can get a dial-in direct account for a $20 to $30 setup fee (sometimes no setup fee at all) and connect rates that are the same as for dial-in terminal accounts (covered in the next section).

Because this is a "dial-in" service, you need a modem, and you'll have to dial a telephone number that the service provider gives you. After you connect to the service provider's computer and log on, however, you can't tell any difference (other than speed) between a SLIP account and a dedicated account. You can transfer files to and from your computer exactly as you would if it were a host computer. In fact, your computer will be identified on the network as a host.

Techno Talk

Permanent's Faster

You'll see one important difference between permanent and dial-in direct connections: working with a permanent connection is much faster than working with a dial-in direct connection. With a permanent connection, you can transfer files from FTP sites more quickly, view Web documents more quickly, even read newsgroup messages more quickly. File transfers and Telnet sessions between your service provider's computer and others on the Internet (as in a permanent connection) are much faster because there's one fewer connection than there is in a dial-in direct connection.

Another important benefit of the dial-in direct account (as compared to the dial-in terminal account) is that you can run multiple sessions at the same time. That is, in the same way that the service provider's computer can let dozens of people work on the Internet at the same time, you will be able to do several different things on the Internet at the same time using multiple program windows. For example, you can transfer files from an FTP site back to your computer using one program, rummage around on the World Wide Web in another program, and run a Telnet session in yet another program.

Don't confuse this service (dial-in direct) with what some service providers call a dial-up connection. A dial-up service (what I call dial-in terminal service) also requires you to dial a telephone number, but it provides more limited service than does SLIP.

Dial-In Terminal Connections

With this type of connection, you have to dial into the service provider's computer. It's confusing that this connection is often called a dial-up service, because you have to dial a call in order to connect to a SLIP or PPP account as well. (To differentiate, some service providers call this a *shell account* or an *interactive service*, which seems only slightly less ambiguous.) I call it a *dial-in terminal* connection because you dial the call to your service provider, and once connected, your computer acts as a terminal.

Unlike with a permanent or dial-in direct connection, your computer won't appear as a host on the network when you use a dial-in terminal connection; it is simply a terminal of the service provider's computer. All the programs you run are actually running on the service provider's computer. That means you can transfer files across the Internet to and from your service provider's computer, but not to and from yours. You have to use a separate procedure, normally a transfer procedure such as Zmodem or Xmodem, to move files between your computer and that of the service provider.

You can still use all the services that would be available on a permanent connection or dial-in direct connection, but those services will be harder to use. You'll be working with a command-line interface—i.e., typing commands. You can kiss your point-and-click interface good-bye if you work with a dial-in terminal connection.

Mail Connections

Many mail connections exist on the Internet. Most large online services have been providing Internet e-mail service to their users for some time. In addition, many BBSs have simple e-mail connections to the Internet (without any other Internet services). With an e-mail connection, you can send mail to the Internet and have friends and colleagues on the Internet send mail to you.

You can even send mail across the Internet to other non-Internet BBS accounts (some BBSs that don't have full Internet access, only an e-mail "gateway"). And it's possible to use Internet's LISTSERV and mailing list systems to take part in Internet discussions on just about any subject through your e-mail connection.

Another form of mail connection is one in which you connect to the Internet in the same way you do with a dial-in terminal connection, but all you're allowed to do is get to the mail system. And finally, you could get a UUCP connection. This is a simple mail connection that uses software intended for this purpose (instead of a general purpose communications program). All you can do is send and receive mail and UseNet newsgroup messages (covered in Chapters 17 and 18).

21

Part 1 ➤ *Untangling the Wires and Getting It Running*

> **Check This Out...**
>
> **What's UUCP?**
> UUCP stands for UNIX-to-UNIX Copy Program. It's a system by which mail can be placed in files and transferred to other computers.

What Sort of Connection Do You Have?

I'm assuming you have (or are going to acquire) one of the first two connections: a permanent or dial-in direct account. I'm not going to cover dial-in terminal connections. Windows 95 provides programs that help you run graphical software on the Internet, which is far superior to using the command-line interface. If you prefer to use a command-line interface or have no option but to use one, I suggest that you read *The Complete Idiot's Guide to the Internet*, which focuses primarily on the dial-in terminal connection. I am also omitting a discussion of mail connections because they are so limited in capabilities. We're interested in getting full Internet access, not an account that lets you send e-mail and nothing more.

In addition, I am going to describe how to use the Windows 95 software to set up a dial-in direct account. But I am not going to describe how to set up your Windows 95 computer to run on a permanent connection because there are many ways to do so, depending on the type of network you are connected to. If your computer is connected to the Internet via a network at work, at college, or through some other organization, talk with the system administrator. Once your administrator sets up your connection, everything will work the same. Running World Wide Web, FTP, and Telnet sessions is the same for permanent-connection users as it is for dial-in direct users.

Let Someone Else Pay

The best way to connect to the Internet is to use OPM: Other People's Money. Many Internet users connect through an organization that has a permanent connection to the Internet. Many large companies have their own computers connected directly to the Internet and allow their employees access to it. IBM, for instance, connects to the Internet and claims that their 250,000 employees can find their way onto the network if they want to. These employees don't have to pay anything to use the Internet; they just have to get permission from the company. Likewise, many governmental departments have Internet access, and many universities have connections and let students access the network for free. Most medium-sized or larger colleges have Internet connections, as do many high schools.

So before you arrange to pay a service provider for Internet access, talk with the person in your organization who's in charge of the Internet connection. You may find that you have to use Internet from a terminal in the organization's building (in the office or from a university building), or you may be able to dial in from home to your organization's computer and then get onto the Internet. This depends on the type of software and hardware that the organization has available.

If you don't know who's in charge of your Internet access (or if your organization is even hooked up), ask around. Ask the head of the computer department, computer center, information services department, or whatever. Ask the people who spend much of their time maintaining, installing, and fixing computers. It may be that only a few people in your organization use the Internet, and you won't get on without a bit of searching and diplomacy. Of course, most small companies won't have an Internet connection, but if you work for a medium-sized or large business, you may be in luck.

There's a drawback to these free accounts, though. You get what's available. If the only thing your college can provide, for instance, is a dial-in terminal account, this book won't help you. We're interested only in the capabilities of the dial-in direct (SLIP, CSLIP, or PPP) account.

> **Check This Out...**
>
> **Not a Student?** Even if you are not a student, you may be able to get onto a college's Internet system. Call your local college to see if they have a connection and find out the requirements for network use. You may find that you can use it if you are even a part-time student (though you probably won't be able to dial in from home). So sign up for Basket Weaving 101.

Find a Free-Net

If you can't get an account through your company or college, the next step is to look for a Free-Net or another form of free system. These are community computing systems, which may be based at a local library or college. With such, you may be able to use the Internet from a terminal at the library, or you may even be able to dial into the system from your home computer. And as the name implies, they don't cost anything. (Well, some may have a small registration fee—$5 perhaps—but if they're not actually free, they are pretty close to it.)

Free-Nets offer a variety of local services, as well as access to the Internet. You may be able to find information about jobs in the area, local events, and recreation. You may be able to search the local library's database, find course schedules for local colleges, or ask someone questions about social security and Medicare.

Part 1 ➤ *Untangling the Wires and Getting It Running*

Free-Nets usually have a menu of options based on the concept of a simulated "town" (see the following figure). It includes the Community Center, Teen Center, and Senior Center. And you'll find an Administration Building, where you can go to register your account on the Free-Net; a Social Services and Organizations Center, where you can find support groups and local chapters of such national organizations as the Red Cross; and a Home and Garden Center, where you can find out about pest control and "Family Preparedness Planning." There might even be a Special Interests Center, where you can chat about UFOs, movies, religion, travel, or anything else. And Free-Nets also have a system that lets you send messages to other users.

A typical Free-Net menu.

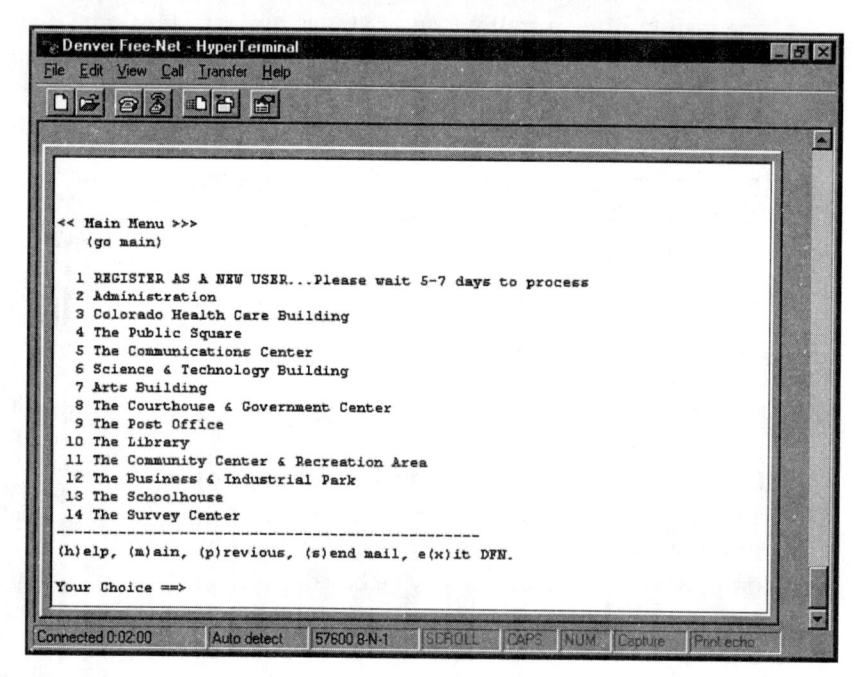

```
<< Main Menu >>>
   (go main)

 1 REGISTER AS A NEW USER...Please wait 5-7 days to process
 2 Administration
 3 Colorado Health Care Building
 4 The Public Square
 5 The Communications Center
 6 Science & Technology Building
 7 Arts Building
 8 The Courthouse & Government Center
 9 The Post Office
10 The Library
11 The Community Center & Recreation Area
12 The Business & Industrial Park
13 The Schoolhouse
14 The Survey Center
-----------------------------------------------------
(h)elp, (m)ain, (p)revious, (s)end mail, e(x)it DFN.

Your Choice ==>
```

Techno Talk

Get it Right! You'll probably see the terms Free-Net, freenet, and FreeNet, as well as other variations. All these terms are service marks of NPTN (National Public Telecommuting Network); they prefer to use the term Free-Net.

Even without their Internet links, Free-Nets are a great community resource, especially for home-bound people such as the elderly and handicapped. (It's a shame that the very people who could benefit most from a computer system such as this are the least likely to have computers. Maybe that will change in the next few years.)

At the time of this writing, a few dozen Free-Nets existed, most of them in the U.S. However, you can also find Free-Nets in New Zealand, Canada, and Finland, and the total number is expected to grow quickly. To find a Free-Net, e-mail **info@nptn.org** or call the NPTN (National Public

Telecommuting Network) at 216.247.5800. If you can't find a Free-Net, maybe you should start one in your town. NPTN can tell you how.

> **Check This Out...**
>
> **The Limitations of Free-Nets**
>
> Not all Free-Nets and other community systems provide full access to the Internet. For security reasons, some may limit certain services. For instance, they may not want you to use FTP to bring possibly virus-laden files into their systems. (I'll talk a little more about viruses in Chapter 12.) And Free-Nets are often very busy and difficult to connect to. You'll probably find that most of these free systems don't currently provide the dial-in direct account you need to use this book; they generally provide dial-in terminal accounts. That may change in the future, but for now that's the way it is.

More Freebies

There are other free sites around (in addition to Free-Nets). Take a look in *Boardwatch Magazine*, *ComputerShopper*, *Online Access*, or another such magazine, which you can find in many bookstores, or check your city's local computer publications and ask other Internet users you run into. You'll find bulletin board systems advertising Internet access, but you'll also find listings of free BBSs with Internet access. For example, Denver has NYX, a system at a local university through which you can get a free account, some Internet access, and even free international e-mail. Not bad. Still, most of these free systems don't provide the dial-in direct connection you need to work with this book.

If you can't figure out where to find a free or almost-free Internet dial-in direct connection, you're going to have to pay. But you want to pay as little possible, and the next chapter explains how.

The Least You Need to Know

When considering an Internet account, keep these things in mind:

➤ There are four main types of Internet connections.

➤ A permanent connection is the best type of connection, but it's expensive. You may have one if you are an employee of a large corporation or a member of an organization (such as a university).

➤ A dial-in direct (SLIP or PPP) connection is the next best thing.

Part 1 ➤ *Untangling the Wires and Getting It Running*

- ➤ This book explains how to install dial-in direct connections, and how to work with dial-in direct and permanent connections.
- ➤ A dial-in terminal connection is still common and easy to set up, but it's hard to use. For this sort of connection, see *The Complete Idiot's Guide to the Internet*.
- ➤ Ask your employer or local college if you can use their Internet connection.
- ➤ Find a Free-Net or another type of free BBS for free Internet access.
- ➤ It's worth a try to check out all of these options, but most free connections don't provide dial-in direct accounts (only dial-in terminal accounts).

Chapter 4

If You Have to Pay: Picking a Provider

In This Chapter

- About The Microsoft Network
- How much will it cost?
- Finding a service provider in your area
- Asking the service provider questions
- Comparing costs

If you've looked around and found no way to get a free account, the next step is to find the service provider with the best rates and the services you need. This chapter strolls around the block of paid providers, so you can see what's for sale.

Where Do I Find Service Providers?

When *The Complete Idiot's Guide to the Internet* was first published, it included a list of service providers. But since that time, the number has grown tremendously, making it impossible to list any significant portion of them. In the Denver area, for instance, the number jumped from just one or two late in 1993 to a couple of dozen in 1995. So, how do you find a service provider? Let's look at a few options.

Part 1 ➤ *Untangling the Wires and Getting It Running*

What About The Microsoft Network?

The first thing you may want to consider is The Microsoft Network (MSN). This is an on-line service that's similar in concept to CompuServe or America Online, though currently much smaller. The following figure shows an example of The Microsoft Network screen.

The Microsoft Network's user-friendly interface.

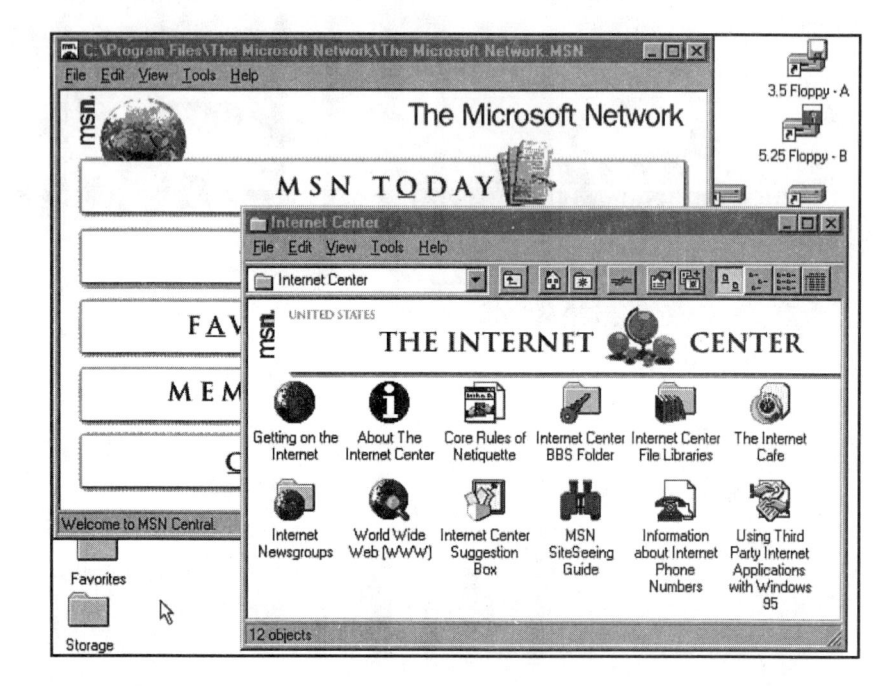

Windows 95 has all the software you need to connect to The Microsoft Network and makes it very easy—far easier than connecting to other service providers. The term "one-click" (as in "one-click Internet access") has become popular in software circles these days. To be honest, you can do very little in the software world with just one click of your mouse. No, you can't install your MSN connection with one click. But the installation routine is fairly simple, and it's much easier than installing a connection for other service providers (as you'll see in Chapters 6 through 8).

So why not use MSN? Four reasons:

➤ You may not be able to get an account. Microsoft announced a few weeks before the launch of MSN that they would initially limit MSN membership to 500,000 people.

➤ At the time of this writing (August, 1995), MSN was a little slow, and the TCP/IP connection was unreliable (which is why Microsoft planned to limit access to the first 500,000 people).

➤ MSN has a reasonable price, but it's not as low as you can find elsewhere.

➤ In order to use MSN's Internet access, you have to dial into one of their TCP/IP phone lines. If there is not one in your area (which is possible), you'll have to pay long distance rates to use MSN's Internet connections.

Here's my personal recommendation: try MSN. If you like it, stay with it. If not, you can always look elsewhere later. You're allowed a free trial, so you'll soon find out if the service is okay (and if Microsoft has managed to iron out the reliability and speed problems). Also, Microsoft plans to change their pricing later, to price Internet access separately from MSN access. At that point, you may find it cheaper to buy MSN access without Internet access (if that's what you want) and get your Internet access from a local service provider.

A Word About Money

At the time of this writing, Microsoft has several payment plans. Of course, this can change at any time, but I'm going to use these plans as a starting point.

Standard $4.95/month, which provides 3 hours of usage a month. Extra hours are $2.50 per hour.

Frequent User Plan $19.95/month, which allows 20 hours of usage a month. Additional hours are $2 per hour.

Charter Member Plan If you are one of the first 500,000 members, you pay $39.95 for the first year, and you get 3 hours of free access a month. Extra hours are $2.50 an hour. (I'll do the math for you. This is the same as the Standard Plan, except you pay $3.33 a month instead of $4.95, and you must pay the entire year up front.)

> **Check This Out...**
>
> **Changes Coming Soon**
> Microsoft says they may soon change the rate structure to create separate prices for their MSN and Internet access portions. They've even stated that this will make it easier for people who want to use MSN but want to use another service provider for Internet access.

You should also note that for these prices, you can access not only the Internet, but all of the MSN services. (If you get an MSN account, you may want to take a look at *Using The Microsoft Network*, also published by Que.)

29

Not only are these prices reasonable, but they reflect a real drop in online charges. In fact, a week or two before the launch of MSN, CompuServe dropped its prices, almost certainly to remain competitive with MSN.

However, you should note that these prices are not the lowest you can find. The additional hourly rate of $2 or $2.50 is not high when compared to that of other online services, but it is a little high when compared to that of true Internet service providers (companies providing access to just the Internet). For instance, my service provider charges $29.95 for the first 25 hours, which is actually a little more than the two best MSN plans. But additional hours are only $1.20. And my service provider doesn't even have the lowest prices. (I stick with them because I'm satisfied with their service and reliability.) You can find much lower prices—even companies selling unlimited access to the Internet for $20 to $40 a month. In other words, you pay a single sum and use the Internet as many hours as you want (or rather, as many hours as you can get onto the system).

A major complaint about the "unlimited access" plans is that while access may not be limited by your bank account, it may be limited by the fact that every time you try to connect, you get a busy tone! That's not to say there aren't excellent unlimited access plans, just that they are only one kind of plan to consider.

I Want Another Service Provider!

So you can't get onto MSN, or you don't want to get onto MSN, or you got on and don't like it. You could try one of the other major online services, of course: CompuServe, America Online, and Prodigy, for example. If you do so, the rest of this book will help you understand the Internet, but information on installation and certain program specifics will be of no use to you. These services provide their own installation programs and Internet utilities. And as you can see in the next two figures, each online service has a unique look and a different way of accessing the Internet.

Chapter 4 ➤ *If You Have to Pay: Picking a Provider*

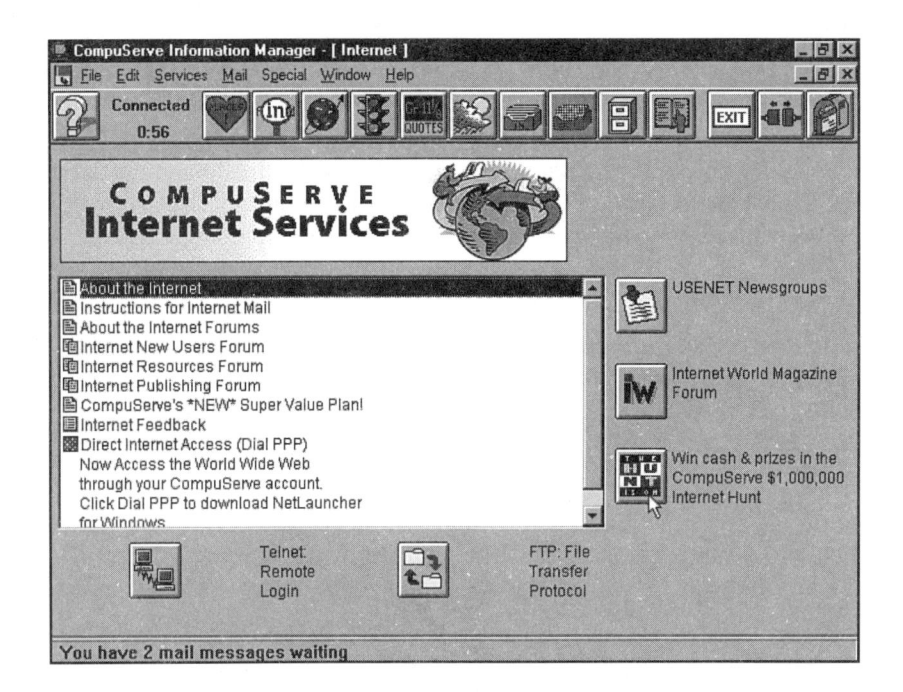

CompuServe's Internet interface.

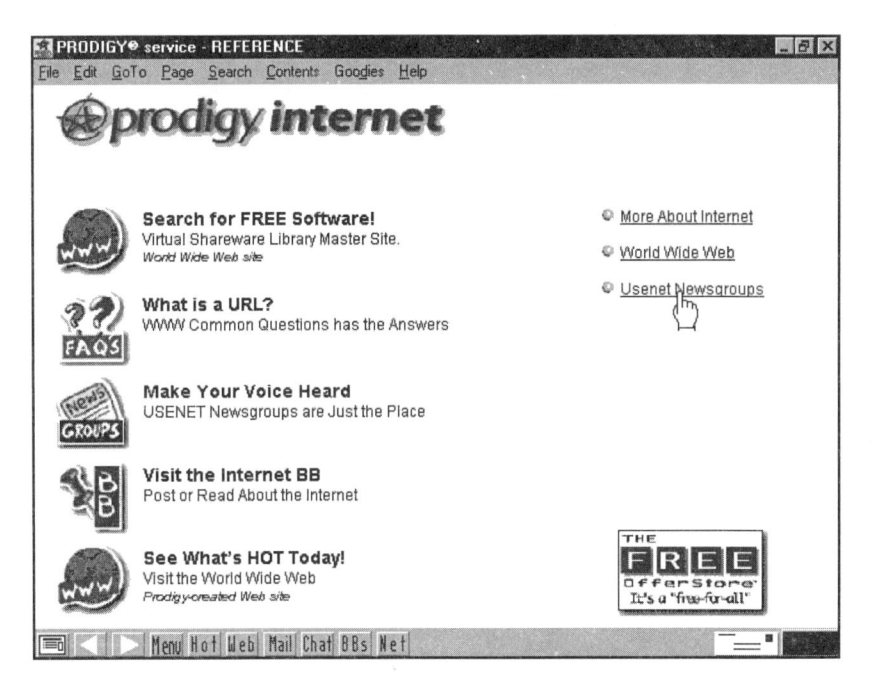

You can also get a connection to the Internet through the Prodigy online service.

If you are searching for the lowest price you can find, these services probably won't help you anyway. However, in most areas, you can find lower prices by using one of the following means:

- Look in your city's local computer publication for ads. Check the local business papers, too, and the business section of the daily paper. Service providers often advertise in these places because so many businesses want to get onto the Internet these days.

- If you already have access to Internet e-mail or you know someone who does, send a message to **info-deli-server@netcom.com** (see Part 4 for information on working with Internet e-mail). In the body of the message, type **Send PDIAL**. This message is received by a special program that automatically returns a message that includes a large list of service providers in the United States, some of which have international access.

- Talk to everyone you know who works with computers. Maybe someone knows of some service providers or already has an account with a provider she would recommend. Better still, you may get an idea of the good ones in your area—and the ones to avoid. Standards vary from excellent to "don't touch that one with a barge pole."

> **Check This Out...**
>
> **Changes Are Inevitable**
>
> It's fair to assume that many, perhaps most, of the service providers in business today will not be in business in two or three years. People who hadn't heard of the Internet two or three years ago are now running companies providing access to the Internet. (Full page ads in Internet magazines with headlines like "Others are making their fortunes selling Internet access—why not you?" haven't helped!)

- You may want to get a copy of the publication *Internet Access Providers* (Mecklermedia, $30). It's an international directory of service providers, regional networks, and bulletin boards with Internet access. You can order it through your local bookstore by calling 800.632.5537 or 203.226.6967 in the U.S., by calling 071.976.0405 in the UK, or by sending e-mail to **info@mecklermedia.com**.)

Explaining What You Want

When you first contact a service provider, make sure you are both talking about the same thing. If you don't understand the account types they are talking about (there are plenty

Chapter 4 ➤ *If You Have to Pay: Picking a Provider*

of variations; many service providers create their own product names), make sure they clarify what they are offering. You want a dial-in direct account, so say "I want a PPP account."

Now earlier I told you that dial-in direct accounts may be SLIP, CSLIP, or PPP. But PPP is the preferred type because it is faster and more stable than SLIP and because the Windows 95 software is set up to run PPP. If you want to run a SLIP account, you'll need extra software, which you can get by buying the Microsoft Plus! add-on package or Windows 95 on CD. If you have Windows 95 on floppy disks, you can still download the SLIP software (I explain how in Chapter 8).

What if the service provider doesn't have PPP accounts? Most will, but if you run into one that doesn't, look elsewhere. If you can't find a PPP account in your area, or if the very best deal is with the SLIP account, you can go with SLIP. You just have to jump through one more hoop to install it. (I explain how to set up a SLIP account in Chapter 7.)

> **Check This Out...**
>
> **Terminology Jumble**
>
> You may hear a service provider use one of these names for the types of service we've been discussing:
>
> Permanent may be called direct, permanent direct, or dedicated service.
>
> Dial-in terminal may be called interactive, dial-up service, or shell account.
>
> Dial-in direct may be called SLIP, CSLIP, PPP, or TCP/IP service.
>
> Mail may be called UUCP, e-mail, or messaging service.

When you're sure you are both talking about the same thing, ask the following questions to compare the rates of different service providers:

➤ **How much is the connect or startup cost?** To start, you may have to pay a setup charge, which is a one-time fee that runs between $20 and $45. Not all service providers charge a setup fee.

➤ **Is there a fixed fee?** The amount you pay per hour can vary tremendously. Some service providers don't charge by the hour; they charge a single monthly fee and provide unlimited time on the Internet ($15 a month for unlimited use,

33

for instance). Also, some service providers charge higher rates for faster modem speeds (though this practice seems to be dying out). Make sure you get the price for the speed of the modem you are using.

- **If there's a fixed fee, is it for limited access?** If the service provider is charging a fixed fee, make sure you know what hours you will be allowed onto the system. Some providers may have a low fixed fee account but will only let you on in the evenings.

- **If it's not an unlimited-access account, how many free hours does it provide?** If the fixed fee is not for unlimited access, it should provide you with a certain number of free hours. For instance, it might be $10 a month for 10 free hours.

- **How much do you charge per hour during weekdays? Evenings? Nights? Weekends?** Many providers charge an hourly rate that varies depending on the time. Find out how much you'll have to pay for additional hours, whatever time you want to connect. Make sure you know what they mean by evening, night, business day, and so on. And remember to check rates for your modem speed.

- **Can I pay for a maximum number of hours, after which all hours are free?** If a service provider charges by the hour, they may have a maximum. For example, once you pay $100 in hourly fees, everything is free for the rest of the month.

- **Do you have a local number?** Ideally you want a service provider with a telephone number in your area code so you don't have to pay long distance charges.

> **Check This Out...**
>
> **POPs** If a service provider says it has a POP (Point of Presence) in your area, it means they have a local telephone number in your area even though they may be located somewhere else. Using a POP, you won't have to pay for long distance calls to connect to the Internet.

- **Is there a surcharge on that local number?** Some service providers charge you extra to use their local number. Ideally you want a *free* local number!

- **Do you have 1-800 access? What is the surcharge? Is it national, or state only?** Some service providers have 1-800 numbers you can use. You'll pay a surcharge (maybe $5–$12/hour), but if you live in the boonies and do not have an Internet number in your area code, you might find it cheaper to use the 1-800 number than to pay long distance charges. The 1-800 number is also convenient for people who want to use the Internet while away from home.

Chapter 4 ➤ *If You Have to Pay: Picking a Provider*

➤ **What modem speeds do you support?** The slower the connection, the more time everything will take, and the more expensive your online work will be—in terms of both the money you pay the service provider and the value of your time. You need a service provider that has at least 14,400 bps modems, preferably 28,800 bps modems. Some now have ISDN access (which I discuss in Chapter 5). Of course, the data-transmission speed you want to use is limited by the speed of your computer's modem. So if you have only a 300 bps modem, it doesn't matter if the service provider does have 28,800 bps modems; your connection will be at 300 bps. (But if you have only a 300 bps modem, you're going to hate working on the Internet. See Chapter 5 to learn more about modems.)

➤ **Do you provide a free shell account?** Some service providers sell you a dial-in direct account (shell account), but if you want dial-in terminal access as well, they charge you extra. Other service providers let you access your account both ways for the same price. If you have a dial-in direct account, why would you want to access your account using a shell account? To carry out administrative tasks such as changing your password or billing method. You'll be able to Telnet into your shell account to carry out these tasks. I cover this in more detail in Chapter 15.

> **Techno Talk**
>
> **Baud vs. bps**
>
> Many people use the term baud instead of bps (bits per second). The two terms are pretty much interchangeable, although they're not exactly the same—and purists will tell you that bps is the more correct of the two when referring to your modem's speed. Baud is named for J. M. E. Baudot, who invented the Baudot telegraph code, and it refers to the modulation and demodulation rate of the modem (the rate at which the modem converts between the computer's digital signal and the phone line's analog signal).

➤ **Do you support ISDN?** ISDN means Integrated Services Digital Network. It's a special form of telecommunications that lets you connect your computer to a very fast line—about four times the speed of a 28,800 bps modem. There are three main problems with this service: most service providers don't yet use it; in many areas of the country it can be difficult to connect ISDN service to your home or business; and it's more expensive than an ordinary line. You don't need ISDN to connect to the Internet, but if you want to spend a lot of time online and need to use that time efficiently, ISDN is worth considering. We'll look at ISDN in more detail in Chapter 5.

> **How much is disk space per megabyte per month?** Your service provider will probably charge you if you store too much stuff on his computer's hard disk. This doesn't have to be a problem, though. A provider may let you use up to 1MB (megabyte) for free, and then charge from 50 cents to two or three dollars a month for each additional MB. These storage prices are more of an issue for dial-in terminal connections, with which you have to store lots of information on the service provider's system. With the sort of connection you are going to use, though, everything is transferred back to your computer, so little gets stored on the service provider's hard disk.

> **How much is domain service?** When you get a dial-in direct account, you can establish your own domain name, or you can use the service provider's. As you'll see in Chapter 5, you are identified on the Internet with two names: a user name, and a domain or host name that identifies where your account is operating. Establishing your own domain name may be free, or it may cost $10 or $20. (I'd recommend that you set up your own domain name; for the pros and cons, see Chapter 5.)

> **Are there any other charges?** There are as many ways to charge you as there are service providers. Check the fine print.

The Least You Need to Know

> The easiest way to connect Windows 95 to the Internet is through MSN.

> If you don't like MSN, you want a cheaper service, or you don't have MSN in your area, find another service provider.

> Remember to check the service provider's modem speed. Some still use slow modems.

> Compare costs carefully; rates vary widely.

> Check the end of this chapter for a series of questions to ask potential service providers.

Chapter 5

Let's Get Physical: What You Need to Get Started

In This Chapter

- The type of computer you need
- How to pick a modem
- Using ISDN
- Account names and passwords
- Getting your own domain name
- The software you need

If you decide the Internet's for you, you need to decide if you have what it takes—i.e., if you have the computer hardware and software you need. The hardware demands are not extreme, but there are a few things to consider. You are going to need the following:

- An Internet account (of course)
- A computer or terminal
- A modem or connection
- A login name

Part 1 ➤ *Untangling the Wires and Getting It Running*

➤ A password

➤ Internet software

> **Check This Out...**
>
> **Internet Accounts** I'm going to use the terms "Internet account" and "Internet connection" (or simply "account" or "connection") throughout this book to mean access to the Internet. You may also see the terms "Internet access" and "Internet service." Basically, these all mean the same thing: the capability to get onto the Internet and use its services.

Your Computer

The first thing you need, of course, is a computer. Not just any computer, but, for the purposes of this book, one running Windows 95. (Why Windows 95? You didn't read the book's title, did you?) If you have Windows 95 installed on your computer and it runs satisfactorily, your computer is ready.

And if you haven't yet bought a Windows 95 computer? Windows 95 will run on a 386, but it runs more comfortably on a 486-66 or a Pentium. (Better still, the next generation of chip—the Sextium, or whatever they plan to call it—is due out about the same time as this book.) You can run Windows 95 with as little as 4MB of RAM...though you'll probably regret it. Get at least 8, preferably more. (You can never have too much RAM!)

Your Modem

If your computer directly connects to a computer with Internet access (usually if you are part of an organization or company that has a direct connection), you don't need to establish the connection yourself. That's up to your system administrator to figure out, and I don't describe setting up such a connection in this book.

If you have to dial into your service provider's computer, though, you need a modem. Modems come in two types: internal and external. An internal modem is a computer board that plugs into a slot inside the computer; the phone line then plugs into a socket on the edge of the modem. Many computers come with an internal modem already installed. An external modem is a box that contains a board much like the internal modem board, but it connects to the outside of your computer by means of a cable running to the computer's serial port (one of the plugs on the back). The phone line then plugs into the modem box.

Chapter 5 ➤ *Let's Get Physical: What You Need to Get Started*

> **Check This Out...**
>
> **Internal vs. External Modems**
>
> Internal and external modems are the same, they are just located in different places. They do vary slightly in price though; external modems are a bit more expensive because they need a box and an extra socket (for power). In addition, external modems take up a serial port, which can be a hassle if you need the serial ports for other purposes (the mouse is usually plugged into one). However, an external modem is much easier to install than an internal one. You install an external modem yourself in a matter of minutes, whereas installing an internal modem requires you (or someone) to take apart your computer—which, quite frankly, many people won't mess with.

The faster your modem, the better. If you have to buy a new modem, I recommend that you don't get anything less than a 14,400 bps modem. Even better, if your budget can stretch that far, get a 28,800 bps modem. If you already have a modem, you may be okay if it's a 9,600 bps modem. If you have anything slower than that, it will be next to useless. Time to buy a new one!

Help! Which Modem Should I Buy?

I can't tell you which modem to buy because your choices are directly related to the type of computer you are using. If you already have a modem and it's fast enough, use it; it'll probably work fine. If you don't have one yet, you might want to talk to your service provider (which you selected back in Chapter 4) and ask for a recommendation. Sometimes modems run into compatibility problems, and it's possible (though unlikely) that the modem you buy will have trouble connecting to the service provider's computer. The service provider should be able to give you a list of modems they know work well, and perhaps even a list of modems that have problems connecting.

You'll probably find that your service provider is using fairly advanced modems with fancy specifications such as V.34, V.32bis, MNP-5, V.42, V.42bis, and so on. (These describe the way in which modems communicate and handle problems during a transmission.) As a result, your service provider might recommend a top-of-the-line modem that costs $300 to $500. Don't do it. You can buy a fast (28,800 bps) high-quality modem for $180 or less or an excellent 14,400 bps modem for far less—and prices are dropping all the time. Try buying from a reputable mail-order company such as MicroWarehouse (800.367.7080), PC Zone (800.258.2088), or Direct Micro (800.288.2887). And note that although you're better off buying a name-brand modem (Zoom Telephonics, US Robotics, Boca Research, Hayes, Practical Peripherals, Motorola, Microcom, or Cardinal, for instance), you don't necessarily have to have "top-of-the-line." Avoid modems that appear to have been built in a foreign toy factory.

Part 1 ➤ *Untangling the Wires and Getting It Running*

> **Check This Out...**
>
> **Faster Modems**
> Doubling the speed of your modem doesn't cut your costs in half. The modem speed merely affects the transmissions between your computer and the service provider's computer (when you upload or download files, for example). Unfortunately, much of your online time will be spent waiting for other computers to do their work or simply reading what you've just transferred. Still, a fast modem will save you money.

There are no guarantees, of course. If there's a bug in your modem's firmware (the software that makes the modem run), you might have problems even if your modem matches your service provider's specifications. Although it's unlikely, this does happen (as thousands of purchasers of fax/modems from a certain major computer manufacturer—who will remain nameless—can attest). But if you buy from a reputable mail-order company and you run into such problems, you can return the modem and try another one.

ISDN Modems?

When I first wrote *The Complete Idiot's Guide to the Internet*, I mentioned that eventually modems wouldn't be necessary because communications from your computer across the phone line would be digital. Well since that time, digital communications using a system called ISDN have grown tremendously in popularity.

ISDN is nothing new. As a matter of fact, it's been around for years, but the phone companies let it sit on the shelf for a few decades. (The acronym means Integrated Services Digital Network, though it's sometimes referred to as *Installable Six Decades from Now*.) Thanks to the Internet, there's now a growing demand for ISDN service.

To use ISDN service, a user needs a special box or card that plugs into his computer. The phone line then plugs into the other end. What's this card or box called? It's often referred to as an ISDN modem! Of course, it's nothing of the sort. As you learned in Chapter 2, modem is short for modulate/demodulate and refers to the process of converting signals from digital to analog (and vice versa) so they can be transferred across phone lines. ISDN is strictly digital: there's no "modeming" going on.

Do you need an ISDN line? Right now, the simple answer is "probably not, and you may not be able to get one anyway." These lines vary greatly in price. In some areas of the country, installation is priced in the hundreds of dollars; in other areas, it may be as low as fifty bucks. The monthly fee varies, too, from around $100 a month to perhaps $30 a month. And of course there are usually "transaction initiation charges," fees for the number of *packets* of data you transmit.

Chapter 5 ➤ *Let's Get Physical: What You Need to Get Started*

Even if you think you need all the speed you can get, you may still not be able to get ISDN. You can call the local phone company, but they may not even know what you are talking about. The last time I called my phone company (US West), they didn't have anyone in Denver who understood ISDN, and they had only a handful of ISDN-trained people throughout their service area. According to Colorado law, US West has to provide ISDN service to any location in Colorado; instead, US West has chosen to allow thousands of Coloradans to file lawsuits against them!

> **Techno Talk**
>
> **Packets?** The Internet's TCP/IP protocol is a *packet switching* system; it breaks all the information your computer sends into small packets of data, each of which is independently addressed and transmitted.

Go ahead and call your phone company; it never hurts to try. But be aware that if you call some phone companies and ask if you can have ISDN service, you get may the answer "Sure. Move to Europe."

I Have a Name

To connect, you need a *login name* (also referred to as a *username, account name, user ID,* and—on The Microsoft Network—*member name*). This is the name of your account: the name you use to access your Internet connection. It tells the service provider who you are so he knows whether to let you on the network (and knows who to bill for the time you spend online). Your login name is also part of the address other users type when they want to send messages to you. This figure shows you what an Internet address might look like.

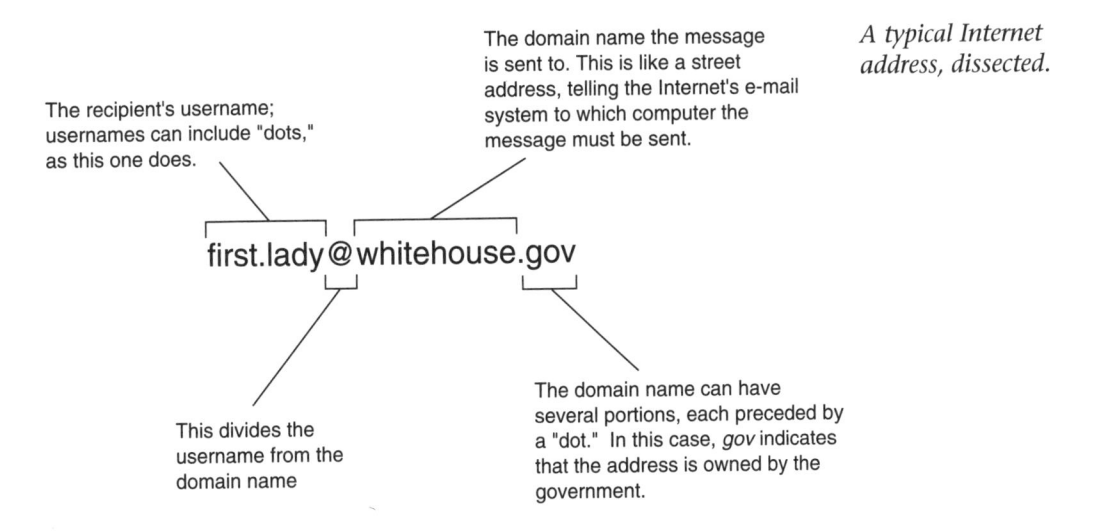

A typical Internet address, dissected.

first.lady@whitehouse.gov

The recipient's username; usernames can include "dots," as this one does.

The domain name the message is sent to. This is like a street address, telling the Internet's e-mail system to which computer the message must be sent.

This divides the username from the domain name

The domain name can have several portions, each preceded by a "dot." In this case, *gov* indicates that the address is owned by the government.

41

Part 1 ➤ *Untangling the Wires and Getting It Running*

A login name is usually made up of the account owner's name, such as pete, pkent, peterk, or peterwk, but you can make yours anything you want. A login name generally contains up to eight characters and, in most cases, is case-sensitive. In other words, Pkent is not the same as pkent, pKENT, or PKENT. You will always have to type your login name in exactly the same way (actually, you'll use the Windows 95 communications software to do it for you).

The Password Is...

You also need a password, a secret "code" you will type when the system asks you to do so. Only *you* are supposed to know your password; the computer assumes that if it receives the correct password, the correct person is trying to log on.

Why do you care if someone else is able to log on as you? Well first of all, you don't want to pay for the time someone else spends working or playing on the Internet. Nor do you want someone reading your messages, sending messages under your name, or communicating in the newsgroups as you (see Chapter 17 for more information about newsgroups). There are people out there who would like to get your password and who know a few (computer) tricks to get it. They work on the basic assumption that your password is easy to figure out because it's a name or a word.

In most cases, passwords can contain up to eight characters (check with your service provider for details). And, like the login name, your password is case-sensitive. If you are using 1n=9YT% as a password, you can't type 1N=9YT% or 1n=9yt%. (It should go without saying that this is only an example. It's not my password!)

Passwords: Pick a Good One

So how do you pick a good password? It shouldn't be a recognizable name or word, so don't use the name of one of your kids or your dog, a description of your job ("bookie" or "boss," for example), the name of your house, or a character from "The Simpsons." It also shouldn't be a meaningful number—especially not your Social Security number or your date of birth.

Here are a few tips for picking a good password:

➤ The best password is a random jumble of characters (1n=9YT%, for example). But because random jumbles are difficult to remember, create what almost appears to be a random jumble, even if it isn't. For example, mix special characters with several short words, such as I&you%in. You could pick three short words at random from the dictionary.

➤ Don't give your password to anyone else; if you do, change it as soon as that person finishes using it.

42

Chapter 5 ➤ Let's Get Physical: What You Need to Get Started

- ➤ Don't type your password while someone is watching; if you must, change it as soon as the person leaves.

- ➤ Change the password regularly, such as every month. (Some systems may force you to do so by stopping you from logging in until you create a new password.)

- ➤ Don't write the password online (in messages, for instance) or anywhere else.

- ➤ The longer the password, the better. Five characters is too short. Ask your service provider the maximum password length (probably eight characters, sometimes more).

When you first set up an account, you may be able to tell the service provider what password you want to use, but they may just assign you one. Log onto the system as soon as possible and change the password. Remember, only one person should know what the password is, and while your paperwork has been lying around the service provider's offices, several people have probably seen it.

> **Check This Out...**
>
> **Forget Your Password?** If you forget your password, don't worry. Call the service provider. Someone there will be able to assign you a new one. Use that new one to log on, and then change the password again. (Many service providers change passwords over the phone way too easily. Others may require some form of identification: your mother's maiden name or your social security number, for example. Pretending to be someone who has forgotten a password is a favorite trick of computer *crackers*.)

Your Domain Name

Whereas your account name identifies your Internet account, your domain name identifies where that account is. For instance, the **msn.com** domain refers to The Microsoft Network, **compuserve.com** is CompuServe, **aol.com** is America Online, **usa.net** is Internet Express, **csn.org** is Colorado SuperNet, and so on. When you get an account with a service provider, that automatically assigns a domain name to you. This domain name becomes part of your e-mail address in the same way that your street name is part of your postal address.

What if you decide you don't like your service provider and you switch to another? You lose your current domain name, which means your e-mail address is wrong—which means you'd better inform all the people you want to receive e-mail from that you have a new address.

Wouldn't it be nice if you could have your own domain name? If you had your own domain name, you could move to another service provider and keep the domain name (like keeping your Post Office box number when you move from one house to another). Well, some service providers will allow you to set up your own domain name. You'll find

43

Part 1 ➤ *Untangling the Wires and Getting It Running*

that most online services do *not* allow you to do this, but many true Internet service providers do. There may be a charge of $20 or $30, or it may be free. (It's no great effort for your service provider; they just submit some information to the organization that administers domain names.)

> **Check This Out...**
>
> **New Domain Charges**
>
> Just before we went to print, Network Solutions, Inc. (the private company that currently maintains the domain-name system, under contract with the National Science Foundation) announced that they plan to begin charging for domain names. You'll have to pay $100, they say, to register and hold the domain name for two years, and $50 a year after that. However, the fee seems exorbitant, and if they have enough complaints, they will change the rate structure.

Once you have a domain name, it's yours. For example, I have an account with Internet Express. My normal e-mail address (the one I would use if I hadn't registered my own domain name) is pkent@usa.net. But that's not the address I give people. I use my pkent@lab-press.com address. The lab-press.com domain name is mine, so if I ever decide to move to another service provider, I take it with me. (It's a matter of getting the new service provider to submit a change request so the computers on the Internet know that mail addressed to that domain should now be sent to the new service provider's system.) Right now it doesn't matter if someone sends e-mail to me at usa.net or lab-press.com; either way, the e-mail gets to me. But if I move to another service provider, the usa.net address won't work anymore.

I recommend that, if possible, you get your own domain name. There are many reasons for changing service providers (remember, many will probably go out of business in the next year or two, anyway). If you have your own domain name, disruption to your e-mail correspondence is nil.

What Are These Domains?

A quick word about the "first-level" domain name, the part right at the end of the name. These identify the type of account someone has or where it is. The following list describes the most often used first-level domains in the United States.

Chapter 5 ➤ Let's Get Physical: What You Need to Get Started

Domain Name	Domain Type
.gov	Government: the White House, Congress, and so on
.edu	Education: universities, colleges, and so on
.com	Commercial enterprises, business
.net	Network-related organizations
.org	Other organizations
.mil	Military

In addition, many first-level domains identify the country in which the account is held:

.uk	The United Kingdom
.jp	Japan
.se	Sweden

Finally, the Software

Now, what software do you need to connect to the Internet with Windows 95? Well, you can go about this little procedure in a number of ways:

- ➤ The quickest and easiest Internet hookup is through The Microsoft Network. You have all the software you need on your Windows 95 disks.
- ➤ If you want to connect to another service provider, you can use the Windows 95 Dial-Up Networking and TCP/IP software to start. Again, this stuff is on the Windows 95 disk. The Microsoft Plus! add-on to Windows 95 has some useful information too, but it's not essential.
- ➤ You can get one of the many Internet software systems on the market: the programs provided by the online services for use solely with those services, or packages such as Internet Chameleon, InterAp, and SuperHighway Access (which you can use to set up a connection to most service providers).

This book explains the first two procedures: how to connect to The Microsoft Network, and how to use the Dial-Up Networking and TCP/IP software that comes on your Windows 95 disks to connect to almost any other service provider.

Once you have your connection up and running, I'll explain how to find more software, freeware, or inexpensive shareware that will help you complete your suite of Internet programs. Because such programs are available online, you can transfer them back to your system directly from the Internet.

Part 1 ➤ *Untangling the Wires and Getting It Running*

The Least You Need to Know

If your organization provides you with an account, don't worry about how you are going to connect; they'll tell you what you need. If you are setting up any other type of account, remember these basic guidelines:

- ➤ If you are getting your own account, you'll need a computer and a fast modem (as fast as possible).

- ➤ Ask your service provider to recommend a modem, and buy one that matches the specifications they give you (though not necessarily the exact modem they recommend).

- ➤ Ask the service provider if they know of any modems that won't work with their system.

- ➤ For dial-in terminal accounts, just about any simple data communications program should work.

- ➤ Pick a sensible password: make it long and seemingly random. Don't select real words, names, or numbers that have a meaning to others.

- ➤ Consider registering your own domain name so you don't have to change your e-mail address if you leave your service provider.

- ➤ The part of the domain name right at the end identifies the type of domain: .com means commercial, .edu means education, .jp means Japan, and so on.

Chapter 6

Connecting to the Internet: The Easy Way

In This Chapter

- ➤ So many options and choices
- ➤ One-click Internet access?
- ➤ Joining The Microsoft Network
- ➤ Getting Internet software from The Microsoft Network
- ➤ Overcoming obstacles

The Many Faces of Internet Access Through Windows 95

Wow, you have lots of options—and other options based on which option you choose. You'll see that you can choose from a number of different ways to set up your Internet access. I don't want to confuse anybody, but what you do next depends on the software you have available. And that depends on whether or not you want to be a member of The Microsoft Network (MSN).

If You Go Through The Microsoft Network...

Let's say you *do* want to be an MSN member. That's one decision down. Now you just have to get some Internet-access software.

➤ If you bought a new computer with Windows 95 installed, you probably already have The Microsoft Network and Internet software installed.

➤ If you have the Microsoft Plus! Pack (a $45 accessory pack for Windows 95), install the Internet Jumpstart Kit from the Plus! installation CD or disk set, and configure it for use with MSN. This is the easiest method; for more information, see the section "Joining MSN with the Microsoft Plus! Software," later in this chapter.

➤ If you don't have the Microsoft Plus! pack, install MSN, subscribe to the service, and then download the Internet software from MSN. You'll learn more about this method in the section "Joining MSN Without the Microsoft Plus! Software," later in this chapter.

If You'd Rather Not...

Now, let's say that you don't want to be an MSN member (perhaps you have found a cheaper Internet service provider, or you think that Bill Gates has enough of your money already) or that you tried it and are unable to join (they are limiting access to the first 500,000 members for a while). Again, that leaves you facing two options for acquiring the Internet software you need:

➤ If you have the MS Plus! pack, install the Internet Jumpstart Kit from the Plus! installation disk, but configure it for use with your service provider, not MSN. (See Chapter 7.)

➤ If you don't have the MS Plus! pack, install the TCP/IP software from your Windows 95 disks. Then configure the TCP/IP connection. (See Chapter 8.)

The latter method actually has some variations because Microsoft has spread the Internet software around a bit. For example, some of the things in the Internet Jumpstart Kit are also on the Windows 95 CD. So even if you don't have the Plus! pack, you can install most of what you need (and you can find the rest online). If you don't have the CD, though—if you bought Windows 95 on floppy disks—you won't find the Internet software at all. It isn't included. Still, you can download everything included in the Jumpstart Kit from various online sources, as I'll explain in Chapter 8.

But wait, there's one more option. Try MSN first by signing up for a free trial. If you don't like it, you can always switch to another service provider later—at which point, you'll have all the software you need, regardless of where it came from.

Chapter 6 ➤ *Connecting to the Internet: The Easy Way*

One-Click Internet Access!

By now, you've probably heard a lot of promises about Windows 95. The most significant one (in my opinion) is that Windows 95 provides "one-click Internet access."

Remember a few years ago when the phrase "user-friendly" was in vogue? It seemed like every program was "user-friendly," at least if you believed the advertising hype. The problem was that most programs were about as friendly as starving pit bulls. What does the term mean, then? Practically speaking, nothing. Apart from the fact that the term itself is a totally unnecessary bit of computer jargon (what's wrong with "easy to use"), it was simply a bloated advertising claim used for products that rarely lived up to the promises.

Back to "one-click Internet access," though, I won't belabor this, because you can probably already see where I'm heading:

> It doesn't matter which method you use to set up your Internet access, and it's going to take you a lot more than one click!

The easiest method probably takes a couple of dozen clicks (that's a guess, I haven't bothered to count), and the most difficult method will give your clicking finger quite a workout. So I give you my rule of thumb about the phrase "one click." When you hear it (in relation to any product, not only Windows 95), just remember the term "user-friendly."

Bought a New Computer?

Microsoft has been encouraging computer manufacturers to install Windows 95 with the MSN and Internet software ready to go. So if you've recently bought a brand new computer, you'll probably find icons on your desktop labeled **The Microsoft Network** and **The Internet**. If so, the software's there, and all you need to do is configure it. Alternatively, if you want to open an MSN account, skip forward in this chapter to "Joining MSN." And if you want to connect to another service provider, go to Chapter 7, "The Jumpstart Kit: Connecting to Other Service Providers."

Joining MSN Without the Microsoft Plus! Software

The rest of this chapter is about setting up Internet access through The Microsoft Network. If you don't want to do that, skip to Chapter 7.

I'm going to start by explaining what to do if you want to join MSN but you don't have the Microsoft Plus! pack. Although the Microsoft Plus! pack provides the quickest and easiest way to set up Internet access to join MSN, most people don't have the Plus! pack. So I'll begin with the second-easiest method.

Part 1 ➤ *Untangling the Wires and Getting It Running*

Do You Have the MSN Software?

The first thing you need to find out is whether you have the MSN software installed. You probably have it if you bought a new computer with Windows 95 already installed. If you installed Windows 95 yourself, you may have to do a little investigating to see if you told the Setup program to include the MSN software.

Minimize all your programs and look on the desktop. If you see an icon labeled The Microsoft Network, it's installed. Alternatively, you can select **Programs** from the **Start** menu. If the MSN software is installed, you'll see **The Microsoft Network** near the bottom of the Programs menu. If you don't have the MSN software installed, you can quickly install it. Follow this procedure:

1. Select **Start**, **Settings**, and **Control Panel**. The Control Panel window opens.

2. Double-click the **Add/Remove Programs** icon in the Control Panel (or click it once and press **Enter**). The Add Remove/Programs Properties dialog box appears.

3. Click the **Windows Setup** tab near the top of the window. After a few moments, a list box appears.

4. Scroll down the list, and click the little check box to the left of **The Microsoft Network**.

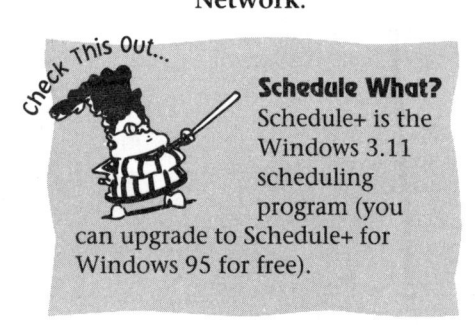

5. You may see a message box telling you that you have Schedule+ 1.0 installed and that once you install MS Exchange (an essential part of The Microsoft Network), group scheduling will be disabled. Close the message box.

6. Click **OK**. Windows 95 copies the files from your installation CD or disks to your hard drive. As it does, follow any on-screen instructions it gives you.

7. When the process is complete, click the **Close** (**X**) button in the upper-right corner of the Control Panel to close the window.

> **Check This Out...**
> **Schedule What?**
> Schedule+ is the Windows 3.11 scheduling program (you can upgrade to Schedule+ for Windows 95 for free).

Joining MSN

The next step is to set up an MSN account. Double-click **The Microsoft Network** icon on your desktop (minimize your applications if necessary so you can see the icon), or select **Start**, **Programs**, and **The Microsoft Network**. After a few moments, you see The Microsoft Network dialog box.

Chapter 6 ➤ *Connecting to the Internet: The Easy Way*

From The Microsoft Network dialog box, follow these steps to set up your account:

1. Click **OK**. The dialog box in the following figure appears, asking for your area or city code and the first three digits of your phone number. (Your area code may already be filled in, depending on the information you provided during Windows 95 setup.)

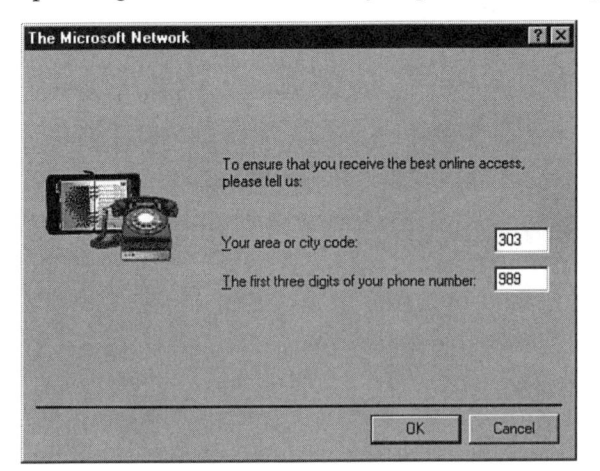

   Enter the first three digits of your phone number.

2. Enter the area code and the first three digits of your phone number and click **OK**. A message box appears, informing you that the program is about to connect to MSN.

3. Click the **Connect** button. The program dials into The Microsoft Network to find an MSN telephone number in your area.

4. After a short while, the program logs off MSN. You'll see a dialog box with three large buttons in the middle and several at the bottom.

5. Click **Price** to see information about current MSN prices and free trials. Then click the **Close** button to return to the previous dialog box.

6. Click the **Details** button to read a short description of MSN. Then click the **Close** button to return to the previous dialog box.

7. Click the **Tell us your name and address** button, and you see the dialog box in the next figure.

51

Part 1 ➤ *Untangling the Wires and Getting It Running*

Enter all your address information.

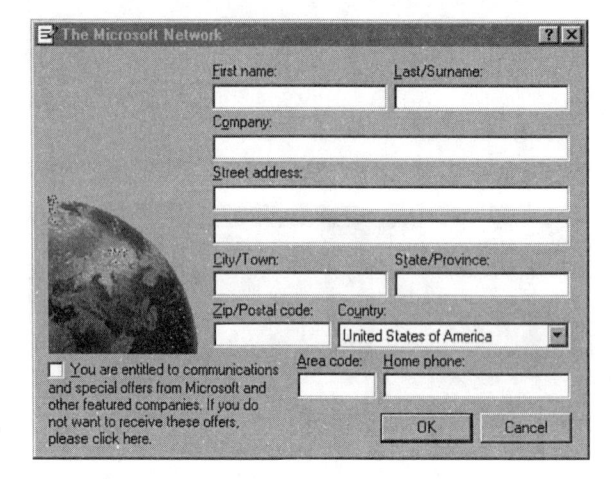

8. Fill in the requested information. As a minimum, you must enter your first and last names, street address, city, and ZIP code. Notice the check box in the lower-left corner. Click this if you don't want Microsoft sending you junk mail or selling your address! Click **OK** to return to the previous dialog box.

9. Click the **Next, select a way to pay** button. In the resulting dialog box (shown in the following figure), you must select a credit card and enter your bank name, card number (you can include dashes in the number if you want), and expiration date. Sorry. No credit card, no account! Modify the **Name on card** text box if necessary, and click **OK** to return to the previous dialog box.

Enter your credit card information.

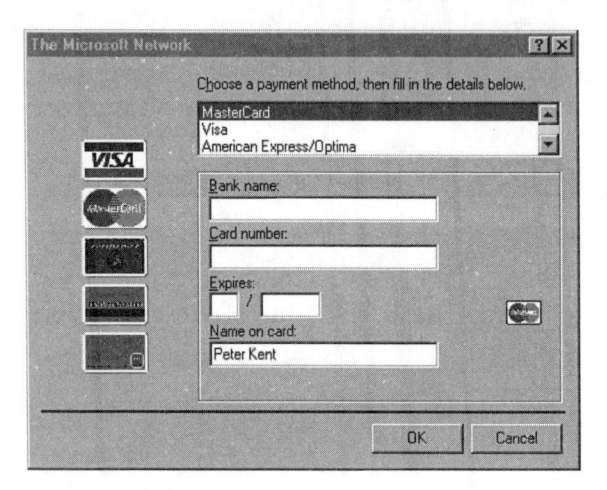

10. Click the **Then, please read the rules** button. (You may be tempted to skip this, but MSN won't let you proceed until you've opened this dialog box.) Read the rules and click the **I Agree** button (assuming you do agree, of course).

52

Chapter 6 ➤ *Connecting to the Internet: The Easy Way*

11. Click **Join Now**. The dialog box shown next will probably show you two telephone numbers, the Primary number and the Backup number. Take a quick look at the numbers to make sure MSN selected numbers in your area code (it should have, unless you mistyped your code earlier).

    If MSN doesn't find a number in your area code, it doesn't fill in these fields. If that happens, or if you need to change a number for some reason, click **Change**. A list of numbers from which you can select appears. Once you have the numbers you want, click **OK**.

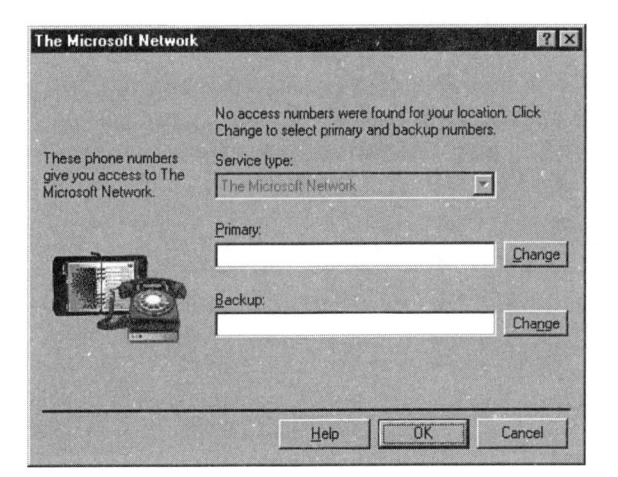

> **Check This Out...**
>
> **Save Your Money** Note that long-distance calls between states are often cheaper than those within a state. Call your phone company for rates.

This dialog box shows your local access numbers.

12. Another message box appears. Click the **Connect** button to dial into MSN again and transfer the information you have entered.

13. After a minute or two, you see the dialog box in the following figure. In the **Member ID** text box, enter your username (your MSN e-mail address). You can use as few as 3 or as many as 64 characters (numbers, letters, hyphens, and underscores; no spaces). In the **Password** text box, enter a password using 8–16 characters (letters, numbers, and hyphens). You can't type the same text or even anything very similar for the membership ID and the password.

> **Techno Talk**
>
> **Advanced Dialing?** Want to enter an advanced dialing procedure (using a credit card from a hotel, for instance)? Is the MSN number that's selected for you a long-distance number, even though it's in your area code? You can click the **Settings** button in this message box to modify the way you dial into MSN. See your Windows documentation for details.

53

Part 1 ➤ *Untangling the Wires and Getting It Running*

Type the membership ID and password you want to use.

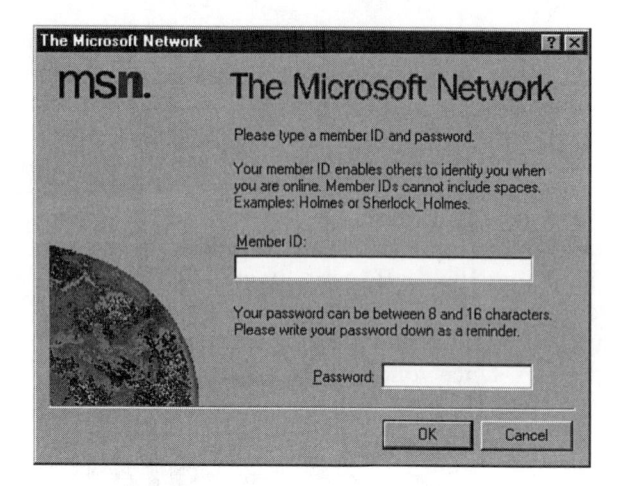

14. Write down your membership ID and password, and then click **OK**. A message box appears telling you that you've completed your setup.

15. Click the **Finish** button.

Getting the Internet Software

Well, you haven't finished yet! No, that one-click Internet access thing is going to require another few dozen clicks, I'm afraid. You've installed the MSN software, but not the Internet-access software. You can download that directly from MSN. (If you bought a new computer and found both The Microsoft Network and The Internet icons on the desktop, you already have the Internet software installed; skip to Chapter 9.)

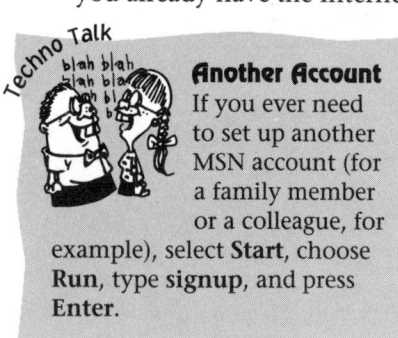

Techno Talk

Another Account
If you ever need to set up another MSN account (for a family member or a colleague, for example), select **Start**, choose **Run**, type **signup**, and press **Enter**.

Start by going to MSN's Internet forum. You can do that from MSN Central (the main MSN window that opens when you log on).

1. To log on to MSN, double-click **The Microsoft Network** icon on your desktop, or open the **Start** menu, choose **Programs**, and choose **The Microsoft Network**. When the Sign In dialog box opens (see the following figure), enter your password and click the **Connect** button. Your member ID should already be there.

54

Chapter 6 ➤ *Connecting to the Internet: The Easy Way*

Here's where you connect to MSN.

> **Save Your Password?**
>
> Notice the Sign In dialog box's Remember my password check box? If you select it, Windows 95 remembers your password and enters it for you. Use this only if you are sure that the only people using your computer are people you trust, or if you have set up a Windows 95 user profile and you log in to Windows 95 using a password.

2. When MSN Central opens, select **Edit**, **Go to**, and **Other Location**. Then type **internet** and press **Enter**.

3. In a few moments, the Internet Center folder opens. Click on the icon that seems like it may lead to the software you need. At the time of this writing, that was the **Getting on the Internet** icon, but that may have changed.

4. Double-click the **Internet Center** icon, and an online document opens.

5. Click the **Upgrade Instructions** icon to display another document.

6. Inside the document that now appears, click the icon next to **Click here to download** (or something similar). MSN begins transferring the software to your computer.

When the download finishes, you are disconnected from MSN. Then the Setup program begins. Take a deep breath, and dive in. Follow this procedure:

1. In the Welcome to Microsoft Network dialog box, click **OK**.

2. When you're prompted, enter the first three digits of your phone number and click **OK**.

55

3. A message box appears, telling you that Setup will connect to MSN and get new numbers. Click **Connect**.

4. In the MSN Sign In dialog box, enter your password if necessary (the Member ID should already be there) and click **Connect**. The program connects, gets the new numbers, and logs off.

5. MSN displays a dialog box showing the new TCP/IP numbers (the Internet-access telephone numbers) that it found. If it didn't find TCP/IP numbers in your area, you have two options: you can decide not to use MSN Internet access, or you can use a long-distance number to connect. To select new telephone numbers, click the **Change** button. (To return to using the normal, non-TCP/IP numbers, open the **Service Type** drop-down list and choose **The Microsoft Network**.)

6. When you finish selecting numbers, click **OK**.

7. When you see a dialog box telling you to restart, close your applications and click **OK**.

That's it. You've installed your Internet software. The next time you connect to MSN, you automatically use the TCP/IP telephone numbers. You'll also find a new icon on your desktop: The Internet. This opens the Internet Explorer, a Web browser, which we'll look at in Chapter 9.

The Internet-Access Numbers

Note that when you install the Internet software, the Setup program provides the MSN software with different phone numbers. To use Internet access, your MSN software has to dial numbers that will provide a TCP/IP connection. (You'll probably remember that TCP/IP means Transfer Control Protocol/Internet Protocol, the communications system used on the Internet.) By default, your MSN software is set up to automatically use these new numbers, with no action on your part. The next time you connect to MSN, you will be connecting to the TCP/IP lines.

If you ever want to stop using the Internet-access service, all you have to do is select different telephone numbers. To do that, access the MSN Sign In dialog box (the box that appears when you double-click the **MSN** icon) and click the **Settings** button to open the Connection Settings dialog box. Then click the **Access Numbers** button, open the **Service Type** drop-down list, and select **The Microsoft Network**. The old non-Internet-access numbers appear in the Primary and Backup text boxes.

Joining MSN with the Microsoft Plus! Software

Okay, now we'll look at the easiest way to set up Internet access. It's still nothing like "one click," but it is quick nonetheless. If you have Microsoft Plus!, you can install all the software directly from the Plus! CD or disks (and save some online time).

Run the **Microsoft Plus! Setup** program and select the **Internet Jumpstart Kit**. Then follow the instructions. At some point, you'll be asked if you want to use the Internet software with MSN. Respond **Yes**, and the setup program makes all the appropriate settings for you. The procedure for setting up your account and selecting the correct access numbers is very similar to the ones in the previous sections. See "Joining MSN" earlier in this chapter for information about setting up your MSN account.

The only real difference in setting up MSN and Internet access using the Plus! pack is that you do it all at once. You don't have to go to the Internet Center to download the Internet software because it's already installed. And when you have your MSN account set up, you can begin exploring the Internet right away. Skip to Chapter 9.

> **Check This Out...**
>
> **MSN's Other Book!**
>
> There's a lot about MSN that I'm not going to cover. This book is about using the Internet itself. You can connect to the Internet through MSN, but MSN also has many services of its own. If you want to learn about these services—the BBSs, chat rooms, online documents, multimedia reference "books," and more—get *Using The Microsoft Network*, also from Que. (And also from me!)

Problems? Surely Not!

Well, you may run into problems. Actually if you've joined MSN, you'll probably find it all fairly straightforward, and you shouldn't run into any problems. However, there are a few cases in which strange things may happen. Let's take a quick look.

Going Back to MSN

Suppose you originally set up Internet access with another service provider (as described in Chapters 7 and 8), but now you've decided that you want to become an MSN member. You can simply install the MSN software in the normal way. However, when you start MSN for the first time, you may see the message box shown in the next figure.

Part 1 ➤ *Untangling the Wires and Getting It Running*

MSN reports a problem with the DNS servers.

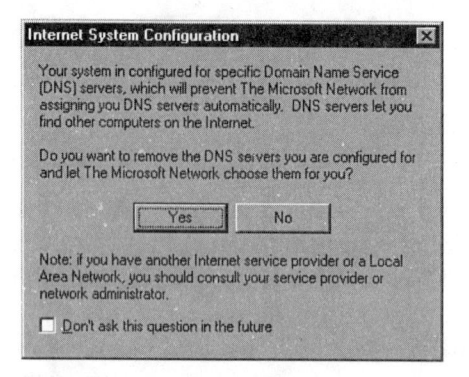

What's this all about? Well, when you set up your connection to the first service provider, you entered DNS (Domain Name System) server IP (Internet Protocol) addresses. DNS servers are computers that provide addressing information to your software to help your programs "navigate" the Internet. When you installed your first Internet connection, you entered the addresses of these servers. But the MSN service wants to provide those addresses for you; it doesn't want the network software to be configured for these addresses.

If you are no longer using your other service provider, click **Yes** and allow MSN to go ahead and make its changes. If you plan to use both service providers, though, you can probably shift the DNS numbers from the Network settings to the Dial-Up Networking properties.

Confused?
This won't make sense to you if you haven't set up Windows 95 for a service provider other than MSN. There again, if you haven't done that, you won't run into this problem. See Chapters 7 and 8 for more information.

These DNS numbers can be stored in two places. You can place them in the Dial-Up Networking properties for a particular service provider, or in the Network settings (opened from the Control Panel). If the numbers are in the Dial-Up Networking properties, they are used only for that connection. If they are in the Network settings, though, they are used for all TCP/IP connections for which DNS numbers have not been defined in Dial-Up Networking.

58

1. Select **Start**, **Programs**, **Accessories**, and **Dial-Up Networking** to open the Dial-Up Networking folder.
2. Right-click the **Connection** icon that represents the connection to your other (non-MSN) service provider and select **Properties**.
3. Click the **Server Type** button.
4. Click the **TCP/IP Settings** button.
5. Click the **Specify name server addresses** option button.
6. Enter the DNS numbers you got from your service provider.

Start MSN again. This time when you see the message, click the **Yes** button to remove the DNS numbers from the Network settings. They remain in the Dial-Up Networking properties but are removed from the Control Panel's Network settings.

It's also possible to keep the DNS numbers in the Network settings. If you click **No** in the message box, MSN uses those numbers. However, that may cause the MSN Internet service to be less reliable and to run slower.

Strange Things Are Happening

There are some bugs with the installation programs in Windows 95 and the Plus! package. If you've tried out a variety of different configurations—installing software for both MSN and another service provider, removing one or the other, or adding one or the other—strange things may start happening. For instance, you may not be able to view the URL (the "address" of a World Wide Web document) of a Favorites or History item when you look in the Properties dialog box (see Chapter 10). Or you may be able to connect to the Internet via your service provider, but when you try to use Internet Explorer, the MSN Connect dialog box might open.

Windows 95 doesn't correctly keep track of everything it removes and adds. If you run into these problems, I suggest that you remove MSN and the Internet Jumpstart Kit, and then reinstall the software. (You don't have to create a new MSN account. When you run the Sign Up program, you'll see a check box asking if you want to create a new account or just set up your computer for an existing account.)

Part 1 ➤ *Untangling the Wires and Getting It Running*

The Least You Need to Know

➤ There are a number of ways to configure Windows 95 for Internet access, so read carefully!

➤ There's no such thing as "one-click" anything!

➤ If you see The Microsoft Network icon on your desktop, the software's already installed. You can set up your account.

➤ The easiest way to set up Internet access is by installing the Internet Jumpstart Kit from Microsoft Plus! and configuring it for The Microsoft Network.

➤ If you don't have the Jumpstart Kit, set up your MSN account, and then download the Internet software from the MSN Internet Center. (Go Internet.)

➤ If you try many different Internet configurations and services, Windows 95 can get confused. You may have to remove the software completely and reinstall to fix this.

Chapter 7

The Jumpstart Kit: Connecting to Other Service Providers

In This Chapter

- The different ways to connect to other service providers
- PPP vs. SLIP
- Getting information from your service provider
- Installing from Microsoft Plus!
- Setting up your TCP/IP software
- Using ping to test your connection
- Setting up a SLIP connection

In Chapter 6, you saw the easy way to connect Windows 95 to the Internet—through The Microsoft Network. Okay, it was nothing like one click, but it took a lot fewer clicks than what you're going to use if you connect to another service provider. In fact, I'd advise that you do some finger exercises before you start. You may want to run down to your local sporting goods store and buy one of those little hand exercisers that rock climbers use.

You can connect to another service provider in any of the following ways (listed from easiest to most difficult):

➤ Install the Internet Jumpstart Kit from the Microsoft Plus! pack. You get the Dial-Up Scripting Tool, the Internet Explorer Web browser, and special software to help you install a SLIP connection. The Jumpstart Kit automatically loads the Dial-Up Networking software from your Windows 95 CD or disks if you haven't already done so.

> **You Can't Stop Here** If you use the Dial-Up Networking software (which you can install directly from the Windows 95 installation CD or disk set), there's a good chance that you'll also need the Dial-Up Scripting Tool to make it more convenient.

➤ Install the Dial-Up Networking software from your Windows 95 CD. Find the Dial-Up Scripting Tool and, if necessary, the SLIP software (they're hidden on the CD; I'll tell you where). Then go online and download Internet Explorer.

➤ Install the Dial-Up Networking software from your Windows 95 disk set. When you use this method, you don't have the Dial-Up Scripting Tool or the SLIP software. However, you can go online and download them, along with Internet Explorer. (See Chapter 8.)

In this chapter, I'm going to explain the first of these methods, how to use the Internet Jumpstart Kit. If you don't have that, skip to the next chapter.

PPP or SLIP?

I advise that you get a PPP (Point-to-Point Protocol) Internet account, which most service providers offer these days. PPP can boast two advantages over SLIP (Serial Line Internet Protocol): PPP accounts are generally quicker and more stable than SLIP accounts, and the Windows 95 software is configured to use PPP.

If you want to use SLIP, you have to install some extra software. This software is available in three places:

➤ **Jumpstart Kit** When you install the Internet Jumpstart Kit from the Microsoft Plus! pack, the SLIP software is also installed.

➤ **Windows 95 CD** It's hidden away, but the SLIP software is on the Windows 95 CD.

➤ **Online** SLIP software is available in a variety of places online: MSN, the Internet, and CompuServe to name a few.

Later in this chapter, I'll explain how to set up a SLIP account, in case you really want to do that (see the section "I Have to Use SLIP"). But if it's at all possible, go with PPP.

Chapter 7 ➤ *The Jumpstart Kit: Connecting to Other Service Providers*

Gathering Information

Whichever method you use, you should start by gathering some information from your service provider. (Do you have a service provider? If not, see Chapter 4 to find out how to get one.) Ever heard of the game 20 Questions?

The first question you should ask is this: Do you have some kind of setup program that will set up my Windows 95 Dial-Up Networking software to connect to your system? The answer will probably be no, especially in the first few months after the release of Windows 95. Perhaps eventually some service providers will offer such a service.

The next question to ask—assuming you got a "no" answer to the first one—is this: Do you have some kind of instruction sheet that tells me what to do? Some service providers already have written instructions that explain what information you should enter into which dialog box. I'm going to help you with that to some degree, but I can't know the particulars—the actual names and numbers—that you must enter.

Question #3 is this: Do you have a script file for the Windows 95 Dial-Up Scripting Tool? If your service provider doesn't seem to know what you are talking about, here's what you tell them: "The Dial-Up Scripting Tool lets you associate a log-in script with a particular service provider in order to help the Dial-Up Networking program connect to that service provider; the script file is an .SCP file." If you are lucky, your service provider will have a script file. (You'll learn more about the Dial-Up Scripting Tool later in this chapter. For now, you can get by just knowing that it saves you a lot of trouble.)

Getting back to the game of questions, you need to get the following information from your service provider:

User name   The name assigned to your account: your account name, user name, account ID, Member ID, Login name, or whatever your service provider calls it.

Password   The password you use to access your account.

Phone number   The telephone number your modem has to dial in order to connect to your service provider.

IP address   The Internet Protocol address, which represents your computer when it's connected to the Internet. Ask your service provider if they "dynamically (or automatically) assign" a number. If they do, their software tells your software what number to use when it connects, and it may vary each time. If the number is not dynamically assigned, ask them what numbers you must enter for the IP Address and the Subnet Mask. With PPP, the IP address is normally assigned automatically, so you are not given a number.

DNS Server Address The number you must enter for your Domain Name Service server. This number identifies a computer that is used to help your software find resources on the Internet. The DNS system is a sort of giant directory in which each DNS server contains a portion of the information needed to route transmissions across the Internet. Ask your service provider if they have an alternate DNS Server Address. Many have only one address, but some provide two or more.

Domain name Your service provider's domain name, which is something like usa.net or mcp.com. The Domain name identifies your service provider's computer to the rest of the Internet.

Domain suffix A suffix added to the domain name. For instance, a domain suffix may be something like ns1.usa.net. (Strictly speaking, the *ns1* bit is the suffix, and the usa.net bit is the domain name; however, you'll enter the suffix and domain name together.) Ask if you have to enter a domain suffix, and if so, ask exactly what you should enter.

Gateway A link from one network to another. Ask if you need to enter a gateway number. It's quite possible that you won't have to (they're more often used when setting up Internet access from a LAN), but some service providers may give you such a number.

Your e-mail address The address you give to other people so they can send e-mail to you. Your e-mail address might be robinhood@sherwood-forest.com, for example.

Internet mail server The address of your mail server. (For instance, mine is mail.usa.net.)

> **Check This Out...**
>
> **Need I Say It Again?** If your service provider can provide you with a PPP account (and most can these days), get a PPP account and forget about this SLIP stuff.

SLIP or CSLIP CSLIP (Compressed SLIP) is a common variation of SLIP. If you have a SLIP connection instead of a PPP connection, ask if the service provider uses SLIP or CSLIP.

Log-in instructions Instructions about how to log on to the service provider's system. You need to know how your particular service provider expects you to log in. For instance, many systems require that you type a command (ppp, for instance) and press Enter to begin running the PPP protocol.

When you are armed with all this information, you are ready to install the software.

Chapter 7 ➤ *The Jumpstart Kit: Connecting to Other Service Providers*

The Easy Way—Using Microsoft Plus!

Let's begin with the easy way. Suppose you want to set up an Internet account with a service provider other than MSN, and you have the Microsoft Plus! software available. Follow this procedure:

1. Place the Microsoft Plus! CD into your CD drive (or put the first floppy disk of the set in your floppy disk drive).

2. Select **Start**, **Settings**, and **Control Panel**.

3. Double-click the **Add/Remove Programs** icon.

4. In the dialog box that opens, click the **Install** button.

5. In the next dialog box that you see, click the **Next** button. Windows 95 looks for SETUP and INSTALL programs on the disk in your floppy disk drive or the CD in your CD drive.

6. When Windows 95 finds a SETUP or INSTALL program, it displays the Run Program dialog box. Look closely at the drive on which it says it found the program to make sure it didn't find the wrong one. (If you have the Microsoft Plus! CD in your CD-ROM drive but you've accidentally left a program disk in your floppy disk drive, it may find the program on the floppy disk first.)

   If the program shown is not the SETUP.EXE program on the Microsoft Plus! disk, click **Browse** to open a typical Windows 95 Browse box. Find the program on the correct disk and double-click it.

7. When the correct program appears in the Run Program dialog box, click **Finish**, and Windows 95 runs the Setup program.

8. In the first message box you see, click **Continue**.

9. In the dialog box that follows, type your name and your organization's name, and then click **OK**. Click **OK** again in the next dialog box to confirm your name and organization.

10. Click **OK** in the Product Number dialog box.

11. Next you see a dialog box that tells you where the Microsoft Plus! files will be placed on your hard drive. Click **OK**.

12. When given the choice of a Typical or a Custom installation, click the **Custom** button.

13. The Setup program displays a dialog box that lists the products available in Microsoft Plus!. Choose the ones you want, and make sure that the **Internet Jumpstart Kit** is selected. Click the **Continue** button, and Setup begins copying the files to your hard disk.

Part 1 ➤ *Untangling the Wires and Getting It Running*

> **Check This Out...**
>
> **Wizard** A *wizard* is a series of dialog boxes that walks you through a procedure (such as installing a program).

> **Check This Out...**
>
> **There's an Easier Way** You can select the **Bring up terminal window after dialing** check box to open a special window in which you can see the text being transmitted between your service provider's computer and your computer during the login procedure. You can then type your user name and password into this terminal window to log in. However, I'm going to show you how to create a login script that will do all this automatically, so don't check the check box.

What happens next depends on the items you chose to install. Let's say you are installing only the Internet Jumpstart Kit. If so, the Internet Setup Wizard dialog box opens.

1. In the first dialog box, click the **Next** button, and the Wizard shows you two options. Click the option button labeled **I already have an account with a different service provider**, and then click **Next**.

2. When the Wizard asks you to enter the name of your service provider, type the name and click **Next**.

3. Next you enter the telephone number you must dial to connect to your service provider. (In a few cases, you might have to open the **Country code** drop-down list and select the country code that you dial to contact your service provider.) Make sure the Bring up terminal window after dialing check box is empty, and then click **Next**.

4. In the next dialog box, enter the **User name** (also known as account name, User ID, and so on) that identifies your account with this service provider, and the **Password** that you use. Type the password very carefully because the Setup program displays asterisks in place of the characters you type (so nobody can look over your shoulder at the screen and see your account password). Then click **Next**.

5. The next dialog box (shown in the following figure) asks you how your IP (Internet Protocol) address is assigned. It's probably assigned dynamically (automatically), in which case you should select the first option button. If your service provider told you to enter IP Address and Subnet Mask numbers, click the **Always use the following** option button and enter those numbers. (Make sure you enter the periods between the individual numbers that make up the IP number.) Then click **Next**.

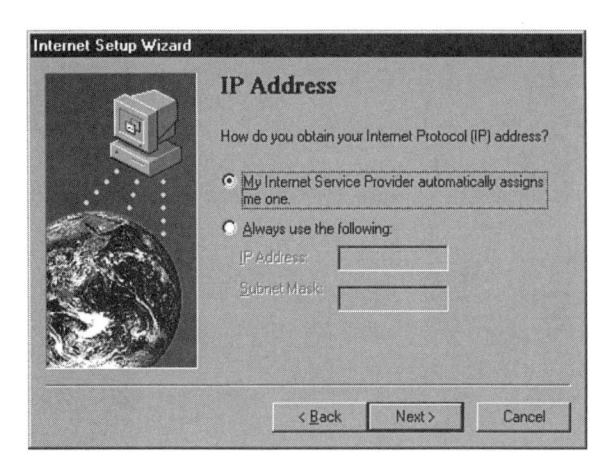

Chapter 7 ➤ *The Jumpstart Kit: Connecting to Other Service Providers*

Enter information about your IP address.

6. The next dialog box (shown in the following figure) asks for your DNS server address. Provide the IP address of at least one DNS server (use two servers if your service provider gave you more than one number). Then click **Next**.

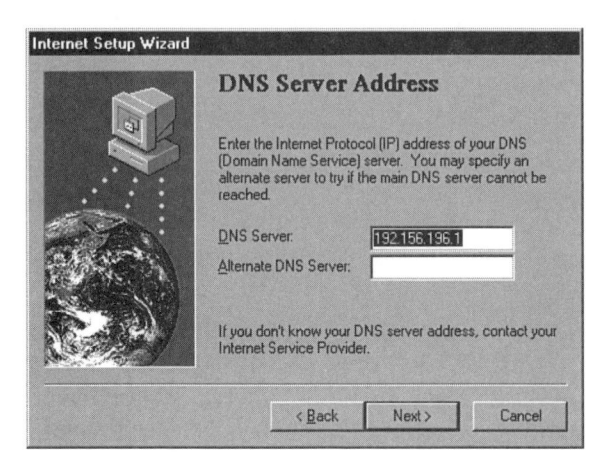

Enter the DNS numbers.

7. The next dialog box (see the following figure) asks if you want to use e-mail. Microsoft Exchange, the e-mail program that comes with Windows 95, uses the information you enter here. (You'll learn more about e-mail in Chapters 21 and 22.) Click the **Use Internet Mail** check box, and then enter your e-mail address and the Internet mail server.

67

Enter your e-mail information.

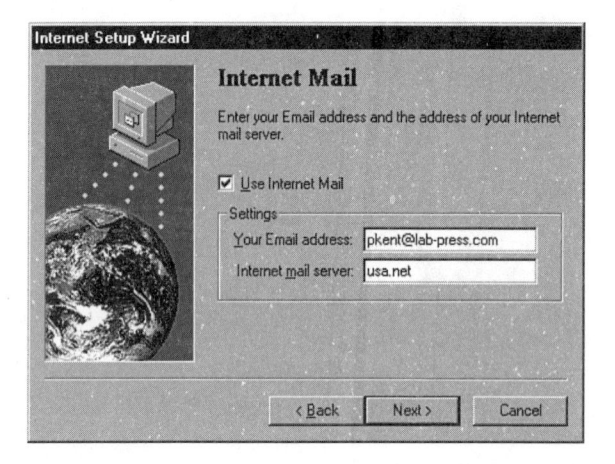

8. The next dialog box asks you which "profile" you want to use for Microsoft Exchange. You should leave the settings in this dialog box alone unless you understand all about profiles. (See Chapter 21 for more information.) Click the **Next** button.

9. Setup displays a dialog box to tell you that you've finished the Internet setup. That's being optimistic. Actually, you've probably got a lot more work ahead of you! (You'll know in a few minutes.) Click the **Finish** button to close the dialog box.

10. When you see a dialog box telling you that you must restart your computer, click **Restart Windows**.

If you want to set up a SLIP account, you're not quite finished. See the section "I Have to Use SLIP," later in this chapter. If you're using PPP, read on.

> **Check This Out...**
>
> **Create a Shortcut** In the Dial-Up Networking folder, right-click the icon that represents your Internet connection and choose **Create Shortcut** from the shortcut menu. Windows places a shortcut on your desktop, so you can quickly start an Internet session by double-clicking on the shortcut.

Does It Work?

Back in Windows, you can quickly check your settings to see if they work. Select **Start**, **Programs**, **Accessories**, and **Dial-Up Networking**. The Dial-Up Networking folder opens, and inside it you find an icon representing the Internet connection you just created. Double-click the icon, and the Connect To dialog box opens. Enter your password (the user name is already entered) and click **Connect**. The program dials into your service provider.

Did you get all the way through to a message that says **Connected at *nn,nnn* bps**? (The *nn,nnn* is the speed of your modem, such as 28,800.) Or did you get a message telling you that **Dial-Up Networking could not negotiate** a compatible set of network protocols, or something similar? If you got the second of these messages, you didn't manage to get all the way through. Why? Because you don't have a login script.

Many users won't have to create a login script, so I put the information on how to do it in the Appendix, "Creating a Login Script," at the end of this book. If you do have to use a script, flip back there, create your script, and then come back here.

> **Check This Out...**
>
> **Watch for This Bug!**
>
> There's a little bug at work in Dial-Up Networking. The problem is this: After you see the message **Dial-Up Networking could not negotiate a compatible set of network protocols**, Dial-Up Networking may simply quit trying to connect. In other words, even if you set up everything correctly and write a good login script, Dial-Up Networking still may not connect properly if it has already had a bad session. The only way around the problem is to restart Windows 95 and try again.

You're Connected, But Is It Working?

Even if Dial-Up Networking tells you that your connection has been made, that doesn't mean that the connection is working correctly. Here's a quick way to test the connection.

Select **Start**, **Programs**, **MS-DOS Prompt**. When the MS-DOS window opens, type **ping** followed by an Internet host name. For example, try **ping usa.net**, **ping ftp.microsoft.com**, **ping ftp.mcp.com**, **ping www.mcp.com**, **ping csn.org**, **ping gopher.sara.nl**, or any other Internet host name you've come across. You can even try to ping your service provider's host name. If one doesn't work, try another (it may be that the host you tried is not operating at the moment). If your connection is working correctly, you should see something like this:

```
C:\WIN95>ping csn.org
Pinging csn.org [199.117.27.21] with 32 bytes of data:
Reply from 199.117.27.21: bytes=32 time=232ms TTL=239
Reply from 199.117.27.21: bytes=32 time=239ms TTL=239
Reply from 199.117.27.21: bytes=32 time=237ms TTL=239
Reply from 199.117.27.21: bytes=32 time=236ms TTL=239
```

The ping command sends a message to a host and asks it to respond. It's a good way to confirm that you can communicate with a host. And if you can communicate with a host, your TCP/IP connection is working correctly!

Part 1 ➤ *Untangling the Wires and Getting It Running*

Still Not Working?

The procedures you have worked through in this chapter will probably be enough to get your connection working. However, this TCP/IP thing is very complicated. It has lots of variations, and you may find that you can't get your connection running this way. You may need to enter more configuration information. Follow this procedure:

1. Select **Start**, **Settings**, and **Control Panel**.

2. When the Control Panel opens, double-click the **Network** icon.

3. In the Network dialog box, click the **TCP/IP** entry and click the **Properties** button. Windows displays the dialog box shown in the following figure.

You can enter more TCP/IP information in this dialog box.

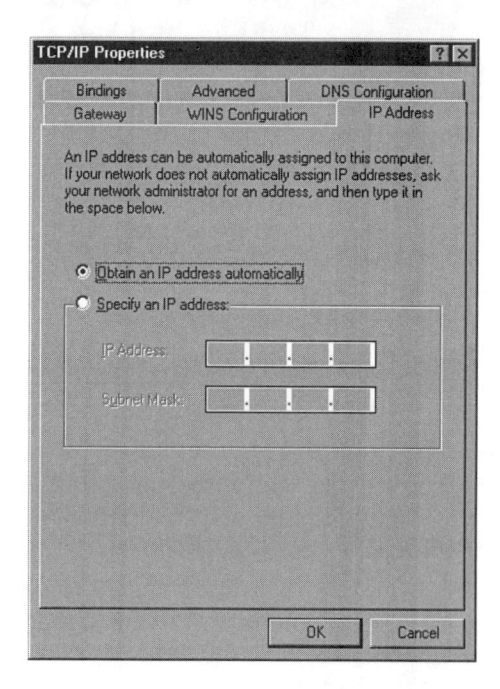

4. If your service provider told you that the IP address would be assigned dynamically or automatically, leave **Obtain an IP address automatically** selected. If you were given an IP address, click **Specify an IP address**. Then type the number into the **IP Address** box. If you were given a Subnet Mask number, enter that, too.

5. Click on the **Gateway** tab at the top of the dialog box. You probably won't need to enter anything in here. However, if your service provider gave you a gateway number, enter it in the **New Gateway** text box and click the **Add** button.

6. Click the **DNS Configuration** tab to see the options shown in the next figure.

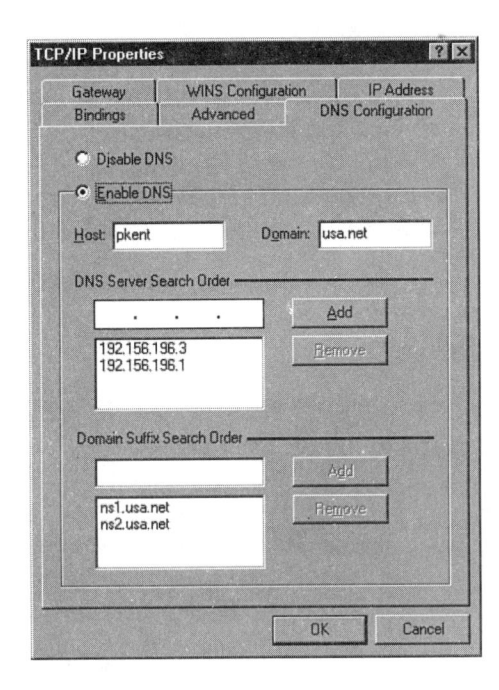

Chapter 7 ➤ *The Jumpstart Kit: Connecting to Other Service Providers*

Enter the Domain Name Service information.

7. You'll almost certainly have to select **Enable DNS**. Most service providers provide one or more DNS numbers that you need to enter.

8. Enter a **Host** and **Domain**. The Host is your computer name. (It doesn't matter what you put here for our purposes; I suggest you just enter your account name.) In the Domain text box, enter your service provider's host name.

9. In the text box below DNS Server Search Order, type the primary DNS server number your service provider gave you. Then click the **Add** button to place the number in the list box. Add any other DNS server numbers they gave you in the same way.

10. If your service provider gave you a domain suffix, enter it in the **Domain Suffix Search Order** text box. (You'll enter the domain name preceded by some other letters and/or numbers.) Then click **Add**.

What About the Other Tabs?

The other tabs in this dialog box (WINS Configuration, Bindings, and Advanced) contain options related to setting up a TCP/IP network. I will not cover that topic in this book; I'll leave it up to your system administrator. Change things on these tabs only if your service provider or system administrator specifically told you to.

71

Part 1 ➤ *Untangling the Wires and Getting It Running*

11. Click **OK** to finish the TCP/IP setup.
12. Click **OK** to close the Network dialog box. In the dialog box telling you that you must restart your computer, click **Yes**.

Now try connecting to your service provider again and try pinging again to see if the connection works. If you're lucky it will. If you're not lucky, you'll have to ask your service provider for help in getting you set up.

I Have to Use SLIP

> **Check This Out...**
> **You're Ready to Go** The SLIP software was installed when you installed the Internet Jumpstart Kit from Microsoft Plus!.

If you really have to use a SLIP connection instead of a PPP connection, you have a few more steps to run through. First of all, you must have used the Internet Setup Wizard to set up your Internet connection. If you haven't already done that, go back to that procedure (covered earlier in this chapter) and work through it. When the Wizard finishes setting up the connection, follow these steps:

1. Select **Start**, **Programs**, **Accessories**, and **Dial-Up Networking**.
2. In the Dial-Up Networking dialog box, right-click the new connection icon and choose **Properties**.
3. In the dialog box that appears, click **Server Type**. You'll see the dialog box shown in the following figure.
4. Open the **Type of Dial-Up Server** drop-down list and select **Slip: Unix Connection** or **CSLIP: Unix Connection with IP Header Compression**, depending on which form of SLIP your service provider uses. (If your service provider has both, the choice is yours. Choose CSLIP.)
5. Click **OK** to close this dialog box. Then click **OK** again to close the Server Types dialog box.
6. Flip back to the Appendix, "Creating a Login Script," and create a login script. Then test your script and connection (which is also covered in the Appendix) to see if it works.

Chapter 7 ➤ *The Jumpstart Kit: Connecting to Other Service Providers*

Note that there are a couple of ways to handle the IP address assigned to your SLIP account. You can tell the Wizard which IP address to use, or you can add a line to your login script, telling Dial-Up Networking to "grab" the IP number from your service provider.

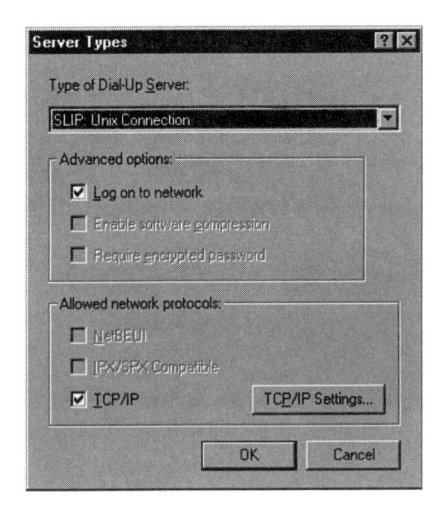

In the Server Types dialog box, you select the type of connection you want to make.

For instance, here's what I see when I dial into my service provider's system and log on using SLIP:

```
Type "c" followed by <RETURN> to continue slip
Annex address is 165.212.158.10. Your address is 165.212.158.117
```

The second number on the last line is my IP address, which my service provider's system assigns to me automatically. However, this number changes (it's dynamic). So although I might get the same number the next time I connect, I probably won't. Therefore, I've added the following line to my SLIP login script to tell Dial-Up Networking to use the second number:

```
set ipaddr getip 2
```

The **2** at the end refers to the position of the number on the line. If I had used a 1, Dial-Up Networking would grab the first number on the line (165.212.158.10) which is wrong, of course. It is the address of the Annex, the computer I'm connecting to.

73

The Least You Need to Know

➤ Microsoft Plus! provides all the Internet software you need. (If you don't have Plus!, see Chapter 8.)

➤ Get a PPP account instead of a SLIP account if possible. PPP is faster and more stable, and it takes slightly less time to set up.

➤ You need to get information such as IP numbers and domain names from your service provider before you can set up your TCP/IP software.

➤ Install the Internet Jumpstart Kit from Microsoft Plus!. Then use the Internet Setup Wizard to set up your software.

➤ When you finish the setup, try to log in. If the login procedure doesn't work, you probably need a login script (see the Appendix).

➤ Use the ping command to see if your TCP/IP connection is really working.

➤ If you have a SLIP connection, you must select SLIP in the Dial-Up Networking Properties dialog box before you try to connect.

Chapter 8

Internet the Hard Way: Installing from Scratch

In This Chapter

- Finding Windows 95 Internet software online
- Installing Dial-Up Networking
- Installing the TCP/IP software
- Configuring the TCP/IP software
- Logging onto your service provider—automatically and manually
- Downloading the Dial-Up Scripting Tool from an FTP site

If you're reading this chapter, we can assume two things:

1. You want to set up an Internet account with a service provider other than The Microsoft Network.
2. You don't have the Microsoft Plus! kit.

So what are you gonna do? Well, first, you're going to answer a couple of other questions.

>Do you have any kind of online access already?

>Do you have the Windows 95 CD?

You see, Microsoft has made a version of the Internet Jumpstart Kit available online. It's not *quite* the same as the one in the Microsoft Plus! pack (at least, not at the time of this writing). It doesn't include the Dial-Up Scripting Tool or the SLIP software, for example. (If you have the Windows CD, you can find those hidden away in a directory on the CD.) However, it does include the Internet Explorer Web browser and the Internet Setup Wizard.

So I'm going to start with the best-case scenario: what you need to do if you do have some kind of online service. Then I'll move on to the worst-case scenario: what you need to do if you have no MS Plus! pack and no online access.

Downloading from the Internet and Online Services

If you already have access (or perhaps have a friend or colleague with access) to the Internet, CompuServe, Prodigy, America Online, or GEnie, find and download Internet Explorer. It's located in the following places:

➤ The Internet's World Wide Web: **http://www.windows.microsoft.com/windows/ie/ie.htm**. (If this URL doesn't work, go to the Internet Explorer home page at **http://www.home.msn.com/** and dig around.) Also try **http://www.windows.microsoft.com**.

➤ The Internet's FTP system: **ftp.microsoft.com/PerOpSys/Win_News/FreeSoftware**.

➤ CompuServe: **GO WINNEWS**

➤ Prodigy: **JUMP WINNEWS**

➤ America Online: keyword **WINNEWS**

➤ GEnie: **MOVE TO PAGE 95**

You may have to dig around a bit to find the file you want. In fact, you may need to ask the sysop or forum manager where you can find the file you need. It's not always easy to find the file. In CompuServe, I found it in library 4 of the WINNEWS forum.

You'll download an executable file (currently it's called MSIE10.exe). Run this file to install the software on your hard disk. Reboot Windows, and then double-click on **The Internet** icon that the installation program placed on your Windows desktop. The Internet Setup Wizard starts. For more information on the Internet Setup Wizard, flip to "The Easy Way—Using Microsoft Plus!" in Chapter 7.

> **Check This Out...**
>
> **Stick with Version 1.0!**
> Just before we went to print, Microsoft released the 2.0 beta version of Internet Explorer. However, at the time of this writing, that version did not include the Internet Jumpstart Kit, which you need for the purposes of this chapter. So download version 1.0 (it's available at the same Web page). You can always go back and upgrade to version 2.0 later.

Chapter 8 ➤ *Internet the Hard Way: Installing from Scratch*

As you learned in Chapter 7, you'll probably also need the Dial-Up Scripting Tool. In addition, if your service provider can't give you a PPP account, you'll need the SLIP software. If you have Windows 95 on a CD, you'll find these programs in the ADMIN\APPTOOLS\DSCRIPT directory on the CD. Read the DSCRIPT.TXT file for installation instructions. After you install these items, go to the Appendix for instructions on creating a login script and, if necessary, see Chapter 7 for information on setting up a SLIP connection.

If you don't have the CD version of Windows 95, you'll have to work a little harder because you won't find these applications on your floppy disks. However, they should be available online at http://www.windows.microsoft.com/windows/software/admintools.htm and the other locations I've just noted. (Look for links and categories such as Windows 95 CD-ROM Extras, Administration Tools, Dial-Up SLIP and Scripting Support.)

Bare Bones—Starting from Scratch

Okay, you've come to the very end, the most complicated setup. You don't want to use The Microsoft Network, you don't have Microsoft Plus!, and you don't have any kind of online access. You don't have friends, either... I mean, um, you don't have friends with online access.

Well, aren't you the lucky one. I wrote the rest of this chapter for you. It explains how to go about getting started without the help of the Internet Setup Wizard. When it comes right down to it, you have everything you need; it's just a bit more trouble to set it all up.

Installing Dial-Up Networking

Let's begin by installing the Dial-Up Networking software. This is the software you'll use to dial your service provider. It may already be installed. Select **Start**, **Programs**, and **Accessories**. Look in the Accessories cascading menu that opens; if you see an entry for Dial-Up Networking, the software is already installed. If you don't see it, follow this procedure to install it:

1. Select **Start**, **Settings**, and **Control Panel**.
2. When the Control Panel opens, double-click the **Add/Remove Programs** icon.
3. Click the **Windows Setup** tab.
4. In the **Components** list, click the **Communications** entry.
5. Click the **Details** button.
6. Click in the **Dial-Up Networking** check box.

77

Part 1 ➤ *Untangling the Wires and Getting It Running*

7. Click **OK** to close the dialog box. Then click **OK** to finish.

8. The Windows Setup program begins copying the necessary files. Insert disks when prompted.

9. When the entire process is complete, restart your computer.

Installing the Networking Components

The next step is to install the TCP/IP network protocol. Follow this procedure.

1. Open the **Start** menu, select **Settings**, and select **Control Panel**.

2. When the Control Panel opens, double-click the **Network** icon. You'll notice that a number of components are already listed in the Network dialog box. When you installed Dial-Up Networking, the Setup program installed the items you see in the following figure.

The Network dialog box already contains any components that were installed when you installed Dial-Up Networking.

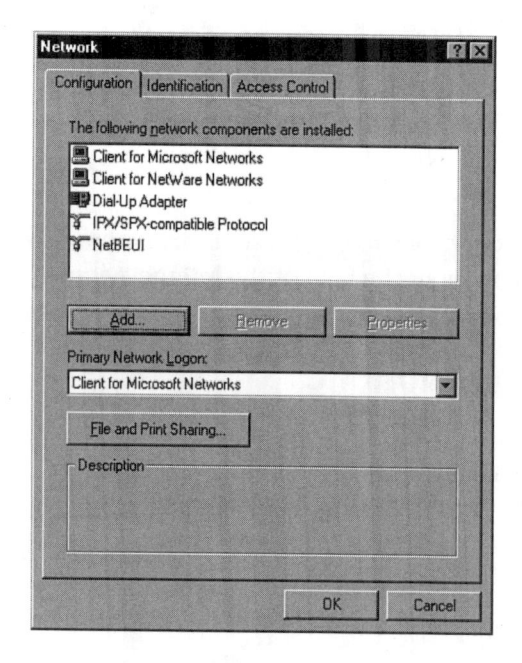

3. In the Network dialog box, click the **Add** button.

4. The Select Network Component Type dialog box (shown in the next figure) appears. Click **Protocol** and click the **Add** button.

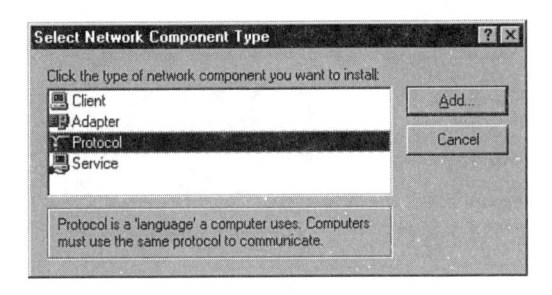

Chapter 8 ➤ *Internet the Hard Way: Installing from Scratch*

The Select Network Component Type dialog box lets you add protocols.

5. In the Select Network Protocol dialog box (below), select **Microsoft** from the **Manufacturers** list and select **TCP/IP** from the **Network Protocols** list. Click **OK** to return to the Network dialog box.

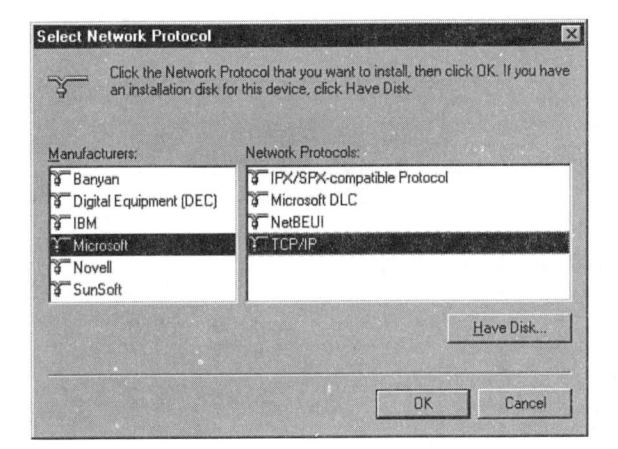

Select the Microsoft TCP/IP protocol.

6. Click the **Identification** tab of the Network dialog box to see the options shown in the next figure.

7. Type a **Computer name** and **Workgroup**. You can ignore the last text box, but you must enter something for the first two. Although for our purposes it doesn't much matter what you enter, this information is necessary if you are connecting to a LAN (for instance). I suggest you enter your login name and the word **Workgroup**.

8. When you finish, click **OK**. The setup program begins copying files from your Windows 95 installation disk to your hard disk.

9. After you copy the files, restart your computer when prompted to do so.

79

Part 1 ➤ *Untangling the Wires and Getting It Running*

On the Identification tab, enter identifying information about your computer.

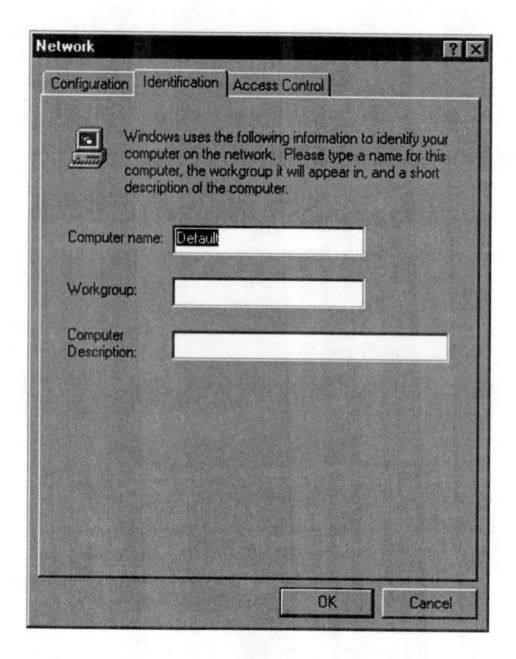

Remove Some Things

When you install Dial-Up Networking, Windows 95 installs a variety of things that you don't need for Internet access: Client for Microsoft Network, Client for Netware Networks, IPX/SPX-compatible Protocol, and NetBEUI. If you are sure you don't need these things (for access to your company's LAN, for instance), click the **Configuration** tab, click the first item, and click the **Remove** button. Repeat for the other items you want to remove.

Setting Up the Connection

Now that you've installed the software you need, you are ready to set up your Internet connection. See "Gathering Information" in Chapter 7 for the questions you need to ask your service provider.

A good service provider should be willing to help you set up this stuff. My service provider, for example, gave its technical-support staff a set of instructions for setting up the Windows 95 TCP/IP software. Other service providers are unwilling or unable to help. Before you attempt to carry out the following configuration by yourself, ask your service provider to help you. If they won't do it, maybe you need another service provider.

80

Chapter 8 ➤ *Internet the Hard Way: Installing from Scratch*

Anyway, once you have all the information you need, follow this procedure:

1. Open the **Start** menu, select **Programs**, **Accessories**, and **Dial-Up Networking**.

2. When the Dial-Up Networking dialog box opens, double-click the **Make New Connection** icon. A wizard opens.

3. Type the name of your service provider into the **Type a name for the computer you are dialing** text box, as shown in the following figure.

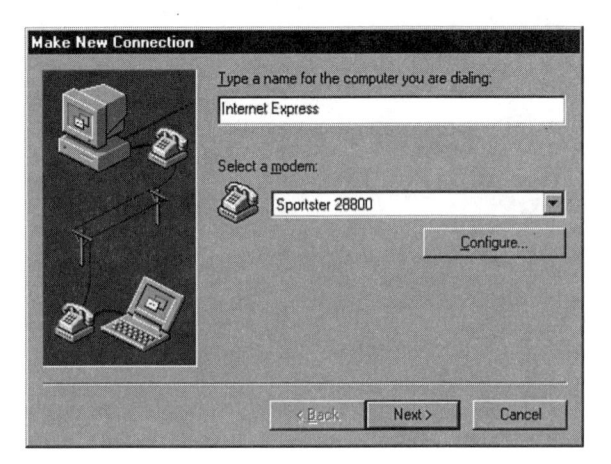

The Make New Connection Wizard helps you create your Dial-Up Networking connection.

4. The Select a modem box will already show a modem. If this is not the correct one, open the drop-down list and select the correct one. Click the **Next** button.

5. Enter the telephone number you dial to connect to your service provider (see the following figure). Note that this number is only the phone number; it doesn't include a number you need to dial to get an outside line or to turn off call waiting, for example. That is done in the modem configuration (see your Windows 95 or modem documentation).

> **Check This Out...**
>
> **Install New Modem Wizard** If you haven't yet installed or configured your modem, you'll see the Install New Modems Wizard instead of the next dialog box. See your Windows 95 or modem documentation for information on how to install the modem.

6. If you have to dial into another country to connect to your service provider (which is unlikely), open the **Country code** drop-down list and select the country you must dial.

7. Click the **Next** button, and you see a message telling you that you've successfully created your connection. That's not exactly true; there's still plenty to be done. Click the **Finish** button.

Part 1 ➤ *Untangling the Wires and Getting It Running*

Enter the phone number your modem has to dial to connect to your service provider.

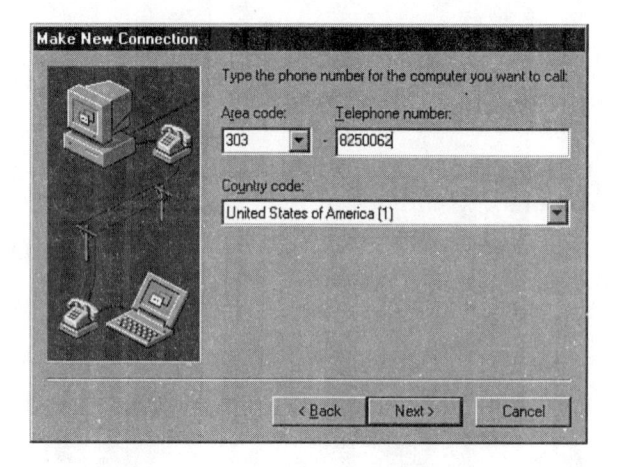

Setting Up the Properties

Unfortunately, you still have a few things to do. Knew it couldn't be that easy, didn't you? Well, move right along to setting up the connection properties.

1. Go back to the Dial-Up Networking window and right-click the icon you just created. Select **Properties** from the pop-up menu (called a "shortcut menu" in Windows 95). You then see the connections properties dialog box shown in this figure.

This box shows the properties for the connection you just created.

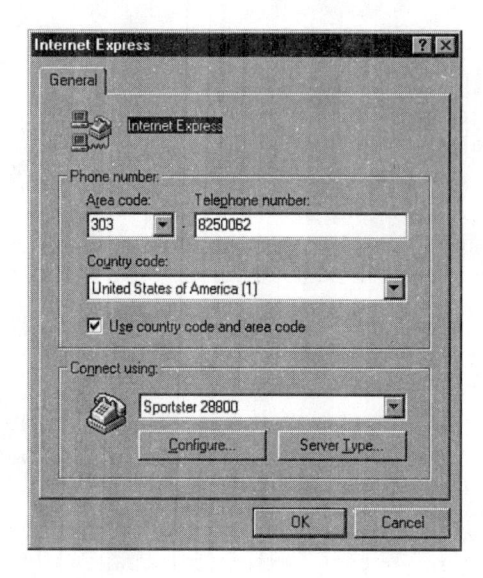

82

Chapter 8 ➤ *Internet the Hard Way: Installing from Scratch*

2. Click the **Configure** button to go to the modem properties dialog box.
3. Click the **Options** tab to see the options in the following figure.

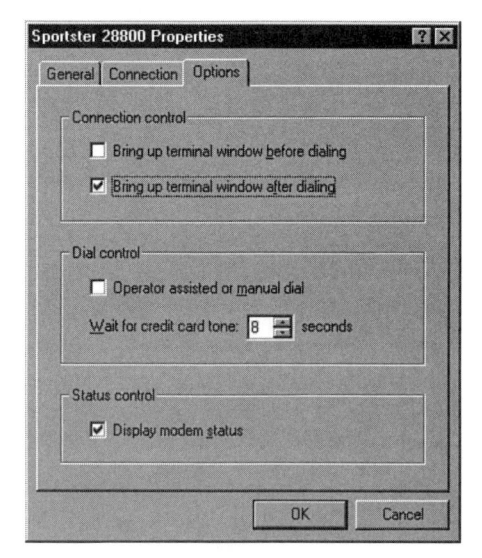

What you do here depends on whether you have the Windows 95 CD.

4. This step depends on whether you have the Windows 95 CD or floppy disks. If you *don't* have the CD, click the **Bring up terminal window after dialing** check box to turn this feature on so you can log on to the service provider manually. Without the CD, you don't have the scripting software. If you *do* have the CD, leave this check box empty. Then click **OK**.
5. Back in the connection properties dialog box, click the **Server Type** button to see the Server Types dialog box (see the next figure).
6. In the **Type of Dial-Up Server** list box, select **PPP; Windows 95, Windows NT 3.5, Internet** (if it's not selected already).

I Want SLIP!

If you have the Windows 95 CD, you can find the SLIP software on the CD in the ADMIN\APPTOOLS\DSCRIPT directory. Read the DSCRIPT.TXT file for installation instructions. If you don't have the CD, you won't have the SLIP software. You'll have to find someone with the CD, or find someone with online access who can get the SLIP software for you (see "Downloading from the Internet and Online Services" earlier in this chapter). When you have the SLIP software installed, see "I Have to Use SLIP" in Chapter 7.

Part 1 ➤ *Untangling the Wires and Getting It Running*

Select the connection type in the Server Types dialog box.

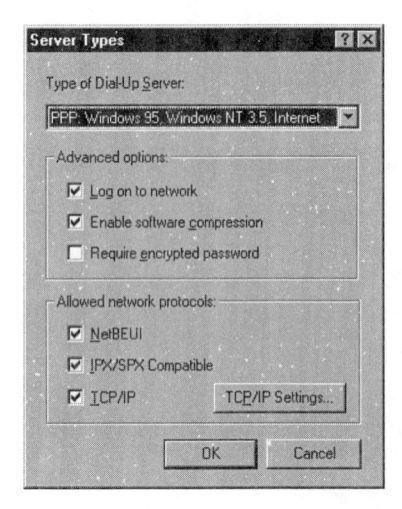

7. Click the **TCP/IP Settings** button to open the TCP/IP Settings dialog box, which you can see in the figure below.

Enter the IP numbers into the TCP/IP Settings dialog box.

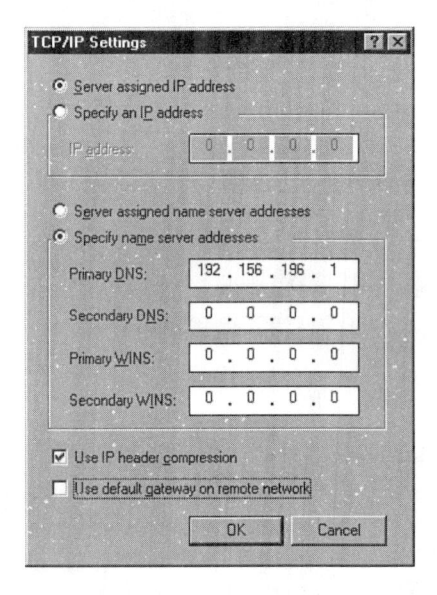

8. If your service provider told you your IP address is assigned automatically, make sure the **Server assigned IP address** option button is selected. If your service provider told you to use a particular IP address, click **Specify an IP address** and type the number into the **IP address** box.

9. If your service provider told you that the DNS name server is assigned automatically (it's probably *not*), leave the **Server assigned name server addresses** option button

Chapter 8 ➤ *Internet the Hard Way: Installing from Scratch*

selected. Otherwise, click the **Specify name server addresses** option button and enter the DNS address your service provider gave you in the **Primary DNS** box. If you were given a second number, enter it into the **Secondary DNS** box.

10. Leave the other items in this dialog box alone unless your service provider told you to change them.

11. Click **OK** to close the dialog box; then click **OK** twice more to return to the Dial-Up Networking window.

Dial-Up Scripting?

What now? Well, you should first go to the section "Does It Work?" in Chapter 7, to see if you can connect to your service provider. And if you can't? If you have to write a log in script? Well, what happens at that point depends on whether or not you have the Windows 95 CD.

If you *do* have the CD, open **Windows Explorer** and view the contents of the CD. Take a look in the **ADMIN\APPTOOLS\DSCRIPT** directory for the **DSCRIPT.TXT** file, and follow the instructions in that file to install the Dial-Up Scripting Tool. Then go to the Appendix and follow the instructions for creating a login script.

> **Tired of Jumping Around?** Look, I hate to keep sending you here and there, but Windows 95's one-click Internet access is *so* simple that it seems to be taking up half this book! The least I can do is conserve space and not repeat myself then. So if I've covered the topic elsewhere, I'll have to get you to flip back a few pages.

If you *don't* have the Windows 95 CD, you'll have to work without dial-up scripting for now. But I will show you how to get that tool a little later (see "Getting the Rest of the Stuff" later in this chapter).

Connecting to Your Service Provider

If you are still reading, it means that you've installed Dial-Up Networking, but not the Dial-Up Scripting Tool (because you don't have the CD). Let's see how you can connect to your service provider manually, that is, without the login script. Follow these steps:

1. In the **Dial-Up Networking** folder, double-click the icon representing the connection you just created. That connection's Connect To dialog box opens (see the following figure). Ignore the User name and Password text boxes this time. Because you are going to log on manually, you'll be entering this information into the Post-Dial Terminal Screen in a moment.

85

Part 1 ➤ *Untangling the Wires and Getting It Running*

No need to bother with the user name and password.

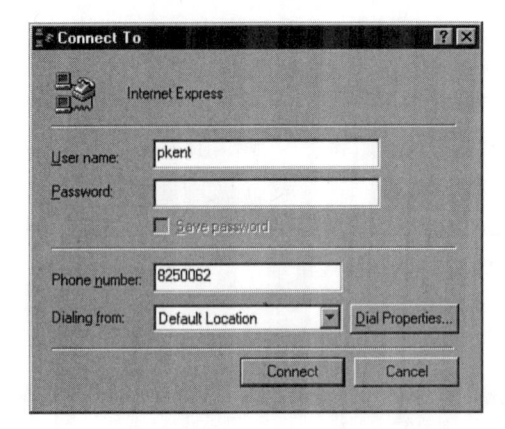

2. Click **Connect**, and Dial-Up Networking begins to dial into your service provider. In a few moments, you'll see the Post-Dial Terminal Screen shown in the next figure.

The Post-Dial Terminal Screen is where you type your login commands.

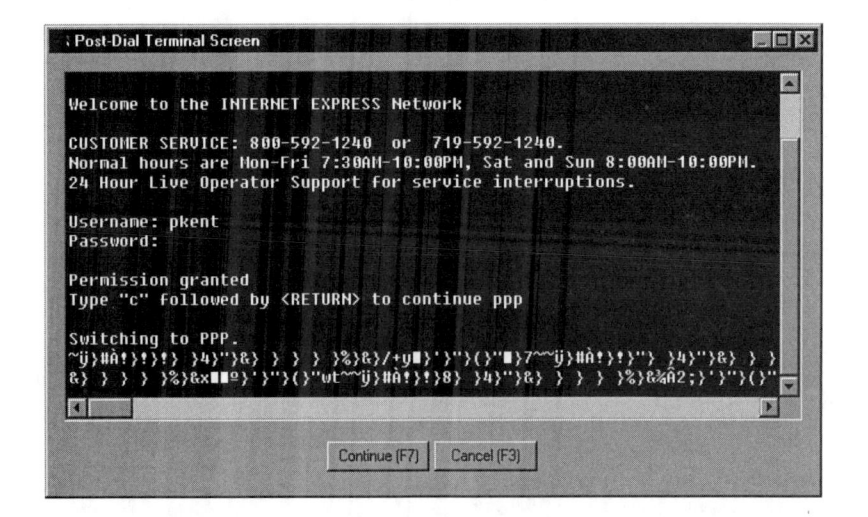

3. Click on the **Maximize** button (next to the X button in the upper-right corner of the window).
4. Type the login commands into this window. You can see from this example that I typed my user name, my password, and the **ppp** command.
5. When your service provider's computer begins the PPP protocol, click the **Continue** button. The Post-Dial Terminal Screen closes, and your session begins.

How do you know the session has begun? After a few moments, you see the Connected to dialog box shown in the following figure.

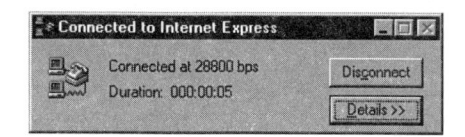

Chapter 8 ➤ *Internet the Hard Way: Installing from Scratch*

This is what you see when you are connected.

This dialog box doesn't actually confirm that the connection is working correctly, only that Dial-Up Networking *thinks* it is. To learn a quick way to verify that you really do have a TCP/IP connection that's working correctly, see "You're Connected. But Is It Working?" in Chapter 7. To disconnect your session, click the **Disconnect** button.

Are you still having problems? I suggest you read "Still Not Working?" in Chapter 7. And remember to ask your service provider for help! Setting these things up is complicated, and there are many variations. You must get everything just right for it to work.

Getting the Rest of the Stuff

You shouldn't have to log in to your service provider manually. You really should have a login script program that automates this process. Microsoft originally forgot to add this feature to Windows 95 (an oversight, so one product manager told me), but they quickly added the feature shortly before Windows 95 was released. Strangely, though, they added it to the Plus! pack and hid it on the Windows 95 CD so it's not part of the standard Windows 95 set of tools. Therefore, if you don't have the Plus! pack or the Windows 95 CD, you don't have dial-up scripting.

Scripting and SLIP

Microsoft has combined the Dial-Up Scripting Tool with the SLIP software. I think their reasoning is that if you have a PPP connection, you probably won't need the Dial-Up Scripting Tool, whereas if you have the SLIP software, you probably will. I believe this reasoning is completely wrong. Microsoft assumes that when you dial into a TCP/IP connection you see a **Login:** prompt, followed by a **Password:** prompt, and that the computer you've dialed into immediately goes into PPP mode. But many, many systems are *not* configured this way. They require that you go through a login procedure quite different from that, and they often require you to type a command to start PPP mode. Thus, many PPP users will need the Dial-Up Scripting Tool. It's a shame it wasn't built into Dial-Up Networking instead of being hidden away.

Dial-up scripting is still available, though, and I'm going to show you how to get hold of it using an Internet system called FTP (File Transfer Protocol). You'll learn much more about this system in Chapter 12. For now, we're going to use the old UNIX program. Well, it's not exactly a UNIX program because it runs in Windows 95's DOS window. But it's a DOS version of the UNIX FTP program, and it will give you a taste of what you are missing by working with GUI programs. (You'll be grateful for the GUI, believe me!)

> **Check This Out...**
>
> **Do You Have Norton Navigator?** I'm going to explain how to use a nasty little command-line program to work with FTP. However, if you've installed Norton Navigator, a set of tools sold by Symantec, you already have an FTP tool; it's built into Norton File Manager. Read your documentation to see how to use it.

For now, just follow instructions, and you'll be okay. Note, though, that this software is available on the World Wide Web (at http://www.windows.microsoft.com/windows/software/admintools.htm) and on CompuServe, America Online, Prodigy, and GEnie. If you can find someone with access to those services to help you, it may be easier to do that than to work with FTP. Another problem is that I know of only one FTP site where the Dial-Up Scripting Tool is available, and if that site is down (as FTP sites sometimes are), you're stuck. (Still, you can always continue using your Internet connection by logging on manually, and come back and get the Dial-Up Scripting Tool later.) You could also use FTP to download Internet Explorer (explained in Chapter 9), and then use Internet Explorer to retrieve the Dial-Up Scripting Tool. (Explorer can operate as an FTP program; see Chapter 12.)

Here's what you need to do. Start by logging on to the Internet. Then select **Start**, **Programs**, and **MS-DOS Prompt**. The DOS window opens. At the DOS prompt, type **ftp** and press **Enter**. You'll see the **FTP>** prompt.

Here is the FTP session. The bold text is what I typed. Type each command at the appropriate place and then press **Enter**.

```
C:\WIN95>ftp ftp.microsoft.com
Connected to ftp.microsoft.com.
220 ftp Windows NT FTP Server (Version 3.51).
User (ftp.microsoft.com:(none)): anonymous
331 Anonymous access allowed, send identity (e-mail name) as password.
Password: (type your e-mail address and press Enter)
230-This is ftp.microsoft.com.  Please see the index.txt file for more
    information
230 Anonymous user logged in as anonymous.
```

Chapter 8 ➤ *Internet the Hard Way: Installing from Scratch*

Use the **dir** command as shown here to see what is in the current directory.

```
ftp> dir
200 PORT command successful.
150 Opening ASCII mode data connection for /bin/ls.
d---------   1 owner    group              0 Jul  3 14:52 bussys
d---------   1 owner    group              0 Aug  9  4:00 deskapps
d---------   1 owner    group              0 Dec 21  1994 developr
----------   1 owner    group           7782 Aug  1 10:03 dirmap.htm
----------   1 owner    group           4441 Aug  1 10:03 dirmap.txt
----------   1 owner    group            712 Aug 25  1994 disclaimer.txt
----------   1 owner    group            860 Oct  5  1994 index.txt
d---------   1 owner    group              0 Aug 31 13:17 KBHelp
----------   1 owner    group        6921254 Sep  6  4:05 ls-lR.txt
----------   1 owner    group         885313 Sep  6  4:06 ls-lR.Z
----------   1 owner    group         677056 Sep  6  4:06 LS-LR.ZIP
----------   1 owner    group          28160 Nov 28  1994 MSNBRO.DOC
----------   1 owner    group          22641 Feb  8  1994 MSNBRO.TXT
d---------   1 owner    group              0 Oct  7  1994 peropsys
d---------   1 owner    group              0 Aug 23 22:55 Products
d---------   1 owner    group              0 Jul 21 12:39 Services
d---------   1 owner    group              0 Sep  1 15:51 Softlib
----------   1 owner    group           5095 Oct 20  1993 support-phones.txt
----------   1 owner    group            802 Aug 25  1994 WhatHappened.txt
226 Transfer complete.
1340 bytes received in 0.82 seconds (1.63 Kbytes/sec)
```

The file you want is currently in the Softlib directory. Use the following commands to change to the directory and see what's there.

```
ftp> cd softlib
250 CWD command successful.
ftp> dir
200 PORT command successful.
150 Opening ASCII mode data connection for /bin/ls.
----------   1 owner    group         115704 Aug 31 11:30 index.old
----------   1 owner    group         115857 Sep  1 16:21 index.txt
d---------   1 owner    group              0 Sep  1  9:34 MSLFILES
----------   1 owner    group           2764 Jun  1 17:35 README.TXT
----------   1 owner    group         248656 Aug 31 12:58 SOFTLIB.EXE
----------   1 owner    group          48654 Dec 21  1994 WDL.TXT
```

```
         ---------  1 owner     group              11407 Mar 18  3:47 WNTDL.TXT
226 Transfer complete.
490 bytes received in 0.27 seconds (1.81 Kbytes/sec)
```

Now you need to enter the MSLFILES directory. (Note, by the way, that at many FTP sites, you must type directory names exactly as they appear—MSLFILES, not mslfiles. At this particular site, that's not necessary.)

```
ftp> cd mslfiles
250 CWD command successful.
```

The directory you are now in contains hundreds of files, including the one you want, DSCRPT.EXE. But before you transfer it, check to see what type of file transfer this site has been set up for.

```
ftp> type
Using ascii mode to transfer files.
```

You *don't* want to do an ASCII transfer (that's just text). So change to binary with this command.

```
ftp> binary
200 Type set to I.
```

Turn on hash marks so you can see that the file is being transferred.

```
ftp> hash
Hash mark printing On (2048 bytes/hash mark).
```

Get the file with the **get** command.

```
ftp> get dscrpt.exe
200 PORT command successful.
150 Opening BINARY mode data connection for dscrpt.exe(57307 bytes).
########...
226 Transfer complete.
57307 bytes received in 26.15 seconds (2.19 Kbytes/sec)
```

When you have the file, you can close the connection to the FTP site and close the MS-DOS window.

```
ftp> bye
221 Thank you for using ftp.micrsoft.com!
C:\WIN95>exit
```

Now go to your Windows directory and find the DSCRPT.EXE file. Create a new directory and move the file into that directory.

Some FTP Tips

The session you just looked at worked at the time of this writing. The problem is, if the files are moved for any reason, the session won't work. The following tips will help you get around:

➤ To open a directory, type **cd** *directoryname* and press **Enter**. Type the directory name exactly as it appears on your screen, using the same upper- and lowercase letters.

➤ To move back to the previous directory, type **cd ..** and press **Enter**. (Note that there's a space after **cd**).

➤ Look for text files; these often contain information that will help you find the file you need. To read one, type **get** *filename* ¦**more** and press **Enter**. The text appears on your screen, page by page. (Press **Spacebar** to move to the next page.)

> **Check This Out...**
>
> ### Where's DSCRPT.EXE?
>
> At the time of this writing, DSCRPT.EXE was available only at the ftp.microsoft.com site in the /Softlib/MSLFILES directory. It will probably remain in this directory. However, it's also supposed to be somewhere in the /peropsys/Win_News directory or a subdirectory of that directory. So if you can't find the file when you follow my instructions, try using the **cd** and **dir** commands to move to the /peropsys/Win_News directory.

If you still can't find the file you need, try to find someone with the CD or with access to the World Wide Web, CompuServe, Prodigy, America Online, or GEnie.

What Now?

Now that you have the file on your computer, go to Windows Explorer and double-click it. Windows expands the contents of the file (it's a compressed "archive" file) and displays it. Read the expanded text file (README.TXT) and follow the instructions for installing the software. Then go to the Appendix and read the instructions for creating a login script.

Part 1 ➤ *Untangling the Wires and Getting It Running*

The Least You Need to Know

- ➤ If you have access to the Internet, CompuServe, Prodigy, GEnie, or America Online, you can download the Internet software.
- ➤ If you download this software, you can return to Chapter 7 and follow the instructions there.
- ➤ If you don't have online access, you can set up a TCP/IP account and then use FTP to grab the Dial-Up Scripting Tool from Microsoft's FTP site.
- ➤ If you have the Windows 95 CD, you'll find the Dial-Up Scripting Tool and SLIP software in the ADMIN\APPTOOLS\DSCRIPT directory.
- ➤ Install Dial-Up Networking; then install the TCP/IP software.
- ➤ If you never get the Dial-Up Scripting Tool, you can always log in to your service provider manually.

Part 2
Working on the Web

The Web. The Internet. What's the difference? The media doesn't seem to know, but there **is** a difference. The World Wide Web is simply one Internet tool among many—it just happens to be the most exciting and popular Internet information tool. When you hear people talking about "surfing the Net," they're usually talking about traveling around on the World Wide Web.

In this section, I'll tell you what the Web is and how to use it. You'll learn how to work with Microsoft's Internet Explorer, the free Web browser you can find in several places. If you are not using Explorer, don't worry. The concepts and most of the techniques are the same with just about any browser. You'll find out how to move around the Web and how to make the most of the Web's multimedia experience.

Chapter 9

Think Global: The World Wide Web

In This Chapter

- ➤ What is the World Wide Web?
- ➤ Finding Internet Explorer
- ➤ Why you don't need Netscape
- ➤ Where to find Netscape if I haven't convinced you
- ➤ Web basics

When I wrote the first edition of *The Complete Idiot's Guide to the Internet* late in 1993, I included a chapter about the World Wide Web. I put it near the back of the book, and it bears little resemblance to the information about Web that appears in this book. Back then, and even well into 1994, the World Wide Web was an Internet backwater, an interesting little system that few people used.

Today, however, it's the Web that is fueling the growth of the Internet. Many people, when they visualize the Internet, are really seeing the World Wide Web. Many people think the Web and the Internet are synonymous, that Web is just another term for the Internet. So what is the Web?

What's the Web?

The *World Wide Web* (also called WWW, The Web, or sometimes even W3) is a hypertext system that helps you travel around the world electronically, looking for information.

WWW is very easy to use—probably the easiest Internet system you'll find. The Web lets you follow a "trail" of links. You select a topic that interests you, and you view related information; from there, you select another topic that interests you, and you view information related to that topic. In this way, you move from one topic to another, hopefully moving closer to where you want to be. (You'll see exactly what I mean in a moment.) If you ever decide you've taken the wrong trail, you can quickly return whence you came.

> **Check This Out...**
>
> ### What Is Hypertext?
>
> If you've ever used a Windows Help file or a Macintosh HyperCard file, you've used hypertext. A *hypertext document* lets you jump from place to place in one document or to other documents using links of some kind. Instead of reading the document from front to back, you can select one piece of text and move to a piece of related text elsewhere in the document. The Web is often referred to as hypermedia, because it's not just text. It also has pictures, sounds, video, and plenty more.

Okay, You've Sold Me—Where's the Browser?

In order to use the World Wide Web, you'll need to get hold of a *Web browser*, a program that displays Web documents. Most of you already have a Web browser: Internet Explorer. If you installed the Internet Jumpstart Kit from Microsoft Plus!, if you joined MSN and then downloaded the Internet software, or if you downloaded the Internet Explorer software from the Internet or another online service, you should see an icon on your desktop labeled The Internet. Double-click on **The Internet** icon, and the browser opens.

If you followed the instructions in Chapter 8 for setting up an Internet connection from scratch, and you didn't download the Internet software from the Internet or an online service, you still have some work to do. You need to install a browser. I advise that you download either Internet Explorer or Netscape. Internet Explorer is a very good browser that is integrated into Windows 95, and it's the browser I'm going to describe in this book. I also mention Netscape because it's currently the most popular browser available (though Internet Explorer is also an excellent browser and is, in some ways, better than Netscape).

All browsers are similar in many ways. Even though I'm working with Internet Explorer in this book, the principles apply to any graphical Web browser. (The alternative to a graphical browser is called a *text-based* browser. Text-based browsers include programs such as Lynx and the line-mode browser, which are used for nongraphical computer systems. Luckily, you don't need to mess with these.)

Grabbing the Program

You saw in Chapter 8 how to use the Windows 95 FTP program to grab files from the Microsoft FTP site. You can do this to grab the Internet Explorer file. (Remember, though, it may be easier to find someone with access to the Web or one of the online services listed in Chapter 8.)

If you really want to try it, here's how to grab the file. Log on to the Internet, open an MS-DOS window, type **ftp ftp.microsoft.com**, and press **Enter**. (Or log on to the Internet, open the **Start** menu, select **Run**, type **ftp ftp.microsoft.com**, and press **Enter**.) The FTP program starts and attempts to connect to the ftp.microsoft.com site. Here's what you'll see:

```
C:\WIN95>ftp ftp.microsoft.com
Connected to ftp.microsoft.com.
220 ftp Windows NT FTP Server (Version 3.51).
User (ftp.microsoft.com:(none)): anonymous
331 Anonymous access allowed, send identity (e-mail name) as password.
Password: nnnnnn                  (type your e-mail address and press Enter)
230-This is ftp.microsoft.com.  Please see the index.txt file for more
    information
230 Anonymous user logged in as anonymous.
```

Type **dir** at the prompt to see a list of the current directory's contents.

```
ftp> dir
200 PORT command successful.
150 Opening ASCII mode data connection for /bin/ls.
d---------   1 owner    group            0 Jul  3 14:52 bussys
d---------   1 owner    group            0 Aug  9  4:00 deskapps
d---------   1 owner    group            0 Dec 21  1994 developr
----------   1 owner    group         7782 Aug  1 10:03 dirmap.htm
----------   1 owner    group         4441 Aug  1 10:03 dirmap.txt
----------   1 owner    group          712 Aug 25  1994 disclaimer.txt
----------   1 owner    group          860 Oct  5  1994 index.txt
d---------   1 owner    group            0 Aug 31 13:17 KBHelp
```

Part 2 ➤ *Working on the Web*

```
----------  1 owner group  6921254 Sep  6  4:05 ls-lR.txt
----------  1 owner group   885313 Sep  6  4:06 ls-lR.Z
----------  1 owner group   677056 Sep  6  4:06 LS-LR.ZIP
----------  1 owner group    28160 Nov 28  1994 MSNBRO.DOC
----------  1 owner group    22641 Feb  8  1994 MSNBRO.TXT
d---------  1 owner group        0 Oct  7  1994 peropsys
d---------  1 owner group        0 Aug 23 22:55 Products
d---------  1 owner group        0 Jul 21 12:39 Services
d---------  1 owner group        0 Sep  1 15:51 Softlib
----------  1 owner group     5095 Oct 20  1993 support-phones.txt
----------  1 owner group      802 Aug 25  1994 WhatHappened.txt
226 Transfer complete.
1340 bytes received in 0.82 seconds (1.63 Kbytes/sec)
```

You need to go into the peropsys directory and see what's in there. So type **cd peropsys**, and then type the **dir** command again.

```
ftp> cd peropsys
250 CWD command successful.
ftp> dir
200 PORT command successful.
150 Opening ASCII mode data connection for /bin/ls.
d---------  1 owner group        0 Oct  7  1994 GEN_INFO
d---------  1 owner group        0 Aug 24  1994 hardware
d---------  1 owner group        0 Aug 24  1994 msdos
----------  1 owner group     1571 Aug 25  1994 readme.txt
d---------  1 owner group        0 Sep  4 12:35 Win_News
d---------  1 owner group        0 Jul 28 12:35 windows
226 Transfer complete.
412 bytes received in 0.17 seconds (2.42 Kbytes/sec)
ftp>
```

Move into the Win_News directory by typing **cd win_news**. Then type the **dir** command again.

```
ftp> cd win_news
250 CWD command successful.
ftp> dir
200 PORT command successful.
150 Opening ASCII mode data connection for /bin/ls.
d---------  1 owner group        0 Aug 20 21:43 archive
```

Chapter 9 ➤ Think Global: The World Wide Web

```
----------  1 owner group    12800 Aug 15 12:14 DATES.DOC
----------  1 owner group    13312 Aug 31 16:19 disktwo.doc
d---------  1 owner group        0 Aug 11 17:09 Docs
d---------  1 owner group        0 Aug 19 18:55 FreeSoftware
d---------  1 owner group        0 Aug 11 17:06 News&Events
----------  1 owner group     1567 Feb  8 12:30 oldreadme.txt
d---------  1 owner group        0 Dec  8  1994 PPT
----------  1 owner group     3859 Sep  4 12:45 README.TXT
d---------  1 owner group        0 Aug  3  8:51 TechnicalInfo&Support
d---------  1 owner group        0 Aug 23 20:45 Windows95CompatibleProducts
d---------  1 owner group        0 Aug 19 18:36 Windows95Information
----------  1 owner group    25088 Sep  1 13:28 winsock.doc
----------  1 owner group   133645 Aug 29  1994 Wintat.zip
226 Transfer complete.
1023 bytes received in 0.49 seconds (2.09 Kbytes/sec)
```

Trust me, you're getting close. Move into the Windows95Information directory.

```
ftp> cd windows95information
250 CWD command successful.
ftp> dir
200 PORT command successful.
150 Opening ASCII mode data connection for /bin/ls.
----------  1 owner group    99328 Aug 15  8:37 AUGUSTQA.DOC
----------  1 owner group  1388935 Jul 25 20:26 autodemo.exe
----------  1 owner group      685 Jul 28 18:29 AUTODEMO.TXT
d---------  1 owner group        0 Aug 23 19:29 InternetExplorer
d---------  1 owner group        0 Aug 19 14:24 ProductComparisons
d---------  1 owner group        0 Aug 11 18:59 ProductOverview
226 Transfer complete.
451 bytes received in 0.22 seconds (2.05 Kbytes/sec)
```

Finally! Now change to the InternetExplorer directory and see what's there.

```
ftp> cd internetexplorer
250 CWD command successful.
ftp> dir
200 PORT command successful.
150 Opening ASCII mode data connection for /bin/ls.
----------  1 owner group   616960 Aug 11 17:10 inetover.doc
```

99

```
             1 owner group        13824 Aug 19 16:47 inetqa.doc
             1 owner group      1097728 Aug 20  9:08 msie10.exe
             1 owner group        14336 Aug  4 16:21 newhtml.doc
226 Transfer complete.
287 bytes received in 0.17 seconds (1.69 Kbytes/sec)
```

See the file MSIE10.EXE in the eighth line of the previous listing? That's the one you want. See what type of file transfer this site has been set up for by using the **type** command.

```
ftp> type
Using ascii mode to transfer files.
```

You don't want to do an ASCII transfer (that's for text only). So change the type to binary with the **binary** command.

```
ftp> binary
200 Type set to I.
```

Then turn on hash marks so that you'll be able to see that the file is being transferred:

```
ftp> hash
Hash mark printing On (2048 bytes/hash mark).
```

To actually get the file, type **get msie10.exe**.

```
ftp> get msie10.exe
200 PORT command successful.
150 Opening BINARY mode data connection for msie10.exe(1097728 bytes).
########...
226 Transfer complete.
1097728 bytes received in 470.71 seconds (2.33 Kbytes/sec)
```

Now that you have the file, you can close the connection to the FTP site and close the MS-DOS window.

```
ftp> bye
221 Thank you for using ftp.micrsoft.com!
C:\WIN95>exit
```

Now go to your Windows directory and find the MSIE10.EXE file. Create a new directory, move the file into the directory, and double-click on the file. Then follow the instructions to install Internet Explorer. (See Chapter 7 for more information.)

Netscape Envy?

I want to warn you...if you use Internet Explorer, you're going to run into people who tell you you're missing out. "You should be using Netscape. It's the best browser there is," they'll tell you.

> **FTP Sites Change!** Remember that FTP sites change often, so the MSIE10.EXE file may not be where it was when I looked (in fact, it may not be called MSIE10.EXE anymore). See Chapter 8's section on FTP for information about finding what you need.

Well I'm here to tell you that you don't need to feel any Netscape envy. I've used both browsers, and I can assure you that Internet Explorer is a very good browser with a lot of advantages.

Yes, Netscape does have a few features that Internet Explorer currently lacks, perhaps the most important of which is the capability to use secure communications. What that means is, if you have the Netscape browser and use it to view a document at a Netscape server, that document can contain special elements that enable you to send encrypted information back to the server.

The obvious example of this in action is when you use the browser to view an online store. The browser creates a form—a document with text boxes, buttons, and so on that's just like a program's dialog box. You type your credit card number into one of these boxes, and then you click on a button. The browser uses information in the document to encrypt the software and sends your encrypted credit card number back to the store. Nobody intercepting the message can read the credit card number and steal it.

> **What's a Server?** A *server* is the program that administers a collection of Web documents. Through the Web browser, you send a request to the server for a particular document, and the server sends it back.

That sounds great, but there are a few reasons you don't have to worry about all this. First, this whole online shopping thing has been grossly exaggerated. Go online and visit a few shopping "malls," and you'll find that many of these "stores" are nothing of the sort. If you want to order, you have to call an 800 number; you often can't order online.

But even if a store is taking orders online, at present it's unlikely that you would be using the Netscape server. So even if you do have Netscape, you still can't send an encrypted credit card number! Of course, that may change. Maybe the Netscape server will soon be all over the place—but Internet Explorer will change too. Microsoft is currently adding security features to Explorer, and they will be present in a new version that's to be released before you read this.

Also, be aware that the Internet changes very quickly. Last year, everyone was talking about Mosaic, the first graphical browser. By the time the name Mosaic was well known, there were easier-to-use programs such as WinWeb, which you rarely hear about these days. Then there was Enhanced NCSA Mosaic, and Super Mosaic, and all sorts of other Mosaics. Then Netscape and InternetWorks appeared. InternetWorks disappeared from the scene (few people ever heard of it, and fewer used it), while Netscape has progressed. All this happened in the span of about a year. So who knows, a year from now Netscape may be in the doldrums, and we'll all be talking about WebNet, or WebWinNet, or WebNetWinView, or whatever (maybe even Internet Explorer). Anyway, my point is, don't think that you have to use Netscape. Internet Explorer is an excellent browser, and it's the one I use for the examples in this book.

If you really *have* to get your hands on a copy of Netscape, though, you can download it from the World Wide Web. Once you learn how to use Internet Explorer, go to **http://www.netscape.com**. (You'll learn how to use a URL—Universal Resource Locator—in Chapter 10).

A Bit More Web Background

Before we move on, let's cover a bit more Web background information. We'll start with the primary "building material" of the HTML document. HTML stands for HyperText Markup Language. HTML documents are computer files that contain ASCII text (just plain old text). But the text contains special codes known as *tags*, which are created using the normal ASCII-text characters but are codes nonetheless. They are not there for you to read; they are there for browsers.

A *browser* is a program that helps you read HTML documents. When your browser opens an HTML document, it looks closely at the codes. They tell the browser what to do with each part of the text—"these few words are a link to another document, this line is a heading, this is the document title," and so on.

When it has read the codes (which happens very quickly), the browser displays the text on your computer screen. It strips out the codes—you don't see them—and formats the text according to what the codes told it to do.

Where Is All This? The Web Server

So where, physically, are these documents stored? On computer systems throughout the world: Chicago, China, Australia, Japan, or anywhere there's a computer connected to the Internet. How do you get to them? A Web server makes them available. This program receives requests from your browser and transmits the Web documents back to you. What term should we use for the actual information stored on the computer? Each individual HTML file is known as a *document* or *page*. You'll also hear the term *site*, which means a collection of documents about a particular subject, stored on a particular computer.

It's More Than Text

The Web is based on text, but there's plenty more than that out there. Just about any form of Internet tool or computer file can be linked to the Web. You'll find pictures, sounds, video, FTP sites (which you'll learn about in Chapter 12), Gopher sites (Chapter 14), WAIS database searches (Chapter 16), and more. Just recently, a new form of data has started arriving on the Web: VRML (Virtual Reality Modeling Language) files. These are 3-D images that you can "walk through" using a special viewer. You can expect to see lots of VRML sites scattered around the Web soon.

You'll usually find that you start by reading a document and then you jump from that document to another document—a picture, an FTP site, or whatever. However, these days, many documents have inline graphics, pictures that appear within the documents. (Yes, I know I said these documents are ASCII text files; the Web documents have special codes that tell your browser which picture to insert into the document. The end result is a document with pictures in it.)

> **Check This Out...**
> **Be Careful with VRMLs** At the time of this writing, the viewers you use to view VRML files are very new and very buggy.

You'll find lots to see and do on the Web, and many special little tricks, fancy tools, procedures that you can use. There's so much to the Web that one could dedicate an entire book to the subject—I did, in fact (*Using Internet Explorer*, also from Que). I've only got a little room here to look at Internet Explorer and the Web (there's lots more on the Internet to cover, too). So although you'll find enough information here to get moving on the Web, you may want to take a trip back to your bookstore to get all the details.

The Least You Need to Know

➤ If you installed the Internet software from MSN or the Jumpstart kit, you already have Internet Explorer, the Web browser.

➤ If you don't have Explorer, go to the Microsoft FTP site to get it.

➤ Explorer is an excellent browser that rivals Netscape. Despite the popular buzz, you don't need Netscape!

➤ The Web is made of servers (programs that provide Web documents) and browsers (the programs used to read those documents).

➤ The Web is based on HyperText Markup Language, which creates text documents for you to read.

➤ Those text documents can contain pictures and can be linked to sounds, video, and just about anything else.

Chapter 10

Let's Surf!: Traveling the World Wide Web

In This Chapter

- ➤ Starting Internet Explorer
- ➤ How you can use the Web when you're not connected!
- ➤ Traveling around the Web
- ➤ Returning whence you came
- ➤ Searching for text
- ➤ Using the cache and refresh features
- ➤ Creating a Favorites list

It's time to begin your journey—a journey of discovery, where no one has gone before. Well, not quite true. Millions have beaten you to the Web, but it's a journey of discovery nonetheless. You'll find all things on the Web: from Shakespeare to *Hustler*, from the U.S. Government to conspiracy theorists. Let's start.

Part 2 ➤ *Working on the Web*

Start Your Engines...

Before you can view the Web, you'll have to open your Web browser. There are a number of ways you can do that. Note that you don't have to connect to the Internet first, as I'll explain in a moment.

Here's a list of several different ways to open Internet Explorer. I know some of these won't make sense to you yet, but by the time you finish this chapter, you will understand URLs, the Favorites and History lists, and desktop shortcuts, and all will be clear.

➤ Double-click **The Internet** icon on your desktop.

➤ Select **Start**, **Programs**, **Accessories**, **Internet Tools**, and **Internet Explorer**.

➤ Select **Start**, **Run**, type a URL (a Web "address"), and click **OK**.

➤ Double-click an entry in your History or Favorites list.

➤ Double-click on a desktop shortcut to a Web page.

➤ If you are an MSN member, click (in some cases double-click) on a link to a Web document. You'll find these links scattered all over MSN.

Using the Web When You're Not Connected

Before we go on, I'd better quickly mention the cache (which I'll cover in more detail later in this chapter). The *cache* is a directory on your hard disk where Internet Explorer saves Web documents. Each time it retrieves a document from the World Wide Web, it places it in the cache. The next time you try to view that document, Explorer pulls it from the cache (depending on how the cache has been configured). Why does Internet Explorer use a cache? To save time. It's much quicker to pull it from the cache than from the Web, especially if you connect to the Internet through the phone lines.

This means that when you first start Explorer, you can "use" the Web without being connected to the Internet. Each time you go to a document that is already in the cache, Explorer pulls it from your hard disk. It's only when you try to view a document that isn't in the cache that Explorer tries to connect to the Internet. When that happens, you see the Dial-Up Networking's Connect To dialog box or Microsoft Network's Sign In dialog box, where you can start your Internet connection.

We're Home!

When the program starts, you see the *home page* (or *start page*, as Internet Explorer calls it). What makes this the home page? It's the page you see when the program starts, okay? It's a sort of home base.

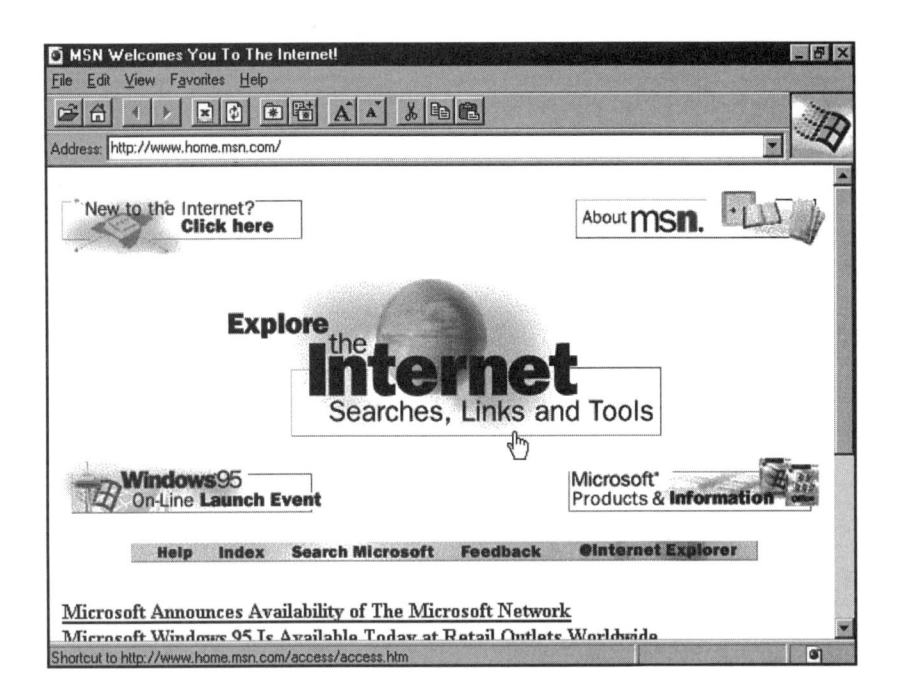

Chapter 10 ➤ *Let's Surf!: Traveling the World Wide Web*

The first thing you see is Explorer's start page.

At the top of the screen, you see a bunch of icons that you can use to speed up your online tasks. The following table shows each of these icons and tells what it does.

Internet Explorer's Toolbar Buttons

Button	Name	Description
	Open Address	Lets you open an HTML file on your hard disk or enter the URL of a page out on the Web.
	Open Start Page	Returns you to the start page.
	Back	Displays the previously viewed page.
	Forward	Displays the next page (the one you just came back from).
	Stop	Stops the current transfer of data from the Web to your browser.
	Refresh	Grabs another copy of the current document from the Web.
	Open Favorites	Displays your list of Favorites, "bookmarks" to Web documents you'll want to return to.

continues

Part 2 ➤ *Working on the Web*

Internet Explorer's Toolbar Buttons   Continued

Button	Name	Description
	Add to Favorites	Adds the current page to your list of Favorites.
	Use Larger Font	Increases the size of the text in the document.
	Use Smaller Font	Decreases the size of the text in the document.
	Cut	Removes the selected text from a text box (the Address text box or a box in a Web form).
	Copy	Copies the selected text, whether from a text box or the Web document itself.
	Paste	Pastes text from the Clipboard to a text box.

> **Techno Talk**
>
> **Home or Start?**
> The term "home page" also means just about any page on the Web (which doesn't make much sense to me, but I don't make the rules). Originally, the home page was the Web document that a browser opened first—its home. Perhaps to avoid this confusion, Internet Explorer's home page has been named the "start page."

Surfing the Web

You're about to start surfing. (That's the Web-geek term for moving around on the Web. Don't ask me why.) Just below the toolbar is the Address bar. This bar displays the Web address (commonly known as a *URL*, or Uniform Resource Locator) of the currently displayed Web document.

In the center of the program window is a document. If you remember, I told you in Chapter 9 that these documents could contain pictures; this document has several. You'll discover, though, that all of them contain links. Point to one, and the mouse pointer changes to a little pointing hand (which you can see in the previous figure). Notice, too, that the status bar changes to show the address of the document or file being "pointed to."

These links are good starting places. Perhaps, the most useful is the big picture in the middle, the **Explore the Internet, Searches, Links and Tools** picture. Click on it, and you go to another document, which contains links to places that will help you search for a particular subject or take you to interesting Web sites.

Chapter 10 ➤ *Let's Surf!: Traveling the World Wide Web*

> **Techno Talk**
>
> **Real URLs**
>
> The status bar at the bottom of the previous figure actually says **Shortcut to http://www.home.msn.com/access/access.htm**. The "Shortcut to" bit is superfluous. I'm not sure why it says this. It's not a shortcut, it's a link, in Web-speak. The word "shortcut" seems to imply a special route, but the status bar calls all links "shortcuts." The URL (http://www.home.msn.com/access/access.htm) is the address and name of the document file to which the link points. (Your browser probably won't display an address like this; I turned on the Show Full Addresses option in the Options dialog box because I think it's clearer that way. See Chapter 11 for more information about changing the way things are shown in your browser.)

Moving Around on the Web

Why don't you try moving around a little? Click a few links here and there, and see where you end up. As you travel through the Web, notice that most links are on text, not pictures. (Each link is underlined and colored blue.) Just click a link and see where it goes. Continue clicking links and wander wherever your fancy takes you. I suggest that you start with the big Explore picture in the middle, and then pick either **A sampler of links** or **Microsoft's Top Ten links** in the document that appears.

> **Check This Out...**
>
> **Stop!** If you start transferring to a document and discover that you really don't want to go there, click the **Stop** button or select **View**, **Stop** (or simply press **Esc**) to cancel the transfer.

Take Me Back

Lost yet? Eventually the question, "How do I get back?" comes to mind. That's easy. Use one of these techniques:

➤ To go to the previous page, click the **Back** button, select **View**, **Back**, or press **Backspace**.

➤ Having gone back to a previous page, go forward again by clicking the **Forward** button or by selecting **View**, **Forward**.

➤ Go all the way home—to the home page or start page—by clicking the **Open Start Page** button or by selecting **File**, **Open Start Page**.

➤ Open the **File** menu and choose one of the documents shown at the bottom of the menu (this is the History list).

109

You'll soon notice that the text links start changing color: from bright blue to purple. The purple links are the ones you've used, which helps you figure out where you've been and where you still need to go. In Chapter 11, I'll show you how to change these colors, or even turn off the color change. These links remain colored differently until the document is no longer in the cache. (It remains in the cache until the cache is full and documents have to be removed to make room for more recent documents; we'll get to that in a moment.)

> **Check This Out...**
>
> **I Can't Use Copy Shortcut**
> Okay, maybe this isn't so handy.... Right now the feature doesn't actually work, but it might in a later version.

Another option is the shortcut menu. When you right-click a link, you get several choices. You can **Open the link** (that's the same as left-clicking it). You can **Open in New Window**, which lets you start another Web session beginning with the document that the link points to. You can **Copy Shortcut**, which enables you to copy the URL to your Clipboard (so you can e-mail it to someone else, for instance). And you can **Add to Favorites** (which you've probably already figured out).

Searching Long Documents

Just as you do in a word processor, you have a Find command to help you dig through long Web documents. Select **Edit**, **Find**, and the Find dialog box opens. Type the word you are looking for, choose **Match case** (if necessary), choose **Start from top of page** to make sure you search the entire document, and then click **Find Next**. Internet Explorer moves the document so that the first line containing the word is at the top of the window.

You can also use the keyboard to move around in documents, by the way. Press **End** to go to the bottom of the document, **Home** to go to the top, and **PgDn** or **PgUp** to move down or up one screen at a time. Use the up and down arrow keys to move up and down a line or two at a time.

It's Faster When You Come Back

Now, time to talk about the cache again. When you go back to a Web document you've already opened, it appears on your screen much more quickly. That's because Internet Explorer isn't taking it from the Internet; it's getting it from the *cache*, an area on your hard disk in which it saves pages. This is really handy. Not only does using the cache speed up working on the Web but, because Internet Explorer doesn't throw away the cached pages when you finish your session, you can come back and view a page later without having to reconnect to the Internet and pay online charges.

Chapter 10 ➤ *Let's Surf!: Traveling the World Wide Web*

By default, these documents are stored in the \PROGRAM FILES\Plus!\microsoft internet\cache directory (or folder, as a directory is called in Windows 95). This cache can get very big—as big as you allow it. Select **View**, **Options** to see the Options dialog box, and then click the **Advanced** tab. You see the dialog box shown in the following figure. The Options dialog box lets you determine the size of your cache. At the top, you see the History information—we'll come back to that.

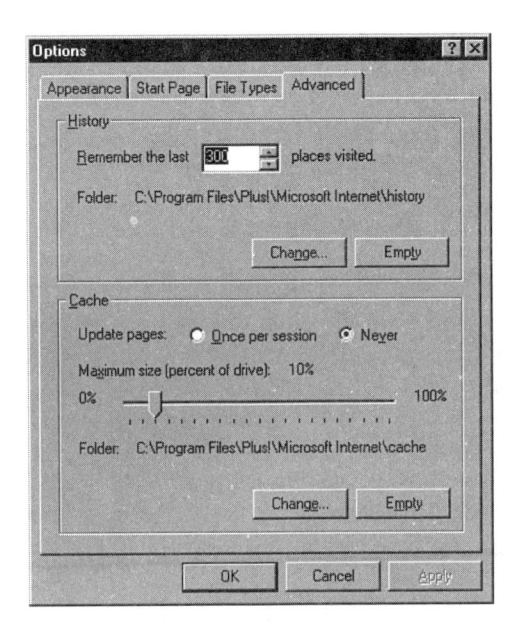

The Options dialog box is where you configure the cache.

Below the History section is the Cache information. Drag the pointer along the **Maximum size** bar to tell Internet Explorer just how much of your drive you want to use for the cache. Initially, this doesn't stop other programs from using that space (though, of course, once the space has been filled up with cached documents, no other program will be able to use it). It just means that Internet Explorer can use that much if it's available.

But which drive? Suppose the drive containing the \PROGRAM FILES\Plus!\microsoft internet\cache folder is almost full, but you have another half-empty drive. First, go to the Windows Explorer—Windows 95's new file-management program—and create a folder for the cache. Then return to Internet Explorer's Options dialog box, click the **Change** button, and select the directory you just created.

Now there are two Update pages option buttons: Once per session and Never. If you choose the **Once per session** option button, Internet Explorer retrieves from the cache only files that it placed there in the current session. For instance, let's say you visited the Rolling Stones Web page (http://www.stones.com/) yesterday. Today you open your browser and go back to the Rolling Stones page. Does Internet Explorer take the page out

111

of the cache? No, not yet, not if Once per session is turned on. It does, however, place a new copy of the Rolling Stones page in the cache, replacing the old one. Say you leave the Stones page and go somewhere else. When you return to the Stones page, Internet Explorer does retrieve it from the cache because it placed a copy of the page there during the current session.

The other option button, Never, tells Internet Explorer not to refresh the page in the cache. For example, consider the Stones example again. When you go to the Stones page today for the first time, Internet Explorer takes it out of the cache, but it does not put a new copy in the cache. The word "Never" is not quite accurate, though. Internet Explorer won't automatically update the pages in the cache, but you can tell it to do so by using the Refresh command (discussed in a moment).

Which of these two options should you use? I prefer Never. It makes my Web sessions much quicker because whenever I tell Internet Explorer to go to a Web page that's already in the cache, it loads it from the cache instead of from the Internet. (It's much quicker to load something from your hard disk than over your phone line!) On the other hand, if I don't remember to use the Refresh command, I won't see any new changes that have been made to the Stones page. Some people may prefer to use the Once per session option so they can be sure they're always looking at the latest page.

Notice the Empty button in the Cache section of the Options dialog box. You can click on **Empty** to delete everything that's in the cache folder (of course, you can also do this from Windows Explorer).

Confused by the Cache? Use Refresh

Refresh is a "cure" for the cache. Do you remember what happens when you return to a Web document that's in the cache? Internet Explorer gets it from the cache, right? Right. That means, however, that you are not getting the latest document. Although that won't always matter, in a few cases, it does matter.

For instance, let's say you want to return to a site you visited several weeks ago. If you have a very large cache, that document may still be in the cache. And if you have the Never option button selected in the Options dialog box, your browser loads the old document from the cache. Think what that can mean if you are viewing a Web document, such as a stock quote page, that changes rapidly. Even if you viewed the page only a few minutes ago, it could already be out of date.

The cure for old, stale Web pages is to refresh them (if you've used other Web browsers, you'll know this as the Reload command). Click the **Refresh** button, or select **View**, **Refresh**. Internet Explorer dumps the current document from the cache and replaces it with the latest version.

Chapter 10 ➤ *Let's Surf!: Traveling the World Wide Web*

The Shortest Route Is a Straight Line...

Now and then, you'll find a URL—a Web address—in a newspaper or magazine. Or maybe someone in a newsgroup mentions one, or a friend e-mails you one. In order to use it, you need to know how to go directly from here to there. You don't want to follow links to this document, you want to go directly to it. There are several ways to do this:

➤ Type the URL into the Address text box and press **Enter**. For instance, type **http://www.mcp.com/** and then press **Enter** to go to the Macmillan Publishing Web site.

➤ Copy a URL into the Windows Clipboard from another application (highlight the text and press **Ctrl+C** or click the **Copy** button), paste it into Internet Explorer's Address text box (press **Ctrl+V** or click the **Paste** button), and press **Enter**.

> **Check This Out...**
>
> ### URL Not Working?
>
> On occasion, you may find that a URL doesn't work. Sometimes this is simply because of a typo. To fix it, try removing the rightmost portion. For instance, if you try **http://www.mcp.com/author/pkent** and it doesn't work, try **http://www.mcp.com/author/**. If that still doesn't work, try **http://www.mcp.com/**. (Yes, you can actually get to my Web page using http://www.mcp.com/authors/pkent.)

➤ Enter a URL into the Address text box (type it or copy it; it doesn't matter) and press **Shift+Enter**. Another Internet Explorer window opens, with the specified Web document inside.

➤ Click the **Open** button or select **File**, **Open**. Type the URL and choose **OK**.

> **Check This Out...**
>
> ### Drop the http://
>
> Every URL has http:// at the beginning, but you can omit this bit when you type the URL. If you type (for example) www.mcp.com, Explorer adds the http:// part for you when you press Enter. However, note that there are other types of URLs, such as ftp:// and gopher:// URLs, which take you to different sorts of systems (you'll learn about these systems in Chapters 12 and 14). When you want to use one of those, you may have to type the full URL. If the address itself begins with ftp or gopher (as in ftp.microsoft.com or gopher.usa.net), you can forget the ftp:// or gopher:// bit. Explorer adds it for you. If the address doesn't start with those words, though, you'll have to type the complete URL.

113

Web Pages on Your Hard Disk

Now and again you may want to open a Web page on your hard disk. How would that get there? Well, you may have created one. (Creating your own Web pages is really quite simple, though I don't have space in this book to discuss it.) Maybe you've saved a page (using **File, Save As**). Maybe you're using Explorer to open different types of image and sound files (which you'll learn about in a moment).

For the purpose of illuminating you on this subject, let's take a closer look at the last method of opening a Web page that was listed in the previous section. Select **File, Open** to see the Open Internet Address dialog box. As you can see in the following figure, the dialog box has an Address box, which functions just like the big Address box in the main window. You can paste or type a URL into it, or you can click the down arrow to select from what I call the "typed" history list (more on this in a few moments). Below that, select the **Open in new window** check box before you choose **OK** to open the specified document in a new window (which is the same as pressing **Shift+Enter** in the main window's Address box).

Use the Open Internet Address dialog box to open Web page files on your hard disk.

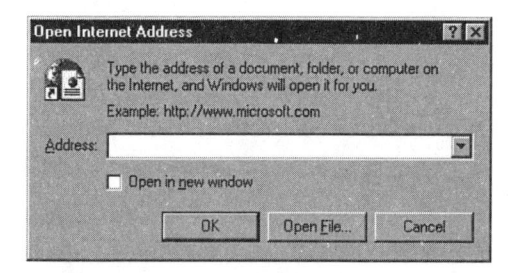

But why use this dialog box when you can use the Address text box in the main window? This dialog box contains a button labeled Open File. Click on **Open File** to see a typical Windows 95 Open File dialog box. At the bottom of this box is a Files of Type drop-down list. Take a look in there, and you'll find that you can open HTM files (Web documents); TXT files (text files); GIF, JPG, and XBM files (graphics files commonly used on the Web); and AU and AIF files (sound files). Of course, you can also select All Files to see files with different extensions. Double-click on the file you want to use, and your browser loads it. (If you open one of the sound files, it loads into Explorer's special sound program.)

Now, Where Was I? Using the History List

A *history list* is a list of Web documents that you've visited before. Almost all Web browsers have history lists, but Internet Explorer's is a little unusual. Most browsers keep a list of sites you've visited during the current session. Internet Explorer saves entries from previous sessions as well.

Chapter 10 ➤ *Let's Surf!: Traveling the World Wide Web*

Earlier in this chapter, you looked at the cache settings in the Options dialog box (View, Options). You can see in that figure that the dialog box also contains History settings. In that example, the history list is set to 300 entries. That means that the Internet Explorer adds entries to the list until there are 300 in the list, and then it removes the oldest ones to make room for the new ones. You can increase this number to 3,000 if you want; you'll be able to go back and find Web documents you viewed weeks ago!

As with the cache, you can empty the history list by clicking the **Empty** button. Each history entry is actually a small text file stored in the \PROGRAM FILES\Plus!\microsoft internet\history folder. Because each entry is so small—about 70 bytes on average—even when the list contains 300 entries, it's still not very large. You can place it in a different folder by clicking the **Change** button.

You can use the history list in a couple of ways. The easiest is to select an entry from the bottom of the File menu. As you visit sites, Internet Explorer adds the document titles to the File menu. If you want to visit a site from a previous session or if you have seen too many documents for them all to be shown in the File menu, select **File, More History**. A special history window, shown in the next figure, appears. (If your history window displays icons instead of a list, you'll probably want to select **View, List**.)

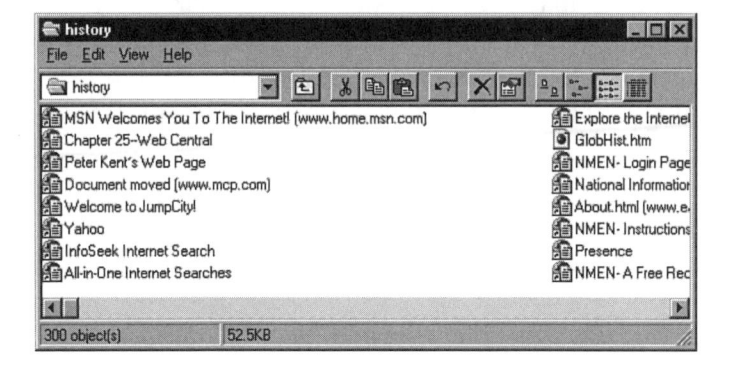

The history list is actually a Windows Explorer window.

This window is actually a Windows Explorer window, showing the contents of the history folder: all those little history files I mentioned. In the history list, you can sort the entries just as you would sort the entries in any Windows Explorer window. Select **View, Arrange Icons, By Date** to see the entries in chronological order, or select **View, Arrange Icons, By Name** to sort them by document title. In addition, because each of the files in the history list is actually a

> **Check This Out...**
>
> **Windows Explorer?** Windows Explorer is Windows 95's new file-management program, which takes the place of Windows 3.1's File Manager.

115

shortcut file, you can simply double-click the document to which you want to return, and Internet Explorer displays that document. (The history window disappears under the Internet Explorer window, but it's still open. You can get back to it by clicking its button on the Taskbar.)

> **Check This Out...**
>
> **Good Housekeeping**
>
> You may want to clean up the history list periodically. To do so, hold the **Ctrl** key and click each entry in the history list that you are sure you don't need. Then select **File, Delete**. You can do all sorts of things in here—anything you can do in the Windows Explorer. You can create desktop shortcuts, copy shortcuts to other directories, rename them, and so on. See your Windows 95 documentation for information on working with the Windows Explorer.

By the way, there's also a GLOBHIST.HTM file in your history directory. GLOBHIST.HTM is a hidden file, so you'll be able to view it only if the Windows Explorer has been set up to display hidden files. To set up Explorer that way, open the Windows Explorer, select **View**, choose **Options**, and click on **Show all files**. Each time a document is added to the history directory, it's also placed as a link inside the GLOBHIST.HTM file. So another way to view your history list is to open this file, which you can do by selecting **File, Open** or double-clicking the file in the history folder.

When you open a file this way, you see a Web document inside the Internet Explorer window. That document contains a list of all the documents you've viewed. Each entry in the document is a link, so you can just click on the text to go to a previously viewed document.

There's another type of history list, too. If you click the Address box's drop-down arrow, you see a list of URLs. These are the URLs that you have typed into the Address box. But this provides a limited history list because it does not contain all the Web documents you've viewed, only the ones you've gone to directly by typing their URLs in the Address box. In other words, if you opened a document by clicking a link, it won't be in this list.

Your Very Own Web Directory

History lists can get very cluttered, and even if you clean them periodically, they often include lots of files you are not really interested in. So there's another way to get back to where you've been: the Web Favorites. This is a collection of shortcuts—again, small text files containing the Web address (URL) that you want to store.

Chapter 10 ▸ Let's Surf!: Traveling the World Wide Web

When you reach a document you think you may want to return to, click the **Add to Favorites** button. (Alternatively, you can select **Favorites, Add to Favorites**, or you can right-click inside the document and select **Add to Favorites** from the shortcut menu that opens.) Whichever method you choose, the Add To Favorites dialog box opens (see the following figure).

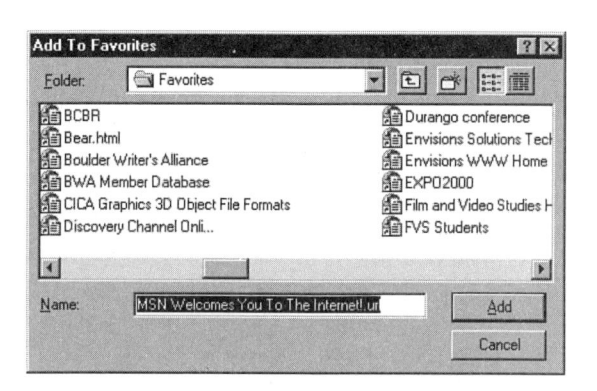

Use the Add To Favorites dialog box to create your own list of favorite Web sites.

The large list box shows the contents of the \Windows\Favorites folder, which is the default location of your Favorites shortcuts. You can modify the entry in the Name text box, if you want. This normally shows the title of the document you are viewing, but you may want to change it to something you'll find easier to remember and recognize later. (Sometimes you'll find documents without titles, in which case Internet Explorer has to use the document's file name, such as GALLERY.HTM or MFR2.HTM—or whatever other unmemorable name it happens to be. In such cases, change the name to something that makes more sense.) Click **Add**, and Internet Explorer creates the file, adding the entry to your Favorites list.

Later when you want to return to one of the documents in your Favorites folder, click the **Open Favorites** button or open the **Favorites** menu and select **Open Favorites**. You see a Windows Explorer window that displays the contents of your Favorites directory. Just double-click the one you want to go to.

As you've probably already noticed, there is another way to choose a Favorite. In the Favorites menu, Internet Explorer shows a few of the items in your Favorites directory. This menu won't necessarily show all of your favorite places, only the first 19. But if the one you want is there, click it.

> **Check This Out...**
>
> **Desktop Shortcuts** You can also add a desktop shortcut to a Web document. To do so, open the **File** menu and select **Create Shortcut**, or right-click in the document and select **Create Shortcut**. A shortcut icon is placed on your Windows 95 desktop. From then on, you can double-click on the shortcut to open Internet Explorer and display the document.

117

Here's another little trick you can use to add a document to your Favorites at the end of your session, or even a week or two later. Simply open the Windows Explorer and drag items from the History folder into the Favorites folder. (If you want to copy an entry from History instead of moving it, press **Ctrl** while you drag.)

Favorites Subcategories

You can customize the way in which your shortcuts are stored by opening the **Favorites** window and selecting **File**, **New**, **Folder**. A new folder icon appears in the window. Type a name for the folder—Music, Multimedia, Business, or whatever else comes to mind—and press **Enter**. Create as many of these folders as you want, each for a different category. You can create subfolders within those folders, too, if you want.

The next time you add a Web document to your Favorites list, you can double-click a folder to place the document in the appropriate category. Later, when you want to return to the page, open the Favorites window, double-click the folder icon, and then double-click the shortcut to the page.

> **Check This Out...**
>
> **Create Folders "On-the-Fly"**
> You can create more folders "on-the-fly" at the same time you add an item to your Favorites list. Notice in the previous figure that the third toolbar button from the right is a picture of a folder. Click on that button to create a new folder.

By customizing the Favorites list and adding folders, you can improve the capabilities of the Favorites menu. I told you earlier that you could have only 19 entries in the Favorites menu. However, that includes the new folders you've created; each folder appears on the Favorites menu as another cascading menu.

By the way, if you are opening a folder from the Favorites window, you may find that another window opens. If you don't like this (if you want the contents of the folder you selected to appear in the same window so you don't have two windows open), you have two options. You can hold down the **Ctrl** key and double-click the folder, or you can select **View**, **Options** and choose **Browse folders** to use a single window that changes when you open each folder option. And one more thing. Sometimes when you open the Favorites window by clicking on the toolbar button, the window doesn't seem to open. When that happens, take a look at the taskbar, and you'll probably find it there.

Chapter 10 ➤ *Let's Surf!: Traveling the World Wide Web*

The Least You Need to Know

- ➤ You can start Internet Explorer in a number of ways. The quickest is to double-click **The Internet** icon on your desktop. (You can also open the **Start** menu, choose **Run**, type a URL, and press **Enter**.)

- ➤ The colored and underlined text on a Web page represents links to other documents; click on the text to go to another document. Many pictures are links, too. (Point at the picture; if the pointer changes to a hand, the picture is a link.)

- ➤ If you click on a link and then change your mind, you can stop a page from appearing by pressing **Esc** or clicking the **Stop** button.

- ➤ Use the **Back** button to return to the previous document.

- ➤ The cache stores documents on your hard disk after you view them, which is why the document appears quickly the next time you view it.

- ➤ Use the history list (on the File menu) to find a document you viewed earlier. Use the Favorites list to create your own directory of Web sites.

Chapter 11

The Web in High Gear

In This Chapter

- ➤ Finding topics that interest you
- ➤ Saving files and creating wallpaper
- ➤ Viewing a Web page's HTML tags
- ➤ Where can I find more viewers?
- ➤ Configuring Explorer to work with viewers
- ➤ Customize Internet Explorer

In the last couple of chapters, I've explained how to move around on the Web. In this chapter, I'll explain how to really get cooking: how to find the information you need, grab things off the Web, play the different types of media that you'll find on the Web, and more.

Where's What I Want?

The Web's a very big place. There are many thousands of different Web sites, with hundreds more going up each day. How can you find what you need? How can you cut through all the extraneous stuff and go right to the information you want to see?

Part 2 ➤ *Working on the Web*

Well, there are plenty of search sites on the Web (special Web documents that help you find any subject). The current Internet Explorer home page has a link called **Explore the Internet; Searches, Links and Tools.** Click on that, and you'll find yourself at a page with several search links. You can also use The All-in-One Search Page, InfoSeek, Lycos, or Yahoo. These pages enable you to search the Web using three well-known search services: InfoSeek, Lycos, and Yahoo. With each of them, you simply type a word (a subject in which you are interested) and click the **Search** button. In a few moments, you see a list of entries that the search service has found. Click on a link in this list, and away you go—straight to the Web document you selected.

You can find loads of search sites. Another place you may want to try is the actual Yahoo site. The page I just described is at the Microsoft Web site; it simply lets you search the Yahoo database. But if you go directly to Yahoo itself (at http://www.yahoo.com/), you'll find that you can also move down through hierarchical lists of Web sites related to Arts, Business and Economy, Computers and the Internet, and so on. The following figure shows Yahoo's opening window.

Yahoo is one of the best-known Web search sites.

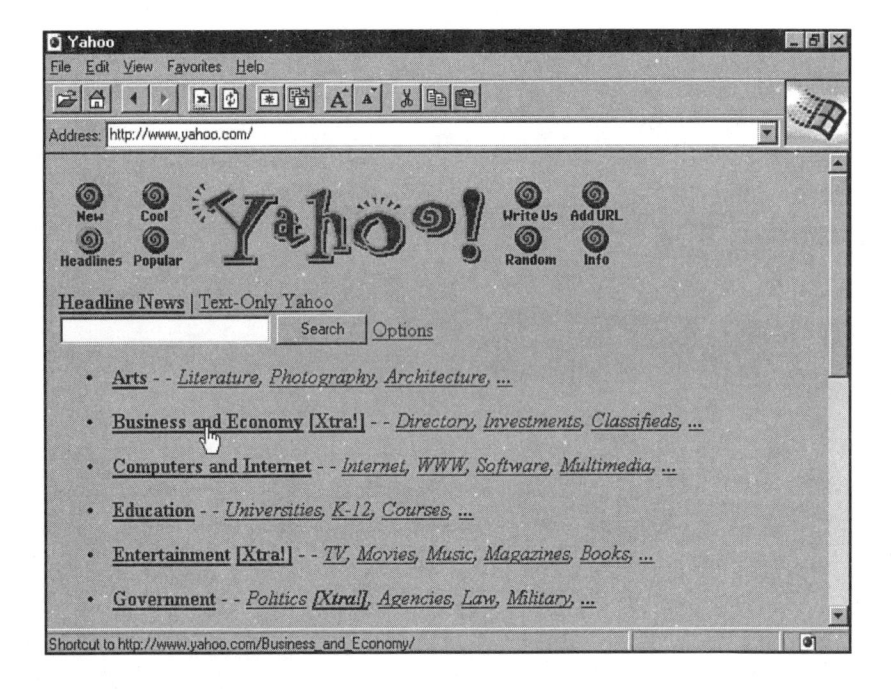

You might also want to try JumpCity at http://www.jumpcity.com/. With JumpCity, you can select a category from a drop-down list to see a list of Web sites, or you can search on a keyword.

Chapter 11 ➤ *The Web in High Gear*

> **Check This Out...**
>
> **Another Good One**
>
> I don't have space to tell you about all the places you can go to search the Web, but you may want to try this one: http://www.mcp.com/authors/pkent/chapt25.htm. This is a sample chapter from my book *The Complete Idiot's Guide to the World Wide Web*, which contains links to loads of places ranging from WebCrawler to Sell it on WWW, and from CommerceNet to The Journalism List.

I've Gotta Keep It! But How?

Suppose you've wandered around the Web for a while, and you've come across something you just have to have. Maybe it's a picture you'd love to use as your desktop wallpaper, a document that would be very handy as research material, or an inline picture that's sorta neat. How can you keep this stuff? Try some of these little tricks:

➤ Place the cursor above and to the left of the text you want to save. (You can't grab pictures like this.) Then press the mouse button and drag the pointer down and to the right. Internet Explorer highlights the text you drag over. Click the **Copy** button or select **Edit, Copy**.

➤ Right-click on the document and select **Select All**. Then right-click on the highlighted text and select **Copy**.

➤ Select **File, Save As**. In the **Save as Type** drop-down list, select **Plain Text** (if you want the text without the HTML codes) or **HTML** (if you want the entire document, HTML codes and all). Give the document a name and click **Save**.

➤ Right-click on a picture. Then select **Copy Picture**, **Save Picture As**, or **Save As Desktop Wallpaper**.

> **Check This Out...**
>
> **It's Not Yours!**
> Remember, much of what you come across on the Web is copyright material. In fact, unless you are sure that what you are viewing is not copyright, you should assume it is. For information about what you can and can't do with copyright material, refer to a book on copyright law. (Many writer's references contain copyright information.)

Copying the Background

A new feature that's becoming popular on Web pages these days is the background pattern. A Web author can add a special background (usually a plain color or some sort of pattern) to his documents. Many Web sites even use a sort of watermark in the background so that the company name or logo, for example, appears behind everything else. If you find a nice background, you can copy it to your system. In fact, you have three choices of how to do that:

123

Part 2 ➤ *Working on the Web*

> **Check This Out...**
>
> **Get Rid of This Wallpaper**
> To remove a wallpaper you created from a background, minimize all your applications, right-click on the desktop, and select **Properties**. Select another wallpaper (or select [None]) in the Wallpaper list box and click OK.

➤ Right-click on the background and select **Save Background As**. In the Save As dialog box, save the background to your hard disk (as a .GIF, .JPG, or .BMP file).

➤ Right-click on the background and select **Set As Desktop Wallpaper**. Explorer creates a file called Internet Explorer Wallpaper.bmp in your Windows folder, and your Windows desktop is replaced with this file.

➤ Right-click on the background and select **Copy Background**. Explorer copies it to the Clipboard so you can paste it into another application.

If these menu options are disabled, the current document is not using a special background.

Viewing the Source

Do you want to see the HTML codes (or tags)? Perhaps, you just want to see what it's all about, or maybe you even want to try to create your own Web pages (copying from other pages that you like is a great way to learn). Right-click inside a Web document—on a blank space, not a picture—and select **View Source** from the shortcut menu. A Notepad window opens, showing you what the original source looks like, tags and all (see the following figure).

This is what the HTML document that creates your home page looks like.

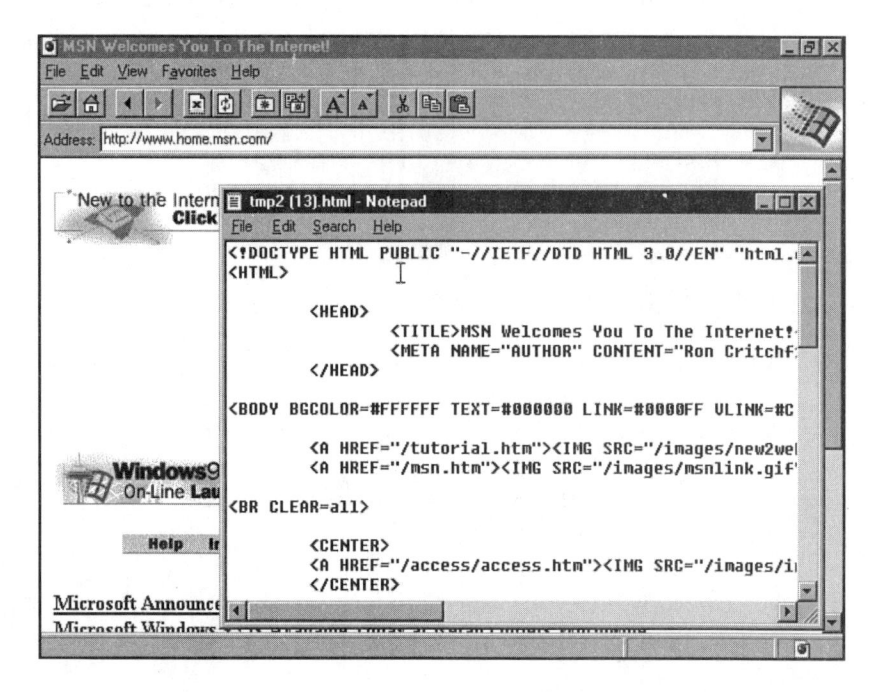

Downloading Files from the Web

Many links on the Web point not to other Web documents, but to computer files of various kinds. In a moment, you'll see how you can play or display graphics, sound, video, and more. Most often, however, you will want to download a .ZIP or .EXE file containing a program. For instance, if you go to a software archive, you can transfer shareware and freeware Internet programs back to your system.

To try it out, type **http://www.windows.microsoft.com/** in the Address box and press **Enter**. You'll come to the Windows 95 site, from which you can download Windows 95 software. Click on the **Free Software** link to find all sorts of free stuff, including the Internet software we looked at in the installation chapters.

To download a file, click on the link. If you click on a link that leads to a file type Internet Explorer recognizes and knows what to do with, Explorer automatically does what it's supposed to: it displays the file or sends it to the appropriate program. If the file is an .EXE file or one that it doesn't recognize, though, you have to tell it what to do. Because each case is slightly different, I'll go over each one separately.

Downloading .EXE Files

If the file you are downloading is an .EXE file (a program file), you see the dialog box shown in the next figure. If you want to save the file to disk, click **Save As**. If you want to save the file to disk (in the Files\Plus!\Microsoft Internet\cache folder) and then run the program, click **Open File**. After the file is transferred, Explorer "opens" it: it runs the program.

Downloading the Windows 95 PowerToys file, powertoy.exe.

Don't Use Open File!

If you clear the Always warn about files of this type check box, the next time you click on a link to an .EXE file, Explorer won't bother to display this dialog box. It will assume that

125

you always want to transfer the file and then run it. However, I advise that you never choose to "Open" files, for a couple of reasons.

➤ You should really check .EXE files with a virus detection program before you use them.

➤ Many .EXE files are archive files. Therefore, when you run them, they automatically extract files—maybe dozens of files—into the folder the .EXE file was placed in. You'll have trouble figuring out which of these files came from the archive you just extracted.

Instead of the Open File button, I advise that you always use the **Save As** option and place the file into a folder of your choice—perhaps one that you created especially for this particular file. Then open the Windows Explorer and run the file from there (after checking for viruses first, of course).

> **Check This Out...**
>
> **Multifile Transfer**
>
> By the way, you can transfer more than one file at a time. If Explorer is transferring a file and you click on a link to another file, you see a message box asking if you want to cancel the current transfer. Click **No**, and you see another dialog box asking if you want to open another window. Click **Yes**, and another Explorer window opens. The window won't show much (just a title, such as Copying file dice2.11.aiff), but Explorer begins transferring the file you selected. Of course, two files will transfer more slowly than one, but you might want to set up several file transfers and then go for coffee.

What if the file you are getting is not an .EXE file—not a normal HTML Web document—but something else? Well, that depends on what the file is and whether Explorer recognizes it. Read on.

Playing Multimedia Files

The Web is more than documents with inline images. There are files of all kinds out there, including documents in many different formats, sound files, graphics, and even video.

Let's say, for instance, that you are visiting the Rolling Stones Web site (I'm sure many of you will—the Stones' Live Audio Clips page had logged more than half a million visits last time I looked). You can get there by typing **http://www.stones.com/** into the Address box and pressing **Enter**, or you can go directly to the Live Audio Clips page using the **http://www.stones.com/audio/index.html** URL.

Chapter 11 ➤ *The Web in High Gear*

The Live Audio Clips page at the Stones site contains links to music. Click on one of these links, and the file is transferred. (Unfortunately, sound files tend to be big, so this will take a while.) When the file finally arrives, what happens? Well, the first thing that Internet Explorer does when it receives any file is try to determine whether it can use the file.

Of course, when Explorer transfers .HTM or .HTML files, it has no problem. (They are the basic Web document files, so it just displays them.) And the same is true when it opens text files. The .HTM and .HTML files are just text anyway, so Internet Explorer has no problem with .TXT files. It can also display .GIF and .XBM files (the original standard inline image files) and .JPG files (another common graphics format on the Web). But what about other things? How about those Stones' sound tracks?

Internet Explorer has a built-in sound application, shown in the following figure. This program plays .AU and .AIF files, two common Web sound formats. So as soon as Internet Explorer finishes transferring the sound file, it opens the sound player and begins playing. When it finishes, you can select **File**, **Save As** to save the sound file on your hard disk, or you can use the buttons and scroll bar to replay the music.

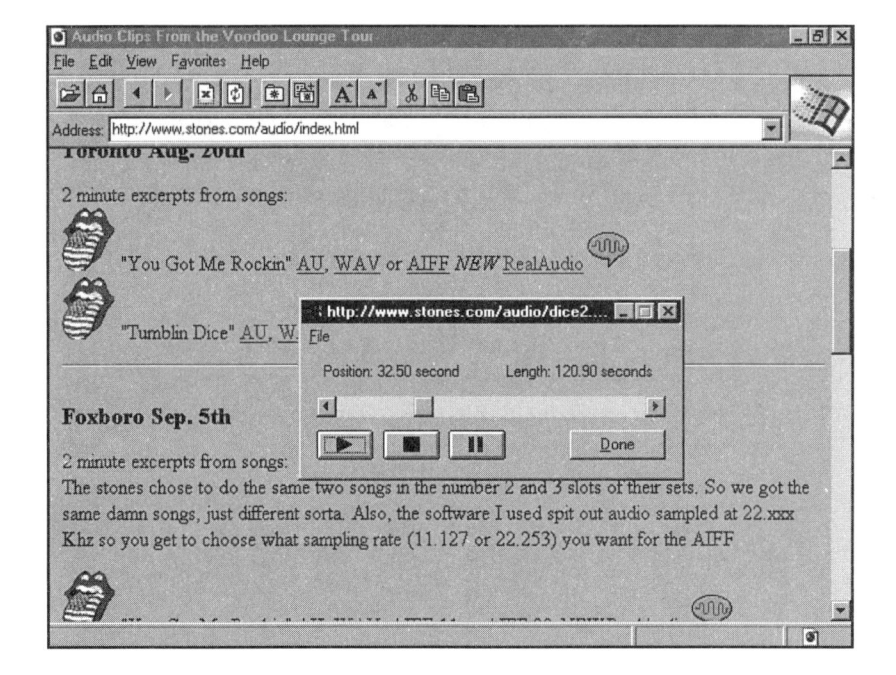

> **Check This Out...**
> **The Right Equipment** Of course, none of this works at all if you don't have a sound board properly installed.

Internet Explorer's built-in sound program will get you rockin'.

127

What about .WAV files? The .WAV format is a common Windows sound format, but until recently it has not been common on the Web. (You'll find plenty of .WAV files now, though, including those at the Stones site.) Because Windows 95 already has a .WAV player called Sound Recorder that's set up, the Internet Explorer sound application doesn't play .WAV sounds. Instead, Sound Recorder opens and plays the music.

When Internet Explorer receives a file that it can't display or play directly, it looks at the Windows 95 file associations. You've probably noticed these throughout Windows 95. To see them from within Internet Explorer, select **View**, **Options** and click the **File Types** tab in the Options dialog box. In the case of the .WAV format, for example, Internet Explorer looks in this list and finds that .WAV is associated with Sound Recorder. So Explorer opens Sound Recorder and gives it the .WAV file. (It won't play immediately; you have to click the **Play** button.)

Explorer goes through this procedure for any file type that it transfers. So as long as you have a program installed that can play a particular file type, and as long as the file type is associated with the program, you can click on a Web link to that file type and display or play it.

Of course, if you don't have the application properly associated with the file type, it won't play. So let's look at how to set up one of these applications—a *viewer* as it's known in the world of the Web.

> **Check This Out...**
>
> **Didn't Get WordPad?** Explorer may not open WordPad or Paint. If you've installed another application that has associated itself with one of these file types, it opens that application instead. For instance, because Word for Windows associates itself with .DOC files, Explorer opens it (instead of WordPad) when you click on a link to a .DOC file.

Adding Viewers

As you've seen, Explorer can handle .HTM, .HTML, .TXT, .BMP, .JPG, .GIF, .WAV, .AU, and .AIF files. In addition, it knows what to do with many other file types. If you click on a link to a .DOC file, for instance, it opens WordPad. If you click on a link to a .PCX file, it opens Microsoft Paint.

But now and again, you'll run across a file type that Explorer has no idea how to handle because nothing has been associated with it. When that happens, you need to install a viewer for each of the file types you want to use. A *viewer* is a program that plays or displays a file type that Explorer can't handle by itself.

Viewers, Anyone?

You can find loads of viewers out on the Internet, and often they are freeware or shareware. Try the following Web sites:

http://www.ncsa.uiuc.edu/SDG/Software/WinMosaic/viewers.htm

http://www.ncsa.uiuc.edu/SDG/Software/WinMosaic/viewers.htm

http://www.law.cornell.edu/cello/cellocfg.html

> **No Room for Carelessness**
>
> Be careful when entering URLs. Note that the first two URLs listed above end in .htm, while the third ends in .html. If you add an "l" that's not needed or miss one that is, you won't get to the document.

Continue your search for a viewer by trying one of these FTP sites. (See Chapter 12 for instructions on getting into FTP sites.)

ftp.winsite.com

ftp.law.cornell.edu in the /pub/LII/Cello/ directory

You'll find that you can already display and play most files you run into, even without getting any new programs. However, you may want to grab GhostScript or GhostView (which display PostScript files) or Adobe Acrobat Reader (which displays and prints .PDF files—Adobe Acrobat hypertext documents—which are growing in popularity on the Internet). Then there's VIDVUE (for .MPG and .AVI animation files) and MPEGPLAY, MFW, and MPEGW (programs that play .MPEG video files).

I Have the Viewer—Now What?

Let's look at a quick example of how to add a viewer. There are two ways to add viewers: automatically and manually. When you run a program's Setup utility, Setup may automatically associate the program with the file type. For example, if you install the RealAudio player (which you can get from http://www.realaudio.com/), the Setup program automatically associates the player with the .RA and .RAM file types.

But some Setup programs don't do this—so you have to do it for them. Don't worry. It's actually quite easy. As an example, you will use the WorldView VRML viewer, available at **http://www.webmaster.com/vrml/wvwin/**. The WorldView VRML viewer displays 3-D images, which are popping up all over the Web now.

After you download the program from the WorldView Web site and install it, you find yourself at the IUMA site (**http://www.iuma.com/IUMA-2.0/vrml/**), a site that has 3-D VRML images. Click one of the links to a VRML file, and the Unknown File Type dialog box appears, informing you that Explorer doesn't recognize the file type. Follow these steps to add a viewer:

1. Click the **Open With** button, and the Open With dialog box appears (see the next figure).

The Open With dialog box appears when you click on a link to a .WRL file at the IUMA site.

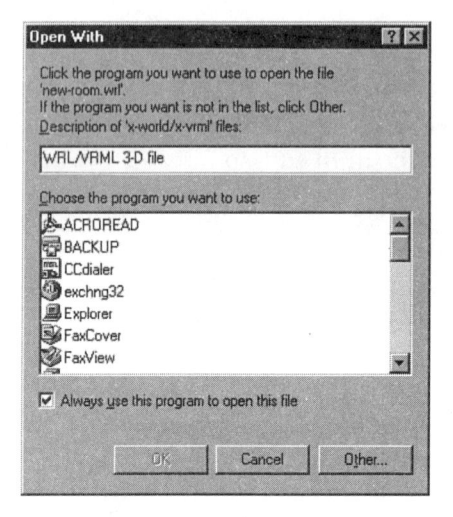

2. Near the top of this dialog box you can see the file name and the file extension (in this case, new-room.wrl). Type **WRL/VRML 3-D file** or something similar in the **Description of** text box. (I like to begin this description with the file extension because that makes it easier to find the association in the list later.)

3. Click the **Other** button, and you see a typical Open dialog box. Select the directory holding the WorldView program that you just installed.

4. Double-click the WorldView program (it's called **WRLDVIEW.EXE**) to place the file name in the Open With dialog box.

5. Click **OK**. The Open With dialog box and the Unknown File Type dialog box close. Then the Confirm File Open dialog box (shown in the next figure) appears.

6. If you want to make sure that Explorer always plays this sort of file without asking you what to do first, click on the **Always warn about files of this type** check box to remove the check mark.

7. Click the **Open File** button. The WorldView program opens and displays the 3-D image.

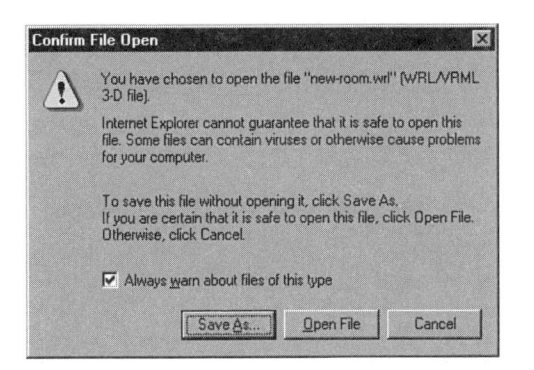

Explorer asks the eternal question, "Now What?"

Next time you click on a link to a VRML file, you won't have to dig your way through this. Instead, your WorldView program automatically opens and displays the 3-D image. (If you don't clear the Always warn about files of this type check box, you will always see the Confirm File Open dialog box, which gives you the option of saving the file to disk instead of viewing it.)

There are two other ways to associate files with programs. You can double-click on a file in the Windows Explorer; if the file type does not have an association, Explorer gives you the chance to associate it with a program. Alternatively, you can choose **View**, **Options** in Explorer, click the **File Types** tab, and then click the **New Type** button. (See your Windows documentation if you want more details about this method. But note that it's more complicated than the method I described, which is the simplest method and will work in almost all situations).

> **Check This Out...**
>
> **Do It Once, Do It Twice** Some file types can come with different extensions: .RA and .RAM both indicate RealAudio. Even if you associate one of the type's extensions with the program using this method, you have to do it again when you run into the same file type using a different extension.

Customizing Internet Explorer

Internet Explorer lets you modify a few settings, some of which you've already seen. Now let's look at the rest of the options. Select **View**, **Options** to open the dialog box shown in the following figure.

At the top of the dialog box, click to remove the check mark from the **Show pictures** check box to turn off inline images. Why? Because inline images are very slow, and turning them off now and again will help you move around the Web much more quickly. (Many Web pages won't work correctly with inline images turned off, though.)

Part 2 ➤ *Working on the Web*

The Options dialog box lets you choose colors and define how URLs are displayed.

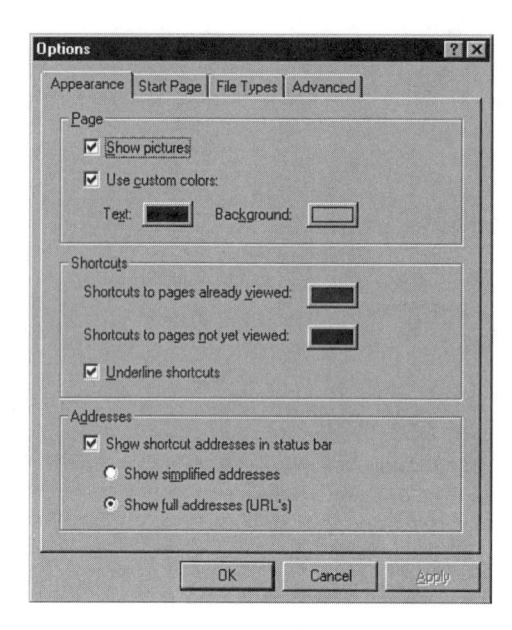

Below that, click the **Use custom colors** check box to modify the text and background colors in the Explorer window. Then click the **Text** or **Background** color button, and a Color dialog box appears. Choose your color and click **OK**. Back in the Options dialog box, click **Apply** to see what your choice will look like. If you like it, click **OK** to save your changes.

The Shortcuts area lets you define what the hypertext links in Web documents will look like. Clear the **Underline shortcuts** check box to remove the link underlining, and then you can modify the link colors. Click the colored buttons to open the Color dialog box. Remember that there are two link colors: one for links that will take you to Web pages you've never been to before (Shortcuts to pages not yet viewed), and one for Web pages that you have been to before. Again, click the **Apply** button to see what the changes look like before you decide to keep them.

Finally, there's the Addresses area of the Options dialog box. When you are working in a Web document and point at a link, the URL for that link appears in the status bar at the bottom of the window (unless you clear the Show shortcut addresses in status bar check box). You also have two options for how Explorer shows these URLs:

> **Show simplified addresses** is the default. A simplified address might be Shortcut to "homepage.html" at www.egallery.com, for instance.
>
> **Show full addresses (URL's)** lets you choose to show the full address (such as Shortcut to http://www.egallery.com/egallery/homepage.html).

I think the idea behind this is that the full URL is somehow confusing, but I don't find the "simplified" address to be of any great utility. (I prefer to take my URLs straight!)

Designating a Home Page

By default, the browser's "home page" (what Internet Explorer calls its start page) is the http://www.home.msn.com/ document. But you can make any page you want your home page. In other words, you can tell Internet Explorer which page to display when it opens and when you click on the Open Start Page toolbar button. In fact, you can even create your own .htm file and use that as a home page. (For more on how to create a simple Web site, see *The Complete Idiot's Guide to the World Wide Web* or *Using Internet Explorer*, both published by Que.)

To set a different Web page as your home page:

1. Open **Internet Explorer** and go to the page that you want to make your home page.
2. Select **View**, **Options** and click the **Start Page** tab.
3. Click the **Use Current** button and click **OK**.

That's it. If you ever want to change back to using the http://www.home.msn.com/ document as the home page, return to the Options dialog box and click the **Use Default** button.

This Could Look Different...

If a Web document is a simple ASCII text document, how does a Web browser know how to display the document? How does it know which piece is a heading and which is body text? And how does it know how each element should be displayed?

The HTML tags inside the source document are instructions to the browser. They tell the browser, for example, which part of the text is a Heading 1 (the <H1> and </H1> tags), which is bold text (<B> and </B>), and so on. They don't tell the browser how to display the text—just what the author intended it to be. So in answer to your question, "how should Heading 1 text be displayed?," the HTML tags don't say.

Unlike some Web browsers, Internet Explorer doesn't let you select the font for each type of text. It does, however, let you choose an overall text size. Select **View**, **Fonts**, and a cascading menu opens, showing you your choices from Largest to Smallest. Simply select one of these, and all the text in the current document changes accordingly. If the text is too small or too large, pick another one.

You can also click the **Use Larger Font** and **Use Smaller Font** buttons at the top of the Internet Explorer window to move up and down through the size range.

There's a Lot More to Learn

You'll be seeing Explorer again later in this book. Explorer can help you work with FTP and Gopher, tools you'll find out about in Chapters 12 and 14. These aren't part of the Web. In fact, they predate the Web. However, most Web browsers can work with these systems because they are so useful. And many Web documents contain links to FTP and Gopher sites. But you've learned quite a bit about the Web proper, and it's time to move on.

The Least You Need to Know

- Many Web sites help you search for subjects. You can select the **Explore the Internet; Searches, Links and Tools** link to use three of them.
- You can save documents as text or HTML files by selecting **File, Save As**.
- Right-click pictures or a background to save it to the Clipboard and use it as files or as desktop wallpaper.
- Right-click a document and select **View Source** to see the underlying HTML tags.
- When you click a link to an .EXE file, Explorer lets you select a folder to save it in.
- Explorer can handle a number of file types; it send files on to other applications to handle the rest.
- You can find freeware and shareware viewers for many file types.

Part 3
Boldly Going Around the Internet

The world seems to have Webmyopia; they can't see the Net for the Web. There's more—much more—to the Internet than the World Wide Web…though the Web is starting to spread its tentacles (if you'll excuse me for mixing my metaphors) throughout the Internet. As Web browsers become more capable, they are providing tools that allow you to use other Internet systems.

The systems you can use include such things as FTP and Archie, which turn the Internet into your own personal computer-file library, and Gopher, a world-wide menu system. In this section, you'll learn about these systems, as well as Telnet (which lets you run programs on other computers), WAIS (a database searching tool), and newsgroups and mailing lists (discussion groups on any subject you can imagine).

Chapter 12

Grabbing the Goodies—Downloading Files with FTP

In This Chapter

- ➤ What is FTP?
- ➤ FTP can be difficult—or easy
- ➤ ftping with your Web browser
- ➤ Clues that will help you find files
- ➤ ftping with WS_FTP
- ➤ Dealing with compressed files
- ➤ Staying safe from viruses

The Internet is a vast computer library. Virtually any type of computer file imaginable is available somewhere on the Internet. You'll find freeware (programs you can use for free) and shareware (programs you must pay a small fee to use) for almost all computer types, as well as music, pictures, video, 3-D images, or hypertext documents of many types. If there's any file type you can imagine, you'll probably find it on the Internet.

But where? We looked at the World Wide Web in Chapters 9 through 11. You'll find plenty of files that you can download from the Web, but there's another system, one that even predates the Web: FTP. FTP, or *File Transfer Protocol*, is an old UNIX system for transferring files from one computer to another. FTP sites all over the Internet contain literally millions of computer files. And although some of these sites are private, many are open to the public.

Let's say, for instance, that you've discovered a really neat file on a computer in Albania, or Australia, or Alabama. Perhaps someone told you where it was, or you saw it mentioned in an Internet directory of some kind, or you saw a message in a newsgroup about it. It might be a public domain or shareware program, a document containing information you want for some research you're working on, a picture, or a book you want to read. Just about anything. You might be told to "ftp to such and such a computer to find this file." That simply means use the FTP system to grab the file.

But how do you get the file from that computer to your computer? In some cases, you may have specific permission to get onto another computer and grab files. A researcher, for instance, may have been given permission to access files on a computer owned by an organization involved in the same sort of research (another university or government department, for example).

In other cases, though, you'll just be rooting around on other people's systems without specific permission. Some systems are open to the public: anyone can get on and grab files that the system administrator has decided should be publicly accessible. This is known as *anonymous ftp* because you don't need a login name to get onto the computer. You simply log in as "anonymous," and you normally enter your e-mail address for a password. (If you were working at the UNIX command line—as many unfortunate people still do—you'd have to type this information. Of course, you are using a program that enters this information for you, though.)

> **Check This Out...**
>
> **Tracking Down a File with Archie** What if you know the file you want, but you have no idea where to look for it? A quick way to track down a file is using Archie. I'll explain all about Archie in Chapter 13.

Before you start, let me give you some guidelines on when you should use FTP. Many systems don't like people digging around during business hours. They prefer you to come in during evenings and weekends. So you may see a message asking you to restrict your use to after hours, or the FTP site may even not let you in at all during certain hours.

The Different Flavors of FTP

Let me give you a little bit of background information about the various versions of FTP. Originally FTP was a command-line program. That meant you typed commands at a prompt and pressed the Enter key. Information then scrolled past on your screen, perhaps too fast for you to read (unless you knew the secret command to make it slow down or stop). You'd have to read this information and then type another command. Although UNIX-geeks got some sort of strange masochistic pleasure out of this sort of thing, real people found FTP to be a painful experience—one that most people avoided. (If you want to see an example of command-line FTP, take a look at Chapter 8.)

Then FTP was automated to some extent. It was possible to get to some FTP sites using Gopher (a system I'll cover in Chapter 14). Gopher allowed you to select files from a menu system instead of typing a command. Still, it was inconvenient for a number of reasons, the most important being that you could access only FTP sites for which some kindly Gopher author had created menus.

Next came graphical FTP programs. (There are plenty around; the best I've seen is WS_FTP, a Windows freeware program.) These allowed you to see lists of files and use your mouse to carry out the operations. Using FTP with such systems was a real pleasure. FTP became easy.

Finally, FTP was incorporated into Web browsers. In other words, you can go to an FTP site using your Web browser; there's usually no need for a special FTP program. The FTP site appears as a document with links in it. You can click on a link to view the contents of a directory, to read a text file, or to transfer a computer file to your computer.

I am going to cover running FTP sessions with a Web browser for a couple of reasons. First, it's a very easy way to work with FTP. Second, you already have a Web browser. However, some FTP sites won't work well through a Web browser, in which cases, you'll want to use WS_FTP. At the end of the chapter, I'll quickly describe WS_FTP and explain where to find it.

Hitting the FTP Trail

As an example, you're going to take a look at the ftp://ftp.usma.edu FTP site because this is where you can find the WS_FTP program. (If you prefer to visit another FTP site, you can follow along; the principles are the same.) I've given you the FTP site name, but not the directory holding the file; you can track it down when you get there.

Techno Talk: What's in a Name

What does all this information mean? First, there's the ftp:// part. This simply tells your browser that you want to go to an FTP site. Then there's the FTP site name (or host name) such as ftp.usma.edu. This identifies the computer that contains the files you are after. After that, there may be a directory name. I haven't given you a directory name in this example, but if I had said "go to ftp.usma.edu/pub/msdos," the /pub/msdos bit would tell the browser which directory to change to in order to find the files.

To start, open your Web browser. (As I have in earlier chapters, I'm assuming that you are using Internet Explorer.) Click in the **Address** text box, type **ftp://ftp.usma.edu** (or **ftp://** and the address of another site you want to visit), and press **Enter**.

Check This Out: A Few FTP Tips

In Internet Explorer, you can quickly select the Address text box by pressing the **Tab** key. And in some cases, you don't need to type the ftp:// bit. If the ftp address starts with ftp, omit ftp://. For instance, instead of typing ftp://ftp.usma.edu, you can type ftp.usma.edu. (Note that this trick won't work in most other browsers.)

Check This Out: Name or Number

The FTP site or host name may be a name (leo.nmc.edu) or a number (192.88.242.239).

In a few moments, with luck, you'll see a screen something like the one in the following figure. Without luck, you'll get a message telling you that you cannot connect to the FTP site. If that happens, see if you typed the name correctly. If you did, the site may be closed, or it may simply be very busy. Try again later.

Notice, by the way, that you didn't have to enter the anonymous login name or your e-mail address as a password. Internet Explorer handles all that for you. If the FTP site is a private site, though, you need a password. Some FTP browsers display a dialog box into which you can type the password. At the time of this writing, though, Internet Explorer doesn't let you connect to private sites. (If that's a problem, get hold of WS_FTP, which you'll learn more about later in this chapter.)

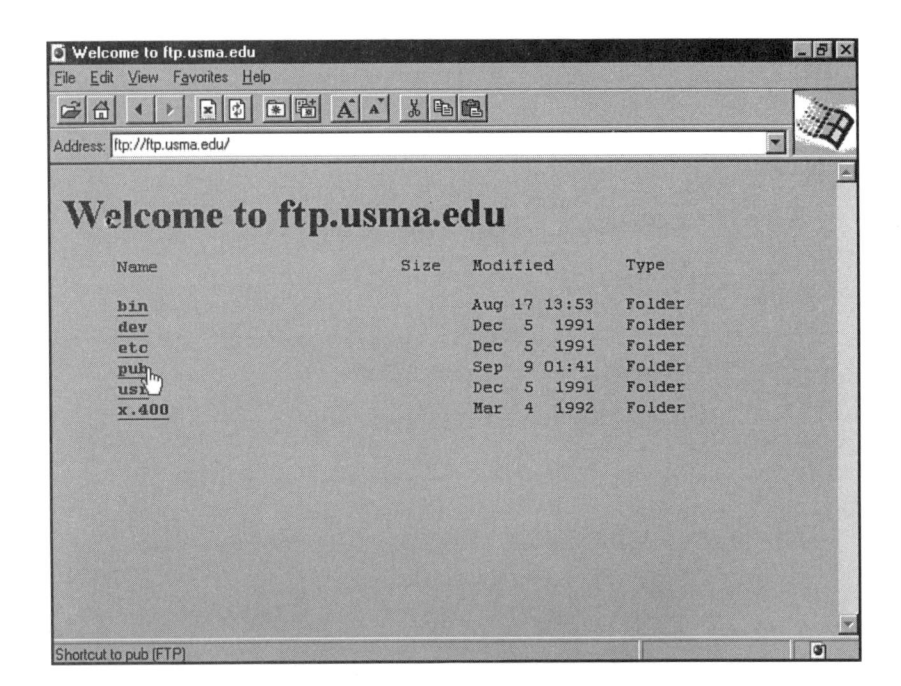

Chapter 12 ➤ *Grabbing the Goodies—Downloading Files with FTP*

```
Welcome to ftp.usma.edu
File  Edit  View  Favorites  Help
Address: ftp://ftp.usma.edu/

Welcome to ftp.usma.edu

Name           Size    Modified         Type
bin                    Aug 17 13:53     Folder
dev                    Dec  5  1991     Folder
etc                    Dec  5  1991     Folder
pub                    Sep  9 01:41     Folder
usr                    Dec  5  1991     Folder
x.400                  Mar  4  1992     Folder

Shortcut to pub (FTP)
```

FTP via a browser. If you've struggled through command-line FTP, you'll love this.

FTP Links

There's another way to get to an FTP site. Many Web authors create links from their Web pages to an FTP site. Click on such a link to go to that site.

What Is All This?

What can you see at the FTP site? Each file and directory is shown as a link. Depending on the browser you are using, you'll see information about the file or directory. Internet Explorer, for example, shows the name of each file or folder on the left side of the window. On the right are three columns: Size, Modified, and Type. The Type column tells what each item is—a *file* or a *folder* (or directory). In the Size column, it displays the file size so you'll know how big a file is before you transfer it. The Modified column tells when the item was created or most recently modified. In the example in these figures, you can see that all the links are directories; there are no files here.

Click a directory link to see the contents of that directory. Explorer displays another Web document, showing the contents of that directory. Notice that it also contains a link back to the previous directory (in Internet Explorer, the Up one level link is located at the top

Part 3 ➤ *Boldly Going Around the Internet*

of the page). The following figure shows what you find if you click the pub link at the ftp.usma.edu. Why pub? Because it's commonly used to hold publicly available files. This time, you can see that there's a file in this directory, along with three more subdirectories.

Traveling through the FTP site, you see the contents of the pub directory (or folder in Windows 95-speak).

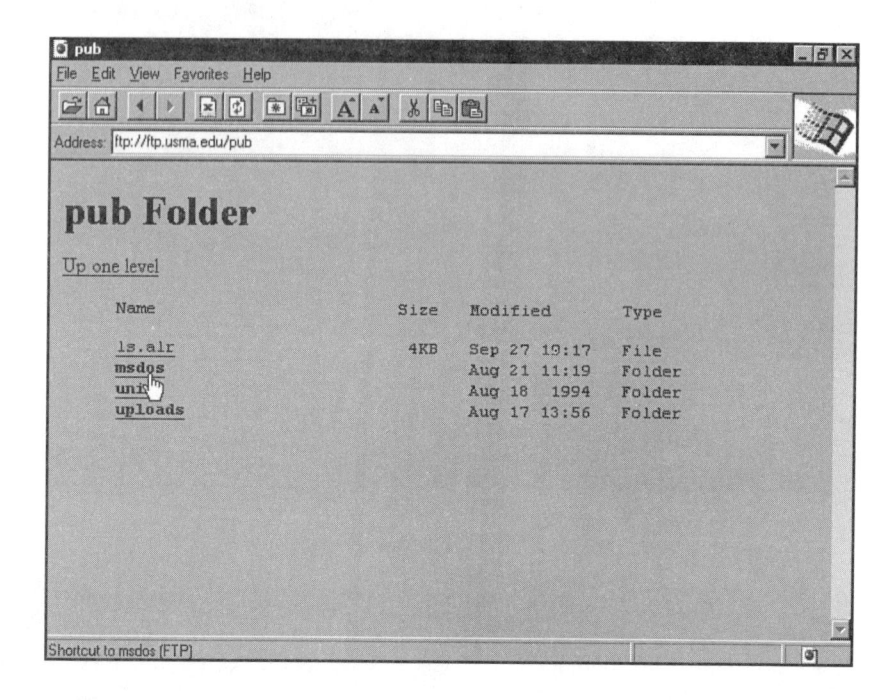

How Do I Find Files? Don't forget Archie! Archie is a system that lets you search an index of FTP sites throughout the world for just the file you need. See Chapter 13 for more information.

What happens when you click a link to a file? The same thing that would happen if you did so from a true Web document. If Explorer can display or play the file type, it will. If it can't, Explorer tries to send it to the associated application. If there is no associated application, Explorer asks you what to do with it, allowing you to save it on the hard disk. This all works in the same way it does when you are at a Web site: Explorer looks at the file type and acts accordingly. (See Chapters 9–12 for more information.)

142

Finding That Pot o' Gold

Now that you're on, you want to find the file you know lies somewhere on this system. (In the example, you're looking for WS_FTP32.EXE, the Windows 95 WS_FTP program.) Where do you start? Well, finding files at an FTP site is often a little difficult. Because these sites are not set up according to any conventions, you often have to dig through whatever directories look like they might contain what you want, until you find that file.

> **Check This Out...**
>
> **FTP Connections Through Web Pages**
> Many FTP sites are now accessible directly through Web documents. For instance, instead of going to **ftp://ftp.winsite.com/pub/pc/win95/** (a well-known shareware archive), you could go to **http://www.winsite.com/**.

Remember, that your Web browser can display text files. When you first get to an FTP site, look for files that say INDEX, README, DIRECTORY, and so on. These often contain information that will help you find what you need. The more organized sites even contain text files with full indexes of their contents—or at least lists of the directories and the types of files you'll find. Click on one of these files to transfer the document to your Web browser. Read the file, and then click the **Back** button to return to the directory.

Look for Clues

You'll often find that directories have names that describe their contents: slip will probably contain SLIP software, mac will have Macintosh software, xwindow will have X Window software, windows will have Microsoft Windows software, gif will contain GIF-format graphics, and so on. If you know what you are looking for, you can often figure out what the directory names mean. In the example, you see msdos, unix, and uploads directories. There's a good chance that what you are looking for is in the msdos directory because it probably contains software designed for IBM-compatible PCs.

In fact, if you enter this directory, you will indeed find WS_FTP32.ZIP (at least it was there at the time of this writing; but these things do get moved around). Click on the **WS_FTP.TXT** file to display a text document that provides a little information about WS_FTP.

Part 3 ➤ *Boldly Going Around the Internet*

It Looks a Little Strange

You often see full FTP site and path information, which takes you straight to the directory you want (ftp.usma.edu/pub/msdos/, for example). If you're used to working in DOS and Windows, FTP site directory names may look pretty strange for two reasons. First, I've used a forward slash (/) instead of a backslash (\) to separate the directories in the path. In the DOS world, you use a backslash; but in the UNIX world—and most of the Internet still runs on UNIX computers—you use the forward slash character instead. Second, the directory names are often long. In DOS, directory names can contain no more than 12 characters (including a period and an extension). In Windows 95 and its programs, directory names can contain as many characters as necessary because the new operating system allows long file and directory names. UNIX computers allow long names, too.

Get the File

When you find the file you want, click on it, and the Confirm File Open dialog box appears. Click the **Save As** button. As you can see in the next figure, the Save As dialog box pops up so you can choose a directory on your computer in which to save the file.

Saving files from an FTP site is a matter of a few clicks.

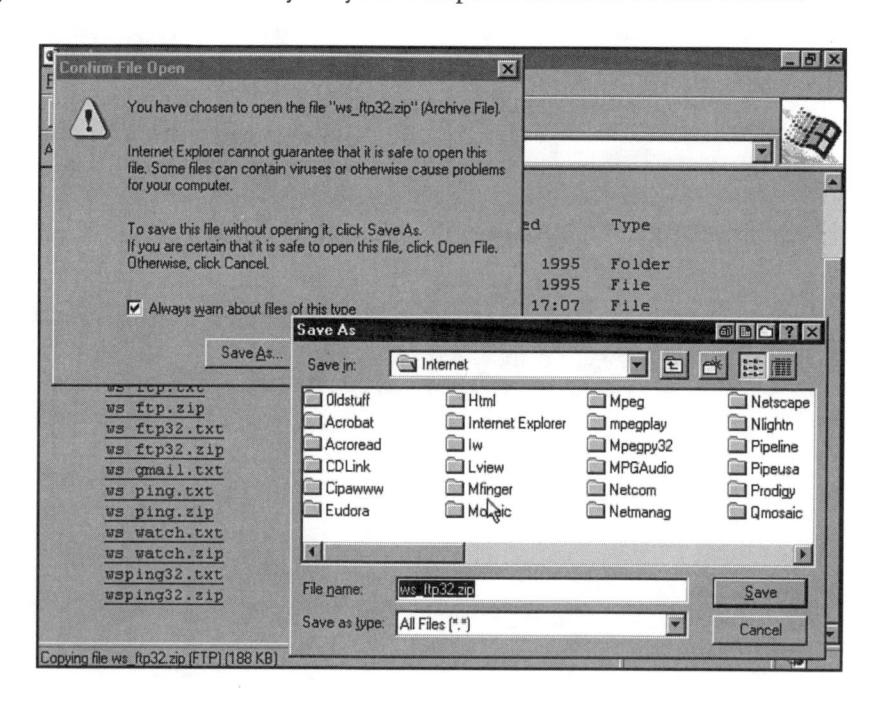

Chapter 12 ➤ *Grabbing the Goodies—Downloading Files with FTP*

Note, by the way, the Always warn about files of this type check box (at the bottom of the Confirm File Open dialog box). Don't clear the check from this check box; if you do, the next time you click on a file with the same extension (in this case, .ZIP), it will be saved without your input and you won't be able to tell Internet Explorer where to place the file.

Of course, different browsers use different methods for saving files. If you are not using Internet Explorer, check your browser's documentation.

Compressed (Squeezed) Files

Many files on FTP sites are compressed. That is, special programs have been used to "squeeze" the information into a smaller area. You can't use these files in their compressed state, but it's a great way to store and transmit them because it saves disk space and transmission time. You can reduce files down to as little as 2% of their normal size, depending on the type of file and the program you use (though 40% to 75% is probably a more normal range). You'll find that most compressed DOS and Windows files are in .ZIP format, a format created by a program called PKZIP. However, you may also see .ARJ (created by a program called ARJ) and .LZH (created by LHARC) now and again, but admittedly that's not very often.

> **Check This Out...**
>
> **Archive Files**
> An *archive* file is one that contains one or more other files, generally in a compressed format. You use archive files to store infrequently used files or to transfer files from one computer to another.

The following table shows some other compressed formats you'll see.

File Formats Commonly Found in FTP Sites

Extension	Compression Program Used
.Z	**compress** (UNIX)
.z	**pack** (UNIX)
.shar	**sh** (UNIX "shell archive")
.Sit	StuffIt (Macintosh)
.pit	PackIt (Macintosh)
.zoo	zoo210 (available on various systems)
.tar	**tar** (UNIX)
.arc	PKARC (DOS; a method that predates PKZIP)

145

> **Check This Out...**
>
> **Same Name, Different Extension**
>
> While digging around in an FTP site, you may notice files that have the same name except for the last few characters; you might find thisdoc.txt and thisdoc.zip, for instance. The first is a simple ASCII text file, and the second is a ZIP file (which is much smaller than the first). If you know you can decompress the file once you have it, get the compressed version. It'll save you time and money.

Finally, there's something called a self-extracting archive. Various programs, such as PKZIP and ARJ, can create files that you can execute (run) to extract the archived files automatically. This is very useful for sending a compressed file to someone when you're not sure if he has the program to decompress the file (or would know how to use it). For instance, PKZIP can create a file with an .EXE extension, which you can run directly from the DOS prompt just by typing its name and pressing Enter, or by double-clicking on the file in Windows 95's Explorer file-management program. When you do so, all the compressed files pop out.

EXE's Okay, But What About ZIP?

If you find a file in two formats, .ZIP and .EXE, you may want to take the .EXE format. The .EXE files are not much larger than the .ZIP files, and you don't have to worry about finding a program to extract the files.

But often, files are available only in .ZIP format. In the example I've been using throughout this chapter, there's a WS_FTP.ZIP file, but no WS_FTP.EXE file. In such a case, you must have a program that can read the .ZIP file and extract the archived files from within.

You may already have such a program. For example, the Symantec Norton Navigator suite of programs comes with Norton File Manager, which can work with .ZIP files. If you don't have such a program, though, I suggest you get hold of WinZIP. You can find WinZIP at http://www.winzip.com/zip/.

Having Trouble Connecting to a Site?

There may be times when you try to connect to an FTP site, and it just won't work. Of course, it may be that the FTP site is simply too busy to let you on (most limit the number of people using them). But sometimes, your browser simply can't manage the site. Perhaps, it's a private site; even if you have a password to enter the site, some browsers (including Internet Explorer at the time of this writing) can't take that password and pass it on. Also, FTP sites come in many "flavors," i.e. many computer types and operating systems. Your browser may simply have trouble communicating. If you run into problems, try WS_FTP.

Try WS_FTP

The very best FTP program around is WS_FTP. I've already shown you where you can find it. Now I'm suggesting that if you run into problems using a particular FTP site, you should download and install WS_FTP. I'm not going to go into great detail about working with this program, but it actually is very easy. Compared to WS_FTP, UNIX FTP is like eating soup with a fork—not particularly satisfying. WS_FTP is what FTP should be. You have all the commands at your fingertips, and you have a library of FTP sites to select from—no more mistyping of FTP host names.

Installing is simple. Just place the files in a folder and create a Start menu entry or a desktop shortcut. Then start your Internet connection, and select the **WS_FTP** program from the **Start** menu or double-click the shortcut. The Session Profile dialog box appears (see the next figure). In this window, you can select an FTP site from the list (it comes with about 20 already configured) or you can enter information about a particular site you want to visit.

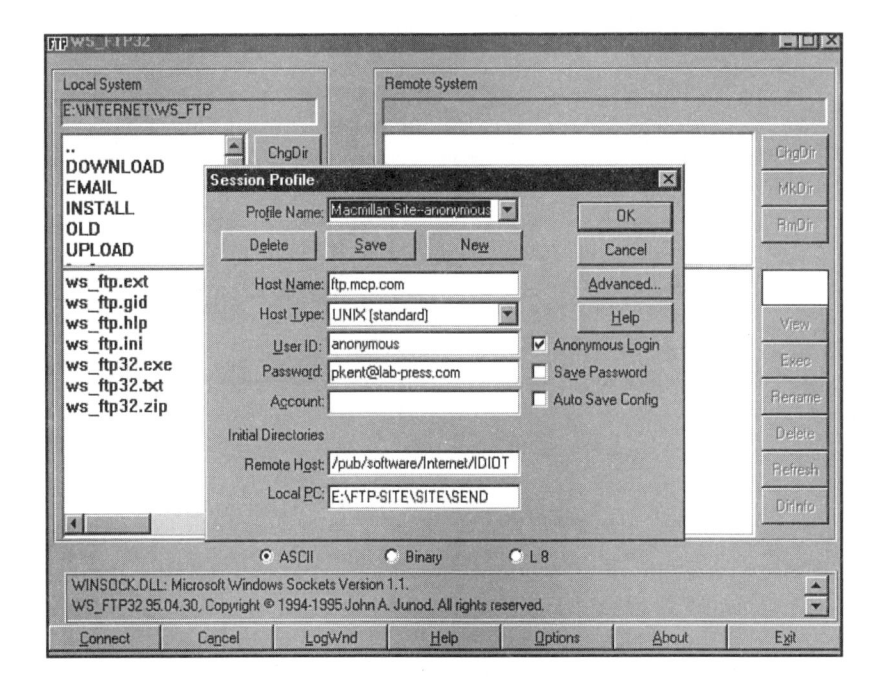

Set up your session profile before you connect.

147

1. Enter a name in the **Profile Name** text box (basically anything that helps you remember what the site contains).

2. Enter the actual FTP site host name in the **Host Name** text box.

3. If you know it, enter the **Host Type** (if you are not sure, ignore this setting and let WS_FTP pick this for you).

4. If you are going to an "anonymous" FTP site, click on the **Anonymous Login** check box. If, on the other hand, you are going to a private site, fill in the **User ID** text box.

5. If this is a private site, enter your password in that text box.

6. If you know which directory you want to go to when you get to the FTP site, enter its name in the **Initial Directories: Remote Host** text box.

7. If you want, you can enter the Local PC directory (the directory on your computer that should appear in the leftmost list box; see the following figure) into which you want transferred files to be placed.

8. Click the **Save** button to save the information.

9. Click **OK** to begin the session.

When WS_FTP connects to the FTP, WS_FTP displays the FTP site directories on the right and the directories on your computer's hard disk on the left (see the following figure). You can move around in the directories by double-clicking or by using the ChgDir button. ChgDir is really handy because if you know where you want to go, it's a lot quicker to type it in and go directly than to go through each directory in the path to get there.

> **Check This Out...**
>
> **Select the File Type** Notice the little ASCII and Binary option buttons below the file list windows? Make sure you select the correct one before transferring a file. Pick **ASCII** for files you know to be ASCII text files; pick **Binary** for anything else.

The two buttons you'll use most are the View and <- buttons. Say, for example, that you find an index file you want to read. You click it and click the **View** button on the right side of the window, and the file is placed into a Notepad window so you can read it. When you find the files you want, press and hold **Ctrl**, click on each file, and then click the <- button to transfer them to your hard disk.

Some of the buttons you probably won't use much—at least not on the FTP site. You can create a new directory and delete a directory (ChgDir and RmDir). If you are using an anonymous login, you won't be able to do this on the FTP site, but you can use them to add and remove directories on your own hard disk. You can also rename and delete files, and even automatically transfer a file and load it into the program with which the file's extension is associated in Windows (use the Exec button).

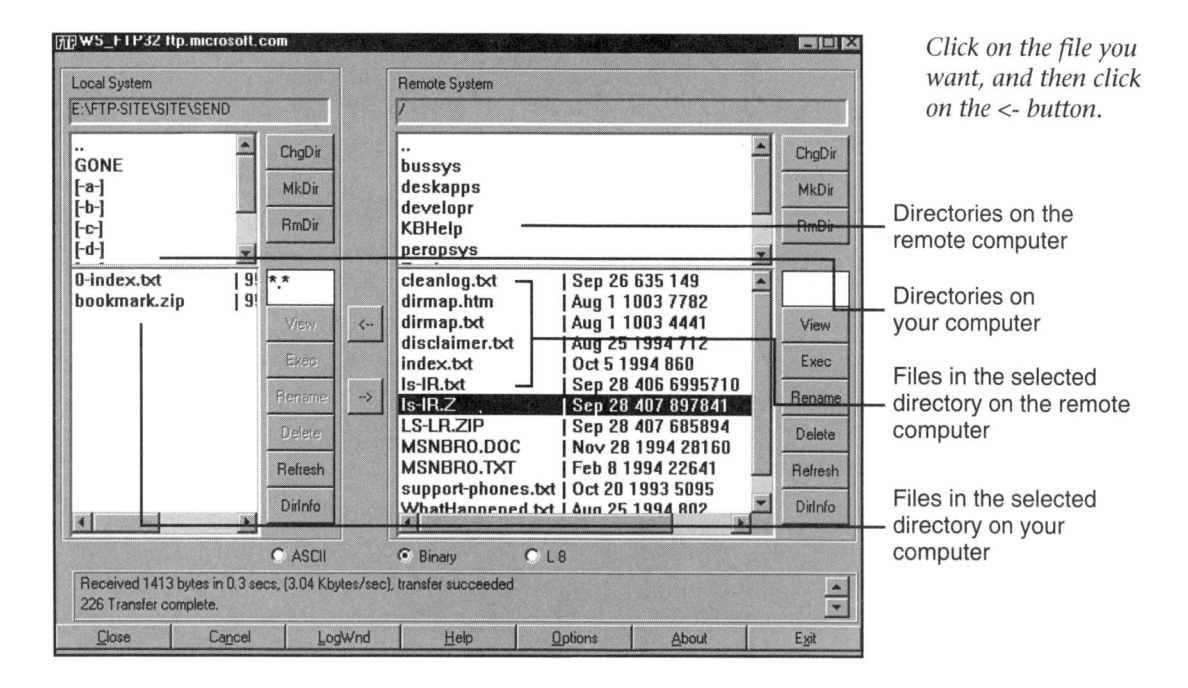

Chapter 12 ➤ *Grabbing the Goodies—Downloading Files with FTP*

Click on the file you want, and then click on the <- button.

- Directories on the remote computer
- Directories on your computer
- Files in the selected directory on the remote computer
- Files in the selected directory on your computer

Sometimes WS_FTP is unable to figure out what type of host it's connecting to. It's usually able to do that, but now and again you'll notice such strange stuff as no directories appearing in the directories list, file dates appearing instead of file names, or partial file names appearing. If you try to transfer one of these strange files to your system, you get a message saying that it doesn't exist. This is easy to fix.

1. First, click the **LogWnd** button to see the session log. The log appears, showing the entire FTP session from the command-line point of view.
2. Go back to the table earlier in this chapter and see if you can find the type of host for this file; usually an FTP site identifies its type.
3. Click the **Options** button.
4. Then click the **Session Options** button in the dialog box that appears.
5. Select the host type from the drop-down list and click the **Save** button.

> **RTFM: Read The Fine Manual** The online help is very good. And because there is so much more to FTP than what I've covered, you should read it. Also, try clicking the right mouse button in the window to see a shortcut menu with various options.

149

It's Alive! Viruses and Other Nasties

If you haven't been in a cave for the past six or seven years, you've probably heard about computer viruses. A *virus* is a computer program that can reproduce itself and even convince unknowing users to help spread it. It spreads far and wide and can do incredible amounts of damage. As is true of real viruses, the effects of a virus on your system can range from almost-unnoticeable to fatal. For example, a virus can do something as harmless as display a Christmas tree on your screen, or it can destroy everything on your hard disk.

Viruses hide out in a variety of places. Boot sector viruses hide in a disk's boot sector (the part of the disk that's read into memory when the computer starts). From there, they can copy themselves onto the boot sectors of other disks. File viruses hide out in program files and copy themselves to other program files when someone runs that program.

Viruses and other malevolent computer bugs are real, and they do real damage. In 1988, 6,000 computers connected to the Internet were infected with a "worm." (The Internet has grown tremendously since then; so the number of victims would surely be higher today.) Similarly, a service provider in New York recently had to close down temporarily after its system became infected.

Viruses Under the Microscope

The term "virus" has become a catch-all for a variety of digital organisms, including these:

Bacteria   Viruses that reproduce but do no direct damage (except using up disk space and memory).

Rabbits   Viruses that reproduce very quickly (hence the name).

Trojan horses   Viruses embedded in otherwise-useful programs.

Bombs   Programs that just sit and wait for a particular date or event, and then wreak destruction; these are often left deep inside programs by disgruntled employees.

Worms   Programs that copy themselves from one computer to another independently of other executable files, and therefore "clog" the computers by taking over memory and disk space.

Unfortunately, security on the Internet is lax. Some computer BBS services (such as CompuServe) check their own systems for viruses regularly. But on the Internet, it's up to each system administrator (of which there are thousands) to keep his or her own system clean. If just one administrator does a bad job, a virus can get through and be carried by FTP all over the world. Some system administrators are reacting by closing off some Internet services (not allowing users to access FTP files, for example).

But having said all that, I've also got to say that the virus threat is also overstated—probably by companies that sell antivirus software. We've reached a stage where almost any confusing computer problem is blamed on computer viruses, and technical support people use it as an excuse not to talk with people. "Your computer can't read your hard disk? You've been downloading files from the Internet? You must have a virus!" In reality, most computer users have never been "hit" by a computer virus, and many who think they have probably haven't. A lot of problems are blamed on viruses these days. Don't get overly worried about it. Take some sensible precautions, and you'll be okay.

Tips for "Safe Computing"

If you are working with just basic ASCII text e-mail and perhaps ftping documents, you're okay. The problem of viruses arises when you transfer programs (including self-extracting archive files) or files that contain mini programs. For instance, many word-processing files now contain macros, special little programs that may run when you open the file.

If you do plan to transfer programs, perhaps the best advice is to get a good antivirus program (they're available for all computer types). Each time you transmit an executable file, use your antivirus program to check it. Also, make sure you keep good backups of your data. Although backups can also become infected with viruses, if a virus hits, at least you can reload your backup data and use an antivirus program to clean the files (some backup programs check for viruses while backing up).

Where to Now?

You'll find thousands of FTP sites all over the world. Here are a few interesting places to start. These two FTP sites contain a lot of Windows shareware utilities.

    ftp.winsite.com/pub/pc/win95/

    ftp.wustl.edu/systems/ibmpc/win3

To find more, go to **http://hoohoo.ncsa.uiuc.edu/ftp/** Web site—the Monster FTP Sites list—to find thousands of FTP sites.

The Least You Need to Know

- ➤ FTP stands for File Transfer Protocol and refers to a system of file libraries.
- ➤ Anonymous FTP is a system the public can use to transfer files.
- ➤ Start an FTP session in your Web browser using the ftp:// URL. For instance, type **ftp://*hostname*** in Internet Explorer's Address text box and press **Enter**.
- ➤ Each directory and file at an FTP site is represented by a link; click the link to view the directory or transfer the file.
- ➤ If your browser can't connect to a particular site, try WS_FTP.
- ➤ Protect yourself against viruses, but don't be paranoid. They're not as common as the antivirus companies want you to think.

Chapter 13

Archie the File Searcher

In This Chapter

➤ What does Archie do?

➤ The different ways to use Archie

➤ Finding an Archie gateway on the Web

➤ Searching for files with your Web browser

➤ Using WS_Archie

➤ Using Archie mail (if you don't want to wait)

➤ Doing descriptive (whatis) searches

Okay, FTP is just great—if you know where a file is located. Sometimes you'll see the FTP site mentioned in e-mail or a document you find somewhere. But what if you know the file you are looking for but have no idea where to go to find it?

Archie to the rescue. Designed by a few guys at McGill University in Canada, *Archie* is a system that indexes FTP sites, listing the files that are available at each site. Archie lists several million files at over a thousand FTP sites and provides a very useful way to find out where to go to grab a file in which you are interested. There's just one problem: Archie's very busy these days and can be very slow.

Try Archie Mail

Archie has a descriptive-index search. That means you can search for a particular subject and find files related to that subject. Because you can't do this using a Web browser, you might want to try Archie mail instead. (You'll learn more about Archie mail later in this chapter.)

More Client/Server Stuff

As are certain other Internet systems, Archie is set up using a *client/server* system. An Archie server is a computer that periodically takes a look at all the Internet FTP sites around the world and builds a list of all their available files. Each server builds a database of those files. An Archie client program—a program running on your computer—can then come along and search the server's database as if it were an index.

It's generally believed in Internet-land that it doesn't matter much which Archie server you use because they all do much the same thing; some have simply been updated more recently than others. This isn't always true. Sometimes, you may get very different results from two different servers. For example, one server might find two *hits* (matches to your search request), while another might find seven.

Getting to Archie

You can choose from several ways to use Archie:

➤ You can use your Web browser to go to an Archie gateway, which is a Web site that helps you search an Archie index.

Archie? What does Archie mean? It's not an acronym (unlike Veronica and Jughead, who you'll meet in Chapter 14). It comes from the word *archive* (as in file archive). Remove the *v* and what have you got? Archie.

➤ You can use a special Archie client program, such as WS_Archie.

➤ You can use e-mail to send questions to an Archie server.

You can also use Archie from the command line in multiple ways, but I'm not going to talk about those more difficult methods. Instead, I'll start with the easiest way to use Archie: through your Web browser. Then I'll give you an overview of the other two methods.

Archie on the Web

Your Web browser is not an Archie client (that is, there is no archie:// URL). Therefore, you have to use an Archie interface (called a *gateway*) on the Web. An Archie gateway provides a link from the Web to Archie servers around the world. You'll find dozens of these gateways on the Web. Open your Web browser (see Chapter 9) and go to **http://web.nexor.co.uk/archie.html** to see a list of them. If that Web site's busy, try one of these other Archie sites:

> http://www.lerc.nasa.gov/Doc/archieplex.html
>
> http://hoohoo.ncsa.uiuc.edu/archie.html
>
> http://src.doc.ic.ac.uk/archieplexform.html

When you arrive at an Archie site, you have to indicate which type of search you want to do: *forms* or *nonforms*. Internet Explorer is a forms-capable browser, as are most other browsers these days. A forms-capable browser can display such forms components as text boxes, command buttons, option buttons, and so on. In most cases, you will select the forms search.

Searching Archie

The following figure shows an example Archie form. This form is from Imperial College in London located at http://src.doc.ic.ac.uk/archieplexform.html. The simplest way to search is to type a file name or part of a file name into the **What would you like to search for?** text box, and then press **Enter** or click on the **Start Search** button. For instance, if you are trying to find the WS_Archie program (which we'll look at later in this chapter), you could type **WSARCHIE** and press **Enter**. (Why not WS_ARCHIE? Because the file you need is called WSARCHIE.ZIP or WSARCHIE.EXE, even though the program name is WS_Archie.)

> **Stop!** To cancel a search, click the **Stop** toolbar button (the one with the X on it).

155

A typical Archie form.

Type the text you want to look for.

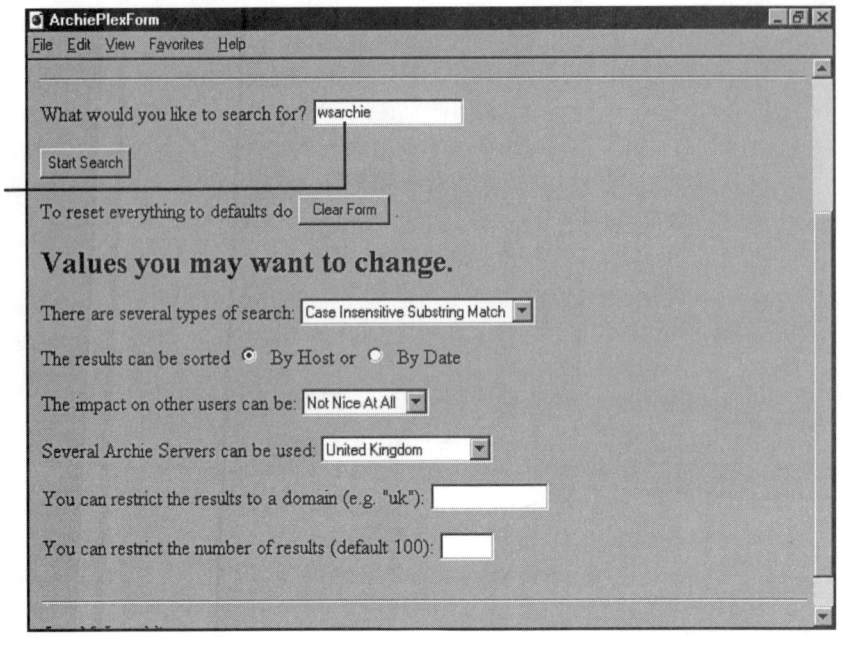

Archie searches are very slow. In fact, it's not unusual for a search simply not to work at all because the Archie server you are working with is busy. (I'll show you how to choose another server in a moment.) If you are lucky, eventually you'll see a screen like the one in the next figure, which shows what the Archie server found: links to the WSARCHIE files. You might see links to the host (the computer that contains the file you are looking for), links to the directory on the host that contains the file you want, or links to the exact file you want. If you click on one of the wsarchie.zip links, Explorer begins transferring the file.

> **Check This Out...**
>
> **Search the Document**
>
> Remember, you can use your browser's Find function (in Internet Explorer, it's Edit, Find) to search the list of files. For instance, you may want to download an EXE file (a self-extracting archive) instead of a ZIP file. If so, search for **.exe** to go directly to the file you need.

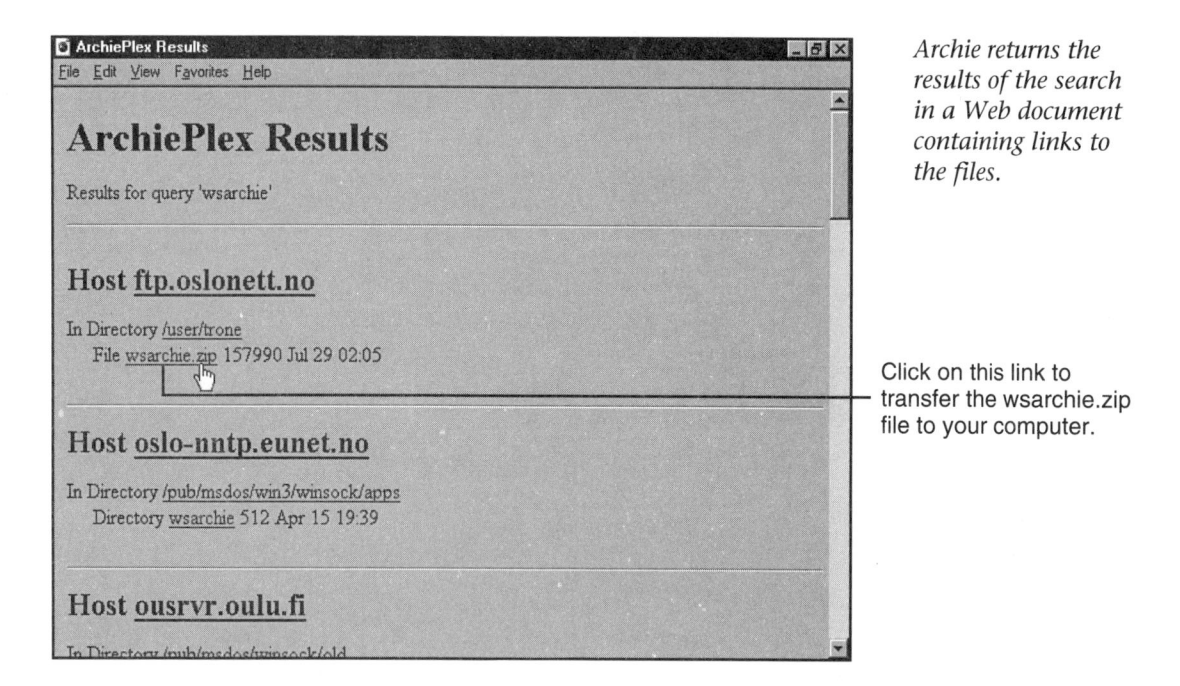

Chapter 13 ➤ *Archie the File Searcher*

Archie returns the results of the search in a Web document containing links to the files.

Click on this link to transfer the wsarchie.zip file to your computer.

Archie's Options

When filling in an Archie form, you can enter more than just the text you want to search for. You can enter the following types of information to provide Archie with more specific options for your search.

➤ **Search type**   There are four types of searches, which I'll explain in a moment.

➤ **Sort by**   The list of files that is returned to you may be sorted according to their file dates or according to the host containing the file. If you use the file date search, it's easier to make sure you get the latest version of the file.

➤ **Impact on other users**   You can tell Archie that you are not in a hurry (so other users can go first) or that you want the results right away. Difficult choice, huh?

➤ **Archie servers**   From this list, you can choose to search any Archie server from anywhere in the world. If the Archie server you try is busy, or if it can't find what you want, try another one. You might want to try a server in a country in which the people are currently asleep; that server might be less busy than those in a country where it's daytime.

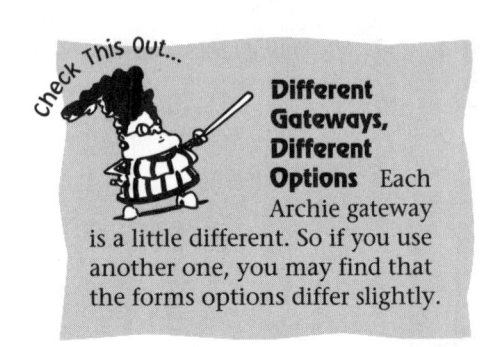

> **Check This Out...**
>
> **Different Gateways, Different Options** Each Archie gateway is a little different. So if you use another one, you may find that the forms options differ slightly.

- **Restrict the results to a domain** You can tell the Archie server that you want to see only files in a particular domain (a particular host-computer type). For example, you might enter UK for FTP sites in the United Kingdom, COM for commercial FTP sites, or EDU for educational FTP sites.

- **Number of results** You can tell the Archie server how many results you want to see. (However, this setting is not always accurate.)

What Are the Search Types?

Before you begin searching for a file name, you should figure out the type of search you want to use. These are your choices:

Exact or **Exact Match** You must type the exact name of the file for which you are looking.

Regex or **Regular Expression Match** You type a UNIX regular expression, and Archie regards some of the characters in the word you type as wild cards. (If you don't understand regular expressions, you're better off avoiding this type of search. In fact, all but UNIX geeks should probably avoid this option.)

Sub or **Case Insensitive Substring Match** This tells Archie to search within file names for whatever you type. It then looks for all names that match what you type, as well as all names that *include* the characters you type. If you search for wsarch, for example, Archie finds wsarch and wsarchie. Note that when you use a sub search, you don't need to worry about the case of the characters; Archie finds wsarch and WSARCH.

Subcase or **Case Sensitive Substring Match** This is like the sub search except that you must enter the case of the word correctly. If you enter wsarch, Archie finds wsarch but not WSARCH.

More often than not, you'll want to use the sub search (Case Insensitive Substring Match), which has probably been set up as the default. It takes a little longer than the other types, but it's more likely to find what you're looking for.

If you use Archie to search for a certain file name, you need to realize that file names are not always set in stone. Because thousands of people are posting millions of files on thousands of computers, file names sometimes change a little. If you have trouble finding something, try a variety of possible combinations.

Chapter 13 ➤ *Archie the File Searcher*

It Doesn't Seem to Work

The Substring Matches don't always find file names that contain what you typed. For instance, if you search for ws_ftp (which we looked at in Chapter 12), Archie may not find ws_ftp32, or it may find only one or two when there are actually many files named ws_ftp32 at many FTP sites. Why? Because it shows you the ws_ftp matches before it shows you the ws_ftp32 matches, and a lot of ws_ftp matches may exceed the find limit (which you entered as the Number of Results option in the Archie form). You can increase the number of results and search again to see if there are any ws_ftp32 files. Or you can do a separate search for ws_ftp32.

Looking for Shareware

If you are looking for shareware, go to **http://vsl.cnet.com/**. This site lets you search for programs by description instead of file name. (It's a Web site, not an Archie gateway, though.)

Getting and Using WS_Archie

If you use Archie a lot, try to get hold of WS_Archie. You may find that you don't like working with Archie through a Web site. (Not only is Archie often busy, but the Web site that contains the gateway is often busy, too.) In addition, you may prefer the way WS_Archie provides the information in the results.

The Web method is very convenient because it creates links to the file you need. WS_Archie can also automate a way for you to get the files you want. To do so, WS_Archie interacts with WS_FTP and orders WS_FTP to go get the file you select.

I showed you how to find WS_Archie a moment ago (by searching Archie with your Web browser). When you find the program, transfer the file into a new directory on your hard disk and install the program from the compressed .EXE or .ZIP file (see Chapter 12). Then open the program and follow these steps to set default options to use in your searches:

1. Select **Options, User preferences**. In the dialog box that appears, select the **Default Archie Server** (the Archie server you want to use in most cases). This should be an Archie server that is close to you. However, if the ones close to you are always busy, you might want to try one in a country that doesn't have a lot of Internet traffic, such as Albania or Arkansas.

159

2. Select the type of search you'll normally want to use, which is probably **Substring**. (The WS_Archie Help file has some good information about Regex searches, if you've been wondering what that's all about.) No need to change the User ID field in this dialog box. Click **OK**.

3. Next, select **Options, FTP Setup**. In the resulting dialog box, enter the path to the WS_FTP program so Archie can automatically launch WS_FTP and grab a file for you. (Don't remove the **%h:%d/%f** at the end of the Command line; that tells WS_Archie to send the information WS_FTP is going to need.)

4. In the Directory list, choose the directory you want WS_FTP to download to.

5. Close this dialog box.

6. Close and reopen the program, and it begins using the defaults you just entered.

Now you're ready to search. Type the name of the file you're looking for in the **Search for** text box. Then click **Search**, and off it goes. The search will probably take a while, and sometimes you may think nothing is happening. In reality, the program is simply waiting. (Read the Help file for an explanation of what the status bar messages mean.)

When Archie finally responds, you see a window like the one in the next figure. If Archie found what you need, click on the file and select **File, Retrieve**. Archie launches WS_FTP, which downloads the file and then closes.

WS_Archie links to WS_FTP to automate downloads.

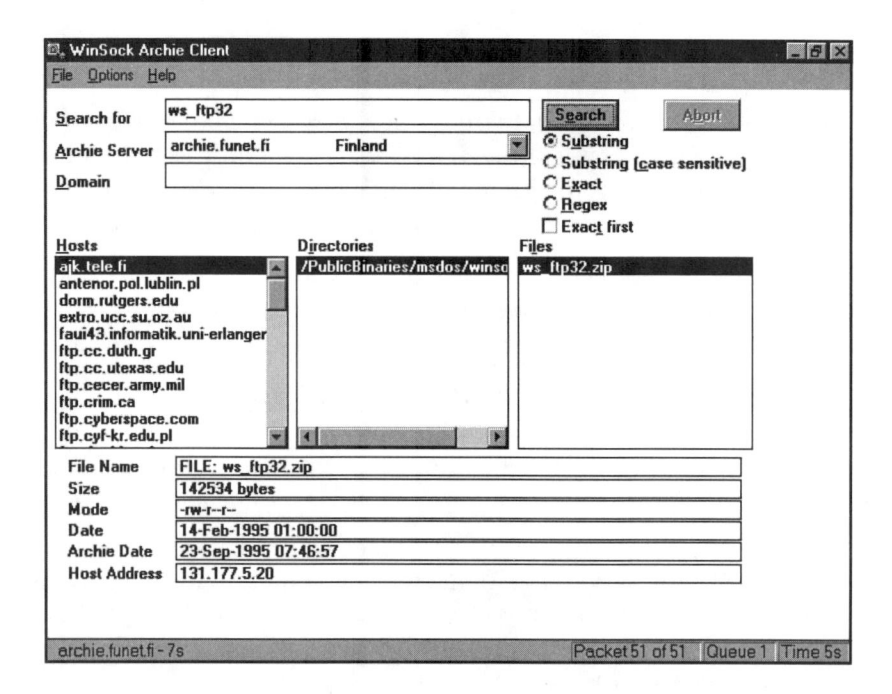

Mail-Order Archie

Archie's real problem is time. It takes a long time to perform a search—if it can even get started. Sometimes the Archie server is too busy to deal with your request.

If you don't want to wait for Archie or spend time trying different Archie servers, you can let your e-mail program send an e-mail message to an Archie server and wait for the response. Eventually, you'll receive a list of files and where you can find them. Then you have to use your Web browser or FTP program to go to the FTP site and download the file.

Some Archie mail responses come in only a few minutes; others may take hours. (This is even true of responses to two different commands in the same e-mail message.) Archie says that if you get no response in two days, there's probably a problem. Use the **set mailto** *emailaddress* command (where *emailaddress* is your e-mail address) to make sure Archie has your correct e-mail address.

Using Archie by mail is actually quite simple. You send a message to **archie@***archieserver* (where *archieserver* is the address of the Archie server you choose). You can choose any Archie server you want. The following table lists the Archie servers.

Archie Servers and Their Locations

Archie Server Address	Location
archie.ans.net	USA, ANS
archie.internic.net	USA, AT&T (NY)
archie.rutgers.edu	USA, Rutgers U.
archie.au	Australia
archie.th-darmstadt.de	Germany
archie.wide.ad.jp	Japan
archie.sogang.ac.kr	Korea

> **Techno Talk**
>
> **Archie List**
>
> To find the latest list of Archie servers, send an e-mail message to an Archie server using this address: **archie@***archieserver* (for example, archie@archie.rutgers.edu). In the body of the message, type **servers** on the first line. See Chapters 20–23 for more information about using e-mail.

Create an e-mail message to the server. Leave the Subject line blank and put all the Archie search commands in the body of the message. (Some e-mail systems don't allow blank Subject lines; if yours doesn't, put the first command in the Subject line.) You can include as many commands in a message as you want. Each command must be on a separate line, and the first character of each command must be the first character on its line. For example, you might enter these commands:

servers

find wsarchie

whatis encryption

The first command, **servers**, asks Archie to send you a list of Archie servers. (The list you get may not be complete; try several different servers to get a complete picture.) The **find** command tells Archie to search for wsarchie. The **whatis** command tells Archie you want to do a *descriptive* search (see the next section). When you finish entering the commands, send the e-mail message.

"Whatis" the Descriptive Index?

You might want to try Archie's **whatis** search command. This command searches a descriptive index, an index of file descriptions. Not all files indexed by Archie have a description, but many do. Whatis may be worth a try if you are having trouble finding what you need. Unfortunately, this command is not currently available through the Web gateways or WS_Archie. You can use it with Archie mail, though.

Suppose you sent Archie an e-mail that contained the command **whatis encryption**. You might get a list of descriptions like this:

```
    codon          Simple encryption algorithm
    des            Data encryption system (DES) routines and a login
                   front-end
    des-no-usa     Data encryption system (DES) code free of US
                   restrictions
```

Sometimes you won't be able to figure out how Archie found some of the files in the resulting list based on the keyword you used. That doesn't matter, as long as some of them look like what you want.

On the left side of each line is a name. If you want to find out where the listed file is, send e-mail back to the server with the command **find** *name* (where *name* is the word on the left side of the line). If you type **find des-no-usa**, Archie lists the DES encryption files that you can download without worrying about U.S. export restrictions.

More E-Mail Commands

You can use these other commands to configure your e-mail search:

- **set search** *type* We talked about the different search types earlier. You can send the **set search** command followed by **exact**, **regex**, **sub**, or **subcase** to tell Archie which type of search you want to do. If you don't specify a search type, the system uses sub.

- **help** You use this command to send for a Mail Archie user's guide.

- **site** *host* You can enter a host IP address (the numbers that describe a host's location) or domain name to have Archie send a list of all the files at that FTP site.

- **quit** This tells Archie to ignore everything that follows in the message. If your mail system inserts a signature file automatically at the end of each message, use **quit** to make sure Archie doesn't think this signature information is another command. Anytime Archie sees a command it doesn't understand, it automatically sends the help information. You don't want to get the help information each time you send an Archie request.

- **set mailto** *mailaddress* If you're not getting answers to your Archie requests, your mail program is probably not inserting enough information in the From line. Use this command (where *mailaddress* is your e-mail address) to specify the path to which you want Archie to send the response.

If you like the idea of working with Archie through the mail, send the **help** command to get the user's guide. There are plenty of little tricks you can use with this system.

The Least You Need to Know

- Archie servers periodically index the available files at thousands of FTP sites. Archie clients can read the indexes.

- The easiest way to use Archie is through a Web page gateway on the Web. See http://web.nexor.co.uk/archie.html for a list of gateways.

- It's important to pick the correct type of search. The simplest is the sub search, which lets you enter part of the file name without worrying about the case you use.

- You may want to try WS_Archie in combination with WS_FTP. When WS_Archie finds a file, select **File**, **Retrieve** to launch WS_FTP and get the file.

- Using Archie by mail can be easy and convenient. Send the message to **archie@***archieserver* (where *archieserver* is the name of the server you choose). Put the commands in the body of the message.

- Use the **whatis** command to search for a file description.

Chapter 14

Digging Through the Internet with Gopher

In This Chapter

- ➤ A bit of Gopher and Web history
- ➤ Why bother with Gopher?
- ➤ Starting a Gopher session
- ➤ Finding your way around Gopherspace
- ➤ Saving text documents and computer files
- ➤ Using Jughead to search a Gopher server
- ➤ Using Veronica to search in Gopherspace

Today, the World Wide Web seems to be "where it's at" on the Internet. Most of the growth in the Internet is occurring on the Web—supposedly it doubles in size every few weeks. But the Web is really quite new. At the end of 1993 and even well into 1994, the World Wide Web was a sideshow on the Internet. Few people knew how to use it, and fewer still bothered. It wasn't hard to use, but there wasn't much incentive; for the vast majority of Internet users, there was no way to display pictures, listen to sounds, play video, or do any of the neat things you've learned to do with Internet Explorer. But don't get me wrong. The Web was not just text and little else, but software for it simply wasn't available.

So what *was* the hot "navigation" system on the Internet in the days before the Web? Gopher.

Let There Be Gopher

If you never used the Internet in the old command-line days, and if Internet Explorer and the other graphical user interface systems that abound are your only taste of the Internet, you don't know just how difficult the Internet can be. (Millions of people *still* use the Internet through a command-line interface—that is, by typing complicated commands to get something done.) Many people who tried to use the Internet just a year or two ago when all the cyberhype began were so turned off by the experience that they went away and never came back. FTP (which you learned about in Chapter 12) was extremely difficult. Telnet (Chapter 15) was pretty clunky—and still is. Even e-mail was barely bearable. All in all, the Internet was *not* a user-friendly place.

Then along came Gopher. This tool was a revolution in simplicity, providing a nice menu system from which users could select options. Instead of having to remember and enter a variety of rather obscure and arcane commands to find what they needed, people used arrow keys to select options from the menu. Those options took the user to other menus or to documents of some kind. In fact, the Gopher system is, in some ways, similar to the World Wide Web. It's a worldwide network of menu systems. Options in one menu link to menus or other documents all over the world. These Gopher menus made the Internet much easier to use—and much more accessible to people other than the long-term cybergeeks.

For a while, Gopher looked like the future of the Internet, at least to a number of people who invested time and money in Internet software. A variety of "graphical point-and-click" Gopher programs (some shareware, some freeware) were published. You may have heard of WinGopher, an excellent Windows program for navigating through the Gopher system.

Then along came the Web. Or rather, along came the graphical Web browsers, which all of a sudden made the Web not only easy to use, but exciting, too. Interest in Gopher subsided rapidly, and everyone rushed off to learn how to create Web documents. So where does that leave Gopher? Still alive and well, actually, for a couple of good reasons. First, many Gopher systems were already set up. And second, because millions of Internet users still don't have access to graphical Web browsers, Gopher is the easiest tool available.

Chapter 14 ➤ *Digging Through the Internet with Gopher*

Gopher servers around the world contain lots of interesting information. And, fortunately, you can get to that information with your Web browser. That's right. Although your Web browser was designed to work on the World Wide Web, you can use the Web to access Gopher.

Enough History. What's Gopher?

The *Gopher* system consists of hundreds of Gopher servers (computers that contain the indexes) and millions of Gopher clients (computers that are running the Gopher menu software, which accesses the server's indexes). Your Web browser is, in effect, also a Gopher client. All servers are public, so any client can access the information from any server.

Graphical Gopher programs exist both commercially and as shareware. You'll probably never use one, though. Working with Gopher through your Web browser works extremely well. Unlike FTP, which works well most (but not all) of the time, your browser handles Gopher sites just fine *all* the time. Okay, there are a few geek things you can do with a true Gopher program that you can't do with a Web browser—such as see details about a menu option—but few people will miss these features. So we're going to take a look at gophering through the Web—with Internet Explorer, of course.

> **Check This Out...**
>
> **Why Is It Called Gopher?**
>
> For three reasons. First, it was originally developed at the University of Minnesota, home of the Golden Gophers. Second, "gofer" is slang for someone who "goes fer" things, and Gopher's job is to "go fer" files and stuff. And third, the system digs its way through the Internet like a gopher in a burrow. By the way, when you use Gopher, you are traveling through Gopherspace.

Let's Gopher It!

So how do you get to a Gopher server? You can start a Gopher session in two ways: by clicking a link in a Web document that some kindly Web author provides, or by typing the gopher:// URL into the Address text box and pressing **Enter**. For example, you can type gopher://wiretap.spies.com/ to get to the Internet Wiretap Gopher server, shown in the following figure.

Part 3 ➤ *Boldly Going Around the Internet*

The Internet Wiretap Gopher is worth a visit; it has loads of interesting documents.

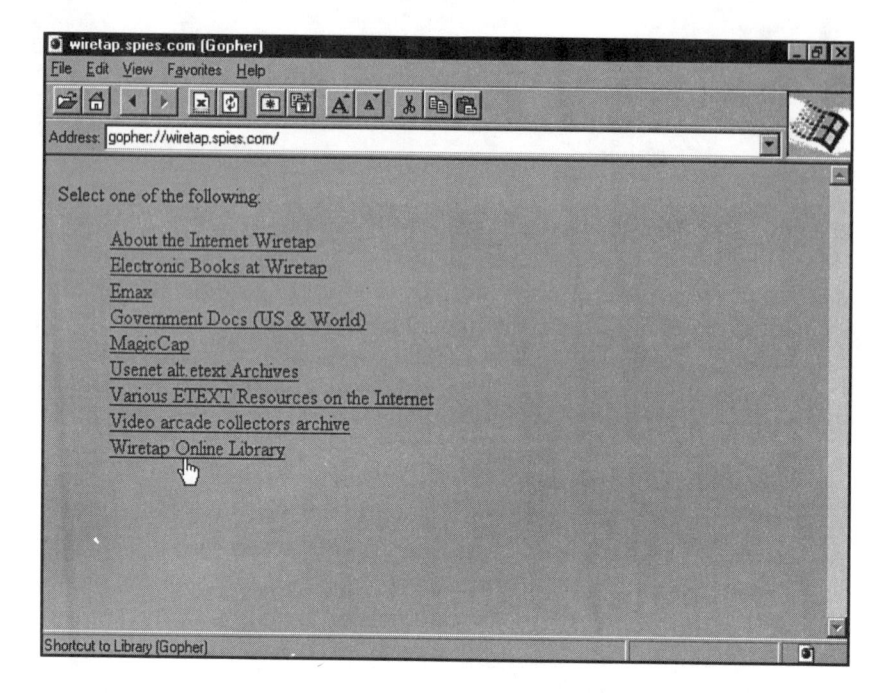

By the way, if you are using Internet Explorer, you usually don't have to enter the gopher:// bit. If the gopher address starts with the word *gopher*, you can type the address and forget the gopher:// part. For instance, you can type gopher.usa.net instead of gopher://gopher.usa.net.

> **Where Can I Start?**
>
> For a list of links to Gopher servers, go to **gopher:// gopher.micro.umn.edu/11/Other%20Gopher%20and %20Information%20Servers**. Or if you don't want to type all that, go to **http://www.w3.org/hypertext/DataSources/ByAccess.html** and click on the **Gopher** link.

You can also include "directories" in the URL. For instance, you can type gopher://earth.usa.net/00/News%20and%20Information/Ski%20Information/ A%20List%20of%20Today%27s%20SKI%20CONDITIONS into the Address box and press Enter to go to the Internet Express Gopher server and automatically select the Colorado

168

Chapter 14 ➤ Digging Through the Internet with Gopher

Ski Information and Ski Conditions menu options. (Too much for you to type? If you visit a Gopher site and find a useful Gopher menu, add it to your Favorites list or Bookmarks; see Chapter 10.)

How, then, do you use a Gopher server with a Web browser? Links represent the Gopher menu options. Click a link to select that option. If the option leads to another menu, the menu appears in the window. If it leads to a file of some kind, the file is transferred in the normal way, and your browser displays or plays it if it can. (Files are treated just the same as they are when you work on a Web site.)

Most of the documents at Gopher sites are text documents. But as you'll remember from Chapter 11, Internet Explorer (and all other Web browsers) can display these text documents within its own window. Of course, you won't find any links to other documents within these text documents (they're not true Web documents, after all). So once you finish, you'll have to use the Back toolbar button to return to the Gopher menu you were just viewing. The following figure shows a text document that I ran across at the Wiretap site. I selected the Electronic Books at Wiretap menu option, and then the Aesop: Fables, Paperless Edition link.

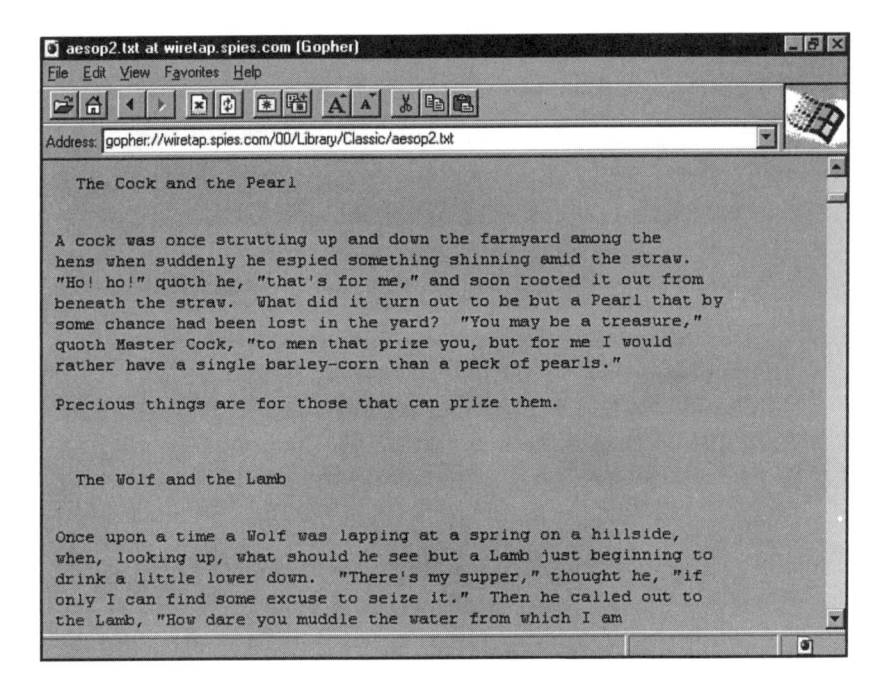

Aesop's fables, from the Wiretap site.

169

Archie's Friends: Veronica and Jughead

Gopher servers have two types of search tools: *Veronica* (Very Easy Rodent-Oriented Netwide Index to Computerized Archives) and *Jughead* (Jonzy's Universal Gopher Hierarchy Excavation And Display). Do these acronyms mean much? No, but *you* try to create an acronym from a cartoon character's name!

> **Techno Talk**
>
> **Searching Gopher Menus** Some Gopher menus are very long. The original Gopher system had a special / command that you could use to search a menu. Similarly, your browser has a Find command. In Internet Explorer use **Edit, Find**.

Veronica lets you search Gopher servers all over the world. Jughead lets you search the Gopher server you are currently working with (though many Gopher servers don't yet have Jugheads).

If you want to search Gopherspace (this giant system of Gopher menus that spread across the Internet), find a menu option that includes Veronica or Jughead. For instance, at the gopher://gopher.cc.utah.edu/ Gopher site, you'll find menu options that say **Search titles in Gopherspace using veronica** and **Search menu titles using jughead**. You might have to dig around to find menus on some sites; sometimes they are several levels down the menu system. (I couldn't find Veronica or Jughead at the Wiretap site we were just looking at.) Many sites don't have Jughead, but virtually all have a link to Veronica.

> **Check This Out...**
>
> **Cartoon Characters** Why Veronica and Jughead? They are characters in the famous Archie cartoon strip. Archie arrived on the Internet first (see Chapter 13). The people who created the Gopher search systems figured Archie needed company, so they named their systems Veronica and Jughead.

Jughead

When you select the Jughead option, you see a few more links. You often find links to other Jughead servers at other sites, and probably a link to information telling you how to work with Jughead. There's also a link to the actual search itself (for instance, at the gopher://gopher.cc.utah.edu site, you can choose **Search menu titles using jughead** and then click **Search University of Utah Menus Using Jughead**). When you click such a link, you go to an index-server form like the one shown in the following figure. Type a word (such as **book**) into the form's text box and press **Enter**. The Gopher system searches for all menu options containing that word.

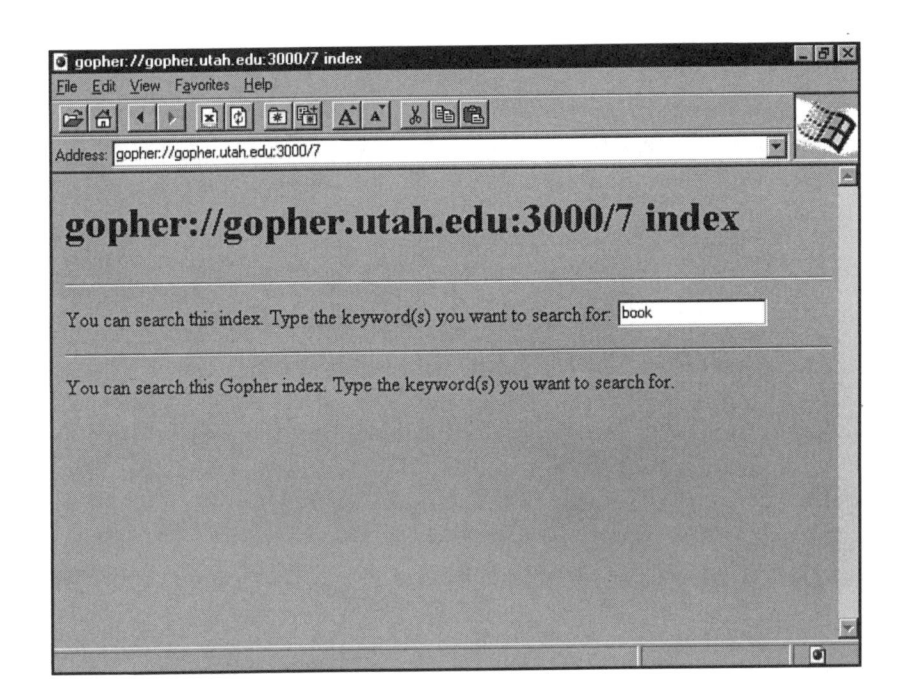

Chapter 14 ➤ *Digging Through the Internet with Gopher*

Type the word you want to find and press Enter.

Soon another Gopher menu appears. This one is created especially for your search: it contains a list of all the items Jughead found for you. (With Jughead, you will probably get a response fairly quickly. Veronica is much slower.) Click on an item to see what it is, or point at it and look in your browser's status bar to see what the link "points" to.

If you don't find what you are looking for, you can click the **Back** toolbar button to return to the form and try again. This time, you might enter **book or publication**, for instance. (A search in which you enter more than one thing to search for is a Boolean search. See the next section.) Press **Enter** to search again.

> **Check This Out...**
>
> **Case Doesn't Matter** You can enter the search statement in upper- or lowercase letters; Jughead doesn't care. It treats **BOOK** and **book** the same way.

171

The Boolean Operators

Jughead allows you to do a Boolean search, which contains more than one thing to search for. In order to run a Boolean search, you have to tell the system what kind of relationship exists between the search criteria. To do so, you can use three Boolean operators when you type your search term: **and**, **or**, **not**. Here's how you use them:

a and b   Searches for a menu item containing word a *and* word b.

a or b   Searches for a menu item containing word a *or* word b.

a not b   Searches for a menu item containing word a but *not* word b.

As you might guess, if you search for **book or publication**, you're going to get a few more menu options. Likewise, if you search for **book or publication or publications**, you get even more.

Pick Any Wild Card—As Long As It's *

You can also use *wild cards* to search. That means that you can use a character to take the place of another character. For instance, if you search for **pub***, you're telling Jughead to search for any word beginning with **pub**. The asterisk simply means "some other stuff here."

> **Check This Out...**
>
> **Wild-Card Rules** Jughead has only one wild card: the * character. You cannot use the ? character, a common wild card in many other systems. You must also use these basic rules: you can't *start* a word with the asterisk, and you can't put an asterisk within a word. (It's ignored if you do.)

So if you tell Jughead to search for **book or pub***, that means "search for the word **book** or any words beginning with **pub**." Your search results might include such words as publication, publications, publicity, public, and publican.

If you search for **book or pub*** instead of typing out **book or publication or publications**, you increase your "hit" rate dramatically. You might end up with hundreds of items. Although you may not want all this extra stuff, some of it might be useful (the **publishers** and **publishing** entries, for example). But **public** and **pubs** give you lots of extra stuff you really didn't want, like **Title 53A - State System of Public Education, Chapter 11 - Students in Public Schools, Part 3 - Immunization of Students.**

More Boolean Stuff

Let's take a quick look at the Boolean stuff again. If you enter several words on a line without one of the Boolean operators (**and**, **or**, or **not**) between the words, Jughead assumes you mean **and**. So, for example, **book and pub*** and **book pub*** mean exactly the same thing: "find entries that contain both the word **book** and a word beginning with **pub**."

There are a few other things to be aware of, though. If Jughead sees any special characters (!"#$%&'()+,-./:;<=>?@[\]^_'{|}~) in the search statement, it treats them as if they were spaces and replaces them with the Boolean operator **and**. For instance, if you tell Jughead to search for **This.file**, it really searches for **this and file**. That's not necessarily a problem, though. If I search for **Pubs_by SCERP_Researchers**, I will still find the correct menu item because Jughead will still search for the words **Pubs**, **by**, **SCERP**, and **Researchers**. (Remember, by the way, that each Jughead is different; so what you find at one Jughead is not the same as what you find at another.)

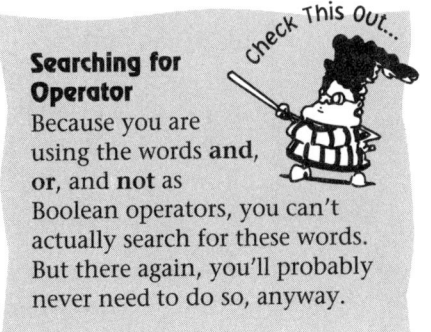

> **Check This Out...**
> **Searching for Operator**
> Because you are using the words **and**, **or**, and **not** as Boolean operators, you can't actually search for these words. But there again, you'll probably never need to do so, anyway.

Special Commands—Maybe

Jughead currently has four special commands you can include in a search string. (At the time of this writing, these commands did not work with Internet Explorer; they may by the time you read this. They should work in other browsers.) You can use these commands:

?all [*what*]   This tells Jughead to include *all* of the hits it finds. Usually it limits the hits to 1,024 (so if it finds 2,000 matching entries, you don't see 976 of them). Mind you, 1,024 is an awful lot, more than you are likely to need. For instance, if you search for **?all book or pub***, Jughead searches for the words **book** and **pub***. If it finds more than 1,024 matches (though it probably won't), it displays all of them.

?help [*what*]   The **?help** command tells Jughead to create a menu option that lets you get to the Jughead help file. You can use the **?help** command by itself, or you can do a search at the same time (such as **?help book or pub***).

?limit=*n* [*what*]   This tells Jughead to limit the number of menu items it gives you. For instance, **?limit=10 book or pub*** tells Jughead to display only the first 10 items it finds.

?version [*what*]   This gives you the Jughead version number. It appears as a menu option: `1. This version of jughead is 1.0.4` (or whatever the actual version number is). You can then click that menu option to read the Jughead help file. You can use the **?version** command by itself, or you can do a search at the same time (such as **?version book or pub***).

You cannot combine these commands. You can use only one in each search. And, as I mentioned before, you may not be able to use them at all in Internet Explorer. (If you do, you may just get a blank page back.) This is a bug, so later versions of Explorer may work with these commands.

Veronica

Working with Veronica is very similar to working with Jughead, with a couple of important differences. First, when you select a Veronica menu option, you choose the server you search. Veronica can search any Gopher server all over the world. Something called a *Veronica server* stores an index of menu options at all of these Gopher servers, so you are actually searching one of these indexes; you get to pick which one.

At the same time, you also have to decide whether you want to limit your search. You can search all menu options, or only menu options that lead to other menus. For example, go to **gopher://gopher.cc.utah.edu** and choose **the Search titles in Gopherspace using veronica** option. You can select **Find GOPHER DIRECTORIES by Title Word(s) (via U of Manitoba)** to look for menu options that lead to other menus (often called *directories* in Gopherspeak) using the University of Manitoba Veronica server. Likewise, you can select the **Search GopherSpace by Title Word(s) (via University of Pisa)** to search all menu options, both "directories" and options leading to files and documents, at the University of Pisa Veronica server.

When you make your selection, you see the same Index Search dialog box that you saw during the Jughead search. Type the word you want to search for and press **Enter**. What happens then? Well, there's a good chance you'll get a message saying ***** Too many connections - Try again soon. ***** (or something similar). If that happens, try another server. If you don't get that message, it might seem like Explorer just waits and waits. The clouds keep moving across the busy icon's background, but nothing seems to happen. These servers are very busy, so it often takes a long time to get a result. When you finally do get a result, though, you'll get a much bigger list than you did from the Jughead search. After all, you are searching the whole world's Gopher servers, not just one.

Veronica Search Details

Veronica searches are different from Jughead searches in a couple of ways. As with Jughead, you can use Boolean searches, and you can use the * wild card. However, the * must appear at the end of the word, not at the beginning or in the middle. (With

Chapter 14 ➤ *Digging Through the Internet with Gopher*

Veronica, putting the ***** inside the word causes the search to abort. Jughead just ignores the asterisk if it's within the word.)

Veronica also has a special **-t** command. You place this within the search string (at the beginning, middle, or end; it doesn't matter), and it defines the *type* of item for which you are looking. For instance, **book -t0** means "search for the word book, but only find text documents." And **book -t01** means "search for the word book, but only find text documents and Gopher menu items." The following table shows you the numbers to use with the **-t** command.

> **Read the Help!**
> For detailed information about Jughead and Veronica searches, read the Help files that you find in the Gopher menus near the Jughead and Veronica menu options.

Veronica's -t Command

Number or Letter	Description
0	Text file
1	Directory (Gopher menu)
2	CSO name server (a searchable database used to track down other Internet users)
4	Macintosh HQX file
5	PC binary file
7	A searchable index
8	Telnet session (see Chapter 15)
9	Binary file
s	Sound file
e	Event file
I	Image file (other than GIF)
M	MIME multipart/mixed message (MIME is a system used by Internet e-mail systems to transfer binary files)
T	TN3270 session (a system similar to Telnet)
c	Calendar
g	GIF image
h	HTML Web document

175

You can also use the **-m** command to specify a maximum number of items to find. For instance, **-m300 book** tells the Veronica server to show up to 300 items that it finds. If you don't use the **-m** command, the Veronica server searches only until it finds the default limit, which is 200 items. Use **-m** to tell the server to find more than the default number.

The Least You Need to Know

- Gopher is a text-based menu system, a real boon to Internet users working with text-based software.
- Working with Gopher through a Web browser is very convenient.
- Travel through Gopherspace by clicking on menu options.
- To save a text document or file, click on the link. Your browser treats it the same way it treats any file on the World Wide Web.
- Use your Web browser's Favorites or Bookmark feature to add a bookmark to any Gopher menu you want to return to later.
- Many Gopher systems now use Jughead, a special search mechanism that enables you to find things on that server.
- Veronica is a powerful tool you can use to search through thousands of miles of Gopherspace at once. Look for a Veronica menu option somewhere in the Gopher menu.

Chapter 15

Telnet: Inviting Yourself onto Other Systems

In This Chapter

- Finding a Telnet program—MS Telnet (and Com*t*)
- Four ways to start Telnet
- Using HYTELNET
- Running your Telnet session
- IBM tn3270 Telnet sites
- Telnetting to your service provider

Millions of computers are connected to the Internet, and some of them have some pretty interesting stuff. Wouldn't it be neat if you could "reach out" and get onto those computers (well, some of them) to take a look at the games and databases and programs on computers around the world?

Well, you can. At least, you can get onto computers whose administrators want you to get on—of which there's a surprisingly high number. A special program called Telnet lets you turn your computer into a Telnet *client* to access data and programs on a Telnet *server* somewhere.

Many Internet users have private Telnet accounts. A researcher, for example, may have several computers he works on regularly, and he may have a special login name and password that the administrators of those computers gave him. But many computers also allow "strangers" into their systems. This is done on a purely voluntary basis, depending on the good will of the people who own or operate a particular computer. If a Telnet server is open to the public, anyone can get on the system and see what's available.

Step 1: Find a Telnet Program

First you need a Telnet program. Telnet programs are one of the weakest features of the Internet. Compared to the wonderful Web browsers and excellent e-mail and FTP programs that are available, the Telnet programs I've run across seem a bit weak.

Part of the problem is that there's a limit to how much a Telnet program can help you. When you telnet, your computer becomes a terminal of the computer you're connected to, and it has to follow that computer's "rules." Because each of the thousands of systems out there on the Internet use slightly different menu systems, command systems, and so on, it's hard to create a really good Telnet program. All the average Telnet program does is provide a window into which you type commands and in which responses appear. In addition, because Telnet isn't a terribly exciting subject (when was the last time you saw a *Time* or *Newsweek* article on the wonders of Telnet?), most software developers ignore it.

Still, if you want to use Telnet, you need a Telnet program. Luckily, you already have one: Microsoft Telnet. Microsoft Telnet comes with Windows 95 and is installed when you install your TCP/IP network software (see Chapters 6 through 8). I'll use that program as my example throughout this chapter.

Other Programs

If you don't like Microsoft Telnet, explore your options. I like Com*t*, a program that lets you use any serial communications program (such as HyperACCESS, CrossTalk, or ProComm) as a Telnet program by "fooling" Windows into thinking a COM port is really a TCP/IP connection. So you end up being able to use all the features in that expensive communications program you bought, such as macros and buttons. With Com*t* installed, you could use the Windows 95 HyperTerminal program as your Telnet program. (And note that many other commercial communications programs now include a Telnet mode.) You can find Com*t* at ftp.std.com/customers/software/rfdmail.

Chapter 15 ➤ *Telnet: Inviting Yourself onto Other Systems*

Let's Go Telnetting!

How do you begin a Telnet session? You have a number of choices.

➤ Click on a **telnet://** link. Sometimes you run across links in Web documents that use the telnet:// URL. When you click on the link, your Telnet program opens and starts the session with the referenced Telnet site.

➤ Type the **telnet://** URL. If your Web browser is open, you can also start a Telnet session by typing telnet:// followed by a Telnet host address, and pressing Enter. For instance, if you type **telnet://pac.carl.org** into Internet Explorer's Address text box and press **Enter**, Microsoft Telnet launches and connects to the Denver Public Library's site. (Type **PAC** and press **Enter** to log on.)

➤ Open the Telnet program. You can open Telnet directly by double-clicking on the **TELNET.EXE** file in the Windows directory in Windows Explorer. (You may want to place a shortcut on your desktop or Start menu so you can open it directly without having to open Internet Explorer first.) When the program opens, select **Connect**, choose **Remote System**, type the Telnet address into the **Host Name** text box, and press **Enter**.

➤ Use the menu system. Open Windows 95's **Start** menu, click **Run**, type **telnet://***hostname* (for instance, **telnet://pac.carl.org**), and press **Enter**.

> **Check This Out...**
>
> **Which Telnet Program?**
> If you use the Web browser methods (the first two), you can choose which Telnet program you want to launch. If you use the Windows Explorer methods (the last two), you can start only the Microsoft Telnet program.

Enough choices for you? Well, whichever method you use, Microsoft Telnet opens and begins the Telnet session.

The HYTELNET Directory: Finding What's Out There

To get a taste for what's available in the world of Telnet, take a look at HYTELNET, the Telnet directory. This used to be available only through Telnet itself, but now you can view the directory at a World Wide Web site, which is more convenient. Open your Web browser and go to **http://library.usask.ca/hytelnet/**. (You can also find a HYTELNET site at http://www.cc.ukans.edu/hytelnet_html/START.TXT.html, but it's rather outdated; there's also one at the Gopher site gopher://liberty.uc.wlu.edu/11/internet/hytelnet.)

From this document, you can launch Telnet sessions on computers all over the place. The following figure shows the first page of HYTELNET. The two most important links in this page are the Library catalogs and Other resources links. They take you to directories of Telnet sites (the other links take you to information about working with Telnet).

179

Part 3 ➤ *Boldly Going Around the Internet*

HYTELNET provides the best way to find Telnet sites.

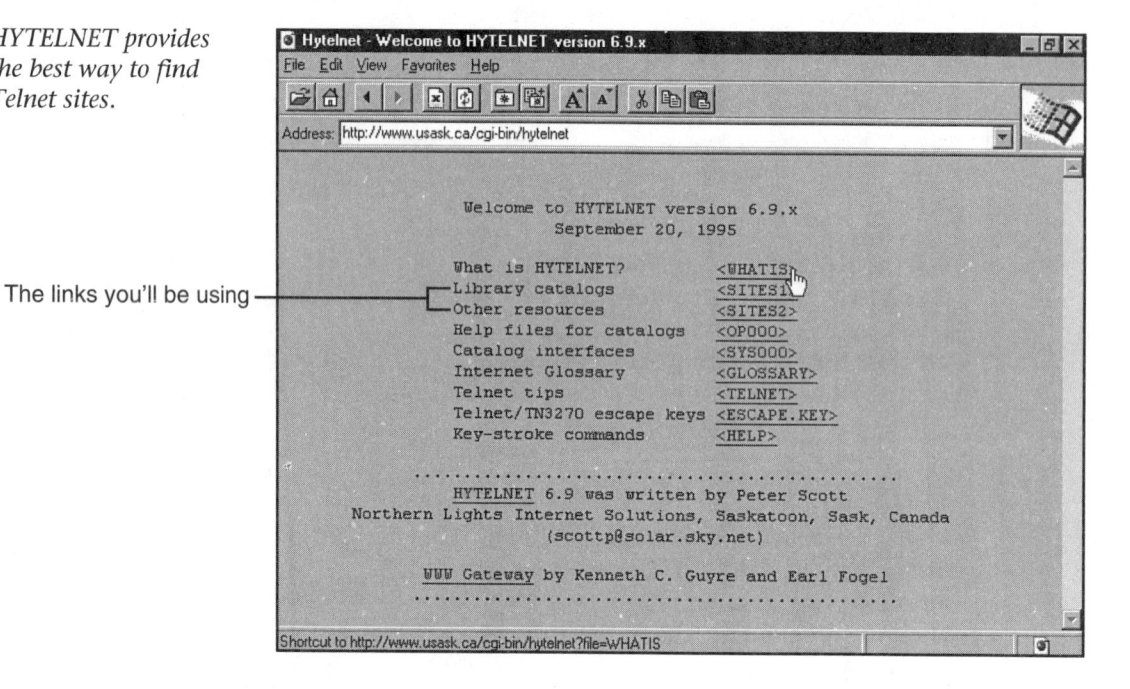

The links you'll be using

```
Welcome to HYTELNET version 6.9.x
           September 20, 1995

What is HYTELNET?           <WHATIS>
Library catalogs            <SITES1>
Other resources             <SITES2>
Help files for catalogs     <OP000>
Catalog interfaces          <SYS000>
Internet Glossary           <GLOSSARY>
Telnet tips                 <TELNET>
Telnet/TN3270 escape keys   <ESCAPE.KEY>
Key-stroke commands         <HELP>

............................................
       HYTELNET 6.9 was written by Peter Scott
Northern Lights Internet Solutions, Saskatoon, Sask, Canada
               (scottp@solar.sky.net)

WWW Gateway by Kenneth C. Guyre and Earl Fogel
............................................
```

More Directories

These Web directories also help you find Telnet and other resources:

http://www.w3.org/hypertext/DataSources/ByAccess.html

http://www.ncsa.uiuc.edu/SDG/Software/Mosaic/MetaIndex.html

You can also search for the word **telnet** at Web search sites (see Chapter 11).

Click on the **Other resources** link, and you're taken to a page that includes links to Databases and bibliographies, Electronic books, Fee-Based Services, NASA databases, and more. If you travel further down the hierarchy of documents, you come to information about individual Telnet services. The next figure shows information you can find about the FDA. The FDA (Food & Drug Administration) Electronic Bulletin Board Telnet site contains news releases, important alerts, information on AIDS, and plenty more. This page shows the Telnet address (fdabbs.fda.gov or 150.148.8.48) and the name (bbs) that you must use to log on once you're connected, as well as a list of commands you can use once you're connected. Note that it also has a link. The Telnet addresses are links. If you click on one, your Telnet program launches and begins the Telnet session.

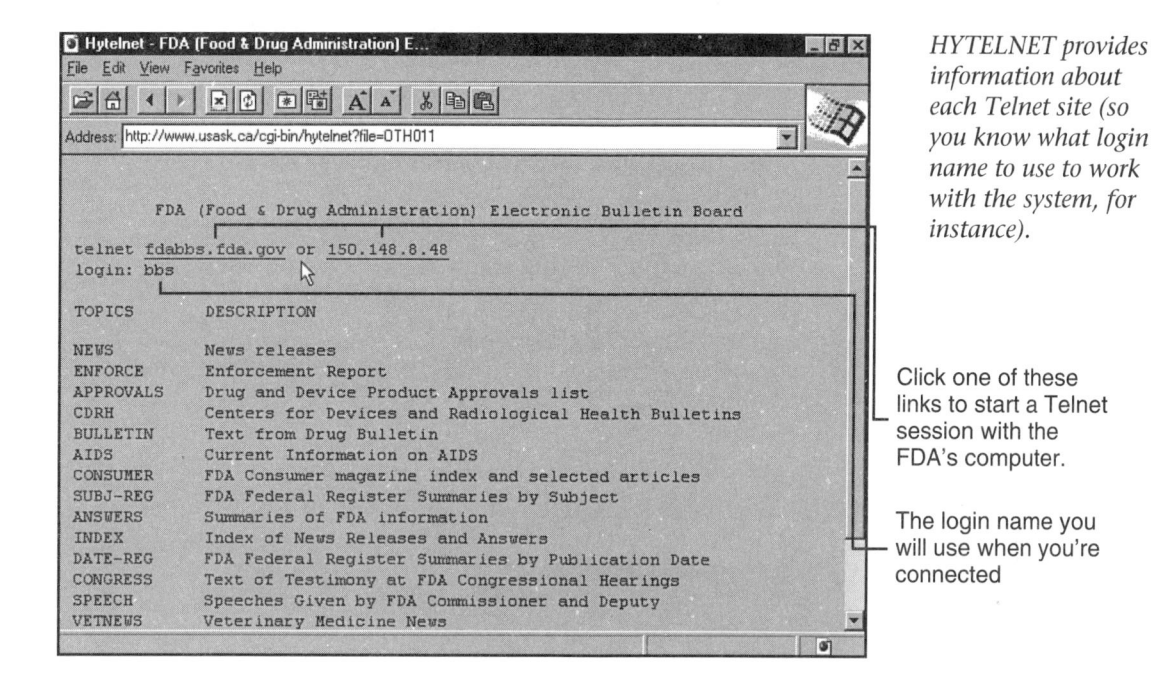

Chapter 15 ➤ *Telnet: Inviting Yourself onto Other Systems*

```
Hytelnet - FDA (Food & Drug Administration) E...
File  Edit  View  Favorites  Help

Address: http://www.usask.ca/cgi-bin/hytelnet?file=OTH011

          FDA (Food & Drug Administration) Electronic Bulletin Board

telnet  fdabbs.fda.gov or 150.148.8.48
login:  bbs

TOPICS          DESCRIPTION

NEWS            News releases
ENFORCE         Enforcement Report
APPROVALS       Drug and Device Product Approvals list
CDRH            Centers for Devices and Radiological Health Bulletins
BULLETIN        Text from Drug Bulletin
AIDS            Current Information on AIDS
CONSUMER        FDA Consumer magazine index and selected articles
SUBJ-REG        FDA Federal Register Summaries by Subject
ANSWERS         Summaries of FDA information
INDEX           Index of News Releases and Answers
DATE-REG        FDA Federal Register Summaries by Publication Date
CONGRESS        Text of Testimony at FDA Congressional Hearings
SPEECH          Speeches Given by FDA Commissioner and Deputy
VETNEWS         Veterinary Medicine News
```

HYTELNET provides information about each Telnet site (so you know what login name to use to work with the system, for instance).

Click one of these links to start a Telnet session with the FDA's computer.

The login name you will use when you're connected

We're In. Now What?

After your Telnet program connects to the Telnet site, you may have to log on. To do so, you need to know the account name you should use. HYTELNET includes the required account name in its description of each Telnet site. Likewise, if you find a Telnet site described in a book or magazine, the account name is often included. However, in some cases, you *won't* have to log on; the computer will let you right in without asking for further information. And in other cases, the introductory screen you see when you first connect may tell you what to use.

When you connect to a Telnet session, you often have to identify the type of computer terminal you are using. Of course, you are using a PC, but your Telnet program can *emulate* (pretend to be) a standard terminal program. By default, it's set to emulate a VT-100 terminal, which is good because the VT-100 setting works in most cases you'll run into. If you run into a site that doesn't like the VT-100 setting—perhaps the text on your screen isn't displayed properly during the session—you can try changing the emulation, but you don't have many choices. Okay, you really have only *one* choice.

Choose **Terminal**, **Preferences** to see the dialog box shown in the following figure. In this dialog box, you can change the emulation to VT-52. You can also modify the settings listed here (even though you probably won't need to).

181

Part 3 ➤ *Boldly Going Around the Internet*

Local Echo	Select this if you can't see the text you type in the session.
Blinking Cursor	Select this to make the text cursor flash on and off, which makes it easier to see.
Block Cursor	Select this to make the text cursor a block (instead of an underline).
VT100 Arrows	Select this to make your keyboard's arrow keys work in the session (so that pressing an arrow key moves a selection bar up and down a text menu, for instance).
Buffer Size	Increase this setting to specify how many lines the session should save. A scroll bar is added to the window so you can scroll up and down to see lines that are not visible in the window.
Fonts and **Background Color**	Click these buttons to access options you can use to change the appearance of the window.

Set up your Telnet session in the Terminal Preferences dialog box.

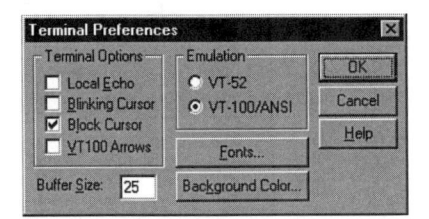

Working in a Telnet Session

As I mentioned earlier, your Telnet program simply provides a way for you to transfer the things you type to the computer you are connected to, and for that computer to send text back to you. In effect, you've turned your computer into a dumb terminal connected to another computer, and you have to follow the rules of that system. And every Telnet system is different.

What you see depends on what type of system is set up on that computer. It might be a series of menus from which you select options, or it might be a prompt at which you type commands. Each system varies a little.

Let me warn you about one thing: Telnet can sometimes be slow—*very* slow. On occasion, you may type something and not see what you have typed for several seconds or even several minutes. This response time depends on two things: the amount of network traffic going to the computer you're connected to and the number of people working on that machine at the time. If you think a particular task is taking too long, you should probably come back later. If it's always slow at a particular Telnet site, try to find another site with the same services.

Chapter 15 ➤ Telnet: Inviting Yourself onto Other Systems

Let's Take a Look at a Site

Let's take a quick look at how one site works. You're going to telnet to the Conversational Hypertext computer, an experimental system owned by the Canadian government. It contains databases that you can "talk" to (you type questions in plain English, and the databases answer you).

Use one of the methods described earlier in this chapter to start the Telnet session. For example, type **telnet debra.dgbt.doc.ca 3000** in the Internet Explorer Address text box and press **Enter**. Microsoft Telnet opens and connects to the Telnet site. At this site, you don't have to enter a login name or password. (How do you know what to use as a login name? If you see a Telnet site listed in a directory, file, or e-mail message, it often tells you to use a particular login name. In other cases, the introductory screen tells you what to use or you are simply connected to the program without logging in.)

> **Check This Out...**
>
> **Microsoft Telnet Bug!**
> There's a bug in Microsoft Telnet. Notice that the Telnet site you just used has a number at the end of the host name. That is the *port* number (some Telnet sites require that you use a port number, but most don't). If you were to open Microsoft Telnet, select **Connect**, choose **Remote System**, type this Telnet address, and press **Enter**, you'd get an error message. You can, however, start the Telnet session at this site from your Web browser or the Run dialog box.

Once you are connected, you see more introductory screens that tell you what the system is and does. Then you see a list of files you can choose from to find the information you want (see the following figure).

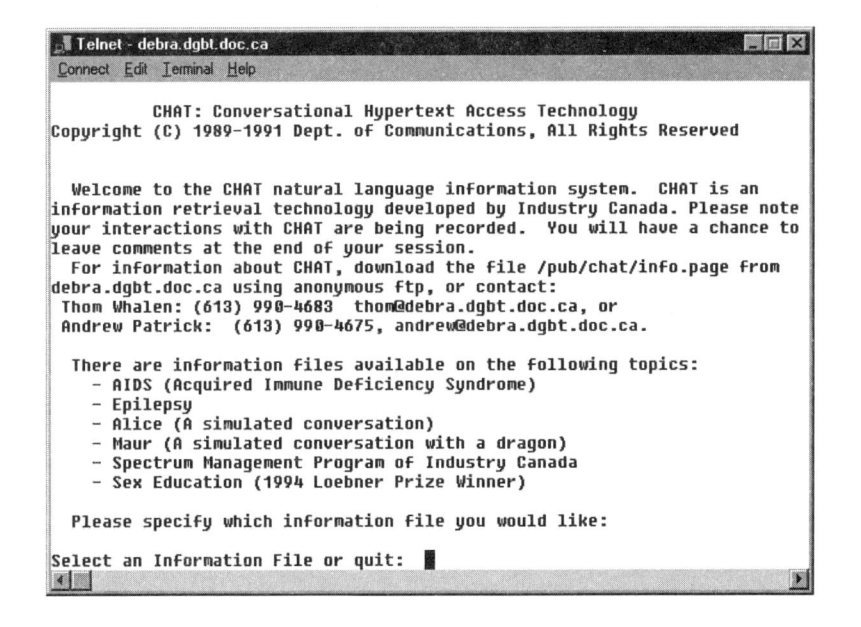

```
Telnet - debra.dgbt.doc.ca
Connect  Edit  Terminal  Help

           CHAT: Conversational Hypertext Access Technology
Copyright (C) 1989-1991 Dept. of Communications, All Rights Reserved


  Welcome to the CHAT natural language information system.  CHAT is an
information retrieval technology developed by Industry Canada. Please note
your interactions with CHAT are being recorded.  You will have a chance to
leave comments at the end of your session.
  For information about CHAT, download the file /pub/chat/info.page from
debra.dgbt.doc.ca using anonymous ftp, or contact:
  Thom Whalen:   (613) 990-4683   thom@debra.dgbt.doc.ca, or
  Andrew Patrick:  (613) 990-4675, andrew@debra.dgbt.doc.ca.

  There are information files available on the following topics:
     - AIDS (Acquired Immune Deficiency Syndrome)
     - Epilepsy
     - Alice (A simulated conversation)
     - Maur (A simulated conversation with a dragon)
     - Spectrum Management Program of Industry Canada
     - Sex Education (1994 Loebner Prize Winner)

  Please specify which information file you would like:

Select an Information File or quit:
```

The Conversational Hypertext Access Telnet site.

183

One of the files listed contains a simulated conversation with a dragon. Let's have a word with that dragon. Type **Maur** and press **Enter**. After a few moments, you see the screen shown in the next figure.

Want to chat with a dragon?

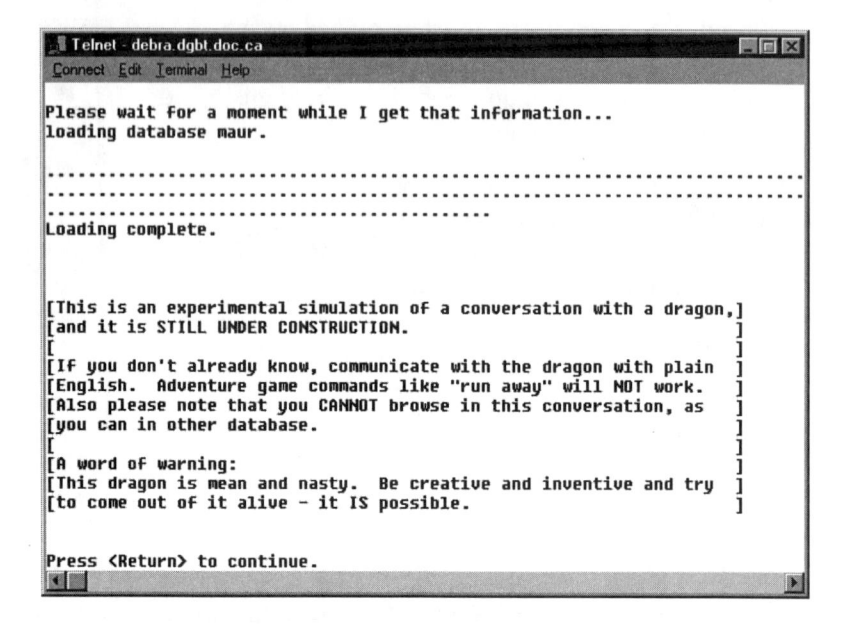

```
Please wait for a moment while I get that information...
loading database maur.
................................................................
................................................................
...............................................
Loading complete.


[This is an experimental simulation of a conversation with a dragon,]
[and it is STILL UNDER CONSTRUCTION.                                ]
[                                                                   ]
[If you don't already know, communicate with the dragon with plain  ]
[English.  Adventure game commands like "run away" will NOT work.   ]
[Also please note that you CANNOT browse in this conversation, as   ]
[you can in other database.                                         ]
[                                                                   ]
[A word of warning:                                                 ]
[This dragon is mean and nasty.  Be creative and inventive and try  ]
[to come out of it alive - it IS possible.                          ]


Press <Return> to continue.
```

Press **Enter**, and the story begins. You see something like this:

```
It seems like you have been wandering through these dark tunnels for years. They hadn't
seemed so bad when you and your companions had entered the deserted mine, led by a rumor
that the Hero's Crown might have come to rest here.
```

Blah, blah, blah...lots more, and then you get this:

```
The voice says:
Well, well, a visitor. It has been a long time since anyone has come
down this way.
You say: who's there?
```

It may take a while, but eventually you'll see this:

```
The voice says:
Long ago my name would have meant something to you. Whole villages fled
at my coming; at least they tried…my name is Maur.
You say: Maur? What kind of stupid name is that?
Maur says: Yes, Maur. You are rather irritating, you pitiful human! I may very
well burn you to a crisp this instant!
```

Chapter 15 ➤ *Telnet: Inviting Yourself onto Other Systems*

```
You say: I'd like to see you try, you over-inflated pile of $%#@
Maur says: See for yourself. (About ten meters into the gloom, ahead of you
and to the right, two huge red reptilian eyes flick open...)
```

Well, the computer may be a little confused by your last statement. Still, it's an experimental system. End your chat by typing **quit** and pressing **Enter**.

Keeping a Record

If you want to keep a record of your session, choose **Terminal, Start Logging**. When the Open Log File dialog box opens, enter a file name, select a directory, and choose **OK**. From that point on (until you close the session or choose Terminal, Stop Logging), all the text that appears on your screen is placed in the log file. If you want, you can copy the text to another document. To copy text from the session, drag the mouse pointer across the text (or choose **Edit, Select All**), and then choose **Edit, Copy**. You can then go to another program (your word processor or e-mail program, for example) and paste that text into another file.

> **Check This Out...**
>
> **Can't See?** If you can't see what you type when you are in a Telnet session, see the information on the **set echo** command (later in this chapter).

Starting Telnet Directly

As you've already seen, you don't have to start a Telnet session from the Web browser; you can start the program directly by running the TELNET.EXE file in the Windows directory. You may want to create a desktop shortcut if you use Telnet often. To do so, open **Windows Explorer**, right-click the **TELNET.EXE** file, choose **Create Shortcut**, and drag the new shortcut from the Windows directory to your desktop. If you create a shortcut, you can start Microsoft Telnet by double-clicking on the shortcut icon.

If you start Telnet in either of these ways, Telnet won't connect to a Telnet site because it doesn't know which one to use. However, Telnet has a little history list that you can use to connect to a site you've used earlier. Open the **Connect** menu and choose one of the previous sessions listed at the bottom of the menu. You can also choose **Connect, Remote System**, and select a host from the Host Name drop-down list (or type a host into the Host Name box), and then click the **Connect** button. Remember the bug I mentioned earlier, though. If you have to include a port name when connecting to a Telnet site (*hostname portname*, such as **debra.dgbt.doc.ca 3000**), you have to start Microsoft Telnet from the Web browser or the Run dialog box.

185

Waving Good-Bye to the Telnet Site

How do you leave the Telnet site? As you know, each computer's system is different. So, of course, each one has a different way for you to "log off." Try **quit**, **exit**, **Ctrl+D**, **bye**, and **done**, in that order. One of those will probably end the session. If they don't, look for some kind of prompt that tells you what you need to type to get out.

It's polite to end a Telnet session using the correct method. But you can also close the connection by closing the Microsoft Telnet window or by choosing **Connect**, **Disconnect**.

IBM Mainframe Telnet Sites

Some Telnet sites are on IBM mainframes running "3270" software. In 3270 mode, you usually type something at a prompt and press Enter or a function key (a *PF key* in 3270-speak). If you try to telnet to a site, and you find that the connection is instantly closed (even before you get to the login prompt), it may be a 3270 site (though, there's no guarantee of it). Likewise, if you log in and see this

```
VM/XA SP ONLINE-PRESS ENTER KEY TO BEGIN SESSION
```

you've definitely reached a 3270 site. Leave the site (select **Connect**, **Disconnect** in Microsoft Telnet). Then telnet to your service provider's system (I'll cover that next), go to the command line, and enter the **tn3270** *host* command.

For example, consider this scenario. You telneted with the command **telnet vmd.cso.uiuc.edu**, and you saw this:

```
Trying 128.174.5.98…
Connected to vmd.cso.uiuc.edu.
Escape character is '^]'.
VM/XA SP ONLINE-PRESS ENTER KEY TO BEGIN SESSION.
```

You know that's the sign of a 3270 site. So leave the session, telnet to your service provider (see the next section for details), go to the command line, and enter this command:

```
teal% tn3270 vmd.cso.uiuc.edu
```

With a bit of luck, you'll see this:

```
VM/XA SP ONLINE
            University of Illinois   Computing Services Office
               3081-KX Serial 24222              VM/XA SP 2.1 9205
```

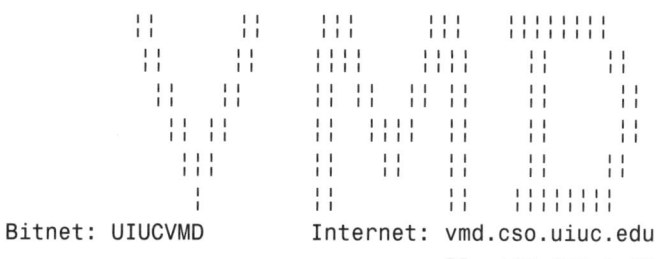

Chapter 15 ➤ *Telnet: Inviting Yourself onto Other Systems*

```
                  | |       | |     | | |      | | |    | | | | | | | |
                  | |       | |     | | |      | | |    | | | | | | | |
                  | |       | |     | | | |    | | | |    | |     | |
                  | |       | |     | | | |    | | | |    | |     | |
                   | |     | |      | | | |   | | | |    | |     | |
                    | |   | |       | |    | | | |       | |     | |
                     | | | |        | |     | | | |      | |     | |
                      | | |         | |      | | | |     | |     | |
                       | |          | |       | | | |    | |     | |
                        |           | |        | | | |   | |     | |
                                    | |         | | | |  | | | | | | | |
          Bitnet: UIUCVMD              Internet: vmd.cso.uiuc.edu
                                                 IP: 128.174.5.98
       Fill in your USERID and PASSWORD and press ENTER
       (Your password will not appear when you type it)
       USERID    ===>
       PASSWORD  ===>
       COMMAND   ===>
                                  RUNNING    VMD
```

You are now in the site using the 3270 mode. You can type ? and press **Enter** to see a help screen, or you can type **logoff** and press **Enter** to end the session.

These 3270 sessions are not very common, so you may never run into one. If you find that you need to work with a 3270 site, see if your service provider can find you some program documentation that explains how to work in this mode. If you really have to use a tn3270 site, you can also look around for a Windows tn3270 emulator. You can find a commercial one at http://www.3270.mcgill.ca/. A freeware program called Windows Sockets 3270 Telnet Application should be available at ftp.ccs.queensu.ca/pub/msdos/tcpip or ftp.sunet.se/pc/windows/winsock/apps. If you can't find an emulator at any of those sites, do an Archie search (see Chapter 13) for the qws3270.zip file.

Telnetting to Your Service Provider

Occasionally, you may need to telnet into your service provider's system. Why? Well, if you need to change your password or change your billing setup, you may find that the only way to do so is through your service provider's menu system. I know it sounds a little weird, but imagine it: You are already connected to your service provider and logged into your account on a SLIP or PPP connection, and then you run a Telnet program and log into your account *again*. You should check with your service provider, though, to see how this will be billed. If you will be billed for two logins, dial into your service provider using serial communications software—such as HyperTerminal—and log in that way.

Open your Telnet program and enter your service provider's host name. When the session begins, you'll have to enter your login name, your password, and any commands required to start your dial-in terminal, or *shell*, account. Then you'll probably see a menu something like the one shown in the following figure.

Part 3 ➤ *Boldly Going Around the Internet*

Select the **A> Administration/Account Info** option to get to an area where you can change your password and view billing information. In addition, take note of the 0> Enter UNIX Shell option. You can select that option to get to a command line where you can run those lovely UNIX programs, including the tn3270 program, if available.

You can Telnet to your service provider to change account information.

Select this option to change your password or look at billing info.

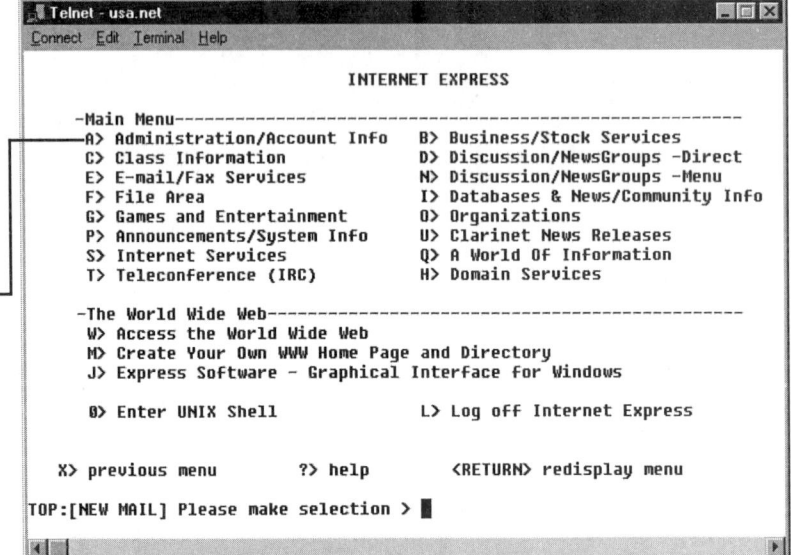

```
 Telnet - usa.net                                              _ □ ×
Connect  Edit  Terminal  Help

                            INTERNET EXPRESS

        -Main Menu------------------------------------------------
        A> Administration/Account Info   B> Business/Stock Services
        C> Class Information             D> Discussion/NewsGroups -Direct
        E> E-mail/Fax Services           N> Discussion/NewsGroups -Menu
        F> File Area                     I> Databases & News/Community Info
        G> Games and Entertainment       O> Organizations
        P> Announcements/System Info     U> Clarinet News Releases
        S> Internet Services             Q> A World Of Information
        T> Teleconference (IRC)          H> Domain Services

        -The World Wide Web---------------------------------------
        W> Access the World Wide Web
        M> Create Your Own WWW Home Page and Directory
        J> Express Software - Graphical Interface for Windows

        0> Enter UNIX Shell              L> Log off Internet Express

        X> previous menu       ?> help        <RETURN> redisplay menu

TOP:[NEW MAIL] Please make selection > █
```

The Least You Need to Know

➤ You already have a Telnet program. Microsoft Telnet is included with Windows 95 (it's installed when you install the TCP/IP networking software).

➤ You can start Microsoft Telnet by entering a telnet:// URL in the Web browser or in the Start menu's Run dialog box, or by clicking on a Web link to a Telnet site.

➤ You can also run the TELNET.EXE file (located in the Windows directory).

➤ Try the HYTELNET site (http://library.usask.ca/hytelnet/). It has links to hundreds of Telnet sites.

➤ When you connect to a Telnet site, you may have to enter a login name and password. HYTELNET tells you what to use. Once you are in, you are on your own. Each Telnet site has its own rules.

➤ If you can't view a site, you may have entered a tn3270 site. You should get hold of a tn3270 program, such as the freeware Windows Sockets 3270 Telnet Application.

➤ If you want to change your password or view billing information, you may need to telnet into your service provider's system.

Chapter 16

Finding Your WAIS Around

In This Chapter

- What is WAIS?
- Different ways to work with WAIS
- The Web WAIS gateway
- Using a Gopher gateway
- The Windows WAIS clients
- The last resort: working in UNIX

It's time to learn about *WAIS* (*Wide Area Information Server*), a system that helps you search for documents containing the information you need on a wide variety of subjects. We looked at searching the Web in Chapter 11. The problem with the Web is, it's a real hodgepodge. Have you heard the computing term "GIGO?" It stands for "Garbage In, Garbage Out." Well, as multimedia master William Horton recently put it, the Web might be described as a "GITSO" system: "Garbage In, Toxic Sludge Out." Sure, there's some really good stuff out there, but there's also a lot of, well, strange stuff. Whatever strikes your fancy—*Babes on the Web*, "grudge" pages, strange unsubstantiated claims about UFOs and politicians, pornography—it's on the Web somewhere.

WAIS is very different. It provides access to some heavy-duty databases, including many from the academic world. You can find databases on agriculture, archeology, biology, and all sorts of other interesting stuff. This isn't just a warehouse for "anything anyone wants to provide." It's designed for serious research.

What Is WAIS?

The WAIS system works like so many other systems on the Internet. There's a client, and there's a server (well, lots of servers, actually). A *client* is a program that can send a request for information to a server. The *server* is the program that has the database you want to search. So in order to search using WAIS, you need to install a WAIS client on your computer. Then you can specify the server you want to search, send your request for information, and wait for a response (which you'll usually get fairly quickly—probably in a few seconds).

> **WAIS in the Web** The WAIS "search engine" program is turning up on the Web. People who create Web pages are using it as a convenient way of allowing their readers to search their Web sites for information. That's not really what this chapter is about.

There are hundreds of WAIS databases, well over 500, in fact. Those databases contain tens of thousands of documents, ranging from the archives of various newsgroups to weather reports, ZIP codes, computer archaeology, and kids' software reviews. Although most of the files contain text documents, you may also find sounds, graphics, and so on. As with other aspects of the Internet, if you can name a subject, it's probably out there somewhere.

The Different Ways to Run WAIS

As you could probably guess (simply because it's part of the Internet), there are several ways to run WAIS:

- ➤ Find a Web *gateway* to WAIS and enter queries into your Web browser.
- ➤ Run WAIS from a Gopher menu option.
- ➤ Set up a Windows-based WAIS client on your own computer.
- ➤ Telnet to a WAIS server and run WAIS from there using UNIX commands.

WAIS is not a widely used system, so there aren't many good programs available for it. The Web is overwhelmingly popular, so Web browsers abound. But you'll have to look a bit further to find a good WAIS program.

Chapter 16 ➤ *Finding Your WAIS Around*

WAIS Conforms to a Standard

In case you're interested, WAIS uses the American National Standard Z39.50: Information Retrieval Service Definition and Protocol Specification for Library Applications standard, revised by the National Information Standards Organization. (No, you don't need to remember that.) Z39.50 is a method for connecting different computer systems and databases. It provides a standard for storing and accessing database information.

The quickest and easiest way to try WAIS is through the Web. You can also try WAIS through a Gopher menu—using your Web browser, of course. (See Chapter 14 for information on using Gopher through your browser.) Alternatively, you might want to use Telnet (see Chapter 15) to connect to a WAIS site or to your service provider's system if they have a WAIS menu option. If you spend much time using WAIS, though, you should install one of the WAIS programs available for Windows. I'll talk about them last.

Web WAIS

Let's start with the simplest way to use the WAIS system, through a Web gateway. Because most browsers (Internet Explorer included) don't have direct WAIS support, you can't search a WAIS database directly from a Web document. And even though there *is* a wais:// URL (see Chapter 10 for information about URLs), most browsers can't use it. Therefore, you mostly use what is known as a *WAIS gateway*, a special Web form into which you enter information that is then sent to a WAIS server. The response from the server is converted to a Web document that is sent to your browser.

One of the best WAIS gateways can be found at WAIS, Inc., the company that created the WAIS system. Use your Web browser to go to **http://wais.wais.com/newhomepages/wais-dbs.html**, where you'll find the WAIS, Inc. Directory of Servers page. (You can also go to **http://wais.wais.com/** to enter the WAIS, Inc. site "at the top," where you can find plenty of information about the WAIS software.)

As you can see in the following figure, this page has two elements: a search area and a list of databases.

Part 3 ➤ *Boldly Going Around the Internet*

The WAIS, Inc. site is the best way to access WAIS on the Web.

The search area

The list of databases

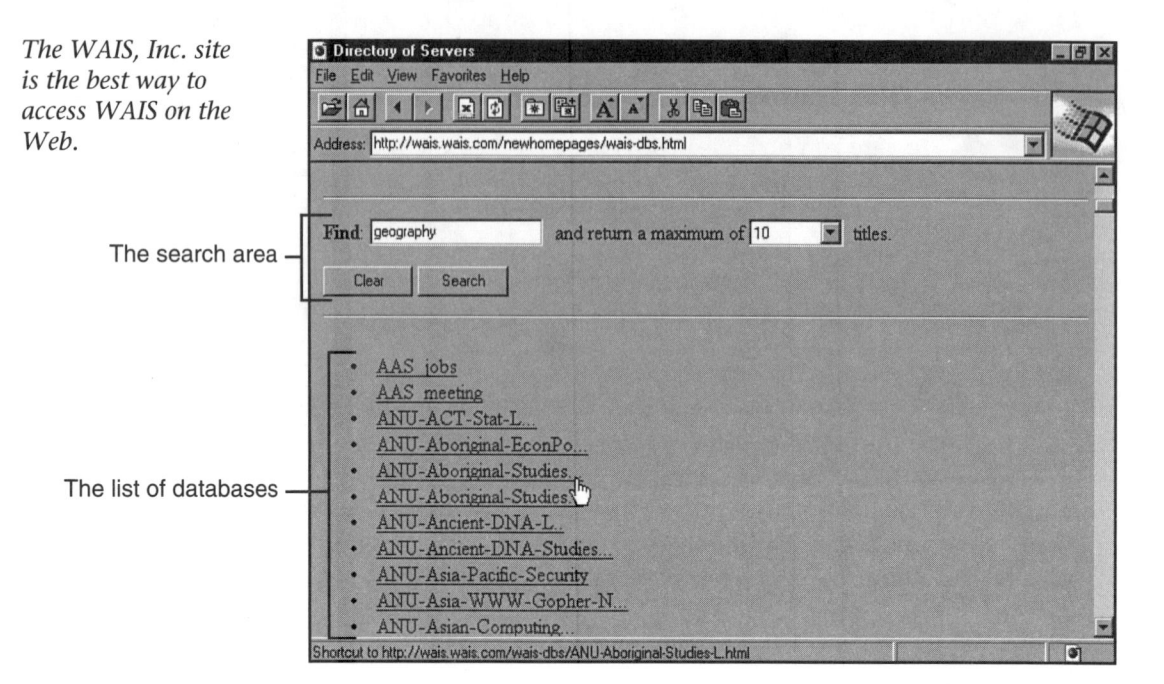

You now have two options. You can search for a useful database by entering search text or by scanning the list. Well, first things first. Let's look at how to search for text. For example, if you wanted to find information about Iceland, you could start by searching for the word "geography" (type the word and then click the **Search** button). Your result is the document shown in the next figure.

Pick Your Keywords

What sorts of keywords can you use? You can type a single word or several words joined with Boolean operators. (The Boolean operators are AND, OR, NOT, and ADJ. ADJ stands for *adjacent*, which means that the second word must immediately follow the first.) You can also type questions and phrases. For detailed information about searching using WAIS, go to **http://wais.wais.com/newhomepages/srchtips.html** or click on the **Help** icon at the WAIS, Inc. site.

Chapter 16 ➤ *Finding Your WAIS Around*

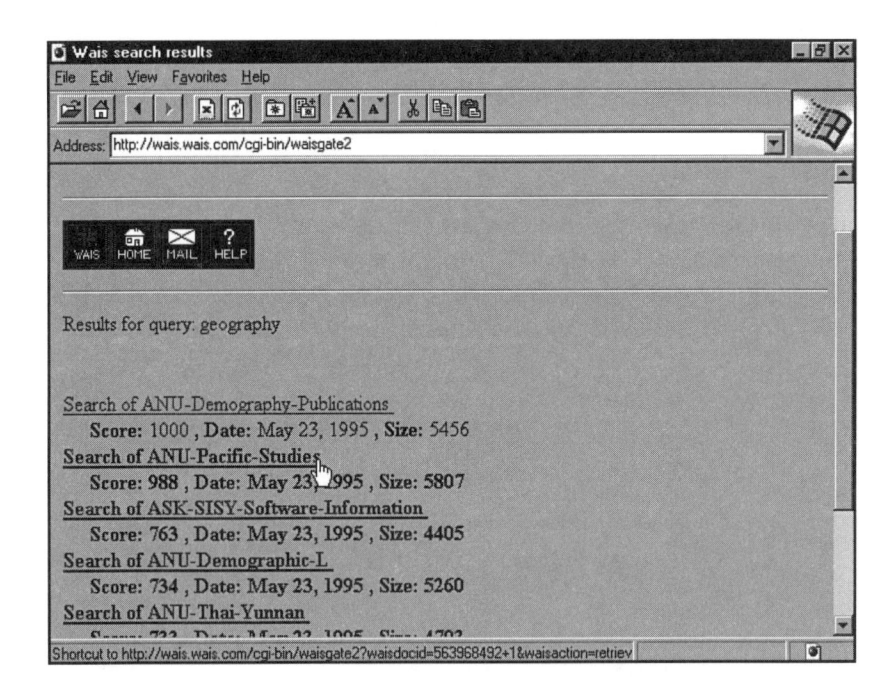

The result of your search for a useful database.

> ### Database List?
>
> You might want to get a list of databases that you can search via WAIS, with a brief description of each. Venturing into this WAIS-land without such a list is like reading a map in Chinese (unless you happen to be Chinese, of course). For instance, while ANU-Asian-Religions.src makes reasonable sense, what is lists.src? Use your browser to go to **gopher://wais.com/00/directory-of-servers/wais-sources.txt**. Read the list, and then save it using the **File**, **Save As** command.

Suppose you searched WAIS for the word "geography," and you got the results screen in the previous figure. You can't see what's at the bottom of the list, but you might imagine that although the ANU-Pacific-Studies database is clearly of no use when searching for Iceland, there might be something more useful lower down. If you find a useful database, click on the database name, and you'll see a document that describes the database and allows you to search it. But guess what? There isn't anything useful. You might need to be a bit more specific. So click the browser's **Back** button to return to the previous page and search again, this time for the word **Iceland**.

193

Part 3 ➤ *Boldly Going Around the Internet*

You're right. That didn't work, either. So return to the **Directory of Servers** page to try your second option: looking through the list for a useful database.

Let Your Eyes Do the Searching

Looking through the list yourself might be tricky. What exactly is ANU-Gesture-L...? How about USDACRIS...? You can click on a database name to see its description. Right near the end, is world-factbook93..., which refers to the CIA World Factbook. To see what that has to say about Iceland, click on the link, and you see a document like the one shown here.

Let's see what the CIA has to say about Iceland.

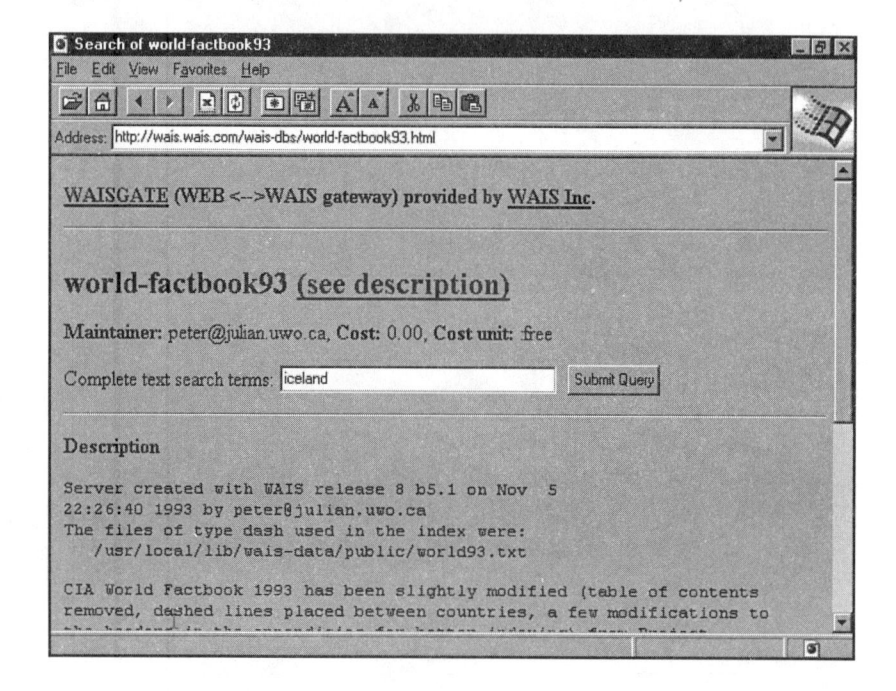

As you can see, this document describes the database you're about to search. If you decide it's the one you need, type the word you want to search for into the text box (uppercase and lowercase doesn't matter), and then click the **Submit Query** button. This time, you're lucky. You find the list of documents shown in the next figure.

194

Chapter 16 ➤ *Finding Your WAIS Around*

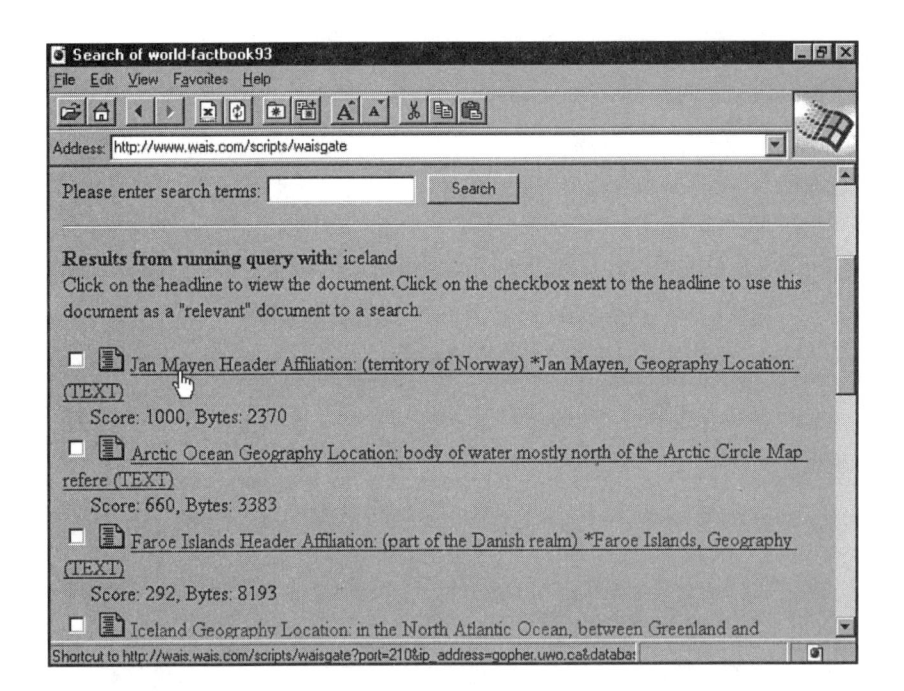

You finally find information about Iceland.

Now you have two more options. You can click on any document to read it, or you can search again to close in on the topic you want. To search again, click in the check boxes to the left of the documents that you want to search further, enter another search word in the text box, and click **Search**. Suppose you search for "population" this time. If you don't find anything—and as a matter of fact, you may find that you can't get much further—you might have to simply open the documents and read them to find what you want. When you find a document that is useful, use the browser's **File**, **Save As** command to save the document, or copy the text to the Clipboard.

As I said, this is probably the best WAIS gateway, but there are others. Try searching for them at Yahoo (http://www.yahoo.com) or another Web search site.

Web—Gopher—WAIS

There aren't that many WAIS gateways on the Web, but there are loads in Gopher. Of course, you don't have a dedicated Gopher program, so you'll use your Web browser to run Gopher to get to WAIS.

Many Gopher servers have links to WAIS servers; use Jughead or Veronica to find them (see Chapter 14). When you find a WAIS entry at a Gopher site, you use it in a way that's similar to using Jughead or Veronica. Simply click on the link, and then enter the search string into the dialog box or form that appears.

195

Part 3 ➤ *Boldly Going Around the Internet*

You'll find other WAIS-related links, such as links to information about how to work with WAIS, links to lists of WAIS servers, and so on. Here's a good place to start: type **gopher://gopher-gw.micro.umn.edu/hh/WAISes** into your Address text box and press **Enter**. At this site, you'll find the **List of all WAIS Sources** and **WAIS Databases sorted by Letter** links. Click one to get to the list of databases. When you find a database that looks like it might be worth searching, click it, and a form appears. Type the word you want to search for and press **Enter**. In a few moments, you see a Gopher menu similar to the one below, showing you what WAIS found.

The results of searching the World Factbook for "Germany"—but through a Gopher site this time.

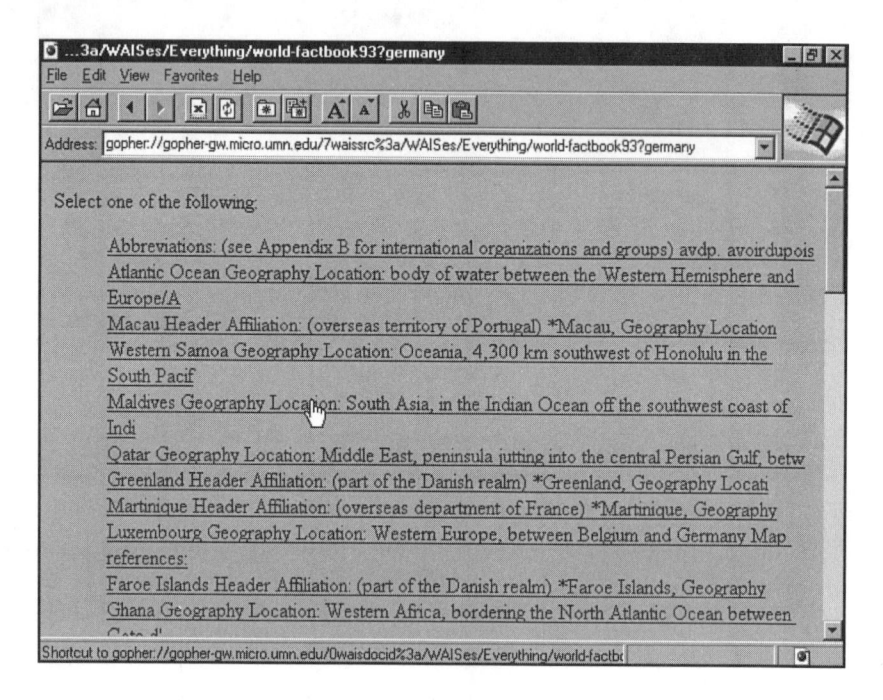

WAIS for Windows—On Your Own Computer

If you want to spend a lot of time using WAIS, you may want to try a WAIS program for Windows. I know of two WAIS "client" programs for Windows. The first is MCC EINet winWAIS, which you can find at http://www.einet.net/EINet/winWAIS.html. (One warning: this site seems a little out of date. You may be able to get a more recent copy at ftp://ftp.einet.net/einet/pc; the most recent I could find was version 2.04.) The second client program is WAIS for Windows (also known as WinWAIS), which is available at ftp://ridgisd.er.usgs.gov/pub/wais/.

Chapter 16 ➤ *Finding Your WAIS Around*

Of the two, I think MCC EINet winWAIS (shown in the following figure) is better. But it doesn't come with a full list of databases, so you have to fool around a little to get one. In addition, neither of them has very good documentation. All in all, I'd say that if you can manage it, stick with using WAIS through the Web. If you use one of these and you spend much time in WAIS, you'll have to bite the bullet and figure out how to deal with these programs.

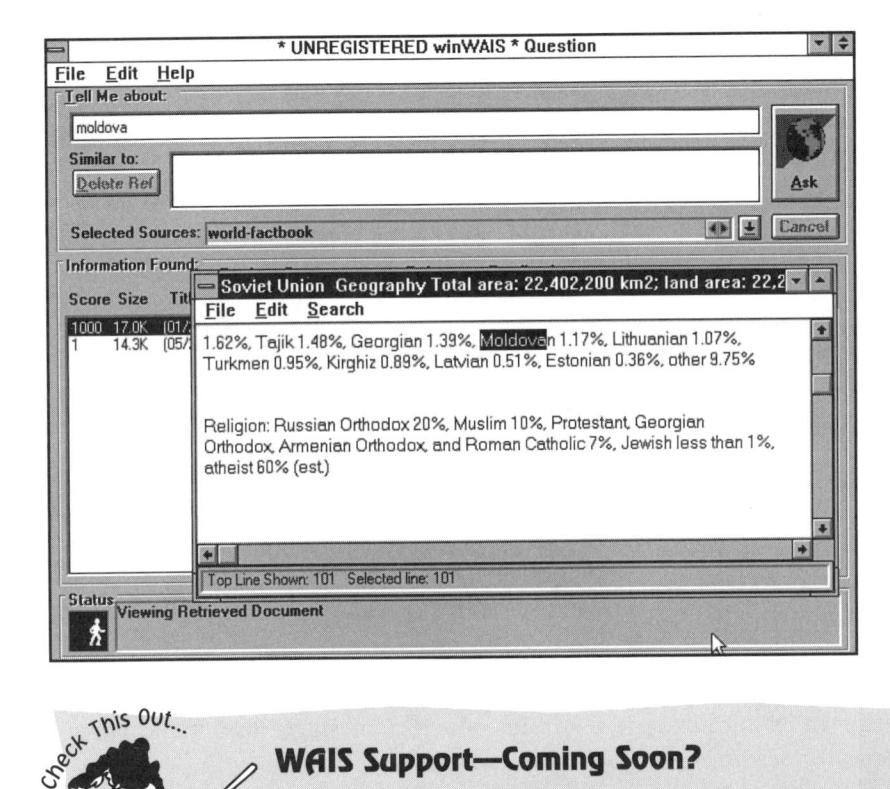

MCC EINet's winWAIS is a dedicated WAIS tool.

WAIS Support—Coming Soon?

Perhaps WAIS support will be added to Internet Explorer later. If so, you'll want to go to **http://www.w3.org/hypertext/Products/WAIS/Overview.html**. From there, you can get to lists of WAIS servers, as well as a searchable index. Some of the links are wais:// links, which you can't use now. However, once Explorer can use the wais:// URL, this method will take you right into the WAIS system.

197

Into the Past—Telnetting to a UNIX-Based Client

There is one more way to use WAIS. If you want full access to WAIS, you can't get the Windows versions to behave, and you would like a little more control than the Web WAIS gateways give you, you can try going through a UNIX client. You can telnet (see Chapter 15) to a site with a WAIS client—even to your service provider, perhaps. Take a look.

Telnet to **wais.com**, **wais.wais.com**, **quake.think.com**, or **nnsc.nsf.net** and log in as **wais**. (To find other WAIS sites that you can telnet to, search for "WAIS" at Yahoo, **http://www.yahoo.com**, or go to the HYTELNET page **http://library.usask.ca/hytelnet/**. Unfortunately, it's currently difficult to find a good WAIS Telnet site.) For example, this is what you see if you telnet to **quake.think.com**. (Don't forget that the bold words are what you are supposed to type.)

```
teal% telnet quake.think.com
Trying 192.31.181.1 …
Connected to quake.think.com.
Escape character is '^]'.
SunOS UNIX (quake)
login: wais
Last login: Tue Nov 16 10:44:41 from forsythe.Stanfor
SunOS Release 4.1.1 (QUAKE) #3: Tue Jul 7 11:09:01 PDT 1992
Welcome to swais.
Please type user identifier: user@host
TERM = (vt100)  (press Enter here)
Starting swais …
```

This may take a little while, but next you see an introductory message. Read it and press **q**, and you see the search screen, which looks something like this:

```
SWAIS                             Source Selection            Sources:  1
#         Server                  Source                      Cost
001:   [  quake.think.com]        directory-of-servers        Free

Keywords:

<space> selects, w for keywords, arrows move, <return> searches, q quits, or ?
```

Chapter 16 ➤ *Finding Your WAIS Around*

A Good Server Is Hard to Find

One problem you'll find with WAIS is figuring out which databases contain what data. The names are often quite obscure. (For instance, what is bib-ens-lyon? It's the Ecole Normale Superieure de Lyon, and it has databases on the sciences—geology, math, physics, chemistry, and so on.) Fortunately, WAIS has a database called the *directory of servers* that you can use to narrow the search a little.

In fact, the directory of servers is probably the first thing you see when you enter WAIS. (It was last time I looked, but at one time a full database listing appeared.) Press **Enter** to select the directory of servers and highlight the **Keywords** line. Type a general keyword, such as **biology**, and press **Enter** again. WAIS searches for databases with biology-related subjects. When it finds matches, it shows you a list something like this:

```
SWAIS                        Search Results                  Item
  #    Score    Source                    Title              Lines
001:   [1000]  (directory-of-se) biology-journal-contents     20
002:   [ 500]  (directory-of-se) Cell_Lines                  117
003:   [ 389]  (directory-of-se) ANU-Ancient-DNA-Studies      90
004:   [ 389]  (directory-of-se) IUBio-fly-clones             59
005:   [ 389]  (directory-of-se) com-books                    99
006:   [ 389]  (directory-of-se) environment-newsgroups       39
007:   [ 333]  (directory-of-se) ANU-Ancient-DNA-L            86
008:   [ 333]  (directory-of-se) ANU-Complex-Systems          67
```

Move the highlight to an entry and press **Spacebar** to see a description of the database's contents. If it's one that you are interested in, press **q** to remove the description, and press **u** to add the database to the main list. Continue in this manner until you find all the databases you want to search. When you finish picking the databases you want, press **s** to return to the first screen (the Source Selection screen).

In the Source Selection screen, deselect the directory of servers (press =), and then select the databases you picked (highlight each entry and press **Spacebar**). When you're ready to search, press **w**, press **Backspace** several times to clear the original search word, and press **Enter**. If Backspace doesn't work, try **Delete**. (You may not be able to see the original search word. Just press **Backspace** until the text cursor is immediately after **Keywords:**, and then type a new search word.)

> **Check This Out...**
>
> **Free...for Now**
> At the time of this writing, all database searches were free. However, notice that some database entries have $0.00/minute in the right column; you may be billed for searches in the future.

The following table lists the commands you can use in the Source Selection screen.

Source Selection Screen Shortcuts

Key or Command	Result
j, or down arrow, or **Ctrl+n**	Moves the cursor down one entry.
J, or **Ctrl+v**, or **Ctrl+d**	Moves the cursor down one screen.
k, or up arrow, or **Ctrl+p**	Moves the cursor up one entry.
K or **Ctrl+u**	Moves the cursor up one screen.
number and **Enter**	Moves to a particular line.
v or **,** (comma)	Displays information about the highlighted database. (Then press **q** and **Enter** to return to the listing.)
Spacebar or **.** (period)	Selects an entry (or deselects a selected entry).
=	Deselects all selections.
Ctrl+j	Selects an entry and moves to the Keywords field.
/*word* and **Enter**	Searches for a listing (where *word* is a word you are searching for).
w and **Enter**	Enables you to enter keywords on which to search (press **Ctrl+c** to cancel).
Enter	Searches selected entries with keywords.
s	Returns to the listing.
h or **?**	Displays the Help screen.
q	Quits.

Use these commands to move the cursor through the list, and press **Spacebar** or **.** (period) to select the entries you want to search. (You can select as many as you want.) If you see an entry you think might be useful, move the highlight to it and press **v** or **,** (comma) to read a description of the database (press **q** and **Enter** to return to the list).

Chapter 16 ➤ *Finding Your WAIS Around*

A little while after you begin the search, you see something like this:

```
SWAIS                             Search Results            Item
  #  Score    Source                       Title           Lines
001:[1000](environment-new)ACTIVE-L vi Re: Report: Exxon Valdez—F   518
002:[ 625](environment-new)hamilton_b Re: Re: When the oil runs out  159
003:[ 578](environment-new)BIOSCI Adm Re: NIH Guide, vol. 23, no. 3  1402
004:[ 516](environment-new)Ron_E._Mad Re: Fwd: 08/94 El Planeta Pla   405
005:[ 484](environment-new)stark@dwov Re: Re: 5HT Levels              503
006:[ 469](environment-new)hamilton_b Re: Re: When the oil runs out  142
007:[ 469](environment-new)cls@truffu Re: (RAN) Oil deal stomps Ind  108
```

Notice the Score column. The higher the score, the more relevant the document is to your particular search. Documents that receive high scores have the search words in the headline or many times throughout. The score is also based on word weighting, term weighting, proximity relationships, and word density.

> **Where Are the Keywords?**
>
> When you press Enter to begin a search, you may notice that the Keywords: field is empty and the text cursor is not at the left side (it's indented a little). Your keywords are still there; you just can't see them. Press **Enter** to continue. Or press **Backspace** to move all the way to **Keywords:** and type a new keyword.

Reading and Saving the Info

You move through this list in the same way you moved through the previous list. However, this time the list is of documents, not databases. You can press **Spacebar** or **Enter** to read the highlighted document.

To be more exact, you *may* be able to read the document. Sometimes documents appear jumbled up slightly, so the lines are not consecutive. If that happens, try this. Go to the list and highlight the document you want to read. Then press ¦ (the vertical "pipe" character), type **more**, and press **Enter**.

What if you want to save the information? You can send the document to yourself (or anyone else, for that matter) using e-mail. Press **m**, and you are prompted for an e-mail address. Type the address and press **Enter**, and that document is on its way. If the WAIS

201

Part 3 ➤ *Boldly Going Around the Internet*

> **Check This Out...**
>
> **Getting Back**
> To get back to the list of databases, press s.

client is on your service provider's computer or on your own computer, you can use the **S** command to save the document in a file.

Is all this too confusing? Do you miss the ease of the Web WAIS gateway? Now you understand the pain of the command line—and the beauty of the graphical user interface.

The Least You Need to Know

- ➤ WAIS means *Wide Area Information Server*. It provides a way to search databases on the Internet.

- ➤ The easiest way to use WAIS is through a Web gateway. Try **http://wais.wais.com/newhomepages/wais-dbs.html**.

- ➤ You can also find plenty of WAIS gateways in Gopher; try **gopher://gopher-gw.micro.umn.edu/hh/WAISes**.

- ➤ Go to **gopher://wais.com/00/directory-of-servers/wais-sources.txt** to find a list of WAIS databases with a short description of each.

- ➤ There are two Windows WAIS clients: MCC EINet winWAIS and WAIS for Windows.

- ➤ If you want full control over your WAIS searches and have trouble setting up the Windows WAIS clients, you may have to telnet to a WAIS client. This is not as easy or intuitive as searching through a Web gateway, however.

- ➤ Telnet to a WAIS client at **wais.com**, **wais.wais.com**, **quake.think.com**, or **nnsc.nsf.net** (log in as **wais** or **swais**). Or, search for **WAIS** at Yahoo to find more Telnet sites.

Chapter 17

Newsgroups: The Source of All Wisdom

In This Chapter

- ➤ What is a newsgroup?
- ➤ What you can find in newsgroups?
- ➤ Finding out what newsgroups exist
- ➤ What is UseNet?
- ➤ Choosing a newsreader so that you can read the messages in the newsgroups

Because it will help if you know what I am talking about, I'll start out this chapter with a few definitions. (Wait! Don't leave! It won't be boring, I promise.)

Are you familiar with bulletin board systems (BBSs)? They're computerized systems for leaving both public and private messages. Other computer users can read the messages you post to a BBS, and you can read theirs. There are tens of thousands of small BBSs around the world, each of which has its own area of interest. For example, many computer companies have BBSs through which their clients can get technical support, and many professional associations have BBSs on which members can leave messages for each other and take part in discussions.

How, then, is that related to an information service such as CompuServe? An information service maintains a collection of many bulletin boards (called *forums* in CompuServe-speak). CompuServe has a few thousand such BBSs. But instead of having to remember several thousand telephone numbers (one for each BBS), you can dial one phone number and access any number of BBSs in the series.

Where does the Internet fit into this picture? As you've already seen, it's a collection of networks hooked together. It's huge, and consequently, it has an enormous number of discussion groups, called *newsgroups* in Internet-speak. There are thousands of them, and at least one exists on any conceivable subject. Each Internet service provider subscribes to a selection of newsgroups—sometimes a very large selection. For instance, my service provider subscribes to around 6,000 (more about subscribing in a moment), America Online subscribes to approximately 12,000, and some providers subscribe to as many as 17,000 different groups. If your service provider subscribes to a newsgroup, you can read that group's messages and post your own messages to the group. (However, you can only work with groups to which your service provider subscribes.)

> **Check This Out...**
>
> **News?** True to its UNIX heritage, the Internet uses the word *news* ambiguously. Often, when you see a reference to "news" in a message or an Internet document, it refers to the messages left in newsgroups (not, as most real people imagine, to journalists' reports on current affairs).

If you've never used a newsgroup (or another system's forum, or BBS, or whatever), you may not be aware of the power of such communications. This sort of messaging system really brings computer networking to life—and it's not all computer nerds sitting around with nothing better to do. (Check out the Internet's alt.sex newsgroups; these people are not your average introverted propeller-heads!) Through newsgroups, I've found work, made friends, found answers to research questions (much quicker and more cheaply than I could have by going to a library I might add), and read people's "reviews" of tools I can use in my business. I've never found a lover or spouse online, but I know people who have (and anyway, I'm already married).

So What's Out There...

You can use newsgroups for fun or real work. You can use them to spend time "talking" with other people who share your interests—whether that happens to be "making and baking with sourdough" (see the rec.food.sourdough group), kites and kiting (rec.kites), or Quentin Tarantino films (alt.movies.tarantino). You can even do some serious work online, such as finding a job at a nuclear physics research site (hepnet.jobs), tracking down a piece of software for a biology project (bionet.software), or finding good stories

Chapter 17 ➤ *Newsgroups: The Source of All Wisdom*

about police work in the San Francisco area for an article you are writing (clari.sfbay.police).

The following newsgroups represent just a tiny fraction of what is available:

alt.ascii-art   Pictures (such as Spock and the Simpsons) created with keyboard characters. You can copy and use them in your own messages.

alt.comedy.british   Discussions on British comedy in all its wonderful forms.

alt.current-events.russia   News of what's going on in Russia right now. (Some messages are in broken English, and some are in Russian, but that just adds romance.)

alt.missing-kids   Information about missing kids.

alt.polyamory   A newsgroup for those with "multiple lovers."

bit.listserv.down-syn   Discussions about Down's syndrome.

comp.research.japan   Information about computer research in Japan.

misc.forsale   Lists of goods for sale.

rec.skydiving   A group for skydivers.

sci.anthropology   A group for people interested in anthropology.

sci.military   Discussions on science and the military.

soc.couples.intercultural   A group for interracial couples.

If you are looking for information on just about any subject, the question is not "I wonder if there's a newsgroup about this?" It is "I wonder what the newsgroup's name is, and if my service provider subscribes to it?"

Can I Get to It?

All those thousands of newsgroups out there take up a lot of room. A service provider getting the messages of 3,000 newsgroups may have to set aside tens of megabytes of hard disk space to keep up with it all. So service providers have to decide which ones they will subscribe to. Nobody subscribes to all the world's newsgroups because many are simply of no interest to most Internet users, and many are not widely distributed. (Some are of regional interest only; some are of interest only to a specific organization.) The system administrators have to pick the ones they want and omit the ones they don't want. And undoubtedly, some system administrators censor newsgroups, omitting those that they believe have no place online.

I've given you an idea of what is available in general, but I can't specify what is available *to you*. You'll have to check with your service provider to find out what they offer. If they don't have what you want, ask them to get it. They have no way of knowing what people want unless someone tells them.

Gimme a List!

You can go to the news.announce.newusers newsgroup to find messages that contain various lists of newsgroups. (You'll find out how to get to a newsgroup in a moment.) Posted to this newsgroup are several messages listing both "official" UseNet newsgroups and "alternative" newsgroups.

In addition, you can use FTP to get lists from the pit-manager.mit.edu FTP site in the /pub/usenet-by-group/news.announce.newsgroup directory. (See Chapter 12 for information about FTP.) You'll find a variety of lists here, including the List of Active Newsgroups, Alternative Newsgroup Hierarchies, and various files listing recent changes. You can also check with your service provider to see if they keep a list of the groups they subscribe to somewhere.

> **Check This Out...**
>
> **I Want to Start One!** Okay, so you have a subject about which you want to start a newsgroup. Spend some time in the news.groups newsgroup to find out about starting a newsgroup, or talk to your service provider about starting a local newsgroup.

Finally, try using your browser to go to http://www.w3.org/hypertext/DataSources/News/Groups/Overview.html. There you'll find a large list of newsgroups with direct links that open the groups. From there, you simply click on a link to open the newsgroup program that your browser is configured to work with (some browsers have built-in newsgroup-viewing capabilities). If you are using Internet Explorer, though, this only works if you have an MSN account because the MSN newsreader is the only one—at present—that you can launch from Explorer.

Another good search site that references newsgroups is the new Jump City (http://www.jumpcity.com/). You select a subject, and you see a list of related Web sites and newsgroups.

Chapter 17 ➤ *Newsgroups: The Source of All Wisdom*

> **Check This Out...**
>
> **Internet Explorer 2.0**
>
> As this book went to print, Microsoft released a beta version of the new Internet Explorer 2.0 program. That program has built-in newsgroup support, so when you click on a link to a newsgroup, the list of messages that people have posted to the newsgroup appears in the browser. You can read the messages right there in the browser window instead of going to the newsgroup window.

Where Do They Come From?

Where do all these newsgroups come from? People all over the world create newsgroups from their own computers. Any host can create a newsgroup, and just about all do. Each host has newsgroups of local interest—about the service provider's services, local politics, local events, and so on.

A large number of newsgroups are part of a system called UseNet. Like the Internet, UseNet is intangible—a network of networks. No one owns it, and it doesn't own anything itself. It is independent of any network, including the Internet (in fact, it's older than the Internet). UseNet is simply a series of voluntary agreements to swap information. Most widely available newsgroups go through UseNet.

> **Techno Talk**
>
> **Moderated Groups** As you'll see in the lists, some newsgroups are *moderated*: someone reads all the messages sent there and decides which ones to post. The purpose is to keep the newsgroup focused and to prevent the discussions from "going astray." Of course, it may look a little like censorship—depending on what you want to say.

What's in a Name?

Let's take a quick look at how newsgroups get their names. Newsgroup names look a lot like host addresses: a series of words separated by periods. This is because, like host names, they are set up in a hierarchical system (though instead of going right-to-left, they go left-to-right). The first name is the top level. These are the top-level UseNet groups:

    comp   Computer-related subjects.

    news   Information about newsgroups themselves, including software you can use to read newsgroup messages, and information about finding and using newsgroups.

207

rec Recreational topics: hobbies, sports, the arts, and so on.

sci Science: discussions about research in the "hard" sciences, as well as some social sciences.

soc A wide range of social issues (such as discussions about different types of societies and subcultures), as well as sociopolitical subjects.

talk Debate about politics, religion, and anything else that's controversial.

misc Stuff. Job searches, things for sale, a forum for paramedics. You know, *stuff*.

Not all newsgroups are true UseNet groups. Many are local groups that UseNet distributes internationally. Such newsgroups are known as *Alternative Newsgroup Hierarchies*, and they have their own top-level groups, such as these:

alt "Alternative" subjects. These are often subjects that many people consider inappropriate, pornographic, or just weird. In other cases, it's just interesting stuff, but the person who created the newsgroup did so in an "unauthorized" manner to save time and hassle.

bionet Biological subjects.

bit A variety of newsgroups from BITNET.

biz Business subjects, including advertisements.

clari ClariNet's newsgroups from "official" and commercial sources; mainly UPI news stories and various syndicated columns (ClariNet is a subscription-based news service).

courts Related to law and lawyers.

de Various German-language newsgroups.

fj Various Japanese-language newsgroups.

gnu The Free Software Foundation's newsgroups.

hepnet Discussions about high energy and nuclear physics.

ieee The Institute of Electrical and Electronics Engineers' newsgroups.

info A collection of mailing lists formed into newsgroups at the University of Illinois.

k12 Discussions about kindergarten through 12th grade education.

Chapter 17 ➤ *Newsgroups: The Source of All Wisdom*

relcom Russian-language newsgroups (mainly distributed in the former Soviet Union).

vmsnet Subjects of interest to VAX/VMS computer users.

You'll see other groups, too, such as the following:

brasil Groups from Brazil (Brazil is spelled with an "s" in Portuguese).

podunk A local interest newsgroup for the town of Podunk.

thisu This university's newsgroup.

(Okay, I made up the last two, but you get the idea.)

Reaching the Next Level

The groups listed in the previous section make up the top-level groups. Below each of those are groups on another level. For instance, there's alt.3d, a newsgroup about three-dimensional imaging. (It's part of the alt hierarchy because, presumably, it was put together in an unauthorized way. The people who started it didn't want to go through the hassle of setting up a UseNet group, so they created an alt group instead—where anything goes.)

> **Check This Out...**
>
> ### How Does It Work?
>
> If you really care how this information ends up on your service provider's computer, here goes. Computers acting as news servers collect the newsgroups from various other places, such as other servers that are part of the UseNet agreements, computers with local newsgroups, ClariNet (a commercial "real" news service that carries news from United Press International), gateways to other networks (such as BITNET), and so on. Then the computers acting as news servers make the information available to your service provider's system. Each server administrator has to make agreements with other administrators to transfer this data.

Another alt group is alt.sex (where anything really does go). This group serves as a good example of how newsgroups can have more levels. Because it's such a diverse subject, one newsgroup isn't really enough. So instead of posting messages to the alt.sex group, you choose your particular favorite area. The specific areas include:

alt.sex.bestiality.barney   Described as "for people with big purple newt fetishes."

alt.sex.fetish.feet   (Self-explanatory.)

alt.sex.motss   Motss means "member of the same sex."

alt.sex.pictures   Described as "Gigabytes of copyright violations."

And there are many more. If you're into it, chances are good that there's a newsgroup for it.

All areas use the same hierarchy. For example, more specialized newsgroups under the main bionet group include bionet.genome.arabidopsis (information about the Arabidopsis genome project), bionet.genome.chrom22 (a discussion of Chromosome 22), and bionet.genome.chromosomes (for those interested in the eucaryote chromosomes).

I'm Ready. How Can I Read These?

Now that you know what newsgroups are, how are you going to use them? Newsgroups store the news messages in text files. Lots of text files. The best way to read the messages you want is to use a *newsreader* to sort and filter your way through all the garbage. (I say the "best way," because believe it or not there really are people who choose to dig through the text files with arcane UNIX commands such as **grep**.)

What newsreader do you have available? Well, if you are a Microsoft Network member, you already have a pretty good newsreader built into the MSN software. There's no need to look further. If you are with another service provider, they may provide you with another program such as WinVN, Free Agent, or OUI. There are also *loads* of commercial newsreaders around, many of which are included with products such as Internet Chameleon, SuperHighway Access, and Internet in a Box.

There are also a few UNIX programs, which you can get by telnetting into your service provider. For example, my service provider has tin, nn, trn, and rn. (Remember, UNIX-types developed the Internet, and there's a UNIX law somewhere that says program names must not use recognizable or easily understood words.) Compared to the point-and-click ease of a good Windows newsreader, these newsreaders are horrible. So I'm not going to bother discussing them.

So which do you use to follow along with this book? In Chapter 18, I'm going to discuss working with the MSN newsreader because so many people already have it. If you are *not* working with MSN, read through the description anyway. You'll find that no matter which newsreader you are working with, the principles are the same. The way that "threading" or "conversations" work, message encoding and encryption, and so on, are similar from program to program. And after I talk about MSN, I'll give you a quick look at several other newsreaders you may want to try.

A Quick Word on Setup

There is one thing you should know before you get started, so I want to quickly discuss setup and subscribing. First, your newsreader must know the location of your *news server*. By now you probably understand the concept of servers and clients. There are Web servers and Web clients (Web browsers), Gopher servers and Gopher clients (programs such as a Web browser that can work in Gopher menus), and WAIS servers and WAIS clients. Not surprisingly, there are also news servers and news clients. The *news server* is the program that gets the newsgroup messages from UseNet and makes them available to a client; your service provider maintains the server. The *news client* is simply the newsreader, the program you use to read the messages.

You must provide most newsreaders with the host name of the news server, which might be news.big.internet.service.com, or news.zip.com, or something like that. Ask your service provider what to use for the news server's host name. (If you are working with MSN, you don't have to worry about this because the MSN newsreader program already knows where to look to find the newsgroup messages.)

The other thing you may have to do is subscribe to the newsgroups in which you are interested. As I explained earlier in the chapter, newsgroups are distributed throughout the world, and a service provider subscribes to the ones they want to make available to their members. Although all of those newsgroups are available on the service provider's system, *you* have to subscribe to them by telling your newsreader which ones you want to read.

Again, you don't have to worry about this if you work with MSN because MSN makes all the newsgroups directly accessible to you. Many newsreaders, however, require you to fetch a list of newsgroups from your service provider (the newsreader has a command you use to fetch and display the list), and then they require you to "subscribe" to the ones you want to use. It's no big deal, you simply choose the ones you want to work with. Until you subscribe though, you can't see the messages.

The Least You Need to Know

- A newsgroup is an area in which people with similar interests leave public messages—a sort of online public debate or discussion.

- There's a newsgroup on just about any subject you can imagine. And if there isn't one, there probably will be soon.

- Newsgroup names use a hierarchical system; each group may have subgroups within it.

- If you are using MSN, you already have a newsreader that enables you to see what's in the newsgroups. It's built into your MSN software. If you are not with MSN, your service provider may provide another type of newsreader.

- There are lots of newsreaders around, such as Free Agent, WinVN, and OUI.

Chapter 18

Getting Your News

In This Chapter

➤ Starting the MSN newsreader

➤ Reading and responding to messages

➤ Marking messages as read

➤ ROT13—encoded messages

➤ Sending and receiving binary files

➤ Using Wincode

➤ Finding other newsreaders: WinVN, Free Agent, and OUI

It's time to see how to work in the newsgroups. We'll start with the MSN newsgroup program, and then we'll take a look at some other programs.

I've chosen the MSN newsgroup program because many Windows 95 users have MSN accounts. Of course you may not have an MSN account, in which case you'll use some other kind of newsgroup program. That program might be WinVN, Free Agent, or OUI (all of which I describe at the end of this chapter); it might be a newsgroup program provided to you by your service provider; or it might be one you received as part of an Internet suite. There are many newsgroup programs around, and although each is a little different, all have certain common characteristics. So we'll take a look at MSN as an example of what a newsgroup program will do. Check your program's documentation for the specific details and to learn about any extra features.

If you are an MSN user, you see icons all over the place representing collections of newsgroups. Many of MSN's BBSs (which is what MSN calls its forums or subject areas) contain icons that represent links to newsgroups; you double-click on the icon to go to the newsgroup. For instance, in the Genealogy forum, double-click on the icon labeled **Genealogy Internet Newsgroups** to open it. Then go to the **soc.genealogy** and **alt.genealogy** newsgroups.

You can also go to the Internet Center, where you can select any of the newsgroups that MSN offers:

1. Select the **Edit**, **Go to**, **Other Location** command.
2. In the dialog box that appears, type **Internet** and press **Enter**.
3. You'll find several icons representing links to different collections of newsgroups. Double-click on one of the icons to open the list of newsgroups.

> **Check This Out...**
>
> ### Where Are the Alt. Groups?
>
> MSN users will find that they can't initially read the alt. groups. Microsoft regards these as a trifle "naughty," so you have to apply for permission to read them. Go to the **Internet Center**, go into the **Internet Newsgroups** forum, and look for an icon that says something like **How to Access all Newsgroups**. This provides information and an electronic form that you can fill out and send to apply for full access. You can only read the messages in this group if you are over 18.

As an example, choose the **Usenet Newsgroups** icon and then the **rec** icon. The following figure shows the windows that appear on your screen, the last of which contains a list of the rec newsgroups. Double-click on one of the rec. icons—rec.animals, rec.answers, rec.scuba, or whatever—and one of two things happen. You may go directly to a newsgroup window that contains a list of messages, or you may see *another* list of newsgroups. Remember the hierarchical system I told you about in Chapter 17? Now you can see it firsthand. Select **rec.audio**, for instance, and you see more newsgroups such as rec.audio.car, rec.audio.pro, rec.audio.tubes, and so on.

Chapter 18 ➤ *Getting Your News*

This is how MSN gives you access to its newsgroups.

First double-click here...
then double-click here...

and then you'll see the newsgroups.

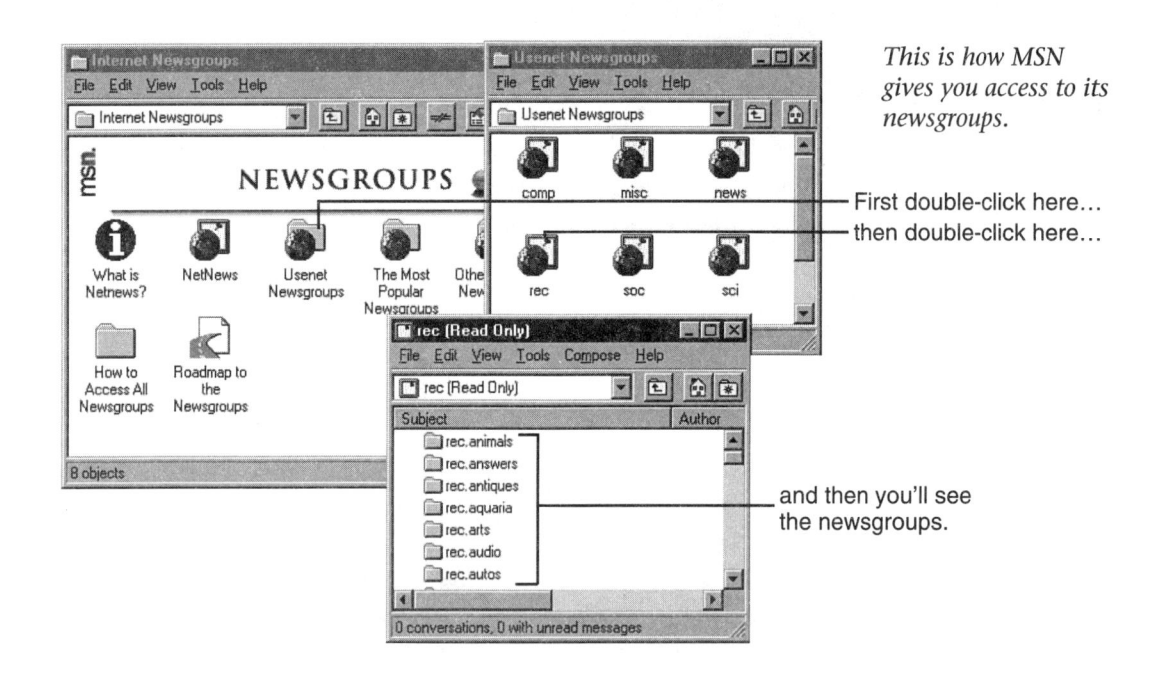

Let's move on to the newsgroup window and then to a list of messages within a newsgroup. The newsgroup window is exactly the same as the MSN BBS windows; you can see an example newsgroup window in the following figure. If you are used to working in MSN's BBS windows, though, you need to be aware that there are some things you can't do. You can't use all the fancy fonts and message formatting here that you can in MSN because the Internet newsgroup system is based on ASCII text. Nor can you insert OLE (Object Linking and Embedding, a Windows data-sharing system) objects or files into your messages (but see "Pictures from Words," later in this chapter).

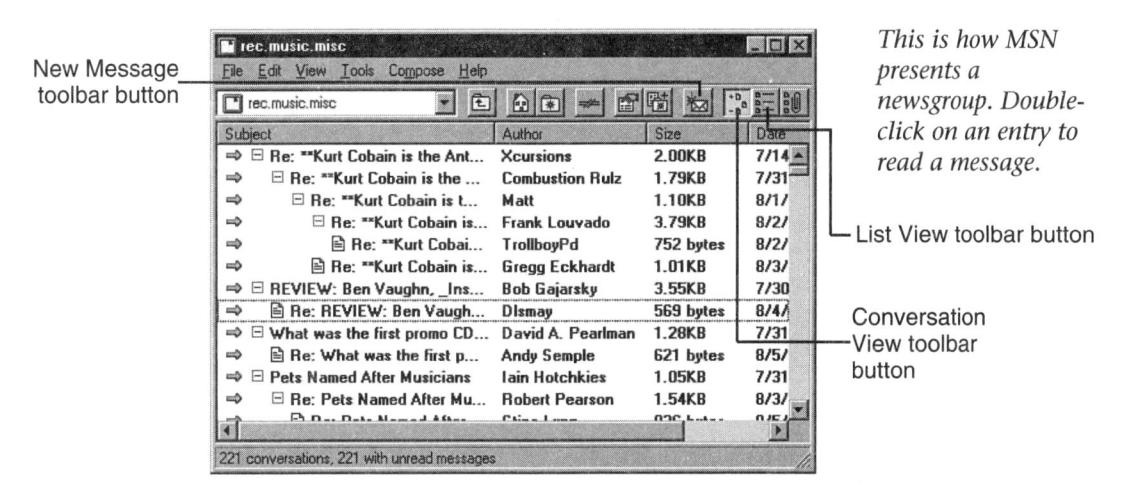

New Message toolbar button

This is how MSN presents a newsgroup. Double-click on an entry to read a message.

List View toolbar button

Conversation View toolbar button

215

Part 3 ➤ *Boldly Going Around the Internet*

> **Check This Out...**
>
> **The Text Looks Strange!** When you view MSN BBS messages, text automatically wraps from line to line as in a word processor. In newsgroups, however, this doesn't happen because each line is, in effect, a separate paragraph. Expand the window size to remove the jagged edge from the right side of the text.

Taking a Look

When you open the newsgroup, a list of messages appears on-screen. At the bottom of the window in the status bar is a message something like **8 conversations, 8 with unread messages**. This *should* mean that there are eight different message threads (or *conversations*—I'll explain that in a moment), and within those threads there are eight different messages.

So what's a *conversation* or *thread*? When you post a message to a newsgroup (by choosing **Compose, New Message**), you aren't replying to anyone. You've just created a thread, or what the MSN newsgroup program refers to as a conversation. Then, a few hours later, someone else reads your message and replies. Because it is a reply, that message is part of the conversation you began. A few minutes later, someone else sends a message to the newsgroup, and it turns out to be not a reply, but a new message. That is the beginning of another thread or conversation. (Note, however, that there's a *long* lag time—a day or more—between someone sending a message to a newsgroup and that message turning up in everyone's newsreader.)

There are three ways to view messages. The default is Conversation View. The previous figure shows a newsgroup window in Conversation View. If your messages don't look like this, click the **Conversation View** toolbar button (shown here) or select **View, Conversation**.

In this view, all messages are grouped together in the conversations they belong to—pretty logical, eh? You can control whether or not you see a conversation by using the little plus (+) and minus (–) signs in the left column. Click the + sign to expand the conversation; MSN shows the first "level" of responses in the conversation. (If you hold the **Shift** key when you click the + icon, MSN shows all levels of the conversation.) Click the – sign to "collapse" a conversation, and MSN removes all the listings below the first level of a conversation. You can also press the + and – keys to expand and collapse conversations.

There's a command that enables you to expand all the conversations in a newsgroup without clicking each + sign. Select **View, Expand All Conversations** to see all levels of all conversations. Likewise, you can select **View, Collapse All Conversations** to collapse all the conversations at once.

> **Message Hierarchies**
>
> In the newsgroup figure shown earlier, you can see a newsgroup with multiple "layers" of responses in a conversation. Why is the alignment of these layers ragged? Why, for instance, is the fifth message indented to the right, and the sixth indented to the left? Each message is indented to the right from the message to which it is a response. Thus the fifth message is a response to the fourth, but the sixth message—although it was sent after the fifth—is a response to the third.

A Different Point of View: List and File Views

Before I go on, let's quickly look at the other two views. First, there's the List View. Click the **List View** toolbar button or select **View, List**. You see that the newsgroup messages are no longer grouped by conversation. Each message in the newsgroup is shown on a line by itself—and there's no indentation of messages and no conversations to expand. How are the messages ordered, then? You put the messages in order by selecting one of the menu options that appears when you select **View, Arrange Messages**. You can place the messages in chronological order (oldest first), in order by size (smallest first), or in alphabetical order by author or subject. Simply click a column heading to sort the messages: click **Author** to sort by author name, **Size** to sort by size, and so on.

There's also a File View, but you can ignore it. It's intended for use in the MSN BBSs, not in the newsgroups. If you select this view in a newsgroup, all the messages disappear from the window.

The Messages Are Gone!

The first time you open a newsgroup, you see all the messages from the newsgroup your service provider (in this case MSN, of course) currently holds. How long a message stays in the newsgroup depends on how busy that newsgroup is and how much hard-disk space the service provider allows for the newsgroup messages—but eventually all messages disappear.

You don't necessarily see all the newsgroup's messages, though. You do when you first enter the newsgroup, but when you return to the newsgroup in a later MSN session, you see all the messages *except* those marked as Read. (Actually, to be more specific, you also see messages that have been marked as Read if they are part of a conversation that includes one or more messages marked as Unread.)

Why didn't I just say "you see all the messages that you haven't read?" Well, there's a slight difference. MSN has no way of knowing which messages you've read because it can't see what you are doing. Instead it has a way of marking messages that it thinks you've read, and it provides you with a way to mark messages as Read even if you haven't read them (in effect, providing a way for you to tell it that you don't want to see the messages).

Marking Your Messages

When you open a message, MSN automatically marks the message as Read. You can manually mark messages in several other ways:

- Click a message and select **Tools, Mark Message as Read**. MSN marks that particular message as Read.
- Click a message and select **Tools, Mark Conversation as Read**. MSN marks all the messages in that conversation (or thread) as Read.
- Select **Tools, Mark All Messages as Read**. MSN marks every message in the newsgroup window as Read.

How can you tell if a message is marked as Read? Messages shown in the newsgroup window with bold text are Unread; the ones that *aren't* bold have been marked as Read. Notice the gray arrow icon in the left column. It indicates that the conversation contains at least one Unread message (even if the first message in the conversation is marked Read).

Why bother marking messages as Read? That tells MSN that you don't want to see those messages when you come back to the newsgroup in a later session. For instance, say you get a couple of messages into a conversation and realize it's pure rubbish (you'll find a lot of messages that have virtually no utility to anyone!). Select **Tools, Mark Conversation as Read**, and you won't see the rest of the messages the next time you open the newsgroup window. Similarly, you might want to quickly read all the messages' Subject lines to find a conversation that interests you. If you don't find anything interests you, you can mark them *all* as Read so you see only new messages the next time.

Notice that there are even commands for marking messages as Unread. Suppose you've read a message, but you want to make sure it appears the next time you open the newsgroup. Click the message and select **Tools, Mark Message as Unread** (or **Tools, Mark Conversation as Unread** if you want to save the entire conversation). There's no Mark All Messages as Unread command, but if you want to do this, choose **Edit, Select All**, and then select **Tools, Mark Conversation as Unread**.

Chapter 18 ➤ *Getting Your News*

> **Check This Out...**
>
> **I Want the Message Back!**
>
> If you ever need to bring a message back, you can use the **Tools, Show All Messages** command to tell MSN to display all the newsgroup messages, even those you've marked as Read. Of course, if MSN no longer holds the message you want to see—that is, if the message has been removed from MSN's hard disks to make more space for new messages—you're out of luck. Note also that if you select this command in one session, it is still on the next time you open the newsgroup; so remember to turn it off before you leave. (In some newsgroups, using this command may display hundreds of messages, which takes a *very* long time.)

Enlightenment: Reading Your Messages

You can probably figure out how to read a message without my help—just double-click it, of course. But as you might guess, there are multiple other ways to do the same thing. Here are all the ways you can open a newsgroup message:

➤ Double-click the message.

➤ Click once on the message and press **Enter**.

➤ Right-click a message and select **Open** from the shortcut menu that appears.

➤ Click a message and select **File**, **Open**.

> **Check This Out...**
>
> **Not All Commands Work**
>
> You'll find that lots of menu commands in the newsgroup window are not appropriate for newsgroups. For instance, View, Refresh is unlikely to do anything. These commands are intended for use in the MSN BBSs.

You can select multiple messages by holding down the **Ctrl** key, clicking on each one, and then using one of the last three methods listed above. When you do this, you get a separate window for each message, which can be a bit confusing. Press **Alt+Tab** to move between the windows, or click on the one you want to read. Once you've read the message, click the **Close** (X) button in the upper-right corner to close the window.

Now take a look at the newsgroup message window, the window that appears when you select a message. You can see an example in the following figure.

219

Part 3 ➤ Boldly Going Around the Internet

The newsgroup window, your path to true wisdom.

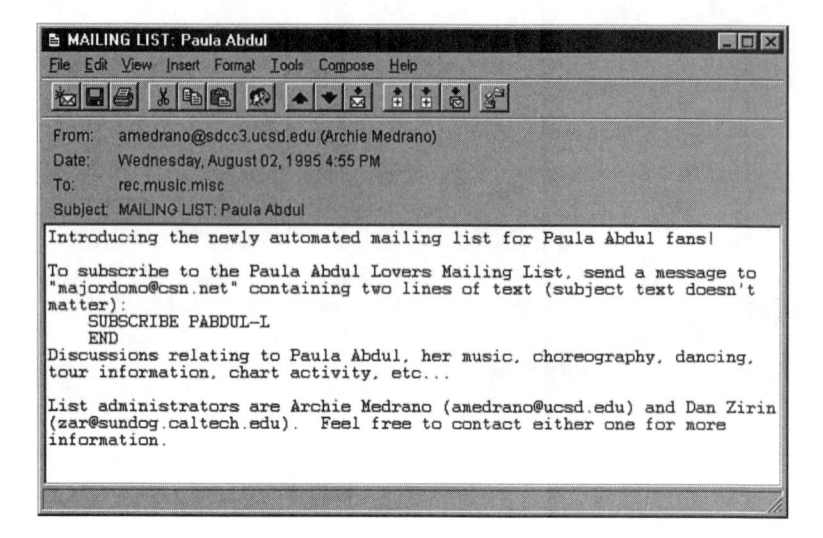

```
MAILING LIST: Paula Abdul
File  Edit  View  Insert  Format  Tools  Compose  Help

From:     amedrano@sdcc3.ucsd.edu (Archie Medrano)
Date:     Wednesday, August 02, 1995 4:55 PM
To:       rec.music.misc
Subject:  MAILING LIST: Paula Abdul

Introducing the newly automated mailing list for Paula Abdul fans!

To subscribe to the Paula Abdul Lovers Mailing List, send a message to
"majordomo@csn.net" containing two lines of text (subject text doesn't
matter):
     SUBSCRIBE PABDUL-L
     END
Discussions relating to Paula Abdul, her music, choreography, dancing,
tour information, chart activity, etc...

List administrators are Archie Medrano (amedrano@ucsd.edu) and Dan Zirin
(zar@sundog.caltech.edu). Feel free to contact either one for more
information.
```

You can read, scroll through, and save a newsgroup message. You can move around in the message using the scroll bar and the keyboard (use Page Up, Page Down, Ctrl+Home, and Ctrl+End). You can also highlight text and save it to the Windows Clipboard using Cut and Copy (from the toolbar or the Edit menu). And don't forget the toolbar buttons, which provide a quick way to use a variety of commands. The following table shows you the buttons you can use to work with messages.

Newsgroup Message Window Toolbar Buttons

Button	Name
	New Message
	Save
	Print
	Cut
	Copy
	Paste
	Reply to BBS

220

Button	Name
▲	Previous Message
▼	Next Message
	Next Unread Message
	Previous Conversation
	Next Conversation
	Next Unread Conversation
	File Transfer Status (not functioning for newsgroups)

Moving Among the Messages

You don't need to close one message window before you open the next message. You can use one of the toolbar buttons or menu commands to move directly to another message. Click the **Previous Message**, the **Next Message**, or the **Next Unread Message** button to move between messages. Each time, the new message replaces the one you are currently viewing in the window.

If you decide that you don't want to read any more messages in the current conversation, you can skip all the other messages by clicking the **Previous Conversation**, the **Next Conversation**, or the **Next Unread Conversation** button. If you prefer, use the equivalent commands in the View menu, or use the keyboard commands to quickly jump between messages (you can find these in the View menu, too).

Saving and Printing

If you run across a message that you think you may need later, you can save it or print it. Simply marking it as Unread isn't good enough, because newsgroups eventually drop all messages, and sooner or later it simply won't be available.

To save a message, click the **Save** toolbar button or select **File**, **Save**. Of course, you can also highlight the text, copy it (press **Ctrl+C**), and then paste it into another Windows application such as a word processor.

221

To print a message, click the **Print** toolbar button to send the message directly to the printer. Or you can select **File, Print** to access the normal Windows 95 Print dialog box, which enables you to choose a printer, select the number of copies, and so on. You can also select the **File, Print Setup** command to choose a printer.

Your Turn: Sending and Responding

There are several ways to send messages or to respond to messages. Use one of these techniques:

➤ To send a message that isn't a response—that is, to start a new conversation—select **Compose, New Message** or click the **New Message** toolbar button.

➤ To reply to someone's message, open the message and select **Compose, Reply to BBS** or click the **Reply to BBS** toolbar button. (Yes, I know this is a newsgroup, not a BBS. But as I mentioned earlier, this is the MSN BBS program.)

➤ To reply to someone privately (to send a message that *doesn't* appear in the newsgroup), select **Compose, Reply by E-mail**.

➤ To send a copy of the original message to someone else, select **Compose, Forward by E-mail**.

If you select one of the e-mail options, Microsoft Exchange's New Message window appears. Otherwise, the newsgroup's New Message window appears.

Working with the New Message Window

The following figure shows MSN's New Message window. Notice that it has its own toolbar with buttons for working with messages. To send a message, follow these steps:

When it's time to have your say, you send a message to a newsgroup.

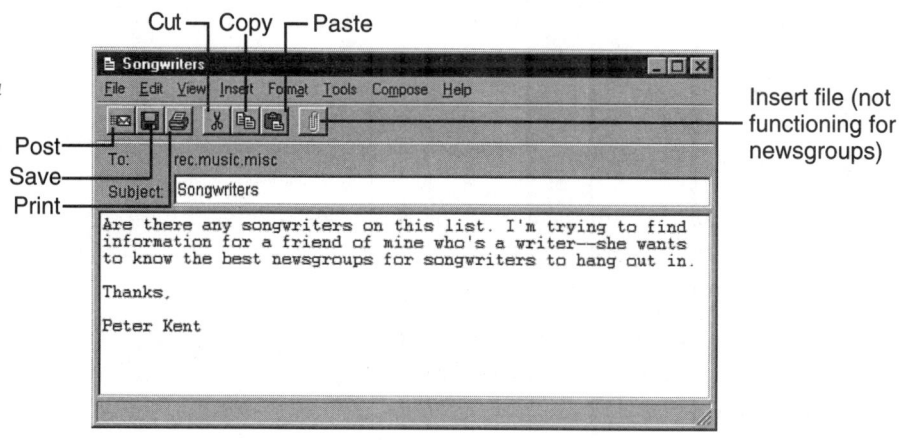

Chapter 18 ➤ *Getting Your News*

1. Enter a message title into the **Subject** text box.
2. Press the **Tab** key and begin typing your message.
3. When you finish, click the **Send** toolbar button or select **File**, **Post Message**. Away it goes.

You won't see the message in the newsgroup window right away. Because of the way that newsgroup messages are distributed, you—and the other people reading the newsgroup—won't see the message in the newsgroup for at least a day and maybe several days.

What's This Gibberish? ROT13

Now and again, especially in the more contentious newsgroups, you'll run into messages that seem to be gibberish. Everything's messed up, and each word seems to be a jumbled mix of characters—almost as if the message is encrypted. Well, it is.

What you are seeing is *ROT13*, a very simple substitution cipher (one in which a character is substituted for another). It's actually very easy to read. ROT13 means "rotated 13." In other words, each character in the alphabet is replaced by the character 13 places further along. Instead of A you see N, instead of B you see O, instead of C you see P, and so on. Got it? So to read the message, all you have to do is substitute the correct characters. Easy.

Of course, there is an easier way. Select **Tools**, **ROT13 Encode/Decode**, and like magic the message changes into real words, as you can see in the following figure.

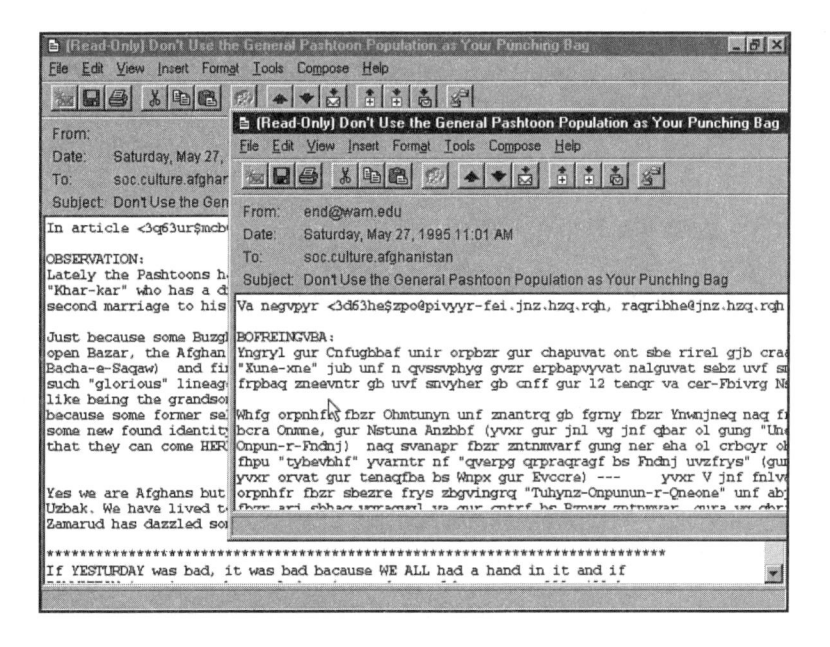

An example of a ROT13 message, with the decoded version behind it.

223

So what's the point? Why encode a message with a system that is so ridiculously easy to break? People don't ROT13 messages as a security measure intended to make them unreadable to all but those with the "secret key." After all, anyone with a decent newsgroup reader has the key. No, ROT13ing (if you'll excuse my use of the term as a verb) is a way of saying "if you read this message, you may be offended; so if you are easily offended, *don't read it!*" ROT13 messages are often crude, lewd, or just plain rude. Offensive. Nasty. Converting a message into ROT13 forces readers to decide whether they want to risk being offended.

I suspect the use of ROT13 is dying out as the Internet grows. Many new users know nothing about ROT13 because many new newsgroup programs don't enable you to read or create ROT13 messages.

Pictures from Words

The newsgroups contain simple ASCII text messages. You can't place any character into a message that is not in the standard ASCII character set (which is made up of the characters you see on your keyboard, plus some symbols). So if you want to send a computer file in a newsgroup message—maybe you want to send a picture, sound, or word processing document—you must convert it to ASCII.

Some of the newer newsreaders can help you do this by automating the process of attaching MIME-formatted files to your messages, or UUENCODING files and inserting them into your messages (see below). Some newsreaders can even convert such files "on the fly" as they read a newsgroup message that contains one, and they automatically display the picture inside the message or convert the file to its original format. For the moment, though, most newsreaders are at a fairly basic, non-sophisticated stage, and they require that you manually UUENCODE computer files that you want to send or manually UUDECODE those that you receive.

MIME

MIME is short for Multipurpose Internet Mail Extensions. It's a system that was originally designed to allow Internet e-mail programs to exchange computer files. When you use a MIME-enabled program to send a computer file, you create an e-mail message and then tell the program to "attach" the file. The program converts the file to ASCII text and sends that text along with the message. The recipient's MIME-enabled program recognizes that the incoming message contains text that is a MIME attachment and converts it back. While most files currently posted to newsgroups are UUENCODED, MIME is becoming more popular because some important newsreaders (such as the newsreader built into the Netscape Web browser) have MIME capabilities.

Chapter 18 ➤ *Getting Your News*

You can place files into newsgroup messages using something called *UUENCODE*. Here's how this system works. First, you take the file you want to send and convert it—UUENCODE it—to ASCII text. Then you copy and paste the text into the message and send it off to the newsgroup. The person reading the message sees a huge jumble of text (see the following figure). If the reader wants to download it from the message, he or she must save the message in a text file (or, in some cases, place it in the Windows Clipboard) and then *UUDECODE* it—convert it from ASCII to its original format. Sound complicated? It really isn't, once you know what you're doing.

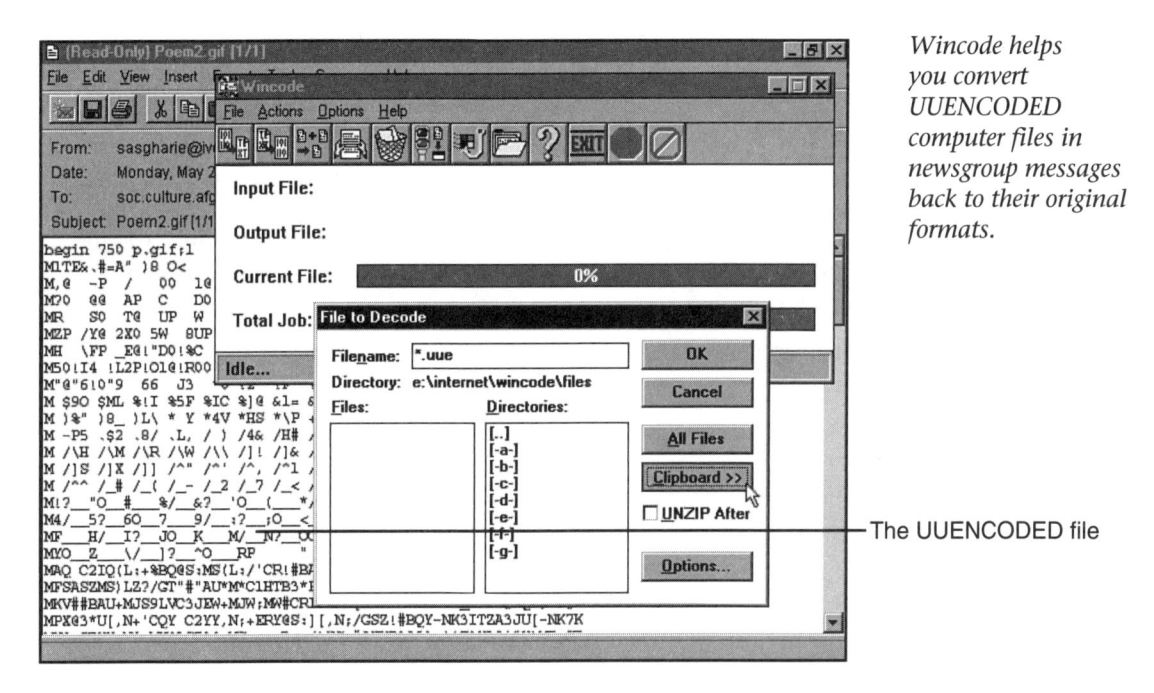

Wincode helps you convert UUENCODED computer files in newsgroup messages back to their original formats.

The UUENCODED file

Perhaps MSN will eventually build UUENCODE and UUDECODE directly into the New Message and BBS windows (some other Internet newsreaders already have these capabilities). For now, however, you need to use a special utility. If you have Norton Navigator, the Windows 95 add-on utility collection from Symantec, you already have a UUENCODE/DECODE utility. In Norton File Manager, select **File**, **UUEncode/Decode**. You can also use a freeware utility called Wincode that you can find on the Internet. You can find it at ftp://ftp.winsite.com/pub/pc/win3/util/. This site is very busy, and you may not be able to get through. You can also try searching for it using Archie (see Chapter 13). Download and unzip Wincode, and read the README.TXT file for information on setting it up.

Part 3 ➤ *Boldly Going Around the Internet*

Practical UUDECODING

Start by grabbing a file from a newsgroup message. This can be a picture, a sound, or anything else that you can place in a computer file. For instance, in the soc.culture.afghanistan newsgroup, I found a UUENCODED picture of an Arabic poem. Here's what to do:

1. Open the message and choose **Edit, Select All** to highlight the entire message.
2. Choose **Edit, Copy** to copy the text to the Clipboard.
3. Open Wincode and select **File, Decode**.
4. In Wincode's File to Decode dialog box, click the **Clipboard** button. Wincode proceeds to decode the text that is in the Clipboard.
5. In this particular example, you see a message saying **Error 045: Illegal DOS input filename**. This means that the file name in the UUENCODED text is not correct. (If you look at the top of the message in the previous figure, you can see that the file name on the first line of the message text is, for some reason, **p.gif;1**. Perhaps Wincode choked on this.)
6. Choose **OK** in this message box, and Wincode displays a text box into which you type a new name.
7. Choose **OK**. Wincode decodes the picture and places it in the FILES subdirectory.

> **Check This Out...**
>
> **Clipboard Bug**
> Wincode's Clipboard system doesn't always work. If you have problems, save the message text in a file, select the file in Wincode's File to Decode dialog box, and choose **OK**.

Many UUENCODED files are split into several messages. You may see Subject lines that say something like Picture.gif 1/3, Picture.gif 2/3, and Picture.gif 3/3, for example. This means that each message contains a portion of the UUENCODED file. In such a case, you need to save each message (select **File, Save**) in a separate text file. This allows Wincode to pick up each message in sequence while it decodes. (See the Wincode instructions for more information.)

MSN Is Not Alone...

There are, of course, many other newsreaders. Your service provider may offer one, for instance, and many commercial Internet suites include them, too. You'll find that although "feature sets" may vary slightly, and you'll use different commands to do different things, the principles are the same. Read the documentation carefully, though; you'll have to tell the program the host name of your service provider's news server and then subscribe to the groups you want to read.

Let's take a quick look at two currently popular products, and one that's likely to become popular.

WinVN

WinVN is a Windows newsreader that's been around for some time. It's a public domain program, so you don't have to open your wallet if you want it. It's fairly easy to use and set up, but it doesn't have any of the advanced features of some other newsreaders. It does, however, have built-in UUENCODING and UUDECODING and ROT13.

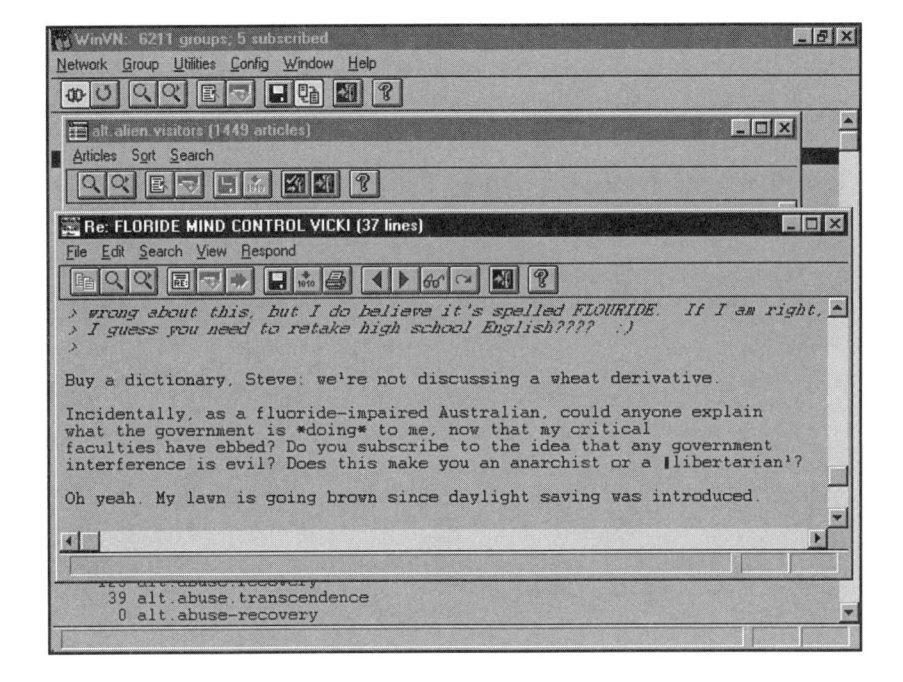

WinVN: it's free, so try it!

Although you can find WinVN all over the place, its "home site" is ftp.ksc.nasa.gov/pub/winvn/. You can also try these two ftp sites: ripem.msu.edu/pub/pc/win/winvn/ titan.ksc.nasa.gov/ and shannon.mee.tcd.ie/winvn/.

Free Agent: Partly Free

Forte produces two newsreaders that are becoming very popular: a free one called *Free Agent*, and one you have to cough up the bucks for that's called simply *Agent*. (Agent has all the features of Free Agent, along with a multilingual spelling checker and free technical support.)

Part 3 ➤ *Boldly Going Around the Internet*

Free Agent provides an excellent way to work with newsgroups.

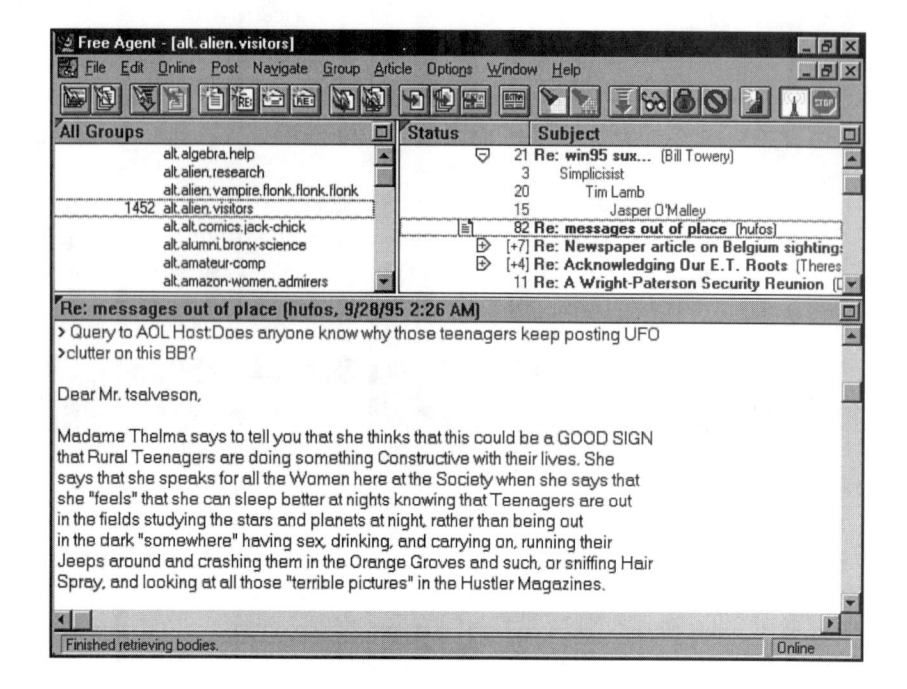

Free Agent is very easy to set up and use. You can subscribe to newsgroups if you want, but you don't have to because it enables you to grab messages from newsgroups you haven't subscribed to.

Free Agent has a few features designed for offline navigation (though not as many as does OUI, described next). An *offline navigator* is a program that helps you cut your online time by automating the things you need to do while online. In other words, you select the newsgroups from which you want to see messages, and then you click on a button. The program quickly logs on, grabs the message headers, and logs off. You then select the messages you want to read and click the button again. The program logs on again, grabs the messages you've selected, and logs off again.

Free Agent has loads of useful features, such as a quick way to copy a Web URL from a message to the Clipboard, the capability to automatically watch a particular thread (in other words, if someone responds to a particular message, Free Agent downloads the message for you without you telling it to), and the capability to ignore a thread (Free Agent doesn't bother to retrieve headers for responses to the marked message). And as does any good newsreader, it also has built-in ROT13 and UUENCODING and UUDECODING.

Free Agent is available in many places, but its home site is http://www.forteinc.com/forte.

Chapter 18 ➤ *Getting Your News*

Newsgroups? Mais Oui!

Finally, a quick look at OUI, the Offline Usenet Interface. This comes from my friends at Dvorak Development, the people who created the NavCIS offline navigator for CompuServe. Like Free Agent, OUI is also an offline navigator for newsgroups; however, its offline features are more advanced.

Aren't all newsreaders offline navigators to some extent? Well, no, they vary greatly. Currently the MSN newsreader enables you to read messages only while you are online, although Microsoft promises to come out with a new version that enables you to open messages and then log off. Some newsreaders let you download the messages you want to read, but let you respond to messages or send new messages only while online. OUI lets you write your messages offline, and then sends them the next time you go online.

In addition, few newsreaders have the "thread management" capabilities of OUI. OUI grabs a detailed picture of newsgroup threads, showing you who responded to which messages and how one message relates to others. Even if another newsreader lets you read a message offline, it probably won't let you view the message *thread* offline (some won't even let you see the thread while online). Working in newsgroups and trying to figure out how all the messages relate can get very confusing sometimes, so thread management is very useful.

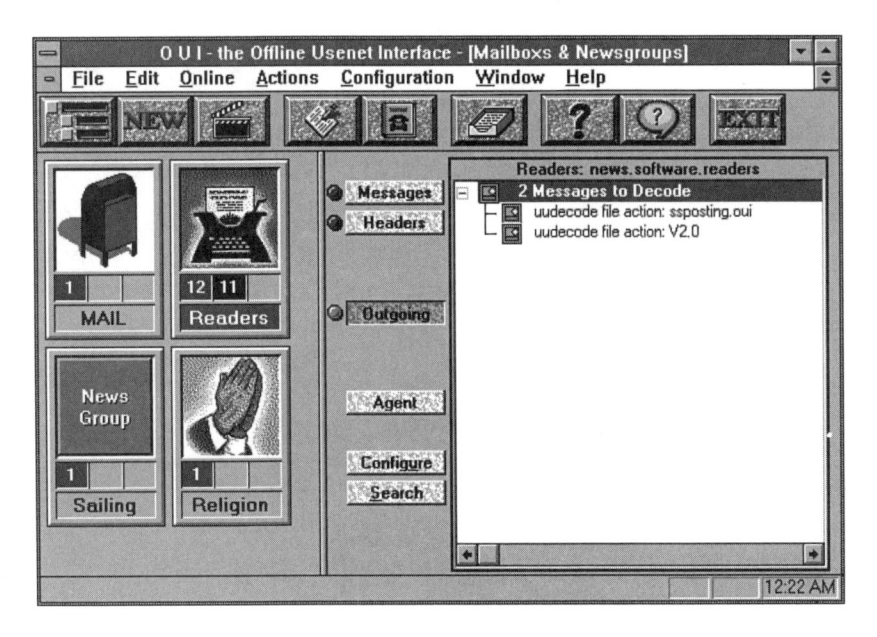

OUI is the first newsgroup with all the features needed for offline navigation.

229

OUI also does something that no other Windows newsreader currently does: it shows you the position of missing messages in the thread. Thanks to the unusual way that newsgroup messages are sent to the UseNet system and then transmitted throughout the world, you often see a response to a message before the original message is available! OUI can figure this out and show you a blank space in the message thread to indicate where something is missing.

You can find OUI at http://www.dvorak.com or ftp.dvorak.com. Try a free 30-day demo to see if you like it. OUI will cost you approximately $40 ($30 if you already own NavCIS). The price includes an image viewer that enables you to quickly display pictures you download from the newsgroups.

By the way, you can also use OUI as an e-mail program. And it has lots of neat features like the capabilities to add sounds, to modify the icons and labels used to identify each group, to UUENCODE and UUDECODE, to use ROT13, and so on. There's also a very cool feature related to UUDECODING. Many pictures posted to newsgroups are encoded and split into several parts (two, three, nine, or however many it takes). If you tell OUI to decode a UUENCODED file in a message, and OUI finds that it's just one part of multipart file, it goes back to the newsgroup and looks for the other parts for you!

A Word of Warning

Newsgroups can be *very* addictive. You can find messages about anything that interests you, angers you, or turns you on. If you are not careful, you can spend half your life in the newsgroups. You sit down in the morning to check your favorite newsgroups, and the next thing you know you haven't bathed, eaten, or picked up the kids from school.

Hang around the newsgroups, and you find people who are obviously spending a significant amount of time writing messages. These people are usually independently wealthy (that is, they work for large corporations who don't mind paying for them to talk politics over the Internet or who don't know that they are paying for them to do so). If you have a job, a family, and a life, be careful.

The Least You Need to Know

- ➤ You can start MSN's newsreader from many places in MSN; try the Internet Center to find links to all the newsgroups.

- ➤ To view the alt. newsgroups, you have to get special permission. You can find information at the Internet Center.

- ➤ A good newsreader lets you view a thread or conversation, which shows how messages relate to each other.

➤ ROT13 is a special encoding system that prevents people from accidentally stumbling across offensive messages. Many newsreaders have a ROT13 command that converts the message to normal text.

➤ You can include binary files in messages by UUENCODING them first. (Pretty soon you'll find newsreaders that use a different method called MIME.)

➤ To decode binary files, you need either a newsreader that can UUDECODE or a utility such as Wincode.

➤ If you are not using MSN, try WinVN, Free Agent, or OUI. The basic principles are the same, but the commands vary.

Chapter 19

Yet More Discussion Groups— Mailing Lists

In This Chapter

➤ *More* discussion groups?

➤ How mailing lists work

➤ Manual and automated lists

➤ LISTSERV mailing lists

➤ Finding lists of interesting groups

➤ Subscribing to mailing lists

Are you getting enough sleep? Are you socializing? Meeting with friends and family? Do you have time to eat and bathe? Yes? Then you're clearly not spending enough time on the Internet. I've already shown you the Web and thousands of newsgroups, along with Telnet, FTP, and WAIS. You'd think that would be enough to keep you quiet 24 hours of the day, but I guess I'm just going to have to give you even more—the mailing lists.

Mailing lists are discussion groups. The difference between a mailing list group and a newsgroup is simply the manner in which messages are distributed. While newsgroups are distributed through a system specifically set up for their distribution, mailing lists are distributed via e-mail.

Part 3 ➤ Boldly Going Around the Internet

If you've already read the chapters on e-mail—Chapters 20 through 23—you already know how to jump in and get started with mailing lists. If you haven't read those chapters yet, you may want to come back to this chapter later.

What's a Mailing List?

Mailing lists work like this. Each mailing-list discussion group has an e-mail address, and you subscribe to the group you are interested in (I'll explain how in a moment). The e-mail address then acts as a mail *reflector*: it receives mail and then sends it on to a list of addresses. So every time someone sends a message to a group of which you are a member, you get a copy of the mail. And every time you send a message to a group, everyone else on the list gets a copy.

There are thousands of mailing lists on the Internet. Here's how you can go about finding the ones that interest you:

➤ Send an e-mail message to **listserv@bitnic.educom.edu**. In the message text, type **list global**. You'll get back an e-mail message that contains a list of thousands of LISTSERV mailing lists. I'll explain what those are in a moment.

➤ Go to the **news.announce.newusers** newsgroup. You can sometimes find a list of mailing lists posted there. (See Chapters 17 and 18 for information about working with newsgroups.)

> **Check This Out...**
>
> **Peered Groups**
> Some LISTSERV mailing lists are shown on the list as "peered." A *peered* LISTSERV group is the same as a *moderated* newsgroup; someone checks the mail and decides what stays and what gets trashed.

➤ Send an e-mail message to **listserv@vm1.nodak.edu** with the command **GET NEW-LIST WOUTERS** in the body of the message. You get back Arno Wouter's text file titled *How to Find an Interesting Mailinglist*.

➤ ftp to the **pit-manager.mit.edu** FTP site, change to the **/pub/usenet-by-groups/news.lists** directory, and find the **Publicly_Accessible_Mailing_Lists,_Part_*n*** files. This lists non-LISTSERV mailing lists. (For information about using FTP, see Chapter 12.)

➤ At the FTP site noted above, take a look in the **/pub/usenet/news.announce.newsusers** directory. You can find a variety of lists there.

> **Busy FTP Site**
>
> The pit-manager.mit.edu site is often very busy. If you can't get through, try again later. Or, look carefully at the message you receive when you are unable to log on. It gives you FTP addresses of other sites that should contain the same files, as well as an e-mail address you can use to find out how you can have the files sent to you via e-mail.

The Types of Lists

There are two basic types of mailing lists:

- Manually administered
- Automated

Some very small mailing lists are set up to be administered by a real person who adds your name to the list. Such lists are often private, with subscription by invitation. Other lists use special programs (mailservers) to automatically add your name to the list when you subscribe. These are often, though not always, public lists that are open to anyone.

Perhaps the most common form of automated list is the LISTSERV list. Named after the LISTSERV mailing-list program, these lists are distributed through the Internet by the BITNET computer network. (Just to confuse the issue, I should state that there are now LISTSERV programs for a variety of different computer systems, and they are used to run mailing lists that are *not* distributed by the BITNET computer network.) Among those other mailing-list programs available, Majordomo is one of the most common.

Some mailing lists are run from UNIX Internet accounts and use a few very simple utilities to make the work easier. For instance, a UNIX user can set up a forwarding utility to automatically forward incoming e-mail to a list of e-mail addresses.

Subscribing to Mailing Lists

Subscribing to manually administered mailing lists is usually as simple as sending a message to the administrator, providing your e-mail address, and asking if you can join the list. You can often reach an administrator by sending e-mail to *listname*-request@*hostname*.

To subscribe to an automated list, you send e-mail to the mailserver program. In the body of the message you enter **SUB *firstname lastname*** (that's your first and last name, of course). To unsubscribe, you use the word **SIGNOFF** instead of SUB.

Note that the address of the list administrator and that of the list itself are usually different (in most cases, but not always). So if the list address is biglist@bighost, that's where you send your e-mail when you want to post messages to the list. But when you want to subscribe, unsubscribe, or do other administrative functions, you normally send e-mail to biglist-request@bighost.

However, there's an exception to every rule, and this time it's the best-known form of mailing list: LISTSERV. While LISTSERV lists also have two e-mail addresses, working with those addresses is a little different, as you'll see right now.

Using a LISTSERV Group

Many people think that mailing lists and LISTSERV groups are one and the same. Not quite. Although LISTSERV groups are a type of mailing list (perhaps the largest category), not all mailing lists are LISTSERV groups. LISTSERV is actually the name of one popular mailserver program, and mailing lists administered by the LISTSERV program are known as LISTSERV groups, LISTSERV lists, or just LISTSERVs. LISTSERV originates on the BITNET network. However, many LISTSERV groups are now based on the Internet itself—on various UNIX hosts.

You can find well over 4,000 BITNET LISTSERV groups, covering subjects such as those listed in the following table.

A Sampling of BITNET LISTSERV Groups

Mailing List	Description
9NOV89-L@DB0TUI11.BITNET	Events centered around the Berlin Wall
AAAE@VM.CC.PURDUE.EDU	American Association for Agricultural Education
AAPOR50@USCVM.BITNET	American Association for Public Opinion Research
AATG@INDYCMS.BITNET	American Association of Teachers of German
ABSLST-L@CMUVM.BITNET	Association of Black Sociologists
ACADEMIA@TECHNION.BITNET	Academia – Forum on Higher Education in Israel
ACADEMIA@USACHVM1.BITNET	Grupo Selecto de Matematicos Chilenos
ACCESS-L@PEACH.EASE.LSOFT.COM	Microsoft Access Database Discussion List
ACCI-CHI@URIACC.BITNET	Consumer Economics and Chinese Scholars

Chapter 19 ▸ Yet More Discussion Groups—Mailing Lists

Mailing List	Description
ADA-LAW@NDSUVM1.BITNET	Americans with Disabilities Act Law
ADD-L@HUMBER.BITNET	Forum for discussion of concerns of drinking and driving
AE@SJSUVM1.BITNET	Alternative Energy Discussion List
CHRISTIA@FINHUTC	A Christian discussion group
H-RUSSIA@MSU.EDU	H-Net Russian History list
H-SHGAPE@MSU.EDU	H-Net Gilded Age and Progressive Era List
HESSE-L@UCSBVM.UCSB.EDU	The Works of Hermann Hesse
ISO8859@JHUVM	A group that discusses ASCII/EBCDIC-character set issues (what fun!)
L-HCAP@NDSUVM1	A group for people interested in issues related to handicapped people in education
OHA-L@UKCC.BITNET	Oral History Association Discussion List
ONO-NET@UMINN1.BITNET	Resource for those interested in the works of Yoko Ono
PALCLIME@SIVM.BITNET	Paleoclimate, Paleoecology for late Mesozoic & early Cenozoic
PFTFI-L@ICNUCEVM.BITNET	Progetto Finalizzato Telecomunicazioni — UO Firenze
PHILOSOP@YORKVM1	The Philosophy Discussion forum
SCAN-L@UAFSYSB.BITNET	Radio Scanner Discussion forum
SCR-L@MIZZOU1.BITNET	Study of Cognitive Rehabilitation, Traumatic Brain Injury
SCREEN-L@UA1VM.UA.EDU	Film and TV Studies Discussion List
SEMLA-L@UGA.BITNET	Southeast Music Library Association Mailing List
SEXADD-L@KENTVM.BITNET	Exchange forum for sexual addiction, dependency, or compulsion
SFER-L@UCF1VM.BITNET	South Florida Environmental Reader
SHAMANS@UAFSYSB.BITNET	Shamans Impact of the Internet on Religion
SHEEP-L@LISTSERV.UU.SE	A list for people interested in sheep

continues

A Sampling of BITNET LISTSERV Groups   Continued

Mailing List	Description
SIEGE@MORGAN.UCS.MUN.CA	Medieval Siege Weaponry List
SKATE-IT@ULKYVM.BITNET	Skating discussion group
SKEPTIC@JHUVM.BITNET	SKEPTIC Discussion Group
SLAVERY@UHUPVM1.UH.EDU	The history of slavery, the slave trade, abolition, and emancipation
SLDRTY-L@LISTSERV.SYR.EDU	Members of Solidarity, a socialist organization, Detroit
SLLING-L@YALEVM.BITNET	Sign Language Linguistics List
SPACESCI@UGA.BITNET	sci.space.science digest
SS-L@UIUCVMD.BITNET	SS-L Sjogren's Syndrome
SWL-TR@TRITU.BITNET	Short Wave Listening in Turkiye
TECTONIC@MSU.EDU	Geology 351 Class
TEX-D-L@DEARN.BITNET	German TeX Users Communication List
TFTD-L@TAMVM1.TAMU.EDU	Thought for the day
TGIS-L@UBVM.BITNET	Temporal Topics on GIS List
THEATRE@PUCC.BITNET	The Theatre Discussion List
TIBET-L@IUBVM.BITNET	Tibet Interest List
TN-L@UAFSYSB.BITNET	Discussion of Cranial Neurolgia Disorders
TNT-L@UMAB.BITNET	TNT Discussion Group
TRANSY-L@UKCC.BITNET	Transylvania University Alumni
TREPAN-L@BROWNVM.BITNET	Weird News List
TVDIRECT@ARIZVM1.BITNET	Professional TV Directors and Producers
UBTKD-L@UBVM.BITNET	UB TaeKwonDo
UIWAGE-L@ECUVM1.BITNET	Unemployment Insurance Wage List
UNCJIN-L@ALBNYVM1.BITNET	United Nations Criminal Justice Information Network
UNIX-WIZ@NDSUVM1.BITNET	Unix-Wizards Mailing List
UNLBIO-L@UNLVM.BITNET	UNL Center for Biotechnology List
UTOPIA-L@UBVM.BITNET	Utopias and Utopianism
VAMPYRES@GUVM.BITNET	Vampiric lore, fact and fiction

Chapter 19 ➤ *Yet More Discussion Groups—Mailing Lists*

Mailing List	Description
VEGAN-L@TEMPLEVM.BITNET	Vegan discussion group
VETTE-L@EMUVM1.BITNET	Corvette Discussion—service info, shows, etc.
VOEGLN-L@LSUVM.BITNET	Discussion list on Eric Voegelin's writing and philosophy
VOICES-L@ORACLE.WIZARDS.COM	Voices In My Head List
VWAR-L@UBVM.BITNET	Vietnam War Discussion List
WCENTR-L@MIZZOU1.BITNET	Moderated Writing Center forum
WEIMING@ULKYVM.BITNET	Chinese Newsletter Distribution List
WHITESOX@MITVMA.BITNET	Chicago White Sox Mailing List
WHR-L@PSUVM.BITNET	Women's History in Rhetoric
WORCIV-L@UBVM.BITNET	World Civilization Committee
WVMS-L@WVNVM.BITNET	NASA Classroom of the Future: WV Mathematics and Science List
XTROPY-L@UBVM.BITNET	Extropians—discussion/development of Extropian ideas
YACHT-L@HEARN.BITNET	The Sailing and Amateur Boat Building List

Now do you have an idea of the wild, wacky, and well-worth-reading mailing lists available to you? (I'm planning to check out the Voices in My Head List.) This is just a tiny portion of what's out there, and it only includes the LISTSERV groups. There are many non-LISTSERV groups, too, which cover a similarly eclectic subject matter.

The LISTSERV Address

Let's take a look at the LISTSERV address. It's made up of three parts: the group name itself, the LISTSERV site, and (usually) **.bitnet**. For instance, the address of the group College Activism/Information List is actnow-l@brownvm.bitnet. Actnow-l is the name of the group, and brownvm is the name of the site. (As you can see from the list above, some of these LISTSERV groups (such as SLAVERY@UHUPVM1.UH.EDU) don't have the .bitnet bit at the end.

A *site* is a computer that has the LISTSERV program, and each site handles one or more LISTSERV groups. In fact, a site may have dozens of groups. The brownvm site, for example, also maintains the forums ACH-EC-L, AFRICA-L, and AGING-L, as well as about 70 others.

Where's the List?

If you want to find the latest list of LISTSERV groups, you can have BITNET send you one. Send an e-mail message to **listserv@bitnic.educom.edu**. In the body of the message (not the subject) type **list global**. That's all you need. You'll automatically get an e-mail message containing the new list.

Let's Do It—Subscribing

> **Check This Out...**
>
> **Worried About Money?** Don't worry, you are not going to have to pay. The vast majority of mailing lists are completely free.

Once you've found a LISTSERV group to which you want to subscribe, you must send an e-mail message to the LISTSERV site (not to the group itself), asking to subscribe to the list. Send a message with the following text in the body (not the subject) of the message:

SUBSCRIBE *group firstname lastname*

For instance, if I wanted to subscribe to the actnow-l list at the brownvm LISTSERV site, I would send a message to listserv@brownvm.bitnet, and in the body of the message I'd write **SUBSCRIBE actnow-l Peter Kent**.

Notice that you send the message to **listserv@***sitename***.bitnet** and that the **SUBSCRIBE** message contains only the *name* of the group (not the entire group address). Also note that you may *have* to put something in the Subject line because some e-mail programs won't let you send e-mail unless you do so. In such a case just type something—anything (**1**, for instance)—in the Subject line. And if your e-mail program automatically inserts a signature (information about you such as your name, street address, and so on) at the end of the message, turn the signature off before you send the message.

You may (or may not) receive some kind of confirmation message from the group. Such a message would tell you that you have subscribed, and it would provide background information about the group and the different commands you can use. Or, you may receive a message telling you how to confirm your subscription. If so, simply follow the instructions in the message. You may receive instructions about working with the mailing list. If you get instructions, read them carefully because they contain important information.

Once you've subscribed, you can either sit back and wait for the messages to arrive, or you can send your own messages. Simply address mail to the full group address (which would be actnow-l@brownvm.bitnet in my previous example).

Enough Already!—Unsubscribing

When you're tired of receiving all these messages (and the volume may very well be overwhelming), you can just unsubscribe. To do so, you send another message to the LISTSERV address. You still send it to **listserv@brownvm.bitnet** (for example), but this time you type **SIGNOFF actnow-l** in the body of the message.

Again, make sure you address your message to **listserv@**, not to the group name itself. And make sure the group name—but not the entire group address—appears after SIGNOFF (the instruction to unsubscribe).

> **Check This Out...**
>
> ### Message Digests
>
> One way to make your mailing lists easier to handle is to get message *digests*. You can send a message to the LISTSERV server (**listserv@** with the command **digest** *listname*, such as **digest techwr-1**). Then, instead of receiving dozens of messages throughout the day, you'll receive one large message at the end of the day that contains all the messages the mailing list received during the day. It has a list of subjects at the top, so you can use your e-mail program's Find command (or save the message in a text file and use your word processor's Find command) to quickly get to the messages that interest you. Note, however, that not all mailing lists can provide message digests.

Getting Fancy with LISTSERV

You can do some pretty neat things with LISTSERV. By sending e-mail messages to the LISTSERV site, you can tell the LISTSERV software how you want to handle your messages. You can ask LISTSERV to send you an acknowledgment each time you send a message (by default most groups won't do this). You can find information about another group member—or tell LISTSERV not to provide information about you to other users. You can tell LISTSERV to stop sending you messages temporarily (when you go on vacation, for example), or you can tell it to send only the message subjects, instead of the entire messages. You can request a specific message, and you can even search the archives for old messages.

In addition, you can combine these commands. For instance, I could send an e-mail message to **listserv@brownvm.bitnet** with these lines in the body of the message:

```
list
query groupname
info ?
```

The **list** command tells LISTSERV to send me a list of the groups handled by this site; **query** *groupname* asks it to tell me what options I have set; and **info ?** tells it to send me a list of information guides. It's a good idea to use **info ?** to find out what user documentation they have available, and then use the **info** *documentname* command to get the site to send you specific documents. (At some sites, sending e-mail to the LISTSERV address with the message **INFO REFCARD** will get you a document outlining the commands you can use.)

> **Remember This!**
>
> When you want to send a message to be read by other group members, you must address it to *groupname@sitename*.bitnet. For all other purposes (to subscribe, unsubscribe, change user options, get more information, and so on), you send the message to *listserv@sitename*.bitnet. If you send administrative-type messages to the group itself, you may get complaints. But hey, you're not alone. Many of us (me included—just a few minutes ago) forget to change the address and send these commands to the wrong address! And these days, some LISTSERV servers recognize when a message contains commands. If so, they intercept the message before it gets to the mailing-list group and send it back to you.

Working with Mailing Lists

Working with a mailing list is quite simple. When a message arrives, you find it in your e-mail inbox with all your normal e-mail. If you read a message to which you want to reply, simply use the reply function of your e-mail program (see Chapter 20 for more information), and it addresses the new message correctly. (At least, in most cases it will. Check the return address that your e-mail program enters for you. With some mailing lists, you'll find that the return address in the header of the message you received is *not* the address to which you are supposed to send messages.) To send a message about a new subject, simply write a new message, address it to the mailing-list address, and send it off.

In some ways, working with mailing lists is not as convenient as working with newsgroups. The newsgroup programs have lots of features for dealing with discussions. Of course your e-mail program will almost certainly let you print and save messages, just as a newsgroup program would. What's missing, though, are the threading functions you get in newsgroup messages, which enable you to quickly see which messages are part of a series of responses. You may also find that messages are sent to you out of order, so you

Chapter 19 ➤ Yet More Discussion Groups—Mailing Lists

may end up reading a response to a message that appears further down in your e-mail inbox. Use the message digest, though, to get the messages in the most convenient form possible.

The Least You Need to Know

- ➤ A mailing list is a discussion group in which messages are exchanged through the e-mail system.

- ➤ Mailing lists may be manually administered or run by a program such as LISTERV or Majordomo.

- ➤ To subscribe to a manually administered list, simply write to the person running the list and ask to join. Or you may need to e-mail to *listname*-**request@***hostname*.

- ➤ To subscribe to an automated but non-LISTSERV list, you normally send a message that includes **SUB** *firstname lastname* in the body. The message normally goes to a different e-mail address. If the list is called biglist@bighost, for example, you probably e-mail to biglist-request@bighost.

- ➤ Subscribe to a LISTSERV group by including the command **SUBSCRIBE** *groupname firstname lastname* in the body of a message you send to **listserv@***sitename*.**bitnet**.

- ➤ To unsubscribe, send a message with the command **SIGNOFF** *groupname* in the body.

- ➤ When you join a group, send a message with the **info ?** command in the body to find out what documentation the group has available.

243

Part 4
E-Mail Made Easy

Is there anyone out there? Yes, indeed. Millions of people are hooked up to the Internet in one way or another, and you can send electronic mail (e-mail) to almost any of them. Pretty staggering, huh? Internet's e-mail system gives you a rapid, cheap link to literally millions of other computer users. In fact, e-mail is the only reason most Internet users ever connect.

Like everything else on the Internet, though, e-mail is not as straightforward as it could be. Addressing messages is a pain, and so is having them returned to you because you typed a period in the wrong place. But don't worry; the chapters in this section break e-mail down into bite-sized pieces. You'll learn about addressing messages, using the different mail programs available, and sending computer files as mail messages. And in case you can't find someone's mail address, I'll give you some tips for tracking it down.

Chapter 20

Please Mr. Postman: An Intro to E-Mail

In This Chapter

- ➤ The e-mail advantage
- ➤ Making yourself understood
- ➤ Addressing the envelope
- ➤ Sending mail to another network
- ➤ E-mail etiquette
- ➤ Choosing an e-mail program

Internet's most popular feature is its e-mail system. Few Internet users use even a small fraction of the vast information resources available to them. But most use the Internet as a cheap and convenient way to send messages to friends across town or to colleagues around the world.

E-mail (short for *electronic mail*) is the process by which you send messages across a computer network. Instead of writing a message on paper, placing it in an envelope, and dropping it in a mailbox, you can send the message from your computer across the Internet to any user anywhere. Many different e-mail programs enable you to do this; I'll talk about them in detail in Chapter 21.

Why Use E-Mail?

> **Check This Out...**
> **Nothing's 100 Percent**
> Sometimes messages take hours to get through, and sometimes—though not often—they get lost.

The advantages of using e-mail are obvious. It's cheap—usually cheaper than sending a message by mail and often cheaper than making a phone call. It's fast. Messages are often delivered in seconds. It doesn't take a week or two for your letter to be delivered to France, and you don't have to wait on hold while the receptionist finds the person you need to contact.

> **Check This Out...**
> **Speedy E-Mail Responses**
> The last time I e-mailed my buddy Al Gore, he received the message and responded within 20 seconds. Well, admittedly, *he* didn't respond personally, but he's been busy. His and Bill's Internet mailboxes receive approximately 30,000 messages a month (though some of them are addressed to Chelsea's cat Socks), to which they respond automatically with a polite message that says "Thanks very much, but I've been busy" or something similar. If you have something to say, you can contact Al at vicepresident@whitehouse.gov. If you'd prefer to chat with Bill, try president@whitehouse.gov.

E-mail is also convenient. For example, a friend told me he uses e-mail to contact a colleague in Japan. He doesn't have to worry about time zones, figure out exactly when his Japanese colleague gets up, or find the overlap between an American day and a Japanese day. Nor does he need to worry about explaining what he wants to a Japanese receptionist. He just sends a message over the Internet and reads the reply the next day.

You can also use e-mail to send the same message to several people at a time. You can create mailing groups, which make it possible for you to write one message and then tell your e-mail program to ship it out to everyone in a particular group. Or you can simply write a message, address it to one person, and "CC" (carbon copy) it to other e-mail users.

Two E-Mail Caveats

Of course, e-mail is not the solution to all the world's ills, and it often can't replace a telephone call or a face-to-face meeting. By its very nature, e-mail has some limitations. You should be aware of them.

None of That Fancy Stuff...

Although e-mail can get your message across, the message is a far cry from a word-processing program's output. When you send text messages with Internet e-mail, they're just that: text. In general, no special formatting is allowed (you can't use bold or italic text, for instance). You can enter carriage returns to format paragraphs and lines, but that's about it.

Things are changing quickly, though. Within some systems, you can format e-mail. For example, if an MSN subscriber sends a message to another MSN subscriber, he or she can use bulleted lists, italic or bold text, color, and so on. Some programs for CompuServe also allow e-mail text formatting. Eventually, these features will reach the Internet proper. For now, however, the majority of Internet e-mail is simple ASCII text.

...And They Can't See Your Face

Many people regard e-mail messages as a form of conversation. Sure, you're communicating through written messages, but somehow these messages are less formal than if they were written on paper. So people often write in a very informal manner as if they were chatting to the recipient. The problem with this is that the recipient can't see your face and can't hear the inflections in your voice. Consequently, what the sender regards as a flippant or sarcastic remark may be taken seriously when the recipient reads the message. (Believe me, I've run into this problem a few times!)

This is both an individual and a cultural problem. Some people (and some cultures) are simply more serious than others. What you feel is "obviously" a joke may not be so obvious to the other person.

It's Corny, But If It Works for You...

Over the past few years, e-mail users have developed a number of ways to clarify the meaning of messages. You might see <g> at the end of the line, for example. This means "grin" and is shorthand for saying, "you know, of course, that what I just said was a joke, right?" You may also see :-) in the message. Turn this book sideways, so that the left edge of this page is up and the right edge is down, and you'll see that this is a small smiley face. It means the same as <g>, of course: "that was a joke, okay?"

249

Part 4 ➤ *E-Mail Made Easy*

Emoticons Galore

> **Techno Talk**
>
> **Emoticons** Many people simply call these character faces "smiley faces," but if you'd like to impress your friends with a bit of techno-babble, you can call them by their technical name: *emoticons*. And if you really want to impress your colleagues, get hold of *The Smiley Dictionary* (Seth Godin). It contains hundreds of these things. You wouldn't have thought so many possible combinations would make sense, would you?

The smiley face is just one of many available symbols, though it is by far the most common. You might also see some of the following emoticons, and you may want to use them yourself. Perhaps you can create a few of your own.

:-(	Sadness, disappointment
8-)	Kinda goofy-looking smile, or wearing glasses
:->	A smile
;-)	A wink
*<|:-)	Santa Claus
:-&	Tongue-tied
:-o	A look of shock
:-p	Tongue stuck out
,:-) or 7:^]	Ronald Reagan

You might even try really weird stuff, such as this smiley cow I found in the alt.ascii newsgroup (refer to Chapters 17 and 18 for more about newsgroups). Look at this from a sideways view.

```
]:o_
 ¦o =
 ¦_o=
```

Or you can get really artistic with something like this (don't turn your head sideways for this one).

```
    ;~; ,          .~.
   ._#_.)       [ _#_ ]
   ( @ @        '^. .^'
    ) .(          \./
    ( v )         /q\
     \¦/          \¦/
     (¦)          (¦)
      ~ ~          ~ ~
```

250

Chapter 20 ➤ *Please Mr. Postman: An Intro to E-Mail*

And lots of people put smiley art in their *signature files* so it goes out with every message they send. This is what one such signature looks like.

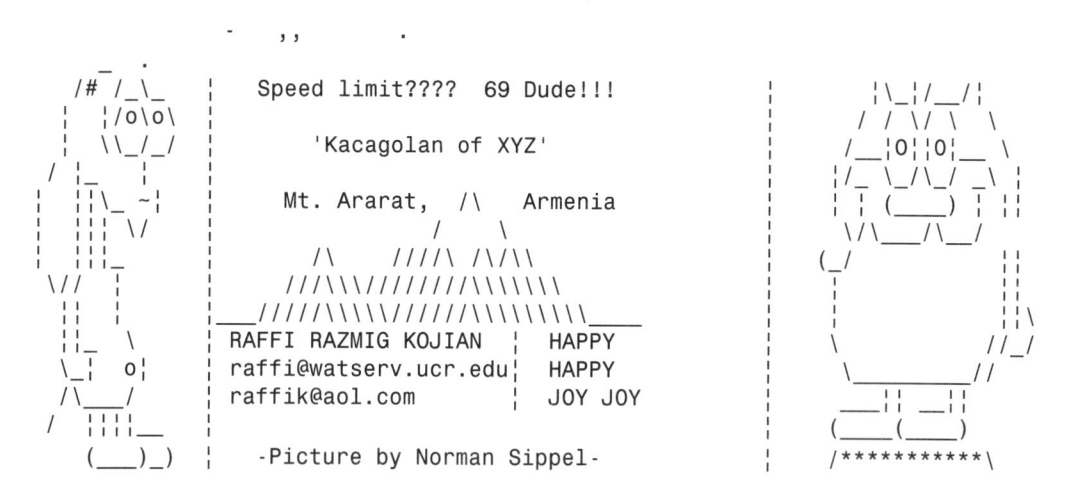

```
        _  .         -  , ,         .
  .    /# /_\_    |  Speed limit????   69 Dude!!!    |   |\_|/__/|
      |  |/o\o\   |                                  |   / / \/ \  \
      |   \\_/_/  |       'Kacagolan of XYZ'         |  /__|0|0|__ \
     /  |_        |                                  | |_  \_/\_/  _\ |
    |   ||\_ ~|   |     Mt. Ararat,  /\   Armenia    |  | |  (___) | ||
    |   ||| \/    |                 /   \            |   \/\__/\_/
    |   ||_       |       /\    ////\ /\/\\          |   (_/    |   ||
    \//    |      |     ///\\\///////\\\\\\          |          |   ||
     ||    |      |___///////\\\\\\//////\\\\\\\\___ |          |   ||\
     ||_   \      | RAFFI RAZMIG KOJIAN  |  HAPPY    |   \            //_/
     \_|   o|     | raffi@watserv.ucr.edu|  HAPPY    |    _____//
     /\_  /       | raffik@aol.com       |  JOY JOY  |     __||_ _||__
    /   ||||_     |                                  |    (___(___)
    (___)_)       |   -Picture by Norman Sippel-     |   /**********\
```

> **Check This Out...**
>
> ### Signatures
>
> Signature files provide a convenient way for e-mail users to add information to the bottom of every message. Many users put their full name and company name, telephone number, address, and so on in the signature file. Some include promotional information for their business or some kind of cutesy saying or quotation.
>
> Many e-mail programs have a way of automatically adding the contents of a signature file to every message that you send. See your program's documentation for more information. (Microsoft Exchange, Windows 95's built-in e-mail program, currently has no automatic signature feature.)

Perhaps this sort of "ASCII art" will die out soon. Many of the newer e-mail programs let you pick the font that is used for message text. ASCII art only works with non-proportional typefaces (the ones in which each letter takes up the same amount of space). If you pick a proportional typeface, the art will no longer look correct; it turns into a jumble of text.

251

Message Shorthand

There are a couple of other ways people try to liven up their messages. One is to use obscure abbreviations, such as the following:

BTW	By the way
FWIW	For what it's worth
FYI	For your information
IMHO	In my humble opinion
IMO	In my opinion
LOL	Laughing out loud (used as an aside to show your disbelief)
OTF	On the floor (laughing) (used as an aside)
PMFBI	Pardon me for butting in
PMFJI	Pardon me for jumping in
RTFM	Read the &*^%# manual
ROTFL or ROFL	Rolling on the floor laughing (used as an aside)
TIA	Thanks in advance
YMMV	Your mileage may vary

The real benefit of using these abbreviations is that they confuse the average neophyte, and they make people feel like they have their own "secret code." They certainly don't save any money; e-mail is so cheap that cutting a message by 15 or 20 characters won't have much affect on the "bottom line" cost.

You'll also see different ways to stress particular words (you can't use bold and italic, remember). You can emphasize a word by using underscores (_now!_) or, perhaps less frequently, with asterisks (*now!*).

Now, Where's That Address?

You might imagine that addressing a message would be simple. However, because the Internet is a conglomeration of so many different networks and provides access to so many different e-mail systems, addressing a message may not be straightforward. Let's take a quick look at a few rules.

Remember that your Internet address is made up of two parts: your login name and your domain name. These two parts are separated by an @ sign. The text to the left of the sign is your login name, and the text to the right is your domain name. Take, for instance, pkent@lab-press.com. The first part, pkent, is the login name, and the second part, lab-press.com, is the domain name. The domain name describes where you can be found on the network; you are given that name when you first open an account. (Chapter 5 covers this in detail, so if you skipped that chapter you might want to backtrack for a moment.) The Internet looks up your domain name, finds the associated number (the address of the computer that is handling your mail), and uses the number to direct your message to the correct place.

> **DNS**
>
> The Internet uses the Domain Name System (DNS) to look up names. The local server (your service provider's e-mail system) starts by contacting a *root server*, a computer that knows the number associated with the highest-level domain in your domain name. For instance, if you are sending a message to joebloe@apotpeel.com, the root server tells your local server which computer is responsible for the .com domain. The local server then contacts the .com computer and asks where apotpeel is. Then, with the complete domain number it needs, the local server uses that information to direct the message to the correct computer and sends it off.

When you send a message through the Internet, all the system initially cares about is the name of the computer (the domain) that collects mail for the person you are trying to reach. (It's kind of like the post office's mail-sorting machines, which look only at ZIP codes.) So if you send a message to joebloe@thiscompany.com, the e-mail system looks only at thiscompany.com. Even if the first part of the address is wrong (if, for example, the login name is really "joblow" and not "joebloe"), the message still goes to the correct domain. However, when the domain checks the login name and finds that it doesn't match any login name in that domain, the message is sent back to you.

E-Mailing to and from CompuServe, AOL, MSN, and More

All the major online services now have Internet connections. In fact they've had Internet e-mail *gateways* for several years. That means that a subscriber to, say, CompuServe or America Online can send e-mail out across the Internet to any other Internet user, and anyone on the Internet can send e-mail into the CompuServe and America Online systems.

To send a message to a member of an online service via the Internet, all you need is the user's online service ID or subscriber name, and the online service's Internet domain name. For instance, let's look at how to send e-mail to someone connected to CompuServe. You'll need the ID (identification number) of the person to whom you want to send the message. A CompuServe ID usually consists of a five-digit number, followed by a comma, followed by two or more digits, such as 71601,1266. However, because you can't put a comma in an Internet address, you have to replace the comma with a period. Then you place the @ sign after the number, and add the CompuServe Internet domain name: compuserve.com. So to send a message to the person who has the CompuServe ID 71601,1266, you end up with the address in the format 71601.1266@compuserve.com.

To send a message from CompuServe to your Internet account, a user would precede your Internet address with **INTERNET:**. For instance, to send a message from CompuServe to joebloe@thiscompany.com, a CompuServe user would enter the following address:

    INTERNET:joebloe@thiscompany.com

Note that with some CompuServe e-mail programs (and there are several to choose from), you don't have to bother with the INTERNET: bit. When the program sees the @ sign, it realizes the address is an Internet address, and it adds the INTERNET: bit for you.

Even More E-Mail Links

You can send messages to a number of other e-mail systems (such as BITNET, Fidonet, Sprintmail, MCImail, and UUCP) through the Internet. Follow these guidelines:

- **Prodigy**   To send a message to a Prodigy information service user, add **@prodigy.com** to the end of the user's Prodigy address.

- **America Online**   To send a message to an America Online information service user, add **@aol.com** to the end of the America Online user's normal address.

- **GEnie**   To send a message to a GEnie information service user, format the address like this: *recipient*__@genie.geis.com__.

- **The Microsoft Network**   To send a message to an MSN user, simply add **@msn.com** to the end of the person's MSN Member ID.

- **BITNET**   BITNET addresses look very similar to Internet addresses: they are in the form *name@host*. You then add **bitnet** to the end. For example, if the address is something like jblow@golden, try **jblow@golden.bitnet**. If that doesn't work, ask your system administrator or service provider for an Internet-BITNET gateway name (a *gateway*, in this context, is a computer that links one network to another). Replace the @ with %, throw away the .bitnet, and add an @ followed by the name of the

Internet-BITNET gateway. For instance, if you were using the cunyvm.cuny.edu gateway, the BITNET address would end up looking like this:

jblow%golden@cunyvm.cuny.edu

➤ **Fidonet**   Fidonet addresses look something like this: Joe Blow 1:6/1.2. To send to Fidonet via Internet, replace the space between the names with a period, replace the space between the last name and first number with an @ (Joe.Blow@1:6/1.2), and then add the letters **p**, **f**, **n**, and **z** in front of the numbers (Joe.Blow@p1:f6/n1.z2). Replace the colon and backslash with periods and add **.fidonet.org**. The final address would be **Joe.Blow@p1.f6.n1.z2.fidonet.org**. (Is this fun, or what?)

> **Check This Out...**
>
> **BITNET, Fidonet, UUNET**
> These are not online services. They are large networks connected to the Internet.

However, the message still might not go through. If it doesn't, replace the @ with % and add **@zeus.ieee.org** at the end (**Joe.Blow%p1.f6.n1.z2.fidonet.org@zeus.ieee.org**).

➤ **MCImail**   Sending messages to MCImail is similar to sending messages to CompuServe. Simply add **@mcimail.com** to the end of an MCImail address. MCImail addresses can be numbers (1111111@mcimail.com) or names (joe_blow@mcimail.com).

➤ **Sprintmail**   If you are given a Sprintmail address, you will probably get two parts: a name and an organization (such as Joe Blow/APOTPEEL). You drop those two items into the following address, using a period between the first and last name:

/PN=Joe.Blow/O=APOTPEEL/ADMD=TELEMAIL/C=US/@sprint.com

➤ **UUNET**   Addresses for UUNET look like Internet addresses: joebloe@golden.uucp. Remove the .uucp, replace the @ with %, and put an @ at the end (joebloe%golden@). Ask your system administrator or service provider for a UUNET-Internet gateway, and add it to the end, which makes the address **joebloe%golden@uu.psi.com**.

You may be given a UUNET path that looks like this:

...!uunet!*host*!*name*

This isn't really an address; instead it shows the route a message takes to reach its destination. When the message reaches uunet, it sends the message on to *host*, which sends it on to the person. Therefore, you have to reverse this: ***name*%*host*@*gateway***.

No, it's not just your imagination. All these different mailing-label schemes really are a royal pain.

255

And More!

The networks I have already mentioned aren't the only ones, they're just the most common. Here are a few more you may run into:

- GEONET (GeoNet Mailbox Systems)
- NASAMAIL
- ENVOY (Telecom Canada)
- BIX (Byte Information eXchange; *Byte* magazine)
- ATT (AT&T)
- MFNET (Magnetic Fusion Energy Network)

Well, you *may* run into these, but you probably *won't*. So I'm not going to describe them all. However, if you do have to send e-mail to one of these systems—and if you can't get the intended recipient to provide a complete and correct e-mail address—get hold of the file MAILGUIDE.TXT. You can find this at ftp.mcp.com (the Macmillan Publishing Internet FTP site) or at the ftp.csd.uwm.edu/pub FTP site by looking for the document internetwork-mail-guide. See Chapter 12 for information on how to use FTP.

> **Check This Out...**
>
> ### Don't Lose Those Addresses!
>
> If someone gives you an e-mail address, don't lose it! Add to your e-mail program's address book all those e-mail addresses you have noted on business cards, letters, or e-mail you receive. Losing an Internet e-mail address is not like losing a telephone number. If you lose a phone number, you can look in the phone book or call information; getting an e-mail address can be much more difficult. I'll discuss some of your alternatives in Chapter 23, but none are foolproof. So if you ever come across an address you think you might need, save it!

Internet Etiquette

There's an etiquette to the Internet (sometimes called *Internetiquette* or just *netiquette*). When you're working with Internet e-mail, newsgroups, and mailing lists (which I covered in Chapters 17 through 19), follow these rules to avoid upsetting people and embarrassing yourself.

Don't write something you will regret later. There have been lawsuits based on the contents of electronic messages, so consider what you are writing and whether you would want it to be read by someone other than the recipient. For example, you never know whether the recipient might forward a message or print it out and pass it around, or if someone else might read it over the recipient's shoulder. And remember, you don't have to use the Internet—there's always the telephone. (Oliver North has already learned *his* lesson!)

Consider the tone of your message. Often, things that are intended to be flippant come off as arrogant, or things intended to be funny come off as sarcastic. When you write, think about how the recipient might interpret your words.

Give the sender the benefit of the doubt. If you receive a message that sounds arrogant or sarcastic, remember that the sender may be trying to be flippant or funny! If you are not sure what a person is saying, ask him or her to explain.

TURN YOUR CAPS LOCK KEY OFF. MESSAGES THAT ARE ALL CAPS ARE DIFFICULT TO READ—AND CAN BE CONSIDERED THE WRITTEN EQUIVALENT OF SHOUTING. YOU ARE NOT USING A TELEX MACHINE, SO WRITE LIKE A NORMAL HUMAN BEING.

Read before you send. This gives you a chance to fix embarrassing spelling and grammatical errors, or to reconsider what you've just said.

Be nice. Hey, there's no need for vulgarity or rudeness (except in certain newsgroups, where it seems to be a requirement for entrance). However, you can get away with a lot more on the Internet than you can on CompuServe, America Online, Prodigy, or any other commercial service, where moderators may reprimand users of bad language.

Which Program Will You Use to Send Mail?

Now we come to the big choice: which e-mail program are you going to use? I'm in a quandary, here. You see, there's a good chance that when you installed Windows 95 you installed something called *Microsoft Exchange*. If you are an MSN member, you definitely have this program. Even if you aren't, you may have installed Exchange because you wanted to use Windows 95's fax program (which is built into Exchange) or because your company wants you to use Exchange for e-mail on your company network.

However, I'm really no fan of Exchange. Its main problem is that it is slow. It can also be rather complicated to set up correctly, perhaps because it's intended to be a communications center from which you send and receive faxes and to which comes all your e-mail from various sources (Internet e-mail, CompuServe e-mail, Microsoft Mail e-mail, Microsoft Network e-mail, and more). I don't use Exchange for my Internet e-mail. Instead, I use a free program called Eudora, which is one of the most popular Internet e-mail programs around. It's much faster and easier to use than Exchange is.

> **Check This Out...**
>
> **Exchange Has Its Advantages**
>
> Don't misunderstand me—I'm not saying you *shouldn't* use Exchange. In fact it has some nice features. It's just that if all you want to do is send and receive Internet e-mail, you can find other programs that are easier to use. I suggest you start by working with Exchange. Later, if you really feel the need, investigate other programs, such as Eudora.

In the next two chapters, you'll learn more about Exchange and Eudora. First I'll explain Exchange because so many readers are likely to be using it. Then I'll look at Eudora—though not in as much detail—because it's probably the first choice for someone who wants something better than Exchange but doesn't want to pay. Move on to Chapter 21 to find out how to get started with Exchange.

The Least You Need to Know

- E-mail can be a quick and inexpensive way to keep in touch with friends and colleagues all over the world.

- <g> means "grin." So does :-). These are called *smileys* or *emoticons*. You can use dozens of emoticons in your e-mail messages. But don't expect everyone to understand them all.

- Addressing most e-mail messages is not a problem. To send e-mail to a member of an online service, you take the person's ID or login name, add an @ sign, and then add the online service's domain name (for instance, PeterKent@msn.com).

- If you do run into problems addressing messages, you can find detailed information in the MAILGUID.TXT file.

- Microsoft Exchange is a communications program that comes with Windows 95. Eudora is a free e-mail program you can download from the Internet.

Chapter 21

Using Microsoft Exchange

In This Chapter

- ➤ Setting up Internet e-mail on Exchange
- ➤ Modifying your address book
- ➤ Password-protecting your Personal Folders
- ➤ Starting Exchange
- ➤ Customizing Exchange

We're going to look at Microsoft Exchange as an example e-mail program. Not everyone can use Exchange, though. If you are working through an online service—such as America Online, Prodigy, or CompuServe—you may not be able to use anything but a program specifically designed for that online service. Because these online services had e-mail systems long before they had Internet access, their e-mail systems are set up differently than true Internet e-mail systems are. Yes, they can send and receive Internet e-mail; but to do so, they use special software and hardware called e-mail *gateways* that interface between the Internet's e-mail system and the online service's system.

Part 4 ➤ *E-Mail Made Easy*

Microsoft Exchange and Internet e-mail programs such as Eudora were designed for true Internet e-mail systems, the systems used by true Internet service providers and not the major online services. The following instructions describe how to set up Microsoft Exchange for use with an Internet mail server. If you are not sure whether you can use Exchange with your Internet service, check with your service provider. (If you are not with a major online service, you probably can.)

Microsoft Exchange has a lot of features, many of which are not relevant to Internet e-mail. Exchange is a multipurpose communications system that enables you to fax, send Internet e-mail, use MSN e-mail, and so on. So I won't explain all of its features (features that are related to faxes and MSN e-mail, for instance). After all, it's the Internet you want to learn about, right? Well then, let's get started.

Setting Up Exchange

The first thing you should do is make sure that you have Exchange set up. If you are using MSN, you do—Exchange is installed automatically for you. In fact, the following information about setting up Exchange does not apply to you because I'm going to describe how to add the Internet Mail service. MSN members don't use Exchange's Internet Mail service; they use its Microsoft Network Online service e-mail system (they can address e-mail to Internet users, and MSN will pass the mail on to the Internet e-mail "gateway"). So you can just skip the following stuff and proceed to the section "Getting Personal with Your Folders."

If you are not using MSN, minimize all your programs and take a quick look at the desktop. If you see an Inbox icon, Exchange is installed. (Perhaps you installed it when you installed Windows 95, or maybe your computer vendor did it for you.)

What if the Inbox icon isn't there? Select **Start**, **Settings**, and **Control Panel**. Double-click on the **Add-Remove Programs** icon and click on the **Windows Setup** tab. Then click on the **Microsoft Exchange** entry in the list box and click **OK**.

A Quick Word About Profiles

Exchange has at least one *profile*. A profile is a set of instructions that tells Exchange which *information services* you want to work with. The information services are the messaging systems—Internet Mail, MSN, Fax, CompuServe, MS Mail, and so on.

You'll probably have only one profile, the MS Exchange Settings profile, which was set up for you automatically when you installed Exchange. You can set up several profiles if you want. (If you want to know more about profiles, check your Windows 95 documentation.) However, most users will work with a single profile quite comfortably.

Chapter 21 ➤ *Using Microsoft Exchange*

Sharing Your Computer?

If you share your computer with other users, you'll probably want to set up your own personal Microsoft Exchange profile. You can set up separate Windows 95 accounts for each user, and a separate e-mail profile for each account. Then each person logs in to Windows 95 using a different password. I'll explain later in this chapter how to password-protect your own e-mail (via the Personal Folders dialog box), but check with your system administrator or check your Windows 95 documentation for information about setting up separate profiles.

So What Have I Got?

To see which services have been installed, right-click on the **Inbox** icon on your desktop and select **Properties**. You'll see the MS Exchange Settings Properties dialog box—the large dialog box in the following figure. In the example, you can see that I have four services set up: Microsoft Fax (the program I use to send and receive faxes), Personal Address Book (the file used to keep address book entries), Personal Folders (the file used to save e-mail messages), and the Microsoft Network Online Service (MSN e-mail). In the dialog box on your screen, you may see other services, too, depending on how Exchange is set up on your computer. The example *doesn't* show Internet Mail. To add Internet Mail, click on the **Add** button, and you'll see the Add Service to Profile dialog box, also shown in the following figure.

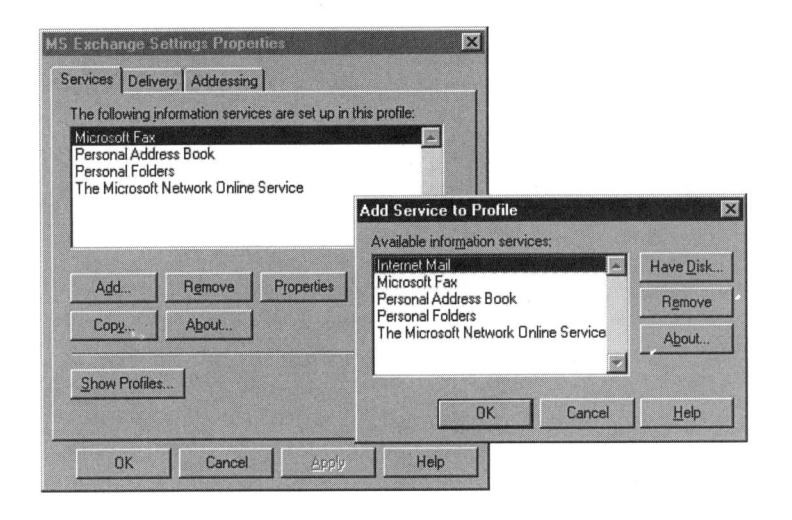

Right-click on the Inbox and choose Properties to see your Exchange services.

Part 4 ➤ *E-Mail Made Easy*

> **Check This Out...**
>
> **Internet Mail**
>
> The Internet Mail service is installed by the Internet Setup Wizard when you choose to install Internet services for a service provider other than MSN. If you already have the Internet Mail service installed, you may want to make sure that it has been installed correctly. Click on the entry in the list box and click on the **Properties** button. Then work through the rest of this section to set the Internet Mail properties.

Click **Internet Mail** in the Add Service to Profile dialog box and click **OK**. The Internet Mail dialog box appears (see the next figure). Enter your basic e-mail information (which is probably all familiar to you by now). One thing you may be unsure of is your Internet mail server's host name; ask your service provider what you should put there.

Enter your basic e-mail information.

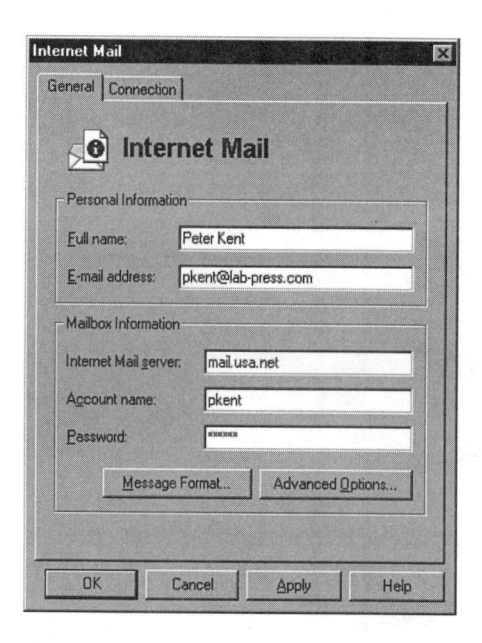

Notice the Message Format and Advanced Options buttons. Only use the Advanced Options button if your service provider gives you a different mail server address for *outgoing* e-mail; if both outgoing and incoming e-mail go through the same server (they usually do), you can ignore this button. The Message Format button enables you to specify whether you want to use MIME or UUENCODE as the default for file transfer. Oops, I'd better explain that.

The Internet has two types of e-mail file transfers. *UUENCODE* is a system that converts binary files—spreadsheet and word processing files, pictures, sounds, whatever—into ASCII text before transmitting the file (I covered UUENCODING in Chapter 18). In some e-mail systems, you have to convert the file yourself and then copy the ASCII text into the body of the message. Other e-mail systems, such as Exchange, do this for you: you tell the program which file you want to send, and it encodes it and places it in the message.

The other form of file transfer is *MIME*, Multipurpose Internet Mail Extension. This system was devised to make file transfers a more fully integrated part of the e-mail system. While UUENCODING began as a sort of *kludge*, a way to "trick" an ASCII-based e-mail system into carrying binary files, MIME was an attempt to turn the e-mail system into a truly "multi-media" mail system. It still converts binary files to ASCII, but it's more fully integrated into the e-mail system. For instance, while the text representing UUENCODED files is fully visible within the e-mail message, a MIME-enabled e-mail program adds the ASCII text after you have finished with the message (you won't see the text representing the file). And when a MIME-enabled program *receives* a message with an attached file, it removes the ASCII text representing the file before you see the message text.

> **Kludge** The word *kludge* is often used in the computer business to refer to a messy fix—something that works but is not very "pretty" or elegant.

Anyway, Exchange allows you to choose which method you want to use. Which should you pick? Whichever most of your correspondents use. If most of the people you'll be sending files to work with MIME, pick that. Or forget it for now, it doesn't matter much; you can return and change it later. And even if you pick one method, you can still send specific files using the other method if you need to.

The Connection Options

Now click on the **Connection** tab at the top of the Internet Mail dialog box, and you see the information in the following dialog box. If you are connecting to the Internet via your company's network, make sure the **Connect using the network** option button is selected. If you are connecting across the telephone lines, make sure the **Connect using the modem** option button is selected. Also, if you are using your modem, make sure that the correct service provider is selected in the Dial using the following connection drop-down list box. This contains a list of the service providers for which you have a Dial-Up Networking connection (see Chapters 7 and 8 for more information).

263

You can ignore the three buttons immediately below the drop-down list box. You use the Add Entry and Edit Entry buttons to create a new Dial-Up Networking connection or to edit the selected one. The Login As button allows you to enter login information—but you've already entered this information (when you created your Dial-Up Networking connection).

Select the Dial-Up Networking connection you are using.

Click here to see the list of providers.

> **Message Headers**
> A message header is the identifying information: the subject, whom the message is from, the date it was sent, and how big it is. This is usually enough information for you to decide whether you want to take the time to download the entire message.

Next, you specify how you're going to manage your e-mail. If you click the **Work off-line and use Remote Mail** check box, each time Exchange checks to see if you have e-mail waiting for you, it uses the Remote Mail program to grab just the message headers, not the entire messages; that way you can decide which messages you want to transfer before you do so. You'll learn more about Remote Mail in Chapter 22.

If you are *not* using Remote Mail, you can click on the **Schedule** button to tell Exchange how often you want to automatically check for e-mail. (If you are using a modem, Exchange automatically dials into your service provider, grabs your e-mail, and logs off; you don't even have to click on the Connect button to start the connection.)

Unfortunately, this all means there are only two options:

➤ You can work offline using Remote Mail. Remote Mail has the advantage of allowing you to view message headers only before you decide whether to transfer mail. But you won't be able to schedule automatic checks.

➤ You can forget about Remote Mail and use the main Inbox window, which is quicker and more convenient—but you'll always get the full messages (you won't get a chance to review the headers first). You have to schedule automatic e-mail checks if you use this method. (You can schedule up to 9,999 minutes, though.)

> **Open Exchange**
> Exchange can carry out these automatic checks only if you have started the program.

Finally, there's the Log File button. Use this button to tell Exchange to keep a record of each mail session (which is handy for troubleshooting if you have problems).

Getting Personal with Your Folders

Your e-mail messages will be stored in something called the *Personal Folders*. These are a series of "folders" inside the MAILBOX.PST file in the \Exchange\ directory on your hard disk. All of your incoming messages and faxes are stored in the Personal Folder's *Inbox* folder, outgoing messages go into the *Outbox*, and so on (as you'll see in Chapter 22).

You can modify a few things related to the Personal Folders. In the **Services** tab of the MS Exchange Settings Properties dialog box, select the **Personal Folders** entry and click the **Properties** button. Exchange displays the Personal Folders dialog box shown in the following figure. At the top of this box is the Path text box, which shows you where the MAILBOX.PST file is stored. Below that, the Name text box lets you rename the Personal Folders (you might call them *My Stuff*, *My Messages*, or whatever you want).

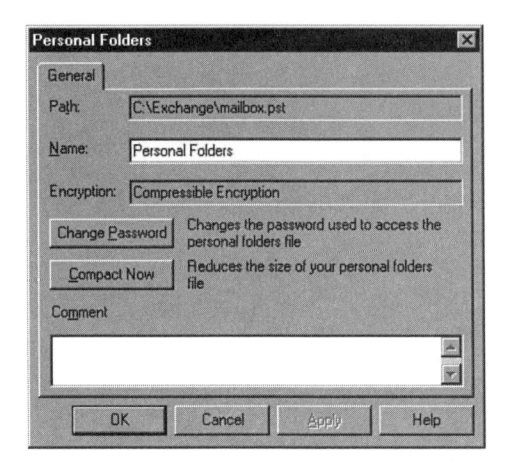

The Personal Folders dialog box enables you to rename your message folders and password-protect your messages.

Part 4 ➤ *E-Mail Made Easy*

The next box, Encryption, shows that the MAILBOX.PST file is encrypted (using Compressible Encryption) so that no one can open and read it in another application. Currently, you can't change this setting.

If you'd like to password-protect your messages—so that only you can open the MAILBOX.PST file—click on the **Change Password** button. You see a dialog box that asks for your Old Password (leave it blank if you don't already have a password) and your New Password. Enter your new password, and then type it again in the Verify Password box (to make sure you typed it correctly the first time).

The Save this password in your password list check box enables you to control how much password protection Exchange uses. If you leave this box deselected, each time you open Microsoft Exchange or each time you try to view the Personal Folders properties, you'll have to enter the password. If you select this check box, you *won't* have to enter the password each time because Microsoft Exchange will assume that if you've already logged in to Windows 95 you should have access to the Personal Folders.

Of course, if you don't use a password to log in to Windows 95, you effectively end up with no password protection at all. (To add a password to Windows 95 itself, you use the Passwords icon in the Control Panel. Ask your system administrator or see your Windows 95 documentation for more information.) For now, you should understand that if someone else logs on to your computer using a different account name and password, Microsoft Exchange won't let him or her into your Personal Folders, even if you select the Save this password in your password list check box. When you finish creating a password, choose **OK**.

> **Check This Out...**
> **Removing a Password** To remove a password, enter your current password into the Old Password box, leave the other boxes blank, and choose **OK**.

Getting back to the Personal Folders dialog box, you have two more options: the Compact Now button and the Comment text box. The MAILBOX.PST file is a database file. When you remove entries from a database—in this case, when you delete messages—the database doesn't shrink. Therefore, you have to compact the database later to remove the "blank" spaces left by the messages. That's what this button enables you to do. And as for the Comment text box, you use it for—you guessed it—comments.

Address Book Options

You can modify a few things related to your address book. On the Services tab of the MS Exchange Settings Properties dialog box, click the **Personal Address Book** entry and click the **Properties** button. You'll see the Personal Address Book dialog box, an example of which you can see in the following figure.

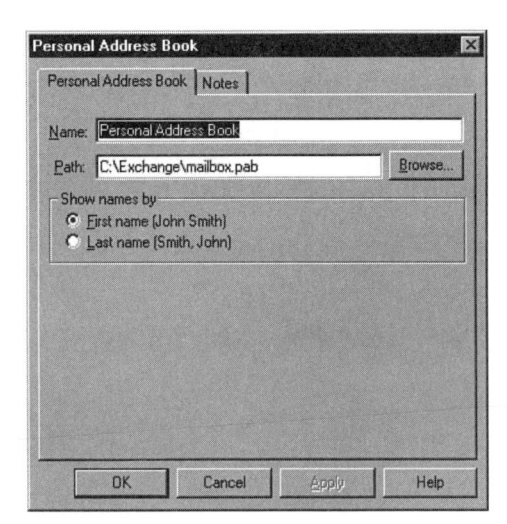

You can change your address book's name, and even create several books.

At the top of this box is the Name text box. You can change the name of your address book, if you want. In the Address Book program, the new name appears in a drop-down list box from which you can select your Personal Address Book.

The Path text box shows you which file contains your address book. By default, this is the MAILBOX.PAB file in your \Exchange\ directory. You can create several address books, if you want. Simply replace the MAILBOX.PAB file name with another .PAB file name—SMITH.PAB, JONES.PAB, or whatever. Then any changes you make will be saved in the new .PAB file.

You use the Show names by options to specify whether you want Exchange to sort and display entries in your address book by first name or by last name. Finally, you can click the **Notes** tab to enter information about the address book, which might be useful if you decide to create several of them; you might have one address book for business and one for personal use, for instance.

That's about all you can set up *outside* Exchange. So let's go inside and take a look.

> **Check This Out...**
>
> **A More Direct Route** As you'll see in Chapter 22, you can also access many of the options you've looked at in this chapter directly from Microsoft Exchange itself, so you can quickly change between address books.

Taking a Look Inside Exchange

Open up Exchange to see what other options you can play with. To open it, double-click on the **Inbox** icon on your desktop or select **Start**, **Programs**, **Microsoft Exchange**. If you did not select the Work off-line and use Remote Mail check box—in other words, if you have scheduled Exchange to grab your e-mail regularly—the program starts, immediately logs on, grabs your e-mail for you, and then logs off. (It will check again according to the schedule you set. For example, if you entered 20, it will check for e-mail again in 20 minutes. If you entered 9999, it will check again in almost 167 hours. Entering this number is a handy way to turn off the automatic e-mail check for most people.)

I'm not going to explain everything you can see in the Exchange window when you open it; I'll get to that in Chapter 22. For now, you're just going to finish setting up the options. First open the **Tools** menu and select **Services**. The Services dialog box appears, listing the services that have been set up for Exchange. You can modify settings for these services as you've already seen. (This is much the same as the MS Exchange Settings Properties dialog box you looked at earlier.)

Then try the **Tools**, **Options** command. This time you see the Options dialog box, which has several tabs. I'm not going to describe all of these, just the ones that directly affect your e-mail (see your Windows 95 documentation for more information).

The General Options

When you first open the Options dialog box, you see the General tab, which is shown in the following figure. It contains options that let you define what Microsoft Exchange does when you receive messages, delete messages, and so on. Let's look at these options in detail:

> **When New Mail Arrives** The following three check boxes enable you to tell Microsoft Exchange what to do when a message arrives in the Inbox.
>
>> **Play a sound** If you select this, Microsoft Exchange will play the New Mail Notification sound defined in the Control Panel's Sounds Properties dialog box.
>>
>> **Briefly change the pointer** If you select this, your mouse pointer will change to an envelope icon for a few moments when new mail arrives.
>>
>> **Display a notification message** If you select this, a message box opens when you receive e-mail. This box lets you immediately open the first message, without going to your Inbox first.

Chapter 21 ➤ Using Microsoft Exchange

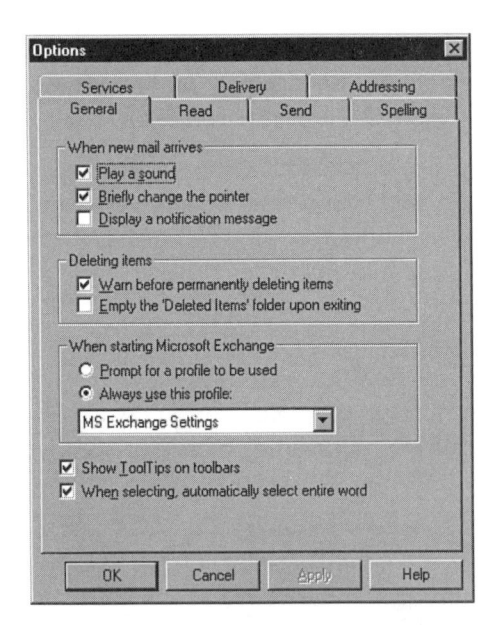

The Options dialog box lets you set up more Microsoft Exchange options.

Deleting items The next two items tell Microsoft Exchange how to handle deleted messages and folders.

> **Warn before permanently deleting items** If you select this, you'll see a warning message before items are deleted from the Deleted Items folder.
>
> **Empty the 'Deleted Items' folder upon exiting** If this is selected when you close Microsoft Exchange, all the messages and folders in the 'Deleted Items' folder will be permanently deleted.

When starting Microsoft Exchange The following two option buttons define what Microsoft Exchange should do when you start the program.

> **Prompt for a profile to be used** This tells Microsoft Exchange to ask you which profile you want to use for the current session.
>
> **Always use this profile** This tells Microsoft Exchange which profile to use automatically each time it opens, so you won't be prompted to select a profile. If you have only one Exchange profile, select this option button.

269

Show ToolTips on toolbars ToolTips are the little boxes that appear when you hold the mouse pointer over a toolbar button. (They display the button's name.) Deselect this check box to turn the feature off.

When selecting, automatically select entire word This tells Microsoft Exchange how you want to select a word in the message. If you choose this option, Microsoft Exchange will use a word-processing feature that automatically selects entire words with minimal mouse movement.

The Read Options

Click the **Read** tab in the Options dialog box, and you see the options that define how Exchange operates while you are reading messages (see the following figure).

You can customize the way Exchange works when you are reading messages.

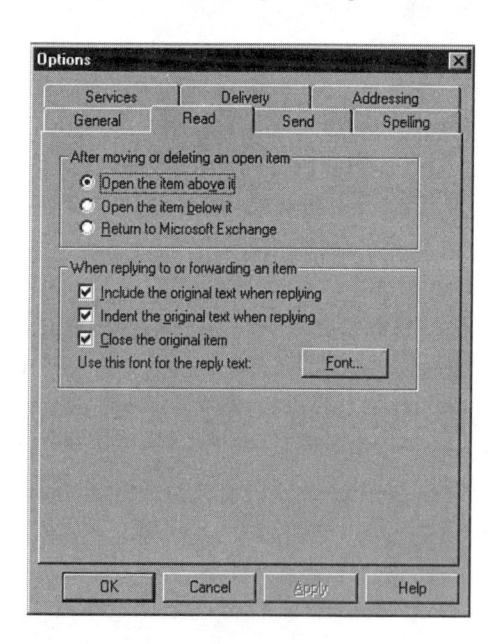

After moving or deleting an open item The three items in this area define what happens when you move or delete a message you are viewing.

  Open the item above it Tells Exchange to display the message immediately above the one you just moved or deleted.

  Open the item below it Tells Exchange to display the next message in the list.

  Return to Microsoft Exchange Tells Exchange to close the message window (you'll be returned to the Microsoft Exchange window).

When replying to or forwarding an item The rest of the options define how to handle message text when replying to or forwarding a message.

> **Include the original text when replying** If you select this, all the text in the original message will be placed into the new message. This is known as *quoting*.
>
> **Indent the original text when replying** Select this if you want to indent the "quoted" message text so that it is offset and more easily identifiable.
>
> **Close the original item** If you select this, the original message is closed when you reply to it or forward it.
>
> **Use this font for the reply text:** By default, when you reply to a message or forward it, the message that you type is blue. That's so that the recipient can quickly tell the difference between the quoted text and the text you add. However, this works only for Microsoft Network, not for Internet e-mail. (Actually, the text will appear blue when you create the message either way, but the color will be removed when the message is sent out across the Internet.)

The Send Options

The Send options enable you to define what Microsoft Exchange should do when you are sending messages. Click the **Send** tab to see the options shown in the following figure.

Most of the options in this dialog box have no effect on your Internet e-mail. You can modify the font you use in your new messages. MSN, for instance, allows you to send messages with different colors and fonts. However, no matter what font you use to create the message, the text becomes plain ASCII text when it's sent across the Internet. How it appears when the recipient reads it depends on how he has set up his own mail program.

If you are sending Microsoft Network e-mail, you can also request a receipt so that you get an automatic message back when the addressee gets your message. However, these settings won't work for Internet e-mail. Nor will the sensitivity and importance settings work; again, these are MSN features, and have no effect on Internet e-mail.

The only option in this area that affects your Internet e-mail is the check box labeled Save a copy of the item in the 'Sent Items' folder. If this check box is selected, by default a copy of each outgoing message (including new messages, replies, and forwarded messages) will be placed in the 'Sent Items' folder so you can refer to it later if you need to. Deselect this check box if you don't want to save a copy of all outgoing messages.

Part 4 ➤ *E-Mail Made Easy*

The Send options, most of which do not relate to Internet e-mail.

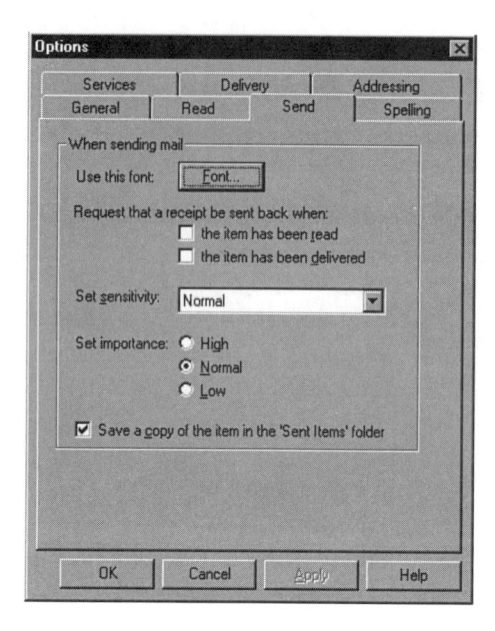

That's about it for now. You've finished setting up Microsoft Exchange. Click the **OK** button, and you're ready to get started. And you'll do just that in the next chapter.

The Least You Need to Know

- ➤ If you are using MSN, you don't need to add the Internet Mail service to Exchange. You'll send Internet e-mail "through" MSN.

- ➤ Right-click on the **Inbox** desktop icon and select **Properties** to add or modify the Internet Mail service.

- ➤ You can use Remote Mail if you want to see message headers before you decide to download your e-mail. If you don't use Remote Mail, though, you can schedule automatic mail transfers.

- ➤ Automatic mail transfers work only if you leave the Exchange program running.

- ➤ You can password-protect your Personal Folders so other people can't read your messages.

- ➤ Open Exchange and select **Tools**, **Options** to define exactly how Exchange operates when you are reading or sending messages.

272

Chapter 22

Working with E-Mail

In This Chapter

- ➤ Sending e-mail
- ➤ Attaching computer files to e-mail messages
- ➤ Working in the Exchange window
- ➤ Retrieving messages using Remote Mail
- ➤ Reading and managing messages
- ➤ If you don't like Exchange, use Eudora

If you've read Chapter 21, you should be ready to send and receive mail. Before you get started, though, I'll make a few background comments. First, if you are an MSN member, remember that you will be sending your Internet e-mail using The Microsoft Network's online service installed in Exchange. Your Internet-bound e-mail will go to the MSN e-mail system, which will recognize the message as an Internet message and will send it to the Internet "gateway." Second, note that Exchange has lots of features that work well with MSN but do not work well with Internet e-mail. For example, in Exchange you can use different fonts and colors, or include pictures. I'm not going to cover any of that, though, because you can't use those features when you send e-mail to non-MSN members (that is, in e-mail going out across the Internet).

Part 4 ➤ *E-Mail Made Easy*

And third, if you have Internet access through a major online service, you will probably have to use a program designed for that service to use Internet e-mail—and you probably won't be able to use Microsoft Exchange. (There are exceptions, however, such as a special add-on to Exchange that allows it to send and receive e-mail via CompuServe.) See your online service program documentation for more on working with e-mail.

In this chapter, you'll start by learning how to send e-mail. You can send a few messages to yourself as a test if you want. You looked at how to open Microsoft Exchange in the last chapter. Therefore, I'll assume that Exchange is open and we can get started.

MSN E-Mail

If you are an MSN member, you have loads of ways to open Exchange (I counted about eight different ones). You can click the **E-MAIL** bar in MSN Central, for instance, or you can click on the **Yes** button in the message box that appears and tells you that you have e-mail waiting.

From Me to You—Sending a Message

You'll begin by sending a message. Open the New Message window by clicking the **New Message** toolbar button or by selecting **Compose**, **New Message**. You'll see the New Message window, shown in the following figure. (Actually this figure is not exactly what you'll see when you first open the window; I selected View, Bcc Box to display the Bcc button and text box. I'll explain what these do in a moment.)

The New Message window after I selected View, Bcc Box.

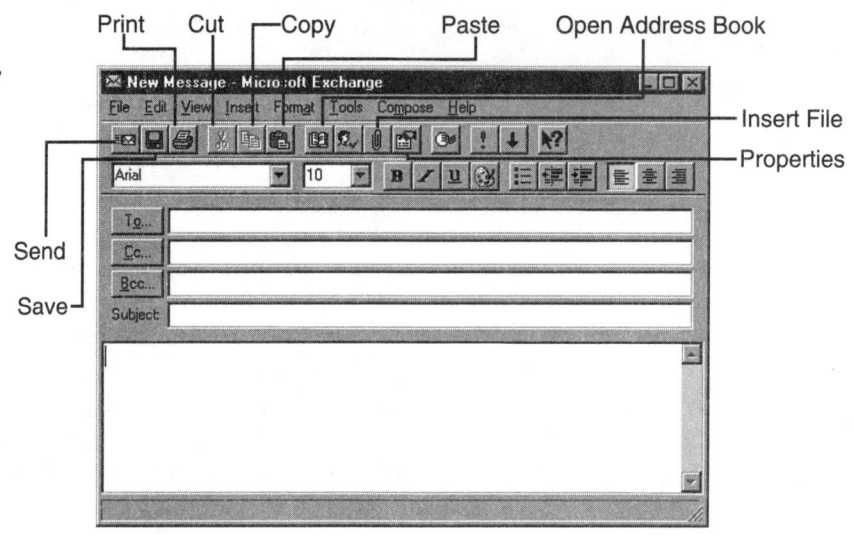

274

Now What Can I Write?

Creating a message is quite simple. Start by typing the address of the person you want to send the message to in the **To** text box. Type the full address, of course, including the @ sign and the domain name (robinhood@sherwood.forest.com, alexandertgreat@alexandria.eg, or whatever). If you'd like to experiment but you don't have anyone's address, type your own. If you want to send the message to several people, you can enter several addresses in the To box. Just separate them with a semicolon and a space (as in joebloe@apotpeel.com; robinhood@sherwood.forest.com).

Now press **Tab** to move into the Cc text box. Here you can enter more e-mail addresses for other people you want to send the message to. However, these are "carbon copies." When the Cc recipients view the message, they'll see that they received a "copy" instead of the original. In a sense, the term is a formality—a throwback to earlier days. After all, an electronic copy of an electronic message is exactly the same as the original.

When you send a message, information about who received the message is placed at the top of the message—you'll see a list of the people whose addresses you entered in the To and Cc text boxes. If you want to send a copy of the message to someone, but you don't want everyone else on the list to know you've sent him or her a copy, you can send a *blind carbon copy*, or *Bcc*. Before you can add Bcc addresses, you must select **View**, **Bcc Box** to display the Bcc text box (which you saw in the earlier figure). Then you press **Tab** to get to the Bcc text box and enter the address(es) as usual.

> **Check This Out...**
>
> **The Address Book** You can click the **To**, **Cc**, or **Bcc** buttons to access the address book—assuming you've added names to the address book, that is. In the address book, you can double-click on any names you want and then click **OK** to add those names to the text box.

Next, press **Tab** to move to the Subject text box. Type a message subject. This is simply a short description of what the message is about; it appears in the list of incoming mail in the recipient's Inbox. (Although you don't have to enter a subject if you don't want to in Exchange, some e-mail programs won't let you send a message unless you include a subject.) Press **Tab** again, and the cursor moves to the large text box, where you type the body of the message.

Formatting Text

Type your message—whatever you want. You can do more than just type, though. You can also format the message (selecting a particular typeface, style, and color) and even place bullets in the message. This won't make any difference if you are sending only Internet e-mail because all that stuff will be removed when the message is sent across the Internet. However, there may be a good reason to use formatting. For example, you might want to if you are sending messages to both MSN members and non-MSN members. MSN will strip the formatting out, leaving simple text, before it sends the message to the Internet for the non-MSN members, but the MSN members who get the message directly will still see the fancy stuff.

Keeping a Copy of the Message

Before you send the message, you might want to save it in a file or print it. To do so, click the **Save** toolbar button or the **Print** toolbar button, or select **File**, **Save** or **File**, **Print**.

You can also save a copy of the message in one of the Microsoft Exchange folders. By default, Microsoft Exchange saves a copy of every message, storing the copy in its Sent Items folder. If you don't want to save a particular message in that folder, click the **Properties** button to open the Note Properties dialog box, and deselect the **Save copy in 'Sent Items' folder** check box. (In Chapter 21, I explained how to change the default so that messages are *not* automatically saved to the Sent Items folder. If you've changed the default, you will have to go to the Note Properties dialog box and select the **Save copy in 'Sent Items' folder** check box when you *do* want Microsoft Exchange to save a particular message there.)

What if you want to save a message in a different folder, though? To do this, choose **File**, **Copy** while the message is open on-screen. A dialog box appears, showing your folders. Double-click a folder name to place the message in that folder.

> **Check This Out...**
>
> **Holding a Message**
>
> You can also move a message into another folder (using the **File**, **Move** command) if you want to ensure that the message is not sent until you are ready. You might want to create a Pending or Postponed folder to hold such messages. Then to open the message and send it later, you double-click it, make any changes, and click the **Send** button. (Use the **File**, **New Folder** command to create a new folder.)

Sending the Message

When you finish with your message, click the **Send** button or select **File**, **Send**. If you are online and are connected to The Microsoft Network, the message is sent immediately. If you're not online, or if you are connected to a service provider other than MSN, the message is placed in Exchange's Outbox folder.

276

Chapter 22 ➤ *Working with E-Mail*

What do you do to send mail out of the Outbox folder, then? Here are a few things you can do:

➤ If you've scheduled automatic e-mail transmissions (see Chapter 21), you can simply allow Exchange to send the mail when it's ready.

➤ In the Exchange window, select **Tools, Deliver Now**. (If you have more than one e-mail system set up, you'll have to select **Tools, Deliver Now Using, Internet Mail** or **Tools, Deliver Now Using, The Microsoft Network**.) Microsoft Exchange sends all the messages in the Outbox folder. Take a minute to retrieve any new incoming messages, and then log off.

➤ If you are an MSN user, log on to MSN and open Exchange. When you open Exchange, it automatically sends the messages in the Outbox folder and retrieves incoming messages.

By the way, Exchange sends only messages that appear in the Inbox in italic text. Any message that is not in italic text will not be sent. For instance, perhaps you created a message earlier and saved it in another folder. You can drag that message into the Outbox, but you can't send it because it isn't in italics. Double-click the message to open it, and then click the **Send** button. The New Message window closes, the message appears in italic text, and Exchange sends the message.

> **Mail Gets Stuck!**
>
> After you send e-mail, look in the Outbox folder. Exchange has a nasty habit of not sending messages when it should! Try selecting **Tools, Deliver Now** (or **Tools, Deliver Now Using, Internet Mail** or **Tools, Deliver Now Using, The Microsoft Network**) to "force" the message out. If that doesn't work, try **Tools, Remote Mail** (or **Tools, Remote Mail, Internet Mail** or **Tools, Remote Mail, The Microsoft Network**). Then, in the Remote Mail dialog box, choose **Tools, Connect and Transfer Mail**. If you see a message saying that the task couldn't be completed, you might need to *reboot* (close your applications, turn your computer off, and then turn it back on) and try again.

Sending Computer Files

Text is not the only thing you can put in an e-mail message. You can include computer files if you wish. As I mentioned in Chapter 18, there are two ways to encode files; you can use MIME or UUENCODE. So which *should* you use? Preferably MIME, but it depends on what the recipient is using. Before you send a file to someone, you should find out which encoding/decoding method he is using. If he can use MIME or UUENCODE, use MIME. If he can only use UUENCODE, you'll have to use that method.

277

Part 4 ➤ *E-Mail Made Easy*

> **Check This Out...**
>
> **Know Your Limits**
> Note that at the time of this writing, MSN members can use only the UUENCODE method (though MIME may be added soon).

Here's how to send a file. From the message window, select **Insert**, **File**. As you can see in the following figure, you have two options: Text only and An attachment. Select the **Text only** option button only if the file you want to insert is an ASCII text file and you want to copy the text from that file directly into the message. If you want to send any other kind of file, select the **An attachment** option button.

For example, select **An attachment**, and then double-click on the file you want to insert (or click once and choose **OK**). The file is inserted into the message, and you see an icon representing the file inside the message area.

> **Check This Out...**
>
> **Shortcut**
> Here's a quick way to insert a file into a message. Position the New Message window so you can see either Windows Explorer or a file on your desktop. Then just drag the file from Explorer or the desktop onto the New Message window.

Now you have to tell Exchange whether to use MIME or UUENCODE to send this message. If you are not using MSN, use whichever you selected when you set up Internet Mail (see Chapter 21). What if you don't want to use the default setting, though? Perhaps you selected UUENCODE, but now you need to use MIME for a particular recipient. You can override the default by selecting **File**, **Properties**. In the Properties dialog box, click on the **Internet** tab. In the Message Format Selection area near the bottom, click on the **Override the profile setting and use** option button, and then choose the correct method from the **Message Format** drop-down list box. (You can do this only if you are using the Internet Mail service, not if you are using MSN's e-mail. If you are an MSN member, simply insert the file using **Insert**, **File** and let MSN handle the rest—it'll use UUENCODE, currently.)

You can insert a file into your message, or you can copy the text from an ASCII text file into your message.

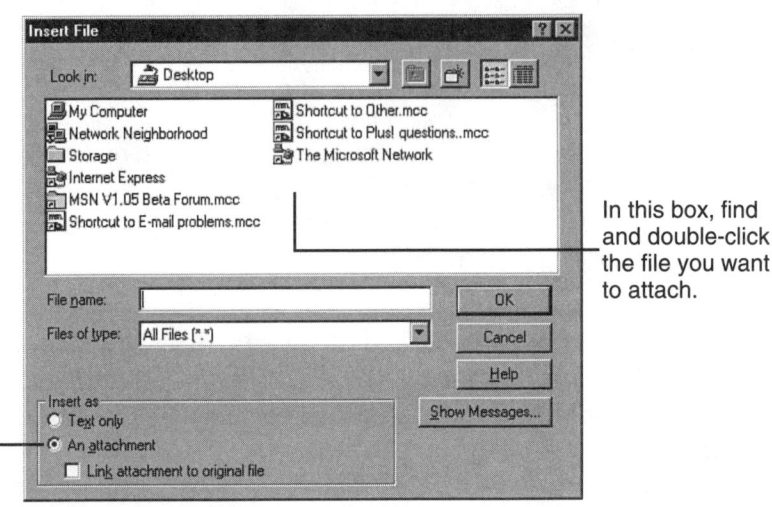

In this box, find and double-click the file you want to attach.

Specify that you want to attach the file to the message.

278

Chapter 22 ➤ *Working with E-Mail*

The Microsoft Exchange Window

The following figure shows an example of the Exchange window (also known as the Exchange Viewer). In the left column, you see a series of folders. At the top is the Personal Folders icon (which you learned a little about in Chapter 21). If you see the Personal Folders icon but no folders below it, click on the + icon to open the list. If you don't see two panes in the Exchange window, click the **Show/Hide Folder List** button (the second one from the left in the following figure) or select **View**, **Folders**.

In the right pane, you see the messages you've received. The first three columns contain various icons. Those three columns are marked with these icons:

Message importance. You may see an icon in this column, but it's unlikely because this is an MSN feature, not an Internet Mail feature.

Message type. The icon shows if the message is a normal e-mail message, a fax, a system administration message, and so on.

Message inclusion. If there's a paper clip icon in this column, the file has some kind of inclusion; if it's an Internet message, the inclusion is a binary file in MIME or UUENCODE format.

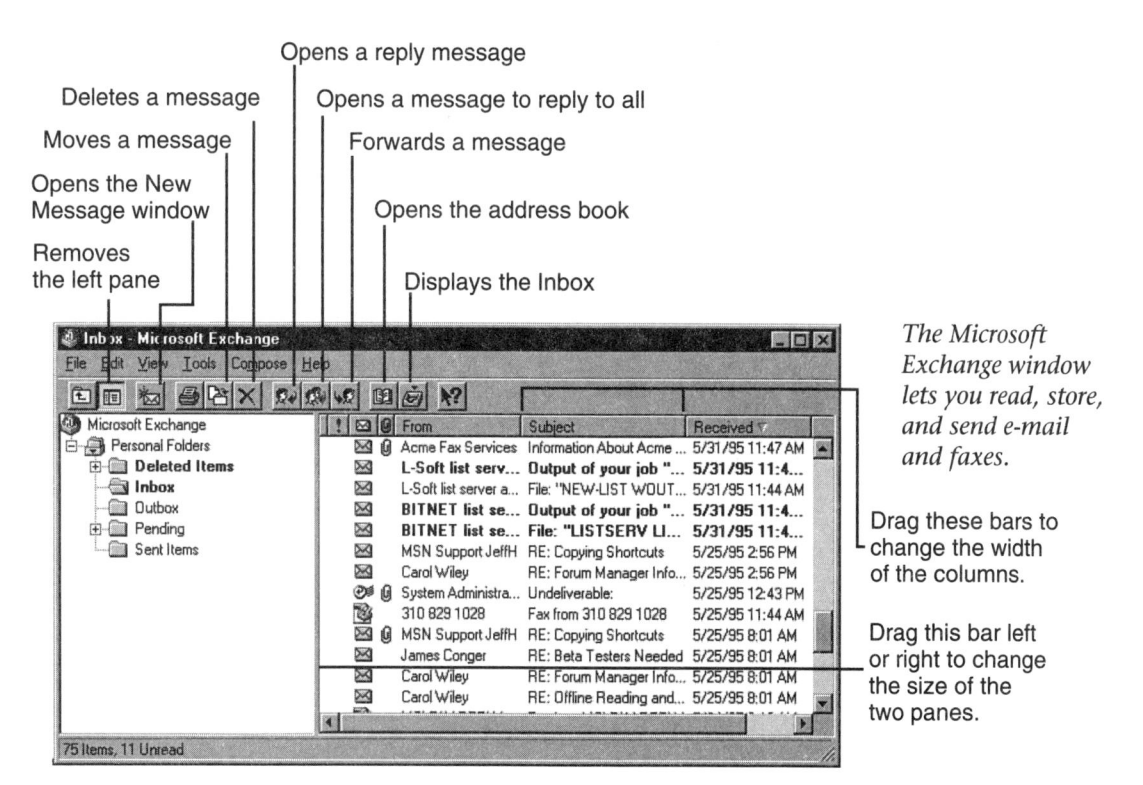

The Microsoft Exchange window lets you read, store, and send e-mail and faxes.

279

There are other columns in the right pane, of course. The From, Subject, Received, and Size columns give you information about your incoming messages. Note that you can drag the bar between the left and right panes to enlarge the space in either pane. Also, you can place the mouse pointer over the dividing line between two columns in the right pane and drag the line to enlarge or reduce a column's width.

How Do I Get My Messages?

How do e-mail messages arrive in your Microsoft Exchange window? A few ways:

> **Check This Out...**
>
> **Auto Open**
> If the Display a notification message check box is selected in the Options dialog box (Tools, Options) when a message arrives, you'll see a message box asking if you want to read the retrieved message now. Choose **Yes**, and the message window opens.

- If you're an MSN member, when you log on you may see a message telling you that you have e-mail and asking if you want to retrieve it. Choose **Yes**, and Microsoft Exchange opens and transfers the message.

- When you select **Tools, Deliver Now** (or, if you have other e-mail services installed in Microsoft Exchange, when you choose **Tools, Deliver Now Using, Internet Mail** or **Tools, Deliver Now Using, The Microsoft Network**), Exchange logs on, sends any outgoing messages, and retrieves any messages that are waiting.

- You can use the Remote Mail system (see the following section) to retrieve them.

- If you set up Exchange to automatically schedule e-mail (see Chapter 22), Exchange periodically logs on and checks for e-mail.

Note, by the way, that the Deliver Now command is really also a "Get Mail" command. You'll use it to both send and retrieve e-mail.

Using Remote Mail

Why would anyone want just the message headers (the From and Subject information), and not the actual messages? Perhaps you subscribe to a number of mailing lists (see Chapter 19) and get dozens—maybe even hundreds—of e-mail messages each day. Perhaps some of the messages are very large, too. Instead of downloading all of the messages, wouldn't it be nice if you could read the message headers and decide which ones you want to download? Or maybe you are on a business trip and want to call in to get your important e-mail. Instead of downloading everything, you might want to pick only the messages you want right now, and leave the rest until you return home. Well, you can do either of these things using the Remote Mail feature. Here's how:

Chapter 22 ➤ *Working with E-Mail*

1. Select **Tools, Remote Mail** (or, if you have installed other e-mail services, choose **Tools, Remote Mail, Internet Mail** or **Tools, Remote Mail, The Microsoft Network**). The Remote Mail window opens.

> **Where's Remote Mail?**
>
> You may find that you have no **Remote Mail, Internet Mail** option. It appears only if you selected Work off-line and use Remote Mail in the Internet Mail Properties dialog box. To do that now, select **Tools, Services**, click **Internet Mail**, click the **Properties** button, and then click on the **Connections** tab.

2. In the Remote Mail window, select **Tools, Connect and Update Headers**, or click the **Update Headers** button. If you are not online, Exchange logs on and grabs any waiting headers. You'll see the headers in the Remote Mail window (shown in the following figure).

3. Read the message headers. Based on the message subjects and who the messages are from, decide which messages you want to keep.

4. Double-click the messages you want to keep. Or select them, and then choose **Edit, Mark to Retrieve** or click the **Mark to Retrieve** toolbar button.

5. You can also retrieve a copy of the message. When you do this, you get the message, but it also remains in the e-mail server so you can retrieve it again later. To retrieve a copy, select the message. Then select **Edit, Mark to Retrieve a Copy** or click the **Mark to Retrieve a Copy** button.

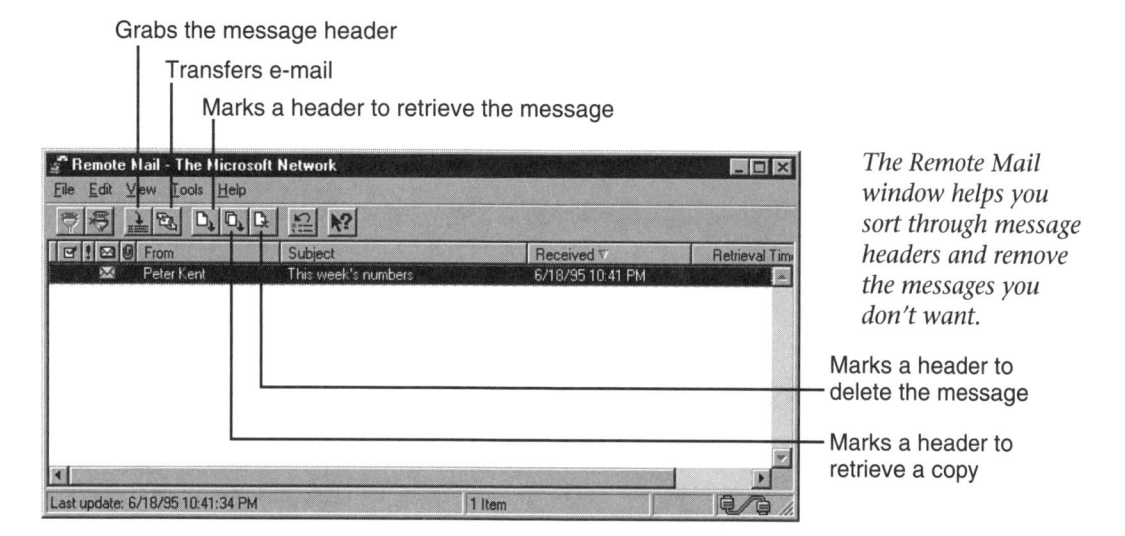

The Remote Mail window helps you sort through message headers and remove the messages you don't want.

- Grabs the message header
- Transfers e-mail
- Marks a header to retrieve the message
- Marks a header to delete the message
- Marks a header to retrieve a copy

281

6. If you find messages you'll never want to retrieve, delete them. Click the message, and then select **Edit, Mark to Delete** or click the **Mark to Delete** button.

7. When you finish reviewing and marking the messages, select **Tools, Connect and Transfer Mail** or click the **Transfer Mail** button. Remote Mail logs on, if necessary, and then carries out your instructions, deleting the messages marked for deletion, retrieving those marked for retrieval, and sending any messages waiting in the Inbox.

8. Close the Remote Mail window and return to the Inbox, where you'll find your messages.

> **Why Retrieve Copies?** If you are traveling, you might find it convenient to retrieve a copy of a message using your laptop. Later, when you return to the office, you can download the original message to your desktop system.

Working with Messages

Now you are ready to work with your incoming messages. There is at least one incoming message (a Welcome! message) in the Inbox after you install Microsoft Exchange. If you don't have anyone sending you messages, send a few to yourself or join a mailing list (see Chapter 19).

When you open Microsoft Exchange, you'll probably find yourself viewing the contents of the Inbox. If (for some strange reason) you do not see the Inbox, click the **Inbox** toolbar button or the **Inbox** folder in the left pane. To read a message, use one of these techniques:

➤ Double-click the message.

➤ Highlight it and press **Enter**.

➤ Right-click it and select **Open**.

➤ Highlight it and select **File, Open**.

Up pops the message in the message window, shown in the following figure. You can use the scroll bars to move through the message, and of course, you can use the normal Clipboard commands to copy text from the message and place it in another Windows application. Note that the message window has its own toolbar.

Chapter 22 ➤ *Working with E-Mail*

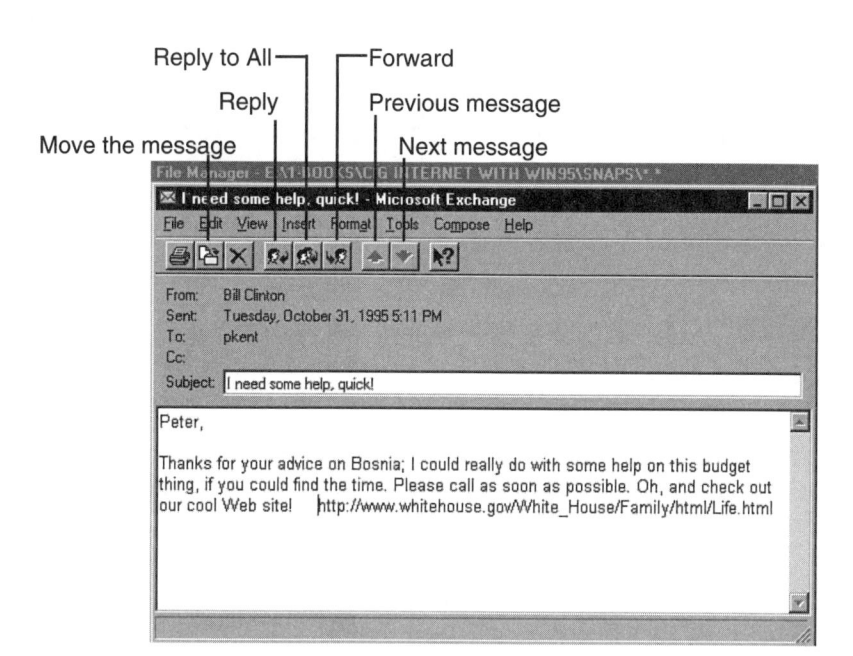

Reply to All
Forward
Reply
Previous message
Move the message
Next message

You view your incoming messages in the message window.

Moving Between Messages

When you've read a message, you can quickly move to the next or the previous one. Click the **Previous** or the **Next** button (or select **View, Previous** or **View, Next**), and the message window displays another message.

You can also delete a message or move it to another folder. Click on either the **Delete** or the **Move Item** toolbar button, or select **File, Delete** or **File, Move**. Depending on how you have configured Exchange, when you delete or move a message, your message window might display another message, or you might automatically return to the Inbox. The settings that control this are located in the After Moving or Deleting an Open Item area of the Options dialog box (see Chapter 21).

There's a File in Here!

What do you do when someone sends you a computer file inside a message? When someone sends you a file, the message contains an icon with the name of the file under it. The file has been converted from the format in which it was transmitted across the Internet (MIME or UUENCODE), and it is ready to use.

You can drag the file icon directly to your desktop, or you can open Windows Explorer and drag it into a directory. You can also double-click it to open it in its source application (if you have that application). If you right-click on the file, you get a shortcut menu.

283

From the shortcut menu, you can select Save As to save it to your hard disk, or you can carry out a variety of other operations such as printing it, renaming it, viewing it in the Windows Explorer Quick View window, or copying it to the Clipboard so you can paste it into a folder on your desktop or in Windows Explorer.

Responding to Messages

Once you've read the message, you may want to respond to it in some way. There are three ways to deal with it that send it back into the e-mail system:

- To reply to the person who sent you the message, click the **Reply to Sender** button or select **Compose, Reply to Sender**.

- To reply to the person who sent you the message and everyone else who received a copy (except Bcc recipients), click the **Reply to All** button or select **Compose, Reply to All**.

- To send a copy of the message to someone else, click the **Forward** button or select **Compose, Forward**.

In each case, a New Message window opens. The New Message window contains the original message text and a place for you to type your reply. (If you prefer not to place the original message text in all of your replies, see the configuration information in Chapter 21.) If you are replying to the message, the address information is already filled in. If you are forwarding the message, you'll have to enter an address the normal way.

More Things You Can Do

I could write a book about Exchange (I'm not going to, but I could). The following list gives you an idea of just a few of the things you can do in this program:

- Create folders and subfolders (**File, New Folder**).
- Move messages between folders (drag-and-drop, or right-click and choose **Move**).
- Copy messages between folders (**Ctrl**+drag-and-drop, or right-click and choose **Copy**).
- Search for a particular message (**Tools, Find**).
- Save messages (**File, Save**).
- Print messages (**File, Print**).

An Alternative: Eudora

If you don't like Exchange, you're not stuck with it. One excellent alternative is Eudora. Eudora is much easier to use than Exchange in many ways—but it doesn't have as many features. People either love Exchange or hate it, it seems. If you are in the latter camp, you should try Eudora. The following figure shows a message window in Eudora.

There are two versions of Eudora, a freeware version and a commercial version. The freeware is excellent, and it's not "crippled" in any way. However, the commercial program does have some nice additional features, such as "file-filtering" (which allows Eudora to handle incoming messages automatically, according to what it finds in the message header), online help, and so on.

> **Check This Out...**
>
> **Crippled?**
> Some manufacturers disable certain features in a freeware program, in an effort to get you to buy the full version.

You can find this program at ftp.qualcomm.com/quest/eudora/windows/ (see Chapter 12 for information about FTP). It's very easy to install and configure; you can have it up and running ten minutes after you download it.

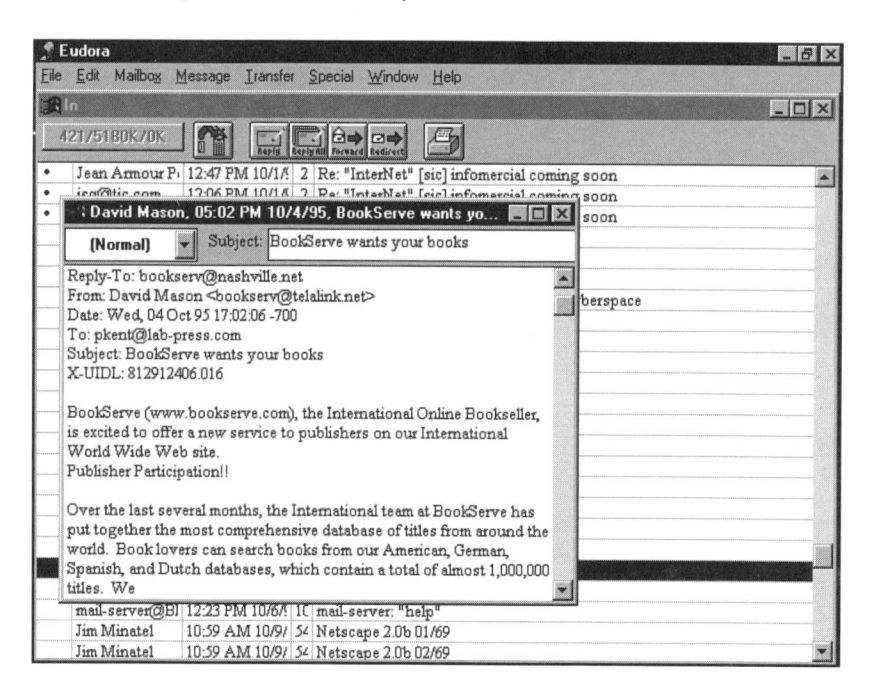

Eudora is a good alternative to Exchange.

285

The Least You Need to Know

- Use **Compose**, **New Message** to write an e-mail message, and click on the **Send** button when you finish writing.

- The message may not be transmitted right away; Exchange may wait until the next scheduled e-mail check or until you use Remote Mail.

- UUENCODE and MIME are two ways of encoding files that you attach to e-mail messages. If you are an MSN member, you can only send attached files using UUENCODE; but MSN handles all the details for you.

- If you are using another Internet e-mail service, you can send files using MIME or UUENCODE; MIME's the preferred method.

- A great alternative to Exchange is Eudora, which you can find at ftp.qualcomm.com/quest/eudora/windows/.

Chapter 23

Return to Sender, Address Unknown

In This Chapter

- Why e-mail gets returned and what to do about it
- Where to look for e-mail addresses
- Using finger to find login information
- Searching Four11's 1.5-million listing
- Searching for newsgroup users
- Using the Yahoo Reference:White Pages category
- Using Netfind

Nothing's simple on the Internet. You might be sure that you've entered the correct e-mail address—you might have even used your mail program to "grab" an address from a message you received—but just when you think you've finished with an e-mail message, it comes back. You look in your Inbox and find something like this:

```
22  Nov  8 Mail Delivery Subs  (1,274) Returned mail: Host unknown
```

You view the message and find a horrendous mess of header lines with comments like:

```
Host unknown (Authoritative answer from name server).
```

Your message has gone out onto the Internet, but nobody knows what to do with it. There may even be occasions when you use a correct address, and the Internet still can't deliver it.

What's Up?

There are four reasons, with some variations, why your mail may not be delivered:

Host unknown The Internet can't find the host that you specified in the e-mail address. Remember that e-mail addresses are in the format *user@host*. For some reason, the Internet can't get through to the host.

User unknown The Internet can get your mail to the host, but the host claims it doesn't recognize the user and sends the mail back.

Service unavailable The address is fine, but the host computer is not accepting mail at the moment. The mail system may be shut down because of hardware or virus problems. Or maybe you sent the message at a time when the host simply doesn't accept mail; some systems refuse mail during certain times.

Can't send The specified host is correct, and the host might be inclined to accept the mail, but the e-mail can't get through to the host. Maybe the network is damaged, maybe the host itself is out of business due to hardware problems, or maybe the host has changed its mail configuration and the information hasn't been passed on to the right people.

Look carefully at your returned mail, and you'll see one of these reasons (or something like it) somewhere in the header. It's usually, but not always, on the Subject line near the top.

Who Didn't Get It?

If you sent a message to several people, you should check carefully to see who didn't receive it. For instance, if you used a mailing list or sent carbon copies to several people, it's possible that the message could have been delivered to some people but not to others. Look carefully at the `Transcript of session follows` section of the header (as shown here) to see who didn't get it.

```
— Transcript of session follows —
550 apotpeel.com (TCP)... 550 Host unknown
```

```
554 <joebloe@apotpeel.com>... 550 Host unknown
(Authoritative answer from name server)
550 ourplace.org (TCP)... 550 Host unknown
554 <fred@ourplace.org>... 550 Host unknown (Authoritative
answer from name server)
```

You can see that this message was sent back from two addresses, in both cases because the Internet couldn't find the host. The message may have gone through to other recipients.

So What's the Problem?

What did you do wrong, then? A number of things could have gone wrong.

You typed the address incorrectly. You may have made a mistake when typing the address. Take a look at the address in the returned message to confirm that you got it right.

> **Check This Out...**
> **An Important Distinction**
> Make sure you didn't type a zero instead of an O, or a one instead of a lowercase L.

A mailer incorrectly modified the domain. A mail server somewhere saw the address, misunderstood it, and added its own domain. If the returned message shows the address you entered along with some higher-level domain stuff that you didn't include in the address, this is what has happened.

You've been given an incomplete address. Some people assume too much when they hand out their addresses: they give you part of it and assume you know where they are and how to complete the highest level of their domain. Generally, you need a complete address only if the mail is leaving your host and going elsewhere. Therefore, if your host sees an incomplete address—without the higher-level domain—it may assume the mail goes to someone in the same domain. (And if a user gets used to giving his address to other local users, he may forget about the higher-level domain part when giving his address to non-local users.)

You used a correct address, but the mailer doesn't know it's correct. There's not much you can do about this except complain. Some mail servers may not have the latest domain information.

The mail program that sent you a message didn't fill out the "From" name correctly. Not all mail programs fill out the From name correctly. They often abbreviate it, stripping out the higher levels of the domain name. The From name is for reference only; it's not used to actually deliver the mail. However, if you use your mail program to "grab" the

From name and put it into your address book (or to reply directly to a message), you're going to have an incorrectly addressed message. If you know the From address is wrong, you should correct it before you use it, of course. Check the body of the message to see if the sender included a signature with his full e-mail address.

Who Ya Gonna Call?

What do you do about these problems? If it's a system problem, in which a mail server does not recognize an address or modifies it incorrectly, there's not much you can do except talk to your service provider. If you can see what the problem is, simply correct the address, strip out all the header garbage you don't need, and send the message again. (You can use your mail program's Forward command to do all this.)

You might also have to try to contact the person some other way (the telephone, remember?) and get the correct address. However, there will be times when you are stuck with a bad address and there's no other way to find the person. That's when things may get tough.

The Internet Directory? There Isn't One

There is no single directory in which you can look up an Internet user's mail address. Finding an address takes a little more work than that. One problem is that the Internet is an amorphous blob that seems unrelated to geography. Although there's no single directory of Internet users, there are many different directories. The problem is, if you've no idea where the person is, you don't know which directory to use.

While researching this book, for example, I came across the names of two people I wanted to talk to about a particular program. I saw their names in a couple of documents, but no addresses were included. Where were these people? It turned out that one was in England and the other was in California. There are a number of different techniques you can employ for finding people.

Talk to the Postmaster

If you are sure a user is at a particular host, you could ask the host's postmaster. To do so, send an e-mail message to **postmaster@***hostname*. Provide as much information about the person as you can, and maybe the postmaster will be able to send you the correct mail address.

Ask Someone Else

Think about who else the person might know: another person with whom the person has worked or with whom you know the person has communicated. Then e-mail that person and ask if he knows where the first person is.

Finger Him

UNIX has a command called **finger** that lets you ask a host about someone whose name you know. Of course, you have to know the person's host system in order to try this. Perhaps you know the host that the user works with, and you need to find the user's account name. There are several ways to use finger:

➤ Use a Web finger gateway, a Web page that lets you enter a finger command and see the response. You can go to http://www.yahoo.com/Computers_and_Internet/Internet/World_Wide_Web/Gateways/Finger_Gateways/ to find a list of gateways (this is at Yahoo), or you can search any of the Web search systems for "finger."

➤ Telnet into your service provider's system (see Chapter 15), go to the UNIX command line, and use the command from there.

➤ Get a Windows finger program. Some commercial Internet suites have finger programs. You can also use the Windows finger shareware, which you can find at the sunsite.unc.edu/pub/micro/pc-stuff/ms-windows/winsock/apps ftp site.

You enter the finger command in this format: **finger *name@host***. For example, if you were looking for someone named Smith at the host named apotpeel.com, your finger search would look something like this:

```
teal% finger smith@apotpeel.com
[apotpeel.com]
Login name: bsmith                    In real life: Bert Smith
Directory: /ftp/./                    Shell: /bin/true
Never logged in.
No unread mail
No Plan.
Login name: gsmith                    In real life: George Smith
Directory: /ftp/./                    Shell: /bin/true
Mail last read Tue Nov  9 10:18:03 1993
No Plan.
```

As you can see, the search came up with two Smiths: Bert and George. Bert has never used his account (see the `Never logged in` line). Sometimes you'll see a `Last login` line or a `Mail last read` line with a date; these give you an idea of how often the person uses the account. So now you have two e-mail addresses you can try: bsmith@apotpeel.com and gsmith@apotpeel.com.

What name are you going to enter with the finger command? You can enter a complete first name, complete last name, or complete login name. (If you enter a login name, you must get the capitalization correct; for first and last names it doesn't matter. Of course, in this case we are looking for the login name so we don't have it anyway.) You can enter **finger** *@host* with no name to see a list of all the people currently logged onto that domain. (You can even enter finger by itself to see a list of all the people currently logged on to your own service provider's system.)

Notice the `No Plan` line at the end of the earlier example. That refers to the user's *.plan file*, a hidden file in his home directory. It is simply a text file that includes any information the user wants to tell people who finger him. Take a look at this example:

```
teal% finger bloe
Login name: joeb                        In real life: Joe Bloe
Directory: /home/clients4/joeb          Shell: /bin/csh
On since Nov  9 09:32:01 on ttyra from ucb-annex.csn.or
Mail last read Tue Nov  9 10:18:03 1993
Plan:
 ================================================================
 ¦   Joe Bloe            ¦Internet:joeb@apotpeel.com ¦
 ¦   2291 S. Coors St.   ¦   CompuServe: 79999,9999  ¦
 ¦   Podunk, CO  80228   ¦    Phone:   303-555-1869  ¦
 ================================================================
```

Joe Bloe has created a text file containing his address, Internet address, CompuServe address, and phone number. You can really track this guy down now. He could have also included a mini résumé telling you what he does if he had wanted.

The finger command also displays the contents of the first line of the .project file (another hidden text file the user may create to provide a little more information). The .project file is likely to be updated periodically, while the .plan file contains more permanent information.

Chapter 23 ➤ *Return to Sender, Address Unknown*

> **Check This Out...**
>
> **I Want a .Plan File!**
>
> Your .plan file has to be stored in your home directory on your service provider's computer. If you are not sure where this is, ask your service provider. You can then create a text file and use FTP to place it into your home directory. The file should be a hidden file; UNIX systems indicate hidden files by placing a period before the file name (thus .plan). You'll have to create a text file on your computer with the text that you want, transfer it to your service provider's system, and then change the name to .plan. But all of this requires a knowledge of UNIX that we haven't covered in this book. Ask your service provider for help.

The finger command won't always work. Some hosts simply don't allow it, and many Internet system administrators believe that it provides too much information and poses a security risk. In some cases, a system only lets you finger someone if you know the person's user name. (It won't let you get a list of all the people named Smith, for instance.) All of these things depend on how each system administrator sets up his system.

Register with Four11!

There's a very good new directory service called Four11 that you may want to register with. The people running this system (SLED Corporation) have taken e-mail addresses from three main sources. They've grabbed information from existing Internet sources—mainly UseNet newsgroups; they've received lists of subscribers from service providers; and they've been given information by people who add details of their own to the directory. So, for instance, you can go to the Four11 directory and add detailed information about yourself—your full name and address, your company name, hobbies, university, and so on—to help people find you.

This directory now has 1.5 million entries, so it's a great place to find people. Use your Web browser to go to http://www.Four11.com/. You enter all your own information (the following figure shows the search form) and then immediately search. You will recieve a password via e-mail so you can return and search in the future.

293

Part 4 ➤ *E-Mail Made Easy*

Four11 provides a directory of 1.5 million people.

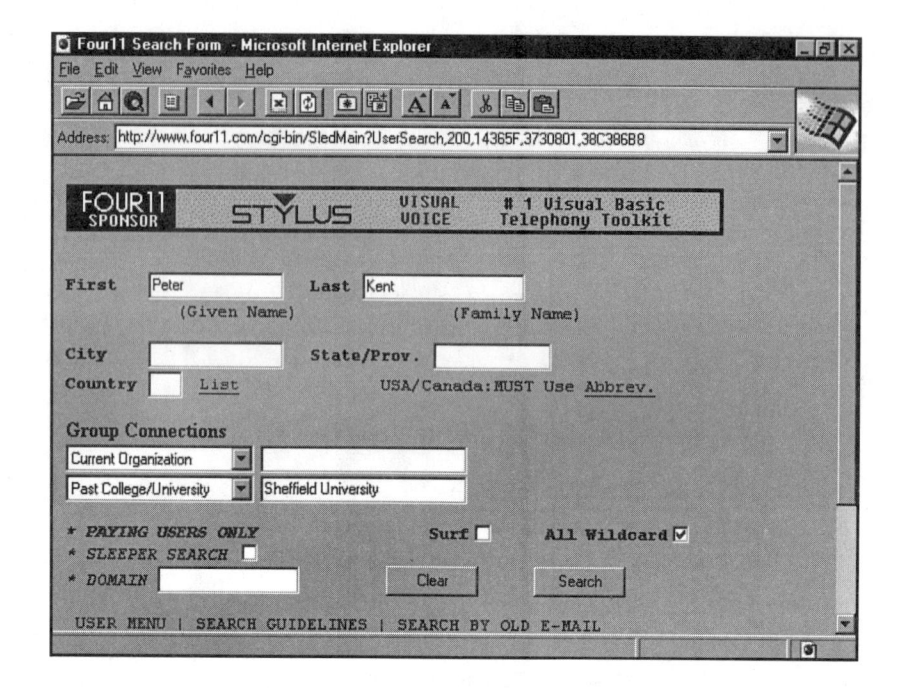

I was impressed with Four11. I managed to find myself in the directory before I'd even registered my information. That may not sound like such a big deal, but I've worked with some other e-mail directories on the Internet where I was unable to find myself. I was pleased that I finally could! Also, it's nice to be able to search for people by the details provided by Four11—to search for people who went to a specific university, for example.

Search for Newsgroup Users

In Chapter 17, you learned about newsgroups. Newsgroup messages provide yet another way of finding certain users. As you learned, in order for you to be able to read these newsgroups, your service provider must subscribe to them. MIT subscribes to most of the newsgroups, and each time a newsgroup message comes into MIT, the system grabs the From: line and saves it. Therefore, if you think the person you are trying to track down uses the newsgroups, you can search MIT's database.

294

Chapter 23 ➤ *Return to Sender, Address Unknown*

To do so, send an e-mail message to **mail-server@rtfm.mit.edu**. In the body of the message enter **send usenet-addresses/***name*, where *name* is the name for which you are searching. Within an hour or two after you send the message, you should receive an e-mail message containing a list of the matches.

> **Check This Out...**
> **For More Information...** You can send the message **send usenet-addresses/help** to get more information about using this system.

There are a few problems with this method, of course. You have to know an exact match from the From: line. Likewise, you can't use a partial name (for example, you can't enter only one name with no spaces). In addition, many people use aliases (in the sense of "fake names") when they post messages in the newsgroups.

Try Yahoo, and Use the White Pages

In Chapter 11, you saw how to use Yahoo to search the World Wide Web for information. Well, why not try Yahoo (and other search systems) to see if it can help you track down the e-mail addresses you need?

For instance, you'll find that Yahoo has a category called Reference:White Pages. You can get there directly by using this URL: http://www.yahoo.com/Reference/White_Pages. The term White Pages in Internet-speak means an e-mail directory of some kind. I found Four11 in this subcategory, along with loads of other useful links including the following:

➤ 1994 WHO is WHO

➤ BEST North America (find researchers)

➤ Book of Transportation Professionals

➤ Christian White Pages

➤ HEP Virtual Phonebook (High Energy Physics sites around the world)

➤ Internet White Pages for the Gulf (of Dubai, not of Mexico)

➤ InterNIC Directory Services

➤ LookUP! Directory Service

➤ NetPages

➤ OKRA – net.citizen Directory (1 million e-mail addresses, similar to Four11)

➤ PH: A More Advanced User Interface (search for e-mail addresses at academic institutions throughout the world)

295

Part 4 ➤ *E-Mail Made Easy*

- ➤ Santa Cruz WWW Whitepages
- ➤ Savannah E-Mail Index (Savannah, Georgia)
- ➤ Singapore White Pages
- ➤ South Carolina White Pages
- ➤ Washington, D.C. Personal Registry
- ➤ World-Wide E-Mail Address Book
- ➤ Index – Hunting for E-Mail Addresses
- ➤ UseNet – addresses index (WAIS)

Some of these services are commercial, so you have to pay to use them. Nonetheless, this is a great way to find an e-mail address. There are also a number of subcategories within the Reference:White Pages category.

- ➤ Netfind (I'll cover that next)
- ➤ Colleges
- ➤ Companies

Use Netfind

The Netfind system has been around for a while. You can use Netfind by telnetting (refer to Chapter 15) to one of the Netfind hosts listed in the following table.

Netfind Hosts

Host	Country
archie.au	Australia
bruno.cs.colorado.edu	USA
dino.conicit.ve	Venezuela
ds.internic.net	USA
eis.calstate.edu	USA
hto-e.usc.edu	USA
krnic.net	Korea
lincoln.technet.sg	Singapore
malloco.ing.puc.cl	Chile

Host	Country
monolith.cc.ic.ac.uk	England
mudhoney.micro.umn.edu	USA
netfind.anu.edu.au	Australia
netfind.ee.mcgill.ca	Canada
netfind.if.usp.br	Brazil
netfind.oc.com	USA
netfind.vslib.cz	Czech Rep.
nic.uakom.sk	Slovakia
redmont.cis.uab.edu	USA

Log into any of these sites using the login name **netfind**. Then, for the latest list plus links to the Telnet addresses, go to **http://www.earn.net/gnrt/netfind.html**.

Lost Addresses

Most search systems will help you find e-mail addresses only of people connected to the Internet through a true Internet service provider (not through an online service). Unfortunately people on the major online services—CompuServe, America Online, Prodigy, and so on—often are not included in these directories. Of course, these services have their own directories, but they are only available to their own members.

You can also search Netfind using a Netfind gateway, at http://www.earn.net/gnrt/netfind.html. (Actually, this is really a Gopher gateway; it allows you to use your Web browser to search a Gopher Netfind directory.) At this Web site you can enter a name, plus a series of key words. For instance, when I entered **kent lakewood colorado**, I got a long list of domains in Lakewood, Colorado. When I clicked on one of the domain names, I got more information. In theory, I should have got the e-mail address of a Kent at that domain, but I got an Illegal instruction message back. Still, you may have more luck. You may also want to try to telnet to a Netfind site and work there.

I've mentioned Netfind because it's one of the oldest, most "venerable" directories. However, you may want to first try the other systems such as Four11 and the various specific directories you can get to from Yahoo.

Part 4 ➤ *E-Mail Made Easy*

The Least You Need to Know

➤ Even when you think you've got the right e-mail address, your message may come back to you.

➤ Check the header of the returned message carefully. It should tell you why the message was returned and who didn't receive it.

➤ The easiest way to get a person's e-mail address is to talk to him. Pick up the phone and call, or get it from someone who knows the person.

➤ If you know the person is at the host that returned the e-mail, send an e-mail message to the postmaster and ask about the person. Address the message to **postmaster@***hostname*.

➤ The **finger** command is a useful way to track someone if you know his or her host name. Not all hosts will send back account information, though.

➤ If you know the user uses the UseNet newsgroups, try MIT's system. It might have the person's address.

➤ Register with Four11 (http://www.Four11.com/) and search there too; it has more than 1.5 million entries.

➤ Try the Reference:White Pages category at Yahoo to find loads of directories you can search.

➤ Netfind is a good way to check host names. However, it may be difficult to find individuals.

Appendix

Creating a Login Script

In Chapter 7, I explained that you may need a login script to connect to your service provider. If that's why you're here, read on. This appendix explains how to go about creating and assigning the script. Yes, it looks a little complicated, but it's not too bad. Take it slowly and take a break or two. It'll be okay.

Creating a Login Script

Microsoft's Dial-Up Networking program is supposed to dial in to your service provider, make a connection, and then establish the TCP/IP connection. The problem is, each service provider works a little differently. With some, you just have to dial in and provide your user name and password, and away you go. You're connected, and the TCP/IP software is running. But many—perhaps most—service providers don't do this.

For instance, when I connect to my service provider, their computer prompts me for my user name and then my password. Then it sends a short message that gives me these three options:

> I can type **c** and press **Enter** to get to my shell account, a simple menu system that can be used by any serial-communications program.
>
> I can type **slip** and press **Enter** to start a SLIP (Serial Line Internet Protocol) connection.
>
> I can type **ppp** and press **Enter** to start a PPP (Point-to-Point Protocol) connection.

Appendix

So how does Dial-Up Networking know all this? It doesn't. So I have to tell it how to handle this—and you will have to, too, if you followed the procedures in Chapter 7 and found that you couldn't connect. To tell Dial-Up Networking what to do, you must create a *login script*, a text file with a set of instructions that tell Dial-Up Networking what it will see and what to do.

Think back to Chapter 7 for a minute. Remember the game of 20 Questions? I told you to ask your service provider if they have a login script file that works with Windows 95's Dial-Up Networking program. If your service provider does have such a script file, all you have to do is place a copy of it in the \Program Files\Plus! directory on your computer and skip to "Assigning the Script File," later in this appendix. If they don't have a script file, you have to create one.

> **Check This Out...**
>
> ### Modify the Login Script?
>
> If your service provider wrote the script file using the **transmit $PASSWORD** and **transmit $USERID** commands, there's no need to change anything in the script. However, if the service provider used the **transmit *username*** or **transmit *password*** commands (where *username* and *password* are the actual user name and password instead of system variables), you'll have to replace the user name and password with your user name and password. Ask your service provider if you need to modify the script in any way.

Watching a Login Procedure

> **Check This Out...**
>
> **Skip This Step?** If your service provider gave you clear and accurate instructions on how to log on, you can skip this step and create the login script from those instructions instead. If the script doesn't work, though, you'll probably need to come back and follow this procedure, to find the correct login sequence.

The first thing you should do is log in to your service provider using a simple serial-communications program such as CrossTalk, Qmodem, or your own personal favorite. If you don't have a favorite, you can use the new HyperTerminal program that comes with Windows 95. Who knows, that may be your favorite! It's actually quite good. (If you haven't installed it, select **Start**, **Settings**, and **Control Panel**. Double-click the **Add/Remove Programs** icon and click the **Windows Setup** tab. You'll find HyperTerminal in the Communications category.)

Follow these instructions:

1. Select **Start**, **Programs**, **Accessories**, and **HyperTerminal**. The HyperTerminal folder opens.

300

Creating a Login Script

2. Double-click the **Hypertrm.exe** icon, and HyperTerminal starts. You'll see the Connection Description dialog box.

3. Type the name of your service provider and click **OK**. The Phone Number dialog box appears.

4. Enter the phone number your modem has to dial to connect to your service provider and click **OK**. HyperTerminal displays the Connect dialog box.

5. Click **Dial**, and HyperTerminal begins dialing into your service provider.

6. When you connect, do everything that your service provider told you you'd have to do to make your connection. Enter your user name, password, and any other commands that are necessary for making your connection.

7. When you are fully logged onto the system, copy all the text that appeared in the window during the session to the Clipboard (choose **Edit**, **Select All** and then choose **Edit**, **Copy**). Then paste it into a word processor or Notepad (with **Edit**, **Paste**).

8. Click the **Close** (X) button to close the HyperTerminal window.

So what did you get? Take a look at the text I saved from my sample session. (The text I had to type appears in bold.)

```
Checking authorization, Please wait...
Connected to port #33[Denver-1]

Welcome to the INTERNET EXPRESS Network

CUSTOMER SERVICE: 800-592-1240   or   719-592-1240.
Normal hours are Mon-Fri 7:30AM-10:00PM, Sat and Sun 8:00AM-10:00PM.
24 Hour Live Operator Support for service interruptions.
```

Username: **pkent**
Password: **nnnnnn** (my password)

```
Permission granted
Type "c" followed by <RETURN> to continue ppp
Switching to PPP.
~ }#_!}!}!} }4}"}&} } } } }%}&DX=_}'}"}(}"â° ~~ }#_!}!}"} }4}"}&} } } } }%}&1_äI}
'}"}(}"_T~~ }#_!}!}#} }4}"}&} } } } }%}&ë_RO}'}"}(}"+3/4~~ }#_!}!}$} }4}"}&} } } }
}%}&hÅ]$}'}"}(}"}+å~~ }#_!}!}%} }4}"}&} } } } }%}&°S}#Ü}'}"}(}""Ä~~ }#_!}!}&} }
4}"}&} } } } }%}&_^éë}'}"}(}"_ù~~ }#_!}!}'} }4}"}&} } } } }%}&}0}?`{}'}"}(}"}%}/
~~ }#_!}!}(} }4}"}&} } } } }%}&Ö(q)}'}"}(}"bª~~ }#_!}!})} }4}"}&} } } } }%}&ë}3}
,}'}"}(}"'R~~ }#_!}!}*} }4}"}&} } } } }%}&}0C-_}'}"}(}"Ç^~~ }#_!}!}+} }4}"}&} }
```

Appendix

What can you tell from this? A number of things:

- When I see the `Username:` prompt, I have to type **pkent** (my account name) and then press **Enter**.

- When I see the `Password:` prompt, I have to type my password and then press **Enter**.

- When I see the message `Type "c" followed by <RETURN> to continue`, I have to type **ppp** and press **Enter**. (No, I don't need to press c, even though that is what the prompt says. The c is used to start my "shell" account.)

I suppose you're wondering what all that garbage at the bottom is. Well, when I typed ppp and pressed Enter, my service provider's computer began the PPP session. PPP is a form of TCP/IP, but HyperTerminal is not a TCP/IP program. HyperTerminal has no idea what the information it is receiving means. That's okay, though, because at this point, I know that I have all the information I need. The service provider's computer sent the message `Switching to PPP`, so I must have done something right.

If you can't get through to your service provider's system in this manner, you need to call your service provider and find out why. I'm going to assume that you've been able to find the information you need and are now ready to write the script file.

You're a Programmer! (Writing the Script)

Open Notepad by clicking on **Start**, **Programs**, **Accessories**, and **Notepad**. In the Notepad window, type your login script. You know how to do that, don't you? You don't? Well, here's an example:

```
proc main
waitfor "username:"
transmit $USERID
transmit "^M"
waitfor "password:"
transmit $PASSWORD
transmit "^M"
waitfor "continue"
transmit "ppp^M"
endproc
```

This is a very simple script, but it works. Let's break it down and determine what it all means:

proc main This must appear at the top of the script. It just means "this is the top of the script, okay?"

Creating a Login Script

waitfor "username:" As you may remember, I also saw that message when I logged on to my service provider's system. I had to wait for the prompt `Username:`. Well, this line tells Dial-Up Networking to wait until it sees that prompt. (Note that I typed **username:** and not **Username:**. The case you use doesn't matter.)

transmit $USERID When Dial-Up Networking sees the `Username:` prompt, it moves to the next line in the script. This line tells Dial-Up Networking to type my user name. **$USERID** means "look at the user name entered during setup, and type that." (You entered your user name in the Internet Setup Wizard.)

transmit "^M" This line means "press **Enter**." ("^M" represents the Enter key; note that it is enclosed in quotation marks.)

waitfor "password:" Of course, this means to wait for the `Password:` prompt.

transmit $PASSWORD Once Dial-Up Networking has seen the `Password:` prompt, it sends my password. Again, **$PASSWORD** means "use the password entered in the Internet Setup Wizard."

transmit "^M" Again, this means "press **Enter**."

waitfor "continue" Wait for the continue prompt (the full prompt was `Type "c" followed by <RETURN> to continue`).

transmit "ppp^M" When Dial-Up Networking sees the continue prompt, it types **ppp** and presses **Enter**. This time the **^M** is added directly after the text you type because you entered the text directly instead of using a *system variable*. There's no need for a separate line for the **^M** command. Note, though, that the text **ppp** and the **^M** are enclosed by quotation marks.

endproc This command tells Dial-Up Networking that the script is finished and that Dial-Up Networking can start the PPP protocol.

There's a lot more to writing scripts. If you really want to get into it, refer to the file called SCRIPT.DOC located in the \Program Files\Plus! directory on your hard disk. (You can open it in WordPad.) This file describes the scripting language, which is by no means easy to figure out. It helps if you have some computer-geek experience.

> **Check This Out...**
> **Don't Sweat It**
> If you are creating an Internet connection from scratch (using the instructions in Chapter 8), don't worry about the user name and password right now. Use the **transmit $USERID** and **transmit $PASSWORD** commands. You'll enter the user name and password later, just before you dial into your service provider.

> **Check This Out...**
> **System Variable?**
> Information the system fills in automatically. $USERID and $PASSWORD are system variables; as such they are treated differently.

303

Appendix

> ### Some Fine-Tuning
>
> I should tell you about a couple of other commands you may want to use: **until** and **set ipaddr getip**. You can add **until** to a **waitfor** command, like this:
>
> waitfor "password:" until 10
>
> This tells Dial-Up Networking to wait 10 seconds (I could have used **until 5**, **until 20**, or whatever I wanted). If the prompt doesn't appear within that time, Dial-Up Networking gives up.
>
> You can use the **set ipaddr getip** command to retrieve your IP command if your service provider's computer sends that information to your computer during login. (For more information on this command, see the section "I Have to Use SLIP," in Chapter 7.)

Most login scripts will probably be fairly simple like mine. As a matter of fact, you can use mine as an example and substitute the correct information. If you need more, refer to the SCRIPT.DOC file. You'll also find sample .SCP files in the \Program Files\Accessories\ directory. You may be able to modify one of them. If you can't figure it all out, ask your service provider for more help. After all, the service provider has to write at least one script, which they use for all their subscribers who want to use Windows 95 software to connect. And if your service provider won't help, find another!

When you finish your script, save it in the \Program Files\Accessories\ directory, using the .SCP extension. For instance, you might call it SCRIPT.SCP. (If you created this script in a word processor instead of Notepad, make sure you save the file in the ASCII format.)

Assigning the Script File

Once you create your script file, you need to associate it with the Dial-Up Networking configuration you created. Here's how:

1. Select **Start**, **Programs**, **Accessories**, and **Dial-Up Scripting Tool**. You see the dialog box shown in the following figure.

2. In the **Connections** list box, click the connection that you created earlier in this chapter. (It may be the only one there. My example shows The Microsoft Network because I also created an MSN Internet connection.)

3. Click the **Browse** button to access a typical Browse dialog box. Find the script file you created (SCRIPT.SCP, for instance), and double-click it to place it in the **File name** text box of the Dial-Up Scripting Tool dialog box.

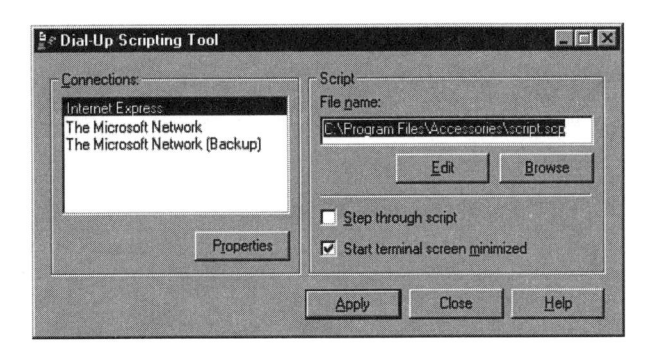

The Dial-Up Scripting Tool lets you tell Dial-Up Networking which script to use.

4. Click the **Step through script** check box.
5. Click the **Apply** button.

Let's See If It Works: Testing the Script

The next thing you have to do is test the script to make sure it works. You selected the Step through script check box in the previous procedure to tell Dial-Up Networking to let you view what's going on—step by step. Follow these steps to test the script:

1. If you have a desktop shortcut to the Dial-Up Networking Connection, double-click the shortcut. If not, select **Start**, **Programs**, **Accessories**, and **Dial-Up Networking**. Then double-click the connection icon in the **Dial-Up Networking** folder.

2. In the Connect To dialog box, enter your **User name** and **Password**, and click **Connect**. The Dial-Up Networking program begins dialing.

About the Password

If you click the Save Password check box, Windows 95 is supposed to save your password for future sessions so that you don't have to enter it each time. However, this feature is a little flaky. If you have set up separate user profiles for Windows 95, it saves this password. (See your Windows 95 documentation for information about user profiles.) If you haven't done that, Windows probably won't save the password (though I've been informed by Microsoft personnel that it should). If it doesn't save the password, you have to enter it each time you log on. You can also place it in your login script (in place of the $PASSWORD system variable) if you want. However, I suggest that you don't use either method unless you are sure that your computer is secure and won't be used by other people.

Appendix

3. When your modem connects to your service provider, Dial-Up Networking displays the dialog boxes shown in the next figure. These windows may be positioned rather awkwardly; you may not be able to see what's going on very well. To fix that, move them into the positions shown in this figure. But do it quickly. If you take too long, your service provider's computer gives up waiting for you and disconnects your modem.

Testing the script.

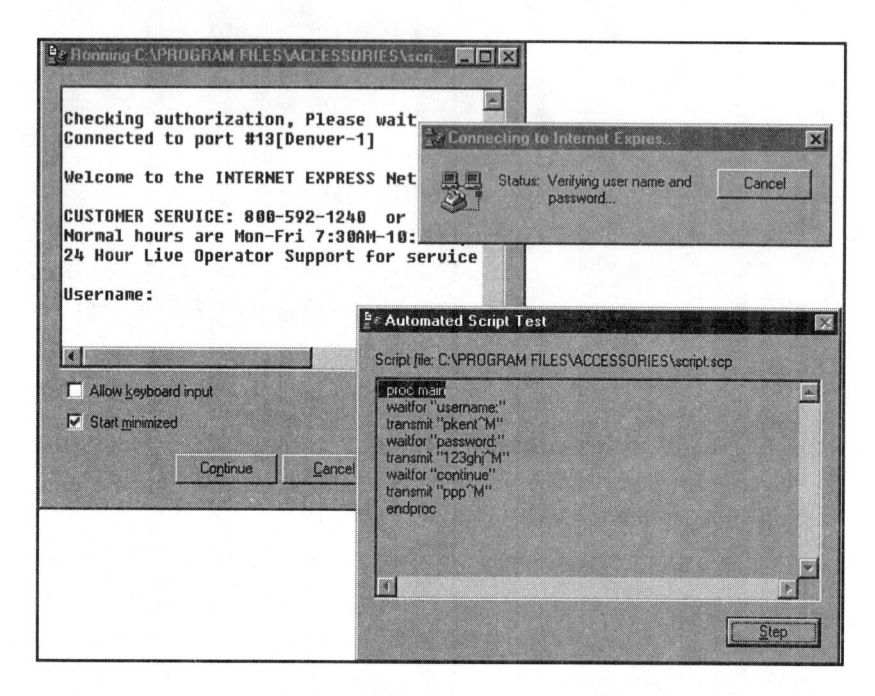

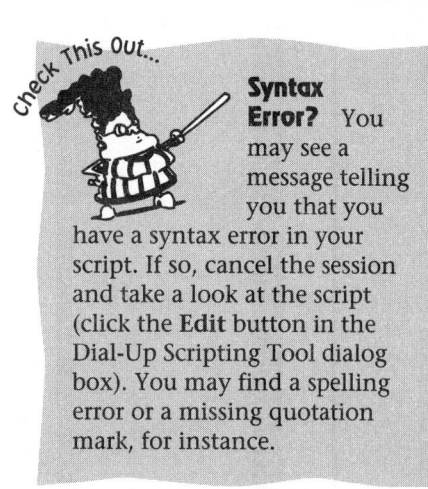

Syntax Error? You may see a message telling you that you have a syntax error in your script. If so, cancel the session and take a look at the script (click the **Edit** button in the Dial-Up Scripting Tool dialog box). You may find a spelling error or a missing quotation mark, for instance.

4. Click the **Step** button in the Automated Script Test window to move through the script step by step. Each time you click the button, the highlight in the window moves to the next line of the script.

5. Watch the effect of your script in the Running-*scriptname* window, where you can see the login session. Each time you click while the highlight is on a transmit command, for instance, Dial-Up Networking should "type" the text that appears after **transmit**. You can watch that happen in the Running-*scriptname* window.

6. Click the **Step** button while the highlight is on the **endproc** command. Both windows close, and Dial-Up Networking begins running the PPP protocol. In a few seconds, you should see the message Connected at nn,nnn bps in the Connected To dialog box (see the following figure).

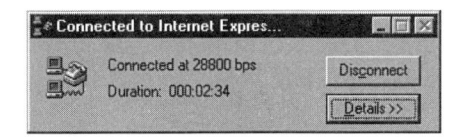

If you get this, you're connected.

7. Click the **Disconnect** button to end the session.

Did everything work correctly? If not, go back and try again. This time, watch the session very carefully and try to figure out where things went wrong. Look for the following errors:

➤ Did you misspell something, and thereby use a transmit command to send the wrong information?

➤ Did a spelling mistake after a **waitfor** command tell Dial-Up Networking to wait for the wrong information?

➤ Did you use the ^M (to press Enter) in the correct places?

➤ Did you leave out any quotation marks?

If you look at your script carefully and watch the session carefully, you should be able to see what's going wrong. And remember to talk with your service provider. You can send them a copy of your login script and have them tell you where you are going wrong.

When your script is working correctly, return to the Dial-Up Scripting Tool dialog box. Click the connection you just tested, and then deselect the **Step through script** check box. Click **Apply** and click **Close**. Try connecting to your service provider again. This time Dial-Up Networking should connect without your assistance.

Check This Out...

Manually Logging In
If you are having problems, you may want to try logging in manually. When you do that, you see your service provider's prompts, and you have to type the responses. (See "Connecting to Your Service Provider" in Chapter 8.)

307

Speak Like a Geek: The Complete Archive

.AU   A sound file format.

.GIF   Graphics Interchange Format. A type of graphics file. The .GIF format was originally developed by CompuServe. Inline graphics in Web documents can only be .GIF, .JPG, or .XBM format. This format is often used in newsgroups, too, when people posting messages want to make pictures available to other people in the newsgroup.

.JPG   The extension generally used for graphics files in the JPEG format.

alias   A name that is substituted for a more complicated name. For example, a simple alias (peterk) may be used instead of a more complicated mailing address (peterk@lab-press.com) or for a mailing list.

America Online   A popular online information system.

anchor   A techie word for an HTML tag that is used as a link from one document to another.

anonymous FTP   A system by which members of the Internet "public" can access files at certain FTP sites without needing a login name; they simply login as ***anonymous***.

Archie   An index system that helps you find files in more than 1,000 FTP sites. The name "Archie" came from the word "archive" and is not an acronym, as you might think.

archive file   A file that contains other, generally compressed, files. Used to store files that are not used often, and files that may be downloaded by Internet users.

ARPAnet   Where the Internet began; the Advanced Research Projects Agency (of the U.S. Department of Defense) computer network, which was the forerunner of the Internet.

article   A message in an Internet newsgroup.

ASCII   American Standard Code for Information Interchange. This is a standard system used by computers to recognize text. An ASCII text file comprises the letters of the alphabet, the punctuation characters, and a few special characters. The nice thing about ASCII is that it's widely recognizable by thousands of programs and many different types of computers.

backbone   A network through which other networks connect.

bandwidth   Widely used to mean the amount of information that can be sent through a particular communications channel.

baud rate   A measurement of how quickly a modem transfers data. Although, strictly speaking, this is not the same as bps (bits per second), the two terms are often used interchangeably.

BBS   See *bulletin board system*.

beta test   A program test based on the premise "this program's virtually finished, we just need a little help getting the rough edges off; let's give it to a few more people."

BITNET   The "Because It's Time" network (really!). A large network connected to the Internet. Before the Internet became affordable to learning institutions, BITNET was the network of choice for communicating.

bits per second   A measure of the speed of data transmission; the number of bits of data that can be transmitted each second (you can think of a bit as equal to one-eighth of a character).

bookmark   A URL that has been saved in some way so that you can quickly and easily return to a particular Web document.

BOOTP   The Bootstrap Protocol. A method used on some networks to connect and start nodes.

bounce   To return e-mail because of some kind of error.

bps   See *bits per second*.

browser   A program that lets you read HTML documents and navigate around the Web.

BTW   An abbreviation often used in online chat or messages to mean "By The Way."

bulletin board system   A computer system to which other computers can connect so their users can retrieve, read, and leave messages and files.

cache   A place where a browser stores Web documents that have been retrieved. The cache may be on the hard disk or in memory, or a combination of the two. Documents you "return to" are retrieved from the cache, which saves transmission time.

CERN   The European Particle Physics Laboratory in Switzerland, which is the home of the World Wide Web. The people there develop lots of Web software and maintain good Web and FTP sites for people looking for information and programs.

chat   Similar to *talk* programs, except that chat systems let large numbers of users chat together. Where a talk program is like a phone call, a chat system is like a party, sometimes with different "rooms" known as channels or groups. The most popular Internet chat system is Internet Relay Chat.

CIX   The Commercial Internet Exchange. An organization of commercial Internet service providers.

client   A program or computer that is serviced by another program or computer (the server). For instance, a Gopher client program requests information from the indexes of a Gopher server program.

compressed files   Computer files that have been reduced in size by a compression program. Such programs are available for all computer systems (for example, PKZIP for DOS and Windows, **tar** and compress for UNIX, and StuffIt for the Macintosh).

CompuServe   A computer information service owned by H&R Block. CompuServe is connected to the Internet.

cracker   Someone who tries to enter a computer system without permission. This is the correct term, though the term hacker is often mistakenly used in its place.

CSLIP   Compressed SLIP. See *Serial Line Internet Protocol (SLIP)*.

cyberspace   The "area" in which computer users travel when "navigating" around on a network or the Internet.

DARPAnet   The Defense Advanced Research Projects Agency network, created by combining ARPAnet and MILNET. A forerunner of the Internet.

DDN   The Defense Data Network. A U.S. military network that is part of the Internet. MILNET is part of the DDN.

dedicated line   A telephone line that is leased from the telephone company and used for one purpose only. On the Internet, dedicated lines connect organizations to service providers' computers, thus providing dedicated service.

dedicated service   See *permanent connection*.

dial-in direct connection   An Internet connection that you access by dialing into a computer through a telephone *line*. When it's connected, your computer acts as if it were an Internet host. You can run client software (such as Gopher or WWW clients), and you can copy files directly to your computer. This type of service is often called SLIP, CSLIP, or PPP. See also *dial-in terminal connection*.

dial-in service   A networking service that you can use by dialing into a computer through a telephone line.

311

dial-in terminal connection   An Internet connection that you can access by dialing into a computer through a telephone line. When it's connected, your computer acts as if it were a terminal connected to the service provider's computer. This type of service is often called Interactive or dial-up. See also *dial-in direct connection*.

dial-up service   A common Internet term for a dial-in terminal connection.

direct connection   See *permanent connection*.

DNS   See *Domain Name System*.

domain name   A name given to a host computer on the Internet.

Domain Name System   A system by which one Internet host can find another so it can send e-mail, connect FTP sessions, and so on. The hierarchical system of Internet host names (*hostname.hostname.hostname*) uses the Domain Name System. The DNS, in effect, translates words into numbers that the Internet's computers can understand. For instance, if you use the domain name firefly.prairienet.org, DNS translates it into 192.17.3.3.

dot address   A term for an IP address, which is in the form *n.n.n.n*, where each *n* is a number (and each number is a byte).

download   The process of transferring information from one computer to another. You download a file from another computer to yours. See also *upload*.

e-mail (or email)   Short for electronic mail, this is a system that lets people send and receive messages with their computers. The system might be on a large network (such as the Internet), on a bulletin board (such as CompuServe), or over a company's own office network.

EARN   The European network associated with BITNET.

EFF   See *Electronic Frontier Foundation*.

Electronic Frontier Foundation (EFF)   An organization interested in social, legal, and political issues related to the use of computers. The EFF is particularly interested in fighting government restrictions on the use of computer technology.

emoticon   The techie name for a smiley. :)

encryption   A means of modifying data so that unauthorized recipients cannot use or understand it.

Enhanced NCSA Mosaic   A Web browser sold by Spyglass. This is a derivation of the original NCSA program.

etext   Electronic text. A book or other document in electronic form, usually simple ASCII text.

Ethernet   A protocol, or standard, by which computers may be connected to one another to exchange information and messages.

FAQ   Frequently-Asked Questions. A document containing a list of common questions and corresponding answers. You'll often find FAQs at Gopher sites, in newsgroups, and at FTP and Web sites.

file transfer   The process of copying files from one computer to another over a network or telephone line. See also *FTP*.

File Transfer Protocol   See *FTP*.

Finger   A program used to find information about a user on a host computer.

flame   An abusive newsgroup message. Things you can do to earn a flame include asking dumb questions, offending people, not reading the FAQ, or simply getting on the wrong side of someone with an attitude.

flamer   A person who writes a flame.

form   A Web form is a sort of interactive document. The document can contain fields into which readers can type information. This information might be used as part of a survey, to purchase an item, or to search a database, for example.

forms support   A Web browser that has forms support can work with a Web form. Not all browsers can use forms.

forum   An individual bulletin board on CompuServe. (In Internet-speak, the term is "newsgroup.")

fragment   Part of a *packet*. Packets can be broken down into small pieces (fragments), transmitted, and then reassembled. See also *packet switching*.

Free-Net   A community computer network, often based at the local library, that provides Internet access to citizens at the library (or sometimes from their home computers). Free-Nets also have many local services, such as information about local events, local message areas, connections to local government departments, and so on.

freeware   Software provided free by its originator. (Not the same as public domain software because the author retains copyright.) See also *shareware*.

FTP   File Transfer Protocol. A protocol defining how files are transferred from one computer to another. FTP is also the name of a program used to move files. You can also use FTP as a verb (often in lowercase) to describe the procedure of using FTP as in, "ftp to ftp.demon.co.uk" or "I ftp'ed to that system and grabbed the file."

gateway   A system that enables two incompatible networks or applications to communicate with each other.

geek Stereotypically, someone who knows a lot about computers. Geeks often spend more time in front of their computers than talking with real people. The word "geek" may have started as a derogatory term, but many geeks are proud of their geekness—and many have become very rich because of it.

GEnie A computer information service owned by General Electric.

Gopher A system of clients and servers that provides a menu system for navigating around the Internet. Most Web browsers can act as Gopher clients. Gopher was started at the University of Minnesota, which has a gopher for its mascot—hence the name.

Gopherspace Anywhere and everywhere you can get to using Gopher is known as Gopherspace.

Gore, Al A vice president who believes the information highway is critical to the U.S.'s future. Gore reportedly wants all United States high schools connected to the Internet in the next few years.

GUI Graphical User Interface (pronounced "goo-ey"). A program that provides a user with on-screen tools such as menus, buttons, dialog boxes, a mouse pointer, and so on.

hacker Someone who enjoys spending most of his life with his head stuck inside a computer, either literally or metaphorically. See also *geek* and *cracker*.

history list A list of Web documents that you've seen in the current session (some browsers' history lists also show documents from previous sessions). You can return to a document by selecting it in the history list.

home page 1. The Web document your browser displays when you start the program. 2. A sort of "main page" at a Web site. Personally, I don't like this second definition, but there's not much I can do about it.

host A computer connected directly to the Internet. A service provider's computer is a host, as are computers with permanent connections. Computers with dial-in terminal connections are not hosts; they are terminals connected to the service provider's host. Computers with dial-in direct connections can be thought of as "sort of" host; they act like hosts when they're connected.

host address See *IP address*.

host name The name given to a host. Computers connected to the Internet really have host numbers, but host names are easier to remember and work with.

host number See *IP address*.

hotlist A list of bookmarks, or URLs, of Web documents that you want to save for future use. You can return to a particular document by selecting its bookmark from the hotlist.

HTML   HyperText Markup Language. The basic "coding" system used to create Web documents.

HTTP   HyperText Transfer Protocol. The data-transmission protocol used to transfer Web documents across the Internet.

hyperlink   See *link*.

hypermedia   Loosely used to mean a hypertext document that contains or has links to other types of media such as pictures, sound, video, and so on.

hypertext   A system in which documents contain links that enable readers to move between areas of the document, following subjects of interest. With most browsers, you use the mouse to click on a hypertext link (usually a blue-colored word or a picture), and you immediately find yourself in a different part of the Web page or on a completely different Web page with related information. The World Wide Web is a hypertext system.

HYTELNET   A directory of Telnet sites. This provides you with a great way to find out what you can do on hundreds of computers around the world.

IAB   See *Internet Architecture Board (IAB)*.

IAP   Internet Access Provider. Another term for service provider.

IETF   See *Internet Engineering Task Force*.

IMHO   An abbreviation often used in online chat or messages that's short for "In My Humble Opinion."

index document   A Web document that lets you search some kind of database.

index server   A special program, accessed through an index document, that lets you search some kind of database.

inline image   A picture inside a Web document. These graphics must be GIF, JPG, or XBM format files.

Integrated Services Digital Network (ISDN)   A digital telecommunications system that everyone's been waiting for but that the telephone companies seem unable to get installed in a decent time frame. ISDN allows voice and data to be transmitted on the same line in a digital format—as opposed to the normal analog format.

interactive service   See *dial-in terminal connection*.

internet   Spelled with a small i, the term internet refers to networks connected to one another. "The Internet" is not the only internet.

Internet   A worldwide network of computer networks that grew out of ARPAnet.

315

internet address   See *IP address*.

Internet Architecture Board (IAB)   The "council of elders" elected by ISOC to get together and figure out how the different components of the Internet will connect.

Internet Engineering Task Force   A group of engineers that makes technical recommendations concerning the Internet to the IAB.

Internet Explorer   A new Web browser from Microsoft. Giving Netscape a run for its money, it's one of the two best browsers around.

Internet Protocol   The standard protocol used by systems communicating across the Internet. Other protocols are used, but the Internet Protocol is the most important one.

Internet Relay Chat (IRC)   See *IRC*.

Internet Society   The society that governs the Internet; it elects the Internet Architecture Board, which decides on technical issues related to how the Internet works.

InterNIC   The Internet Network Information Center. This NIC, run by the National Science Foundation, provides various administrative services for the Internet.

IP   See *Internet Protocol*.

IP address   A 32-bit address that defines the location of a host on the Internet. Such addresses are normally shown as four bytes separated by periods (for example, 192.156.196.1). See also *dot address*.

IRC   Internet Relay Chat. A popular chat program. Internet users around the world can chat with other users in their choice of IRC channels.

ISDN   See *Integrated Services Digital Network (ISDN)*.

ISOC   See *Internet Society*.

JPEG   A compressed graphic format often found on the World Wide Web. (These files use the .JPG or .JPEG extension.)

Jughead   Jonzy's Universal Gopher Hierarchy Excavation And Display tool. A Gopher search tool similar to Veronica. The main difference between Veronica and Jughead is that Jughead searches a specific Gopher server, while Veronica searches all of Gopherspace.

KIS   See *Knowbot Information Service*.

Knowbot   A program that can search the Internet for requested information. Knowbots are in an experimental stage.

Knowbot Information Service   An experimental system that helps you search various directories for a person's information (such as an e-mail address).

LAN See *Local Area Network*.

leased line See *dedicated line*.

link A connection between two Web documents. Links are generally pieces of text or pictures that you can click on to make the browser request and display another Web document.

linked image An image that is not in a Web document (that's an inline image) but is "connected" to a document by a link. Clicking on the link displays the image.

LISTSERV lists Mailing lists (using mail reflectors) that act as newsgroups. Messages sent to a LISTSERV address are sent to everyone who has subscribed to the list. Responses are sent back to the LISTSERV address.

Local Area Network (LAN) A computer network that covers only a small area, often a single office or building.

logging off The opposite of logging on; telling the computer that you've finished work and no longer need to use its services. The procedure usually involves typing a simple command such as **exit** or **bye**.

logging on Computer jargon for getting permission from a computer to use its services. A logon procedure usually involves typing in a user name (also known as an account name or user ID) and a password. This procedure makes sure that only authorized people use the computer. Also known as logging in.

login The procedure of logging on.

lurk To read newsgroup or LISTSERV messages and not respond to them. Nobody knows you are there. Despite the creepy connotation of the word "lurk," lurking is a good way to become familiar with a newsgroup before contributing to it.

lurker Someone who is lurking.

mail reflector A mail address that accepts e-mail messages and then sends them on to a predefined list of other e-mail addresses. Such systems make distributing messages to a group of people easy and convenient.

mail robot An e-mail system that automatically carries out some sort of procedure for you.

mail server 1. A program that distributes computer files or information in response to e-mail requests. 2. A program that handles incoming e-mail for a host (as in POP3 mail server).

mailing list A list of e-mail addresses in a designated named group. You can send a single message to everyone in that group by entering just one name (the name of the mailing list) as the To address. Also refers to discussion groups based on the mailing list. Each message sent to the group is sent out to everyone on the list. (LISTSERV groups are mailing list groups.)

MB   Abbreviation for megabyte.

MCImail   An e-mail system owned by MCI.

megabyte   A measure of the quantity of data. A megabyte is a lot when you are talking about files containing simple text messages, but it's not much when you are talking about files containing color photographs.

MILNET   A U.S. Department of Defense network connected to the Internet.

MIME   Multipurpose Internet Mail Extensions. A method that lets you send computer files as e-mail.

mirror site   An FTP site that is a "mirror image" of another FTP site. Every week or two, the contents of the other FTP site are copied to the mirror site. The point is that if you can't get into the original site, you can go to one of the mirror sites.

modem   A device that converts digital signals used by your computer into analog signals for transmission through a phone line (modulation), and converts the phone line's analog signals into digital signals your computer can use (demodulation).

Mosaic   The first popular GUI Web browser; from the NCSA.

MPEG   A computer video format. With the right software and (in some cases) hardware, you can play MPEG video files on your computer.

MUD   A type of game popular on the Internet. MUD means Multiple User Dimensions, Multiple User Dungeons, or Multiple User Dialogue. A MUD is a text game in which each player has a character and the characters communicate through your typed messages.

navigate   To move around on the Web using a browser. When you jump to a Web document, you are navigating.

navigator   A program that helps you find your way around a complicated BBS. Several navigator programs are available for CompuServe, for instance. Navigators can save you money because they enable you to prepare for many operations (such as writing mail) offline, and then go online quickly to perform the operations automatically. True Internet navigators are currently in a developmental stage and are not widely use.

NCSA   National Center for Supercomputing Applications. The people who make the World Wide Web browser called Mosaic.

netiquette   Internet etiquette. The correct form of behavior to use while working on the Internet and UseNet. Can be summed up as "Don't waste computer resources, and don't be rude."

Netnews   See *UseNet*.

Netscape   The Web's most popular browser, which was created by some old NCSA programmers who started a company called Netscape Communications.

Network Information Center   A system providing support and information for a network.

Network News Transfer Protocol (NNTP)   A system used for the distribution of UseNet newsgroup messages.

newbie   A new user. The term may be used to refer to a new Internet user, or a user who is new to a particular area of the Internet. Because everyone and his dog is getting onto the Internet, these loathsome creatures have brought the general tone of the Internet down a notch or two, upsetting long-term Internet users who thought the Internet was their own personal secret.

news server   A computer that collects newsgroup data and makes it available to newsreaders.

newsgroup   The Internet equivalent of a BBS or discussion group (or "forum" in CompuServe-speak) in which people leave messages for others to read. See also *LISTSERV lists*.

newsreader   A program that helps you find your way through a newsgroup's messages.

NIC   See *Network Information Center*.

NNTP   See *Network News Transfer Protocol*.

NOC   Network Operations Center. A group that administers a network.

node   A computer "device" connected to a computer network. That device might be an actual computer, or it might be something else such as a printer or router.

NREN   The National Research and Education Network.

NSF   National Science Foundation. A U.S. government agency, the NSF runs the NSFNet.

NSFNet   The National Science Foundation network. A large network connected to the Internet.

online   Connected. You are online if you are working on your computer while it is connected to another computer. Your printer is online if it is connected to your computer and ready to accept data. (Online is often written "on-line," though the non-hyphenated version seems to be gaining acceptance these days.)

packet   A collection of data. See also *packet switching*.

Packet InterNet Groper (PING)   A program that tests whether a particular host computer is accessible to you.

packet switching   A system that breaks transmitted data into small packets and transmits each packet (or package) independently. Each packet is individually addressed and may even travel over a route different from that of other packets. The packets are combined by the receiving computer.

permanent connection   A connection to the Internet that uses a leased line. The computer with a permanent connection acts as a host on the Internet. This type of service is often called direct, permanent direct, or dedicated service, and it is very expensive to set up and run. However, it provides a very quick high-bandwidth connection.

permanent direct   See *permanent connection*.

PING   See *Packet InterNet Groper*.

point of presence   Jargon meaning a method of connecting to a service locally (without dialing long distance). If a service provider has a POP in, say, Podunk, Ohio, people in that city can connect to the service provider by making a local call.

Point-to-Point Protocol (PPP)   A method for connecting computers to the Internet via telephone lines; similar to SLIP (though it's currently less common).

POP   See *point of presence* and *Post Office Protocol (POP)*.

port   Generally, "port" refers to the hardware through which computer data is transmitted; the plugs on the back of your computer are ports. On the Internet, "port" often refers to a particular application. For instance, you might telnet to a particular port on a particular host. The port is actually an application.

Post Office Protocol (POP)   A system for letting hosts get e-mail from a server. This is typically used when a dial-in direct host (which may only have one user and may only be connected to the Internet periodically) gets its e-mail from a service provider. The latest version of POP is POP3. Do not confuse this with point of presence (POP).

posting   A message (article) sent to a newsgroup, or the act of sending such a message.

postmaster   The person at a host who is responsible for managing the mail system. If you need information about a user at a particular host, you can send e-mail to **postmaster@*hostname***.

PPP   See *Point-to-Point Protocol (PPP)*.

Prodigy   A computer information service.

protocol   A set of rules that defines how computers transmit information to each other, enabling different types of computers and software to communicate with each other.

public domain software   Software that does not belong to anyone. You can use it without paying for it, and you can even modify it if the source code is available. See also *shareware* and *freeware*.

reflector, mail   A kind of public mailing list. Messages sent to a mail reflector's address are sent on automatically to a list of other addresses.

reload (or refresh)   A command that tells your browser to retrieve a Web document even though you have it in the cache.

remote login   A BSD (Berkeley) UNIX command (**rlogin**) that is similar to Telnet.

rendered   An HTML document that is being viewed in a Web browser. The browser renders it into a normal text document. You don't see the codes, only the text that the author wants you to see. An unrendered document is the source HTML document with codes and all.

rlogin   See *remote login*.

ROT13   Rotation 13. A method used to encrypt messages in newsgroups so you can't stumble across an offensive message. If you want to read an offensive message, you'll have to decide to do so—and go out of your way to decode it.

router   A system used to transmit data between two computer systems or networks using the same protocol. For instance, a company that has a permanent connection to the Internet will use a router to connect its computer to a leased line. At the other end of the leased line, a router is used to connect it to the service provider's network.

Serial Line Internet Protocol (SLIP)   A method for connecting a computer to the Internet using a telephone line and modem. (See *dial-in direct connection*.) When connected, the user has the same services provided to the user of a permanent connection.

server   A program or computer that services another program or computer (the client). For instance, a Gopher server program sends information from its indexes to a Gopher client program.

service provider   A company that provides a connection to the Internet. Service providers sell access to the network for greatly varying prices. Shop around for the best deal.

shareware   Software that is freely distributed, but for which the author expects payment from people who decide to keep and use it. See also *freeware* and *public domain software*.

shell account   Another name for a simple dial-in terminal account.

signature   A short piece of text transmitted with an e-mail or newsgroup message. Some systems can automatically attach text from a file to the end of a message. Signature files typically contain detailed information on how to contact someone: name and address, telephone numbers, Internet address, CompuServe ID, and so on.

Simple Mail Transfer Protocol (SMTP)   A way to transfer e-mail between computers on a network.

SLIP   See *Serial Line Internet Protocol (SLIP)*.

smiley   A symbol in e-mail and newsgroup messages used to convey emotion or simply for amusement. Create smileys by typing various keyboard characters. For example, :-(means sadness. Smileys are usually sideways; turn your head to view the smiley. The correct term is "emoticon."

SMTP   See *Simple Mail Transfer Protocol (SMTP)*.

source document   An HTML document, the basic ASCII file that is rendered by a browser.

stack   See *TCP/IP stack*.

tags   The "codes" inside an HTML file.

talk   A program that lets two or more UNIX users on the same host or different hosts type messages to each other. When a user types a character, that character is immediately transmitted to the other user. Common talk programs include talk, ntalk, and YTalk.

tar files   Files compressed using the UNIX tape archiver program. Such files usually have file names ending in .tar.

TCP/IP   Transfer Control Protocol/Internet Protocol. A set of protocols (communications rules) that control how data is transferred between computers on the Internet.

TCP/IP stack   The software you must install before you can run TCP/IP programs across a dial-in direct connection. You might think of the TCP/IP stack as an Internet driver. In the same way you need a printer driver to send something from your word processor to your printer, you need the TCP/IP stack to send information to (and receive information from) your dial-in direct programs.

Telnet   A program that lets Internet users log on to computers other than their own host computers, sometimes as far away as the other side of the world. Telnet is also used as a verb, as in "telnet to debra.doc.ca."

the Web   See *World Wide Web*.

tn3270   A Telnet-like program used for remote logins to IBM mainframes.

Trojan Horse   A computer program that appears to carry out a useful function, but which is actually designed to do harm to the system on which it runs. See also *virus*.

UNIX   A computer operating system. Many hosts connected to the Internet run UNIX; however, Windows NT is growing in popularity, and we'll soon see plenty of Windows 95 hosts.

upload   The process of transferring information from one computer to another. You upload a file from your computer to another. See also *download*.

URL Uniform Resource Locator. A Web "address."

UseNet The "User's Network." A large network connected to the Internet. The term also refers to the newsgroups distributed by this network.

UUCP UNIX to UNIX Copy Program. A system by which files can be transferred between UNIX computers. The Internet uses UUCP to provide a form of e-mail in which the mail is placed in files and transferred to other computers.

UUCP network A network of UNIX computers connected to the Internet.

uudecode If you use uuencode to convert a file to ASCII and transmit it, you'll use uudecode to convert the ASCII file back to its original format.

uuencode A program used to convert a computer file of any kind (sound, spreadsheet, word processor, or whatever) into an ASCII file so that it can be transmitted as a text message. The term is also used as a verb, as in "uuencode this file." There are DOS and UNIX uuencode programs. In Windows, there's a program called Wincode that can uuencode and uudecode files.

Veronica The Very Easy Rodent-Oriented Net-wide Index to Computerized Archives. A very useful program for finding things in Gopherspace.

viewer A program that displays or plays computer files that you find on the Web. For instance, you need a viewer to play video files you find. These are sometimes known as *helpers*.

virus A program that uses various techniques to duplicate itself and travel between computers. Viruses vary from simple nuisances (they might display an unexpected message on your screen) to serious problems that can cause millions of dollars' worth of damage (such as crashing a computer system and erasing important data).

VT100 The product name of a Digital Equipment Corporation computer terminal (DEC). This terminal is a standard that is "emulated" (duplicated) by many other manufacturers' terminals.

W3 See *World Wide Web*.

WAIS See *Wide Area Information Server (WAIS)*.

Web server A program that makes Web documents available to browsers. The browser asks the server for the document, and the server transmits it to the browser.

Web site A collection of Web documents about a particular subject on a host.

Webspace The area of cyberspace in which you are traveling when you work on the Web.

White Pages Lists of Internet users available in Yahoo (a WWW search system).

Whois A UNIX program used for searching for information about Internet users.

Wide Area Information Server (WAIS) A system that can search databases on the Internet for information in which you are interested.

World Wide Web A hypertext system that allows users to "travel through" linked documents following any chosen route. World Wide Web documents contain topics that you can select to move to other documents. See also *hypertext*.

WWW See *World Wide Web*.

X.500 A standard for electronic directory services.

XBM X Bitmap graphics format. A bitmap from the UNIX X Window system. These are simple images, one of only two types that can be used as inline graphics (the other is .GIF).

Ytalk Currently one of the best UNIX talk programs. Unlike the basic talk program, YTalk lets several users talk together at once. It can also communicate with other types of talk programs.

Index

Symbols

* (asterisk) wild card, 172
? wild cards (Jughead), 173
@ (at), e-mail addresses, 252-253

A

abbreviations (e-mail shorthand), 252
access numbers, 56
accessing
    Archie, 154
    Internet, 49, 80-81
        Dial-Up Scripting Tool, 88-91
        installing, 76-77
        MSN (Microsoft Network), 48
        new computers, 49
        properties, 82-85
        software, 48
    OUI (Offline Usenet Interface), 230
    see also connecting
accounts
    access numbers, 56
    connecting to the Internet
        fees, 22-23
        Free-Nets, 23-25
    domain names, 43-45
        fees, 44
        first-level domain types, 44-45
    e-mail, fingering, 291-293
    MSN (Microsoft Network)
        additional, 54
        addresses, 51
        joining, 50-54
    membership ID, 54
    passwords, 53
    names, 41-42
    PPP (Point-to-Point Protocol), 62
    service providers, setting up, 65
    shell accounts, 321
    SLIP (Serial Line Internet Protocol), 62
    types of, 4
acquiring Internet software, 54-55
Add Remove/Programs Properties dialog box, 50
Add Service to Profile dialog box, 262
Add to Favorites command (Favorites menu), 117
Add To Favorites dialog box, 117
addresses
    address book options, 267
    Archie servers, 161
    customizing Internet Explorer, 132
    DNS server address, 64
    e-mail, 64, 256
        incorrect, 289
        lost, 297
        mailing lists, 317
        parts of, 252-253
        President of the US, 248
        reflectors, 317
        troubleshooting, 289
        Vice President of the US, 248
    Internet directories, 290
    Internet Explorer, 132
    IP (Internet Protocol), 316
        address, 63, 70, 73
    LISTSERVs, 239
MSN (Microsoft Network) accounts, 51
URL (Uniform Resource Locator), 113
advanced dialing Microsoft Network, 53
Advanced Research Projects Agency (ARPAnet), 309
    networks, 14
alt (alternative newsgroup), 208-209, 214
    newsgroup names, 208-209
Always warn about files of this type check box, 130
America Online, 309, 254
    e-mail, 253-254
American Standard Code for Information Interchange (ASCII), 310
anchors (defined), 309
anonymous FTP (File Transfer Protocol), 309
AOL (America Online), 254
    e-mail, 253-254
Archie, 4, 309
    accessing, 154
    client/server system, 154
    e-mail, 161-163
        commands, 163
        Whatis command, 162
    gateways, 155
    mail, 154
    searching, 155-156
        e-mail, 161-163
        options, 157-158
        search types, 158-159
    servers
        finding, 155
        locations, 161
        performing searches, 155-159
    WS_Archie, 159-160
archive files, 309

ARPAnet (Advanced Research Projects Agency network), 14, 309
Arrange Messages command (View menu), 217
articles (defined), 309
ASCII (American Standard Code for Information Interchange), 224-225, 310
  decoding (UUDECODING), 323
  encoding (UUENCODING), 323
assigning script files, 304-305
associating files with programs, 131
asterisk (*) wild card, 172
at symbol (@; e-mail addresses), 252-253
attachments (file messages), 283-284
AU (sound file formats), 309
automated mailing lists, 235
  LISTSERV lists, 235
  subscribing to, 235

B

"Because It's Time" network (BITNET), 310
backbones (defined), 310
background color
  Internet Explorer, customizing, 132
  VT-100 setting, 182
bacteria (defined), 150
bandwidths (defined), 310
baud rate, 35, 310
Baudot, J.M.E. (inventor of telegraph code), 35
BBS (bulletin board systems), 8-9, 310
  computers as, 9
  defined, 203
  forums, 313
  navigators, 318
  owners of, 13
  starting requirements, 8
Bcc box command (View menu), 275
beta tests, 310
biological subjects newsgroup, 208
bionet (alternative newsgroup), 208
bit (alternative newgroup), 208

BITNET ("Because It's Time" network), 310
  computer network (LISTSERV lists), 235
  e-mail, 254
bits per second (bps), 35, 310
biz (alternative newsgroup), 208
blind carbon copies, 275
blinking cursor (VT-100 setting), 182
block cursor (VT-100 setting), 182
Boardwatch Magazine, 25
bombs (defined), 150
bookmarks, 310
  hotlists, 314
boolean searches, 172-173
boot sector viruses, 150
BOOTP (Bootstrap Protocol), 310
bounces (defined), 310
brasil (alternative newsgroup), 209
Browse dialog box, 304
browsers, 4, 96-97
  defined, 102, 310
  Enhanced NCSA Mosaic, 312
  forms support, 313
  Gopher, 168-169
  history lists, 114-116
  Internet Explorer, 96, 101-102, 316
    cache, 110-112
    dowloading, 76-77
    opening, 106
    updating, 76
  Mosaic, 318
  Netscape, 96, 101-102, 319
  rendering, 321
  servers, 101
BTW (By The Way), 310
buffer size (VT-100 setting), 182
bulletin board systems, *see* BBSs
business subjects newsgroup, 208
buttons
  Internet Explorer toolbars, 107-108
  New Type (Internet Explorer), 131
  Open File, 125-126
  Open File (Internet Explorer), 130
  Open With (Internet Explorer), 130
  Save As, 125-126

Use Default (Internet Explorer), 133
Use Larger Font (Internet Explorer), 134
Use Smaller Font (Internet Explorer), 134
buying modems, 39-40

C

cache, 110-112, 310
  defined, 106
  emptying, 112
  history lists, 114-116
  refresh button, 112
caps lock, 257
carbon copies
  e-mail
    blind carbon copies, 275
    messages, 275
case insensitive substring match searches, 158
case sensitive substring match searches, 158
CERN (European Particle Physics Laboratory), 310
chats, 311
  IMHO (In My Humble Opinion), 315
  IRC (Internet Relay Chat), 316
choosing, *see* selecting
CIX (Commercial Internet Exchange), 311
ClariNet news service, 208
  Archie, 154
  clari (alternative newsgroup), 208
clients, 311
  defined, 190
  news, 211
  UNIX-based, telnetting to, 198-202
  WAIS programs for Windows, 196
clipboard button, 226
codes
  FTP (File Transfer Protocol), connecting to, 97-101
  viewing, 124
Collapse All Conversations command (View menu), 216
Color dialog box, 132
commands
  Archie, 163
  Compose menu
    Forward, 284
    Forward by E-mail, 222

326

Index

New Messages, 216, 222, 274
Reply to All, 284
Reply to BBS, 222
Reply to E-mail, 222
Reply to Sender, 284
Connect menu
  Disconnect, 186
  Remote System, 185
Edit menu
  Copy, 123, 301
  Find, 110, 156
  Go To, 55, 214
  Mark to Delete, 282
  Mark to Retrieve, 281
  Mark to Retrieve a Copy, 281
  Paste, 301
  Select All, 185, 218, 226
Favorites menu (Add to Favorites), 117
File menu
  Create Shortcut, 117
  Decode, 226
  Delete, 116, 283
  More History, 115
  Move, 276, 283
  New Folder, 118, 276
  Open, 114, 116, 219
  Open Start Page, 109
  Post Message, 223
  Print, 222, 276
  Print Setup, 222
  Properties, 278
  Save, 221, 276
  Save As, 114, 123, 193
  Send, 276
  UUEncode/Decode, 225
Insert menu (File), 278
Jughead, 173-174
Options menu
  FTP Setup, 160
  User Preferences, 159
Ping, 69
Source Selection screen (directory of servers; WAIS), 200
Start menu
  Programs, 50
  Run, 54, 179
  WS_FTP, 147
Terminal menu
  Preferences, 181
  Start Logging, 185
Tools menu
  Connect & Transfer Mail, 277, 282
  Connect & Update Headers, 281
  Deliver Now, 277

Find, 284
Mark All Messages as Read, 218
Mark Conversation as Read, 218
Mark Conversation as Unread, 218
Mark Message as Read, 218
Mark Message as Unread, 218
Options, 268
Remote Mail, 277, 281
ROT13 Encode/Decode, 223
Services, 268
Show All Messages, 219
Veronica, 174-176
View menu
  Arrange Messages, 217
  Bcc box, 275
  Collapse All Conversations, 216
  Conversation, 216
  Expand All Conversations, 216
  Folders, 279
  Fonts, 133
  Forward, 109
  List, 217
  Next, 283
  Options, 111, 128
  Previous, 283
  Refresh, 112
  Stop, 109
comp (UseNet group), 207
Complete Idiot's Guide to the World Wide Web URL, 123
Compose menu commands
  Forward, 284
  Forward by E-mail, 222
  New Messages, 216, 222, 274
  Reply to All, 284
  Reply to BBS, 222
  Reply to E-mail, 222
  Reply to Sender, 284
composing (e-mail messages), 222, 275
compressed files, 145-146, 311
  ZIP files, 146
CompuServe, 311
  e-mail, 253-254
  forums, 313
  defined, 204
computers
  accessing the Internet, 49
  as BBSs (bulletin board services), 9
  compressed files, 311

crackers, 311
dial-in services, 311
downloading, 312
Ethernet, 312
files, sending, 277-278
hackers, 314
logging off, 317
logging on, 317
nodes, 319
requirement for running Windows 95, 38
routers, 321
servers (defined), 321
sharing, 261
ComputerShopper, 25
Comt, 178
configuring Exchange, 260
Confirm File Open dialog box, 130, 144
Connect & Transfer Mail command (Tools menu), 282
Connect & Update Headers command (Tools menu), 281
Connect menu commands, 185-186
Connect To dialog box, 68, 106
Connect to Transfer Mail command (Tools menu), 277
Connected To dialog box, 307
connecting
  computers (Ethernet), 312
  dial-in direct connection, 311
  dial-in terminal connection, 312
  FTP (File Transfer Protocol)
    codes, 97-101
    links, 141
    troubleshooting, 140, 146-149, 235
    WS_FTP program, 147-149
  Internet, 80-81
    Dial-Up Scripting Tool, 88-91
    domain names, 43-45
    IAB (Internet Architecture Board), 316
    login names, 41-42
    modems, 38-41
    passwords, 42-43
    properties, 82-85
    SLIP (Serial Line Internet Protocol), 321
    software, 45
    see also connections

327

Internet Mail services, 263-265
   modems, 263
online, 319
point of presence, 320
service providers, 85-87
   accounts, 65
   Jumpstart Kit, 66-68
   TCP/IP, 70-72
   troubleshooting, 68-69
SLIP (Serial Line Internet Protocol), 72-73
Telnet
   direct connections, 185
Telnet sites, 181
WAIS, 190-191
see also accessing
Connection Description dialog box, 301
connections, 18-22
   dial-in direct, 19-20
      advantages, 20
      disadvantages, 20
      SLIP (Serial Line Internet Protocol), 19-20
   dial-in terminal, 21
   fees, 3-4
   free accounts, 22-23
      finding, 25-26
      Free-Nets, 23-25
   ISDN (Integrated Services Digital Network), 40-41
   mail, 21
   permanent, 18-19
      advantages, 20
      TCP/IP (Transfer Control Protocol/Internet Protocol), 19
   permanent connections, 320
   types, 4
   see also connecting to the Internet
Conversation command (View menu), 216
conversations, 216
   views, 216
Copy command (Edit menu), 123, 301
copying
   backgrounds of Web pages, 123-124
   files (FTP), 313
   messages, 276
   pictures on World Wide Web, 123
   Telnet sessions, 185
cost, *see* fees
courts (alternative newsgroup), 208

crackers, 311
Create Shortcut command (File menu), 117
CSLIP (Compressed Serial Line Internet Protocol), 64, 311
customizing
   Internet Explorer, 131-134
      addresses, 132
      background color, 132
      hypertext links, 132
      turning off inline images, 131
   LISTSERVs, 241-242
      options, 242
cyberspace, 311

D

DARPAnet (Defense Advanced Research Projects Agency), 311
data
   encryptions, 312
   packets, 319
databases
   lists of
      obtaining, 193
      viewing, 194
   WAIS, 190
      directory of servers, 199-201
      running, 190-202
      standard, 191
      see also WAIS
   WAIS (Wide Area Information Server), 324
   Yahoo, 122
DDN (Defense Data Network), 311
de (alternative newsgroup), 208
Decode command (File menu), 226
decoding (UUDECODING), 226, 323
dedicated connections, *see* permanent connections
dedicated lines, 311
Delete command (File menu), 116, 283
deleting history lists, 116
Deliver Now command (Tools menu), 277
dial-in direct
   accounts, 4
   connections, 19-20, 311
      advantages, 20

      disadvantages, 20
      SLIP (Serial Line Internet Protocol), 19, 20
dial-in services, 311
dial-in terminal
   accounts, 4
   connection, 21, 312
      dial-up service, 312
Dial-Up Networking, 68-69, 299-300
   folders, 85
   installing, 77-78
   passwords, 305
   Ping command, 69
   properties, 82-85
   scripts
      testing, 305-307
      writing, 302-304
   shortcuts, creating, 68
Dial-Up Networking dialog box, 72, 81
Dial-Up Scripting
   FTP (File Transfer Protocol), 88-91
   tool, 85, 88-91, 304
      SLIP (Serial Line Internet Protocol), 87
Dial-Up Scripting Tool dialog box, 307
dial-up services, 312
   see also dial-in terminal connections
dialing up service providers, 68-69
dialog boxes
   Add Remove/Programs Properties, 50
   Add Service to Profile, 262
   Add To Favorites, 117
   Browse, 304
   Color, 132
   Confirm File Open, 130, 144
   Connect To, 68, 106, 307
   Connection Description, 301
   Dial-Up Networking, 72, 81
   Dial-Up Scripting Tool, 307
   Exchange Settings Properties, 261, 265
   File to Decode, 226
   Find, 110
   Internet Mail, 262
   Internet Setup Wizard, 66
   Microsoft Network, 50
   Network, 70, 79
   Note Properties, 276
   Open Internet Address, 114
   Open Log File, 185
   Open With, 130

Index

Options, 111, 128
Options (Microsoft Exchange)
   General Options, 268-270
   Read Options, 270-271
   Sending Options, 271-272
Personal Address Book, 267
Personal Folders, 266
Product Number, 65
Properties, 278
Run Program, 65
Save As, 124, 144
Select Network Component Type, 78
Select Network Protocol, 79
Server Types, 72, 83
Session Profile, 147
Sign In, 55
TCP/IP Settings, 84
Unknown File Type, 129-130
Welcome to Microsoft Network, 55
wizards, 66
digests (messages), 241
directories
   cache (defined), 106
   HYTELNET, 179-182, 315
   Internet, 290
   Internet Access Providers, 32
   Knowbot Information Service, 316
   names, 144
   World Wide Web, 180
disappearing messages, 217-218
Disconnect command (Connect menu), 186
disconnecting from Telnet, 186
discussion groups, *see* mailing lists; newsgroups
disks
   hard (World Wide Web), 114
   saving files to, 125
   sound files, 127
   space, comparing rates of service providers, 36
displaying
   documents, 133-134
   LISTSERVs, 241-242
      options, 242
   messages, 219
   World Wide Web (WWW), 108

DNS (Domain Name Services), 64, 253, 312
   root servers, 253
documents, 103
   displaying, 133-134
   Gopher, 169
   home pages, 314
   hypermedia, 315
   hypertext, 315
      defined, 96
      links, 132
   indexing, 315
   links, 317
   saving
      WAIS, 195
      World Wide Web (WWW), 123
   searching, 110
   source documents, 322
   WAIS
      reading, 201-202
      saving, 201-202
   see also files; pages; sites
domain names, 43-45, 64, 312
   DNS (Domain Name Services), 253
   server address, 64
   e-mail addresses, 252-253
   fees, 44
   first-level domain types, 44-45
   troubleshooting, 289
domain service, comparing rates of service providers, 36
domain suffix, 64
dot address, 312
   see also IP (Internet Protocol), 316
downloading, 312
   files, 125
   .EXE files, 125
   multimedia, 126-128
   multiple files, 126
   troubleshooting, 125-128
   viruses, 151
   .WAV, 128
   WS_FTP program, 149
   Internet, 55-56
   Internet Explorer, 76-77
DSCRPT.EXE, 91

E

e-mail, 5, 248
   addresses, 64, 256
      address book, 267
      DNS (Domain Name Services), 253

      incorrect, 289
      lost, 297
      parts of, 252-253
      President of the US, 248
      troubleshooting, 289
      Vice President of the US, 248
AOL (America Online), 254
Archie, 161-163
   commands, 163
   Whatis command, 162
BITNET, 254
bounces (defined), 310
computer files, sending, 277-278
connection, 21
defined, 312
domain names, 289
emoticons, 250-251, 312
errors (Error 045: Illegal DOS input filename), 226
Exchange, 268
   defined, 259-260
   Internet Mail services, 262
   Remote Mail, 280-282
Fidonet, 255
fingering, 291-293, 313
folders, personal, 265-266
formatting, 249
from line, 289
GEnie, 254
IMHO (In My Humble Opinion), 315
Internet directories, 290
Internet Mail services
   connecting to, 263-265
   MIME (Multipurpose Internet Mail Extension), 263
   UUENCODING, 263
mailing lists, 317
   finding, 234
MCImail, 255, 318
messages
   blind carbon copies, 275
   carbon copies, 275
   composing, 275
   copying, 276
   disappearing, 217-218
   displaying, 219
   files, 278, 283-284
   incoming, 282
   mailing lists, 242
   marking, 218
   MIME files, 224
   moving, 283
   New Message window, 284
   posting, 320

329

printing, 221-222, 276
reading, 219-221
replying, 222, 284
responding, 222
ROT13 (rotated 13), 223-224
saving, 221-222, 276
sending, 222-223, 274, 276-277
shorthand, 252
signatures, 321
troubleshooting, 277
UUDECODING, 226
UUENCODING, 224-225
MIME (Multipurpose Internet Mail Extensions), 318
MSN (Microsoft Network), 254, 274
Netfind, 296-297
newsgroups (mailing lists), 234-235
online services, 256
passwords, changing, 266
pictures (ASCII files), 224-225
POP (Post Office Protocol), 320
postmasters, 290, 320
Prodigy, 254
programs, choosing, 257-258
receiving
  online services, 253-254
  troubleshooting, 288-289
reflectors, 317
  defined, 234
Remote Mail, 265
returned, 288
  host unknown, 288
  sending, 288
  services unavailable, 288
  user unknown, 288
robots, 317
sending online services, 253-254
servers, 317
signatures, 251
smileys, 322
Sprintmail, 255
text, formatting, 275-276
troubleshooting, 289-290
  service providers, 290
users, searching for, 294-295
White Pages, 295-296
Yahoo, 295-296
zeros, 289
EARN (defined), 312

Edit menu commands
  Copy, 123, 301
  Find, 110, 156
  Go To, 55, 214
  Mark to Delete, 282
  Mark to Retrieve, 281
  Mark to Retrieve a Copy, 281
  Paste, 301
  Select All, 185, 218, 226
educational newsgroup (k 12), 208
EFF (Electronic Frontier Foundation), 312
electronic mail, *see* e-mail
emoticons, 250-251
  defined, 312
  smileys, 322
emptying cache, 112
encoding
  UUENCODING, 224-225, 323
    Error 045: Illegal DOS Input filename, 226
    Internet Mail services, 263
encryptions, 312
errors
  Error 045: Illegal DOS input filename, 226
  syntax, 306
etext (electronic text), 312
Ethernet, 312
etiquette on the Internet, 256-257
Eudora, 285
exact searches, 158
Exchange, 268
  address book options, 267
  defined, 259-260
  e-mail, 257-258
    Remote Mail, 265, 280-282
    Eudora, 285
  general options, 268-270
  Internet Mail services
    connecting to, 263-265
    MIME (Multipurpose Internet Mail Extension), 263
    UUENCODING, 263
  opening, 265
  passwords, changing, 266
  profiles
    defined, 260
    information services, 260
  read options, 270-271
  sending options, 271-272
  services, 261-263

set up, 260
  Inbox icon, 260
  windows, 279-280
  messages, 280
Exchange Settings Properties dialog box, 261, 265
EXE files, 146
  downloading, 125
  DSCRPT.EXE, 91
exiting Telnet, 186
Expand All Conversations command (View menu), 216
Explorer, 316
  adding viewers, 129-131
  customizing, 131-134
    addresses, 132
    background color, 132
    hypertext links, 132
    turning off inline images, 131
  documents, displaying, 133-134
  downloading files, 125
    EXE files, 125
    multimedia files, 126-128
    multiple files, 126
    troubleshooting, 125-126
  Find function, 156
  home pages, 133
    creating, 133
extensions, 146
.JPG, 309
external modems, 39

F

FAQ (Frequently-Asked Questions), 313
favorite web sites, 116-118
  subcategories, 118
Favorites menu commands (Add to Favorites), 117
fees
  connecting to the Internet
    free accounts, 22-23, 25-26
    Free-Nets, 23-25
  connections, 3-4
  domain names, 44
  service providers
    comparing rates, 33-36
    finding lowest fees, 32
    MSN (Microsoft Network), 29-30
Fidonet, 255
File command (Insert menu), 278

Index

File Manager, 88
File menu commands
  Copy, 276
  Create Shortcut, 117
  Decode, 226
  Delete, 116, 283
  More History, 115
  Move, 276, 283
  New Folder, 118, 276
  Open, 114, 116, 219
  Open Start Page, 109
  Post Message, 223
  Print, 222, 276
  Print Setup, 222
  Properties, 278
  Save, 221, 276
  Save As, 114, 123, 193
  Send, 276
  UUEncode/Decode, 225
File to Decode dialog box, 226
File Transfer Protocol, *see* FTP
File view, 217
files
  archive, 309
  ASCII (e-mail), 224-225
  associating with programs, 131
  compressed, 145-146
    ZIP files, 146
  compressed files, 311
  downloading, 125, 312
    .EXE files, 125
    multimedia, 126-128
    multiple files, 126
    troubleshooting, 125-128
    viruses, 151
    .WAV, 128
    WS_FTP program, 149
  EXE, 146
    DSCRPT.EXE, 91
  extensions, 146
    .JPG, 309
  finding
    Archie, 153-163
    FTP sites, 143-145
  formats in FTP sites, 145
  FTP (File Transfer Protocol), 313
  grabbing, 97-101
  messages, 283-284
    inserting, 278
  MIME files, 224
  multimedia, 126-128
  .plan files, 292-293
  saving
    to disks, 125
    FTP sites, 144
  scripts, assigning, 304-305
  signatures, 251
  tar files, 322
  TELNET.EXE, 185
  UUDECODING, 226
  UUENCODING, 224-225
  viruses, 150
  ZIP, 146
  see also documents
files, *see* documents
Find command (Edit menu), 110, 156
Find command (Tools menu), 284
Find dialog box, 110
Find function (Internet Explorer), 156
finding
  Archie servers, 155
  files
    Archie, 153-163
    FTP sites, 143-145
  free accounts, connecting to the Internet, 25
  Free-Nets, 24
  Gopher server links, 168
  mailing lists on Internet, 234
  programs (Telnet), 178
  service providers, 27-32
    comparing rates, 33-36
    lowest fees, 32
  sites, 121-123
  viewers
    FTP sites, 129
    Web sites, 128-129
  WAIS servers, 199-201
  WAIS Windows programs
    FTPs, 196
    URLs, 196
  WS_Archie, 159
  see also searching
fingering e-mail, 291-293, 313
fj (alternative newsgroup), 208
flames, 313
folders
  Dial-Up Networking folder, 85
  personal
    e-mail, 265-266
    inbox, 265
    outbox, 265
  Sent Items folder, 276
Folders command (View menu), 279
fonts (VT-100 setting), 182
Fonts command (View menu), 133
form searches
  Archie, 155-156
    options for searching, 157-158
    search types, 158-159
formatting
  e-mail, 249
  LISTSERVs, 241-242
  options, 242
  text, 275-276
forms, 204, 313
  searches, 155
  support, 313
Forward by E-mail command (Compose menu), 222
Forward command (Compose menu), 284
Forward command (View menu), 109
fragments, 313
Free Agent newsreader, 227-228
Free-Nets, 23-25, 313
  finding, 24
  limitations, 25
  menus, 24
freeware, 313
  newsgroup (gnu), 208
FTP (File Transfer Protocol), 4, 313
  CERN (European Particle Physics Laboratory), 310
  connecting to
    codes, 97-101
    troubleshooting, 235
  Dial-Up Scripting, 88-91
  history of development, 139
  mirror sites, 318
  newsgroup lists, 206-207
  Norton Utilities, 88
  sites
    anonymous FTP, 309
    Archie, 153-163
    changing, 101
    compressed files, 145-146
    file formats, 145
    finding files, 143-145
    links, 141
    saving files, 144
    troubleshooting, 140, 146-149
    typing, 140
    viewing, 129, 141-142
    Windows shareware utilities, 151
    WS_FTP program, 139, 147-149
    ZIP files, 146
  tips, 91
FTP Setup command (Options menu), 160

331

G-H

Graphics Interchange Format (.GIF), 309
gateways, 313
    e-mail (online services), 253-254
    service providers, 64
    WAIS, 191
General Options (Microsoft Exchange Options dialog box), 268-270
GEnie, 254, 314
German language newsgroup, 208
gibberish (ROT13), 223-224
global lists (LISTSERVs), 240
gnu (alternative newsgroup), 208
Go To command (Edit menu), 55, 214
Gopher, 4, 167, 314
    documents, 169
    Gopherspace, 314
        Veronica (Very Easy Rodent-Oriented Net-wide Index to Computerized Archives), 323
    history, 166-167
    Jughead (Jonzy's Universal Gopher Hierarchy Excavation and Display tool), 316
    name, 167
    searching
        Jughead, 170-174
        Veronica, 174-176
    servers, 167
        finding links to, 168
    starting sessions, 167-168
    WAIS searching, 195-196
grabbing files, 97-101
graphics
    GUI (Graphical User Interface), 314
    JPEG (Joint Photographic Experts Group), 316
    XBM (X Bitmap graphics format), 324
    GUI (Graphical User Interface), 314
        Mosaic, 318

hackers, 314
hardware (ports), 320
headers (messages), 264
help command (Archie), 163
Herzfeld, Charles (director of ARPAnet), 14
hierarchies (messages), 217
history lists, 114-116, 314
    deleting, 116
holding messages, 276
home pages, 108, 314
    creating, 133
    defined, 106
    Internet Explorer, 133
    navigating, 109
    saving to hard disks, 114
    World Wide Web (favorite sites), 116-118
host address, *see* IP (Internet Protocol; addresses)
host numbers, *see* IP (Internet Protocol; addresses)
hosts, 314
    names, 314
    Netfind, 296-297
hotlists, 314
HTML
    codes, viewing, 124
    tags (anchors), 309
HTML (HyperText Markup Language), 102
    defined, 315
    documents, 103
    pages, 103
    sites, 103
    source documents, 322
    tags (defined), 322
HTTP (HyperText Transfer Protocol), 315
hyperlinks, *see* links
hypermedia (defined), 315
hypertext
    defined, 96, 315
    hypermedia, 315
HYTELNET, 315
    directory, 179-182
    URL, 179-182

I

IAB (Internet Architecture Board), 14, 316
IAP (Internet Access Provider), 315
IBM mainframe (Telnet sites), 186-187
IEEE (Institute of Electrical and Electronics Engineers) newsgroup, 208
IETF (Internet Engineering Task Force), 14
images (inline), 315
    turning off, 131

IMHO (In My Humble Opinion), 315
Inbox folders, 265
Inbox icon, 260
incoming messages, 282
index documents, 315
index servers, 315
indexers
    Archie, 153-163, 309
info (alternative newsgroup), 208
information services
    Exchange, 261-263
    Internet Mail services, 262
        connecting to, 263-265
        MIME (Multipurpose Internet Mail Extension), 263
        Remote Mail, 265
    profiles, 260
inline images, 315
    turning off, 131
Insert menu commands (File), 278
inserting (file messages), 278
Install New Modem Wizard, 81
installing
    Dial-Up Networking, 77-78
    Internet access, 54-56, 76-77
        online services, 76-77
    networking components, 78-79
    service providers (accounts), 65
    TCP/IP (Transfer Control Protocol/Internet Protocol), 78
instructions
    logging on service providers, 64
    profiles (defined), 260
interactive services, *see* dial-in terminal connections
internal modems, 38-39
Internet
    access numbers, 56
    accessing, 49
        Dial-Up Scripting Tool, 88-91
        installing, 76-77
        MSN (Microsoft Network) software, 50
        new computers, 49
        software, 48
    accounts
        PPP (Point-to-Point Protocol), 62
        SLIP (Serial Line Internet Protocol), 62

Index

chats, 311
  IRC (Internet Relay Chat), 316
connecting to, 18, 22, 80-81
  IAB (Internet Architecture Board), 316
  properties, 82-85
dedicated lines, 311
dial-in direct connection, 311
dial-in terminal connection, 312
dial-up services, 312
directories, 290
domain names, 312
downloading, 55-56
e-mail, 248
  addresses, 252-253, 256
  defined, 312
  emoticons, 250-251, 312
  fingering, 313
  formatting, 249
  lost addresses, 297
  MIME (Multipurpose Internet Mail Extensions), 318
  online services, 253-254
  postmasters, 320
  President of the US, 248
  Remote Mail, 265
  shorthand, 252
  signatures, 251
  smileys, 322
  Vice President of the US, 248
  see also e-mail
etiquette, 256-257, 318
Internet Engineering Task Force, 316
Internet Explorer
  cache, 110-112
  downloading, 76-77
  opening, 106
Internet Mail services, connecting to, 263-265
InterNIC, 316
IP (Internet Protocol) address, 63
Jumpstart Kit, installing, 66-68
mail servers, 64
mailing lists, finding, 234
messages
  ASCII files, 224-225
  caps lock, 257
  disappearing, 217-218
  Error 045: Illegal DOS input filename, 226

mailing lists, 242
MIME files, 224
printing, 221-222
reading, 219-221
replying, 222
responding, 222
ROT13 (rotated 13), 223-224
saving, 221-222
sending, 222-223
UUDECODING, 226
UUENCODING, 224-225
MILNET, 318
MSN (Microsoft Network), accessing, 48
Netfind, 296-297
newsgroups (UseNet), 214-215
  alternative groups, 214
  conversations, 216
  messages, 216
  threading, 216
noncommercial system, 13
origins, 14
phone system, 10
postmasters, 290
reasons for using, 15-16
service providers, 12-13
  comparing rates, 33-36
  Dial-Up Scripting Tool, 85
  MSN (Microsoft Network), 28-30
  selecting, 27-32
  terminology, 32-36
SLIP (Serial Line Internet Protocol), 321
software, acquiring, 54-55
White Pages, 295-296
World Wide Web (WWW), 96
  browsers, 96-97
  contents, 103
  favorite sites, 116-118
  home pages, 106
  HTML (HyperText Markup Language), 102
  servers, 101
  URL (Uniform Resource Locators), 113
  Yahoo, 295-296
internet (defined), 315
internet address, *see also* IP address
Internet Architecture Board (IAB), 14
Internet Engineering Task Force (IETF), 14, 316

Internet Explorer, 96, 101-102, 316
  adding viewers, 129-131
  cache, 110-112
  customizing, 131-134
    addresses, 132
    background color, 132
    hypertext links, 132
    turning off inline images, 131
  documents, displaying, 133-134
  downloading files, 76-77, 125
    .EXE files, 125
    multimedia files, 126-128
    multiple files, 126
    troubleshooting, 125-126
  Find function, 156
  history lists, 114-116
  home page, 133
    creating, 133
  opening, 106
  toolbar buttons, 107-108
  updating, 76
Internet Explorer 2.0 (newsgroup support), 207
Internet Mail dialog box, 262
Internet Mail services, 262
  connecting to, 263-265
  modems, 263
  Remote Mail, 265
  UUENCODING, 263
Internet Protocol, 316
Internet Setup Wizard dialog box, 66
Internet Society (ISOC), 9, 14, 316
InterNIC, 316
IP (Internet Protocol)
  addresses, 63, 70, 73, 316
  dot address, 312
IRC (Internet Relay Chat), 316
ISDN (Integrated Services Digital Network), 40-41, 315
  comparing rates of service providers, 35
ISOC (Internet Society), 9, 14, 316

J-K-L

.JPG (file extensions), 309
Japanese language newsgroup, 208

333

joining
  MSN (Microsoft Network)
    accounts, 50-54
    Microsoft Plus! software, 57
  OUI (Offline Usenet Interface), 230
  service providers, 57-59
JPEG (Joint Photographic Experts Group), 316
Jughead, 170-174
  boolean searches,172-173
  commands, 173-174
  wild-card searches, 172
Jughead (Jonzy's Universal Gopher Hierarchy Excavation and Display tool), 316
JumpCity site (URL), 122
Jumpstart Kit, installing, 66-68

k12 (alternative newsgroup), 208
keyword searches (WAIS), 192-194
KIS (Knowbot Information Service), 316
kludge, 263
Knowbot Information Service, 316

LAN (Local Area Network), 317
law newsgroups, 208
leased line, *see* dedicated lines
links, 317
  connecting to FTP sites, 141
  images, 317
List command (View menu), 217
List view, 217
lists (newsgroups), 206-207
LISTSERVs
  addresses, 239
  customizing, 241-242
    options, 242
  groups, 236-239
    global lists, 240
    moderated, 234
    peered, 234
  lists, 317
    automated mailing lists, 235
  mailing lists, 234
  messages
    lurking, 317
    sending, 240, 242
  subscribing to, 240
  unsubscribing, 241

local echo (VT-100 setting), 182
locating
  mailing lists, 234
  Remote Mail, 281
logging off, 317
  Telnet, 186
logging on, 317
  instructions (service providers), 64
  login scripts, 69
  logins, 317
  manually, 307
  passwords, 42-43
  process, 300-302
  Telnet sites, 181
  user IDs, 41-42
login names, 41-42
  e-mail addresses, 252-253
login scripts, 69
  creating, 299-300
  modifying, 300
lost addresses, 297
lurking, 317

M

-m commands (Veronica), 176
magazines
  Boardwatch Magazine, 25
  ComputerShopper, 25
  Online Access, 25
mail, *see* e-mail
mailing lists, 5, 317
  automated, 235
    LISTSERV lists, 235
    subscribing to, 235
  BITNET computer network, 235
  defined, 234-235
  LISTSERVs, 234
    addresses, 239
    customizing, 241-242
    global lists, 240
    groups, 236-239
    lists, 317
    moderated groups, 234
    peered groups, 234
    sending messages, 242
    subscribing to, 240
  manually administered, 235
  messages, receiving, 242
  messages digests, 241
  newsgroups (UseNet), 208, 319
  reflectors (defined), 234
  subscribing, 235-236

manually administered mailing lists, 235
Mark All Messages as Read command (Tools menu), 218
Mark Conversation as Read command (Tools menu), 218
Mark Conversation as Unread command (Tools menu), 218
Mark Message as Read command (Tools menu), 218
Mark Message as Unread command (Tools menu), 218
Mark to Delete command (Edit menu), 282
Mark to Retrieve a Copy command (Edit menu), 281
Mark to Retrieve command (Edit menu), 281
marking messages, 218
MCImail, 255, 318
megabytes (MB), 36, 318
members
  e-mail, searching for, 294-295
  names, 41-42
membership ID, 54
menus (Free-Net), 24
message
  printing, 221-222
  saving, 221-222
message window toolbar buttons, 220-221
messages
  articles (defined), 309
  blind carbon copies, 275
  carbon copies, 275
  composing, 275
  conversations, 216
  copying, 276
  digests, 241
  disappearing, 217-218
  displaying, 219
  Error 045: Illegal DOS input filename, 226
  Exchange window, reading, 280
  files, inserting, 278
  flames, 313
  gibberish (ROT13), 223-224
  headers, 264
  hierarchies, 217
  holding, 276
  incoming, 282
  LISTSERVs, customizing, 241
  mailing lists, receiving, 242
  marking, 218
  MIME files, 224

334

Index

missing (OUI), 230
moving, 221, 283
New Message window, 284
pictures (ASCII files), 224-225
posting, 320
printing, 276
reading, 219-221
Remote Mail, 280-282
replying, 222, 284
responding, 222
returned, 288
saving, 276
sending, 222, 274, 276-277
  computer files, 277-278
  LISTSERVs, 240, 242
  New Message window, 222-223
  troubleshooting, 277
shorthand, 252
signatures, 321
syntax errors, 306
text, formatting, 275-276
UUDECODING, 226
UUENCODING, 224-225
viewing, 216
  File view, 217
  List view, 217
Microsoft Exchange, *see* Exchange
Microsoft Network dialog box, 50
Microsoft Network, *see* MSN (Microsoft Network)
Microsoft Telnet, *see* Telnet
MILNET, 318
  DARPAnet (Defense Advanced Research Projects Agency), 311
  DDN (Defense Data Network), 311
MIME (Multipurpose Internet Mail Extensions)
  defined, 224, 318
  files, 224
  Internet Mail services, 263
mirror sites, 318
misc (UseNet group), 208
missing messages (OUI), 230
modems, 38-41
  buying, 39-40
  defined, 318
  external, 39
  Install New Modem Wizard, 81
  internal, 38, 39
  Internet Mail services, connecting to, 263

ISDN (Integrated Services Digital Network) *see* ISDN
speed, 39
  comparing rates of service providers, 35
moderated LISTSERV groups, 234
modifying (login scripts), 300
More History command (File menu), 115
Move command (File menu), 276, 283
moving
  messages, 221, 283
  World Wide Web (WWW), 109
    backspacing, 109-110
MPEG (Motion Pictures Experts Groups), 318
MSN (Microsoft Network), 28-29
  access numbers, 56
  accounts
    additional, 54
    addresses, 51
    joining, 50-54
    membership ID, 54
    passwords, 53
  advanced dialing, 53
  changing service providers, 57-59
  downloading, 55-56
  e-mail, 253-254, 274
  fees, 29-30
  Internet, accessing, 48
  Microsoft Plus! Pack, 48
  joining, 57
  troubleshooting, 59
MSN (Microsoft Network) Sign In dialog box, 55
MUD (Multiple User Dungeons), 318
multimedia files, 126-128
  downloading, 126-128
Multiple User Dungeons, *see* MUD

N

names
  directories, 144
  domain, 43-45
    DNS (Domain Name Services), 253
    e-mail addresses, 252-253

fees, 44
first-level domain types, 44-45
domain names, 64, 312
  troubleshooting, 289
file extensions, 146
FTP sites, 140
  typing, 140
Gopher, 167
host names, 314
login names, 41-42
  e-mail addresses, 252-253
newsgroups
  alternative, 208-210
  UseNet, 207-210
user names, 66
  service providers, 63
National Public Telecommuting Network (NPTN), 24
National Science Foundation (NSF), 14
navigating
  home pages, 109
  World Wide Web (WWW), 109
    backspacing, 109-110
navigators, 318
  offline navigators, 228-229
Netfind, 296-297
netiquette, 256-257, 318
Netscape, 96, 101-102, 319
Network dialog box, 70, 79
Network Information Center, 319
networks, 9-10
  backbones (defined), 310
  components, installing, 78-79
  cyberspace, 311
  DDN (Defense Data Network), 311
  defined, 9
  Free-Net, 313
  LAN (Local Area Network), 317
  UseNet, 207
    newsgroup names, 207-208
New Folder command (File menu), 118, 276
New Message command (Compose menu), 216, 222, 274
New Message window, 284
  messages, sending, 222-223

335

New Type button (Internet Explorer), 131
news (UseNet group), 207
news servers, 319
newsgroups, 5
  alternative groups, 214
  articles (defined), 309
  defined, 204
  Error 045: Illegal DOS input filename, 226
  FTP site, 206
  hierarchy, 209-210
  Internet Explorer 2.0 support, 207
  lists of, 206-207
  mailing lists
    automated, 235
    LISTSERV mailing lists, 234
    LISTSERVs, 239, 317
    subscribing, 235-236
  names
    alternative, 208-210
    UseNet, 207-210
  news clients, 211
  news servers, 211
  newsreaders, 210-211
  OUI (Offline Usenet Interface), 229-230
  subscribing to, 211
  types, 204-205
  URL, 206
  warning, 230
newsgroups (UseNet), 214-215, 319
  conversations, 216
  lurking, 317
  mailing lists, 317
    BITNET computer network, 235
    defined, 234-235
    LISTSERVs, 236-239, 240, 242
    manually administered, 235
    messages, 242
    messages digests, 241
  message window toolbar buttons, 220-221
  messages
    ASCII files, 224-225
    disappearing, 217-218
    displaying, 219
    flames, 313
    hierarchies, 217
    mailing lists, 242-243
    marking, 218
    MIME files, 224

printing, 221-222
reading, 219-221
replying, 222
responding, 222
ROT13 (rotated 13), 223-224
saving, 221-222
sending, 222-223
UUDECODING, 226
UUENCODING, 224-225
origination, 207
OUI (Offline Usenet Interface) messages, 230
searching, 294-295
threading, 216
newsreaders, 210-211, 319
  ASCII files, 224-225
  Free Agent, 227-228
    offline navigator, 228
  MIME files, 224
  offline navigators, 229
  UUDECODING, 226
  UUENCODING, 224-225
  WinVN, 227
Next command (View menu), 283
NNTP (Network News Transfer Protocol), 319
NOC (Network Operations Center), 319
nodes (computers), 319
nonforms searches, 155
Norton File Manager, 88
Norton Navigator, 88
Note Properties dialog box, 276
Notepad, 302-304
NPTN (National Public Telecommuting Network), 24
NREN (National Research & Education Network), 319
NSF (National Science Foundation), 14, 319
NSFNet (National Science Foundation network), 319
nuclear physics newsgroup, 208

O

offline navigators, 228-229
online, 319
Online Access, 25
online services, 256
  AOL (America Online), 253-254, 254, 309

BITNET, 254
CompuServe, 253-254, 311
e-mail, sending, 253-254
Fidonet, 255
gateways, 253-254
GEnie, 254, 314
Internet Explorer, downloading, 76-77
MCImail, 255, 318
MSN (Microsoft Network), 253-254
Prodigy, 254, 320
Sprintmail, 255
Open command (File menu), 114, 116, 219
Open File button, 125-126
Open File button (Internet Explorer), 130
Open Internet Address dialog box, 114
Open Log File dialog box, 185
Open Start Page command (File menu), 109
Open With button (Internet Explorer), 130
opening
  Exchange, 265
  Internet Explorer, 106
  messages, 219-221
  see also starting
Options command (Tools menu), 268
Options command (View menu), 111, 128
Options dialog box (Microsoft Exchange), 111
  General options, 268-270
  Read options, 270-271
  Sending options, 271-272
Options menu commands
  FTP Setup, 160
  User Preferences, 159
OUI (Offline Usenet Interface), 229-230
  accessing, 230
  messages, missing, 230
  threading, 229
Outbox folders, 265

P

packets, 319
  fragments, 313
  switching, 319
    fragments, 313
pages, 103
  backgrounds, copying, 123-124

336

Index

home pages, 108, 314
   defined, 106
   navigating, 109
   see also documents; sites
passwords, 42-43, 63, 66
   changing, 266
   Dial-Up Networking, 305
   MSN (Microsoft Network) accounts, 53
   removing, 266
   saving, 55
   selecting, 42-43
Paste command (Edit menu), 301
payment, *see* fees
peered LISTSERV groups, 234
permanent accounts, 4
permanent connections, 18-19, 320
   advantages, 20
   TCP/IP (Transfer Control Protocol/Internet Protocol), 19
personal address book options, 267
Personal Address Book dialog box, 267
personal folders
   e-mail, 265-266
   inbox, 265
   outbox, 265
Personal Folders dialog box, 266
phone numbers
   access numbers, 56
   service providers, 63
phones
   dedicated lines, 311
   dial-in services, 311
picking, *see* selecting
pictures
   copying on World Wide Web, 123
   UUDECODING, 226
PING (Packet Internet Groper), 319
Ping command, 69
plugs (ports), 320
podunk (alternative newsgroup), 209
point of presence, 320
POP (Post Office Protocol), 320
ports, 320
Post Message command (File menu), 223
post-dial terminal screen, 86
posting messages, 320

postmasters, 290, 320
PPP (Point-to-Point Protocol), 62, 320
Preferences command (Terminal menu), 181
preparing e-mail messages, 222, 275
Previous command (View menu), 283
prices, *see* fees
Print command (File menu), 222, 276
Print Setup command (File menu), 222
printing messages, 221-222, 276
problems, *see* troubleshooting
Prodigy, 254, 320
Product Number dialog box, 65
profiles
   defined, 260
   sharing computers, 261
programs
   associating files with, 131
   bombs (defined), 150
   clients, 311
      defined, 190
   Comt, 178
   crackers, 311
   e-mail, choosing, 257-258
   finding Telnet, 178
   Knowbot, 316
   servers (defined), 190
   worms (defined), 150
   WS_FTP, 139, 147-149
Programs command (Start menu), 50
properties (Internet, connecting to), 82-85
Properties command (File menu), 278
Properties dialog box, 278
protocols, 320
   BOOTP (Bootstrap Protocol), 310
   Ethernet, 312
   FTPs (File Transfer Protocols), 137
      history of development, 139
      tips, 91
   Internet Protocol, 316
   POP (Post Office Protocol), 320
   PPP (Point-to-Point Protocol), 62, 320

   SLIP (Serial Line Internet Protocol), 19-20, 62, 87
      connecting to, 72-73
      IP address, 73
      software, 83
   TCP/IP (Transfer Control Protocol/Internet Protocol), 19, 322
providers
   service providers
      accounts, 65
      changing, 57-59
      CIX (Commercial Internet Exchange), 311
      connecting, 85-87
      connecting to, 68-69, 80-81
      CSLIP (Compressed Serial Line Interface Protocol), 64
      defined, 321
      Dial-Up Networking, 77-78
      Dial-Up Scripting Tool, 85-87
      dialing up, 68-69
      DNS (Domain Name Services), 253
      domain names, 64
      domain suffix, 64
      e-mail, 290
      e-mail addresses, 64
      gateways, 64
      hosts, 314
      IAP (Internet Access Provider), 315
      Internet mail servers, 64
      IP (Internet Protocol) address, 63, 70
      Jumpstart Kit, 66-68
      log-in instructions, 64
      logging on, 300-302
      login scripts, 69
      passwords, 63, 66
      phone numbers, 63
      point of presence, 320
      PPP (Point-to-Point Protocol), 62
      properties, 82-85
      selecting, 63-64
      SLIP (Serial Line Internet Protocol), 62, 64, 72-73
      TCP/IP (Transfer Control Protocol/Internet Protocol), 70-72
      user names, 63, 66
public domain software, 320

Q-R

quit command (Archie), 163
quitting Telnet, 186

rabbits (defined), 150
Read Options (Microsoft Exchange Options dialog box), 270-271
reading
  documents (WAIS), 201-202
  messages, 219-221
    Exchange window, 280
    marking, 218
  newsgroups, 210-211
rec (UseNet group), 208
receiving e-mail
  online services, 253-254
  troubleshooting, 288-289
reflectors, 317
  defined, 234
refresh button (cache), 112
Refresh command (View menu), 112
refreshing, 321
regex searches, 158
regular expression match searches, 158
relcom (alternative newsgroup), 209
reloading, 321
remote login, 321
Remote Mail, 265, 280-282
  locating, 281
  windows, 282
Remote Mail command (Tools menu), 277, 281
Remote System command (Connect menu), 185
removing passwords, 266
rendering, 321
Reply to All command (Compose menu), 284
Reply to BBS command (Compose menu), 222
Reply to E-mail command (Compose menu), 222
Reply to Sender command (Compose menu), 284
replying to messages, 222, 284
resources, 10
  finding free accounts for Internet connections, 25
responding to messages, 222, 284

returned e-mail
  host unknown, 288
  sending, 288
  services unavailable, 288
  user unknown, 288
robots (e-mail), 317
root servers, 253
ROT13 (rotated 13)
  defined, 321
  messages (gibberish), 223-224
ROT13 Encode/Decode command (Tools menu), 223
routers, 321
Run command (Start menu), 54, 179
Run Program dialog box, 65
running WAIS, 190-202
Russian language newsgroup, 209

S

Save As button, 125-126
Save As command (File menu), 114, 123, 193
Save As dialog box, 124, 144
Save command (File menu), 221, 276
saving
  documents
    WAIS, 195, 201-202
    World Wide Web (WWW), 123
  files
    disks, 125
    FTP sites, 144
  messages, 221-222, 276
  passwords, 55
  sound files to disks, 127
  World Wide Web (WWW) pages to hard disks, 114
Schedule+ (defined), 50
sci (UseNet group), 208
screens (post-dial terminal screen), 86
scripting
  Dial-Up Scripting Tool, 85, 87, 88-91, 304
  passwords, 305
  testing, 305-307
scripts
  files, assigning, 304-305
  login scripts, 69
    creating, 299-300
    modifying, 300
  writing (Notepad), 302-304

search tools
  Jughead, 170-174
    boolean searches, 172-173
    wild-card searches, 172
  Veronica, 174-176
    -m command, 176
    -t commands, 174-176
searching
  Archie, 155-156
  e-mail, 161-163
  options, 157-158
  search types, 158-159
  by program description, 159
  documents, 110
  Gopher
    Jughead, 170-174
    Veronica, 174-176
  mailing lists (Internet), 234
  newsgroups (UseNet), 294-295
  WAIS, 191-195
    database lists, 193
    Gopher, 195-196
    keywords, 192-194
    troubleshooting, 201
    URL, 192
    using directory of servers, 199-201
    viewing database lists, 194-195
  World Wide Web (WWW), 121-123
    saving documents, 123
  WS_Archie, 159-160
  see also finding
security
  passwords, 42-43
  user IDs, 41-42
  viruses, 150-151
Select All command (Edit menu), 185, 218, 226
Select Network Component Type dialog box, 78
Select Network Protocol dialog box, 79
selecting
  modems, 39-40
  passwords, 42-43
  service providers, 27-32, 63-64
    comparing rates, 33-36
    terminology, 32
self-extracting archives, 146
Send command (File menu), 276

Index

sending
    computer files, 277-278
    e-mail (returned), 288
    messages, 222, 274, 276-277
        LISTSERVs, 240, 242
        New Message window, 222-223
        troubleshooting, 277
Sending Options (Microsoft Exchange Options dialog box), 271-272
Sent Items folder, 276
Serial Line Internet Protocol, *see* SLIP
Server Types dialog box, 72, 83
servers
    Archie
        finding, 155
        locations, 161
        performing searches, 155-156
        searching, 157-159
    defined, 101, 190, 321
    e-mail, 317
    Gopher, 167
        finding links to, 168
        Jughead, 170-174
        Veronica, 174-176
    indexing, 315
    news, 211
    news servers, 319
    WAIS, 197
        finding, 199-201
    World Wide Web (WWW), 323
service providers, 12-13
    accounts, setting up, 65
    changing, 57-59
    CIX (Commercial Internet Exchange), 311
    comparing rates
        1-800 access, 34
        disk space per megabyte, 36
        domain service, 36
        ISDN (Integrated Services Digital Network), 35
        modem speed support, 35
        shell account access, 35
    connecting, 85-87
    connecting to, 80-81
        troubleshooting, 68-69
    CSLIP (Compressed Serial Line Interface Protocol), 64

defined, 19, 321
Dial-Up Networking, installing, 77-78
Dial-Up Scripting Tool, 85-87
dialing up, 68-69
DNS (Domain Name Services), 253
domain names, 64
e-mail
    addresses, 64
    troubleshooting, 290
fees
    comparing rates, 33-36
    finding lowest fees, 32
gateways, 64
hosts, 314
IAP (Internet Access Provider), 315
Internet mail servers, 64
IP (Internet Protocol) address, 63, 70
Jumpstart Kit, installing, 66-68
log-in instructions, 64
logging on, 300-302
login scripts, 69
    modifying, 300
MSN (Microsoft Network), 28-29
    fees, 29-30
networking components, installing, 78-79
newsgroups, 204
    hierarchy, 209-210
    types, 204-205
    see also newsgroups
passwords, 63, 66
phone numbers, 63
point of presence, 320
PPP (Point-to-Point Protocol), 62
properties, 82-85
selecting, 27-32, 63-64
    Internet Access Providers (directory), 32
SLIP (Serial Line Internet Protocol), 62, 64
    connecting to, 72-73
TCP/IP (Transfer Control Protocol/Internet Protocol), 70-72
telnetting to, 187-188
terminology, 32
user names, 63, 66
services (dial-in services), 311
Services command (Tools menu), 268, 281
services unavailable, 288

Session Profile dialog box, 147
set mailto command (Archie), 163
set search command (Archie), 163
shareware, 321
    freeware, 313
    Windows utilities (FTP sites), 151
sharing computers (profiles), 261
shell accounts, 321
    service provider access, 35
shortcuts
    creating, 68
        starting Telnet, 185
    URL (Uniform Resource Locators), 109
shorthand (e-mail), 252
Show All Messages command (Tools menu), 219
Show full addresses option (Internet Explorer), 132
Show pictures check box (Internet Explorer), 131
Show simplified addresses option (Internet Explorer), 132
signatures (e-mail), 251, 321
sites, 103, 323
    Complete Idiot's Guide to the World Wide Web, 123
    defined, 239
    finding, 121-123
    FTP (File Transfer Protocol)
        Archie, 153-163
        changing, 101
        compressed files, 145-146
        file formats, 145
        finding files, 143-145
        links, 141
        names, 140
        newsgroup lists, 206-207
        saving files, 144
        troubleshooting connections, 140
        typing names, 140
        viewing, 141-142
    Gopher documents, 169
    JumpCity, 122
    mirror, 318
    Telnet, 183-186
        IBM mainframe, 186-187
    viewers, finding, 128-129
    WAIS, connecting to, 190-191

339

World Wide Web (WWW)
  favorites, 116-118
  Yahoo, 122
  see also documents; pages
SLIP (Serial Line Internet
  Protocol), 19-20, 62, 64, 321
  CSLIP (Compressed Serial
    Line Internet Protocol),
    311
  connecting to, 72-73
  Dial-Up Scripting Tool, 87
  IP address, 73
  software, 83
smileys, 250-251, 312, 322
SMTP (Simple Mail Transfer
  Protocol), 321
soc (UseNet group), 208
software
  connecting to the
    Internet, 45
  freeware, 313
    newsgroup (gnu), 208
  Internet
    accessing, 48
    acquiring, 54-55
    MSN (Microsoft Network),
      48, 50
      accessing the Internet, 50
  public domain software,
    320
  shareware, 321
  SLIP (Serial Line Internet
    Protocol), 83
sound files
  saving to disks, 127
  .WAV files, downloading,
    128
sounds (UUDECODING), 226
Source Selection screen
  directory of servers
    (WAIS), 199
  commands, 200
Sprintmail, 255
stacks (TCP/IP), 322
Start Logging command
  (Terminal menu), 185
Start menu commands
  Programs, 50
  Run, 54, 179
  WS_FTP, 147
start pages, *see* home pages
starting
  BBSs (bulletin board
    systems) requirements, 8
  Gopher sessions, 167-168
  Internet Explorer, 106

Telnet
  creating shortcuts, 185
  direct connections, 179
  links, 179
  Web browsers, 179
  Windows 95 menu
    system, 179
  Telnet sessions, 179
Stop command (View menu),
  109
subcase searches, 158
subcategories (favorites), 118
subscribing
  LISTSERVs, 240
    unsubscribing, 241
  mailing lists, 235-236
  newsgroups, 211
substring matches, 159
suffixes (domain suffix), 64
surfing the World Wide
  Web, 108
syntax errors, 306

T

-t commands (Veronica),
  174-176
tags (HTML)
  anchors, 309
  defined, 322
  viewing, 124
talk (UseNet group), 208
talks, 322
tar files, 322
TCP/IP, 70-72
  access numbers, 56
  installing, 78
  IP address, 70
  login scripts, 299-300
TCP/IP (Transfer Control
  Protocol/Internet Protocol),
  19, 322
  access numbers, 56
  stacks, 322
TCP/IP Settings dialog box, 84
telecommunications (ISDN),
  315
telephone numbers
  Internet Access Providers
    (directory), 32
  National Public
    Telecommuting Network
    (NPTN), 24
telephones
  dedicated lines, 311
  dial-in services, 311

Telnet, 5, 322
  disconnecting from, 186
  finding programs, 178
  HYTELNET directory,
    179-182
  logging on, 181
  service providers, telnetting
    to, 187-188
  sites, 183-186
    IBM mainframe,
      186-187
  starting
    creating shortcuts, 185
    direct connection, 179
    links, 179
    Windows 95 menu
      system, 179
    starting sessions, 179
Telnet sites (HYTELNET), 315
TELNET.EXE file, 185
Terminal menu commands
  Preferences, 181
  Start Logging, 185
testing scripts, 305-307
text
  etext (electronic text), 312
  formatting, 275-276
thisu (alternative newsgroup),
  209
threading, 216
  OUI (Offline Usenet
    Interface), 229
toolbars
  Internet Explorer buttons,
    107-108
  message window toolbar
    buttons, 220-221
tools
  Dial-Up Scripting Tool, 85,
    88-91, 304
  Jughead (Jonzy's Universal
    Gopher Hierarchy
    Excavation and Display
    tool), 316
  searching
    Jughead, 170-174
    Veronica, 174-176
Tools menu commands
  Connect & Transfer
    Mail, 282
  Connect & Update
    Headers, 281
  Connect to Transfer
    Mail, 277
  Deliver Now, 277
  Find, 284
  Mark All Messages as
    Read, 218

Index

Mark Conversation as Read, 218
Mark Conversation as Unread, 218
Mark Message as Read, 218
Mark Message as Unread, 218
Options, 268
Remote Mail, 277, 281
ROT13 Encode/Decode, 223
Services, 268, 281
Show All Messages, 219
transferring files, *see* downloading, files
Trojan Horse, 322
  defined, 150
troubleshooting
  dial-up networking, 69
  downloading files, 125-128
  e-mail, 289-290
    from line, 289
    receiving, 288-289
    service providers, 290
  messages, sending, 277
  Microsoft Plus! Pack, 59
  newsgroups, 230
  searching WAIS, 201
  service providers, connecting to, 68-69
  URLs (Uniform Resource Locators), 129
  Windows 95, 59
turning off inline images, 131
typing FTP site names, 140

U

Underline shortcuts check box (Internet Explorer), 132
UNIX
  clients, telnetting to, 198-202
  defined, 322
unknown
  host (e-mail), 288
  user, 288
Unknown File Type dialog box, 129-130
unsubscribing (LISTSERVs), 241
updating Internet Explorer, 76
uploading, 322
URL (Uniform Resource Locator), 113, 323
  Archie servers, 155
  Complete Idiot's Guide to the World Wide Web, 123

finding WAIS Windows programs, 196
hotlists, 314
http://, 113
HYTELNET, 179-182
JumpCity, 122
newsgroups, 206
searching WAIS, 192
shortcuts, 109
troubleshooting, 129
viewers, 128-129
  VRML, 129
World Wide Web (WWW), 108
Yahoo database, 122
see also addresses
Use custom colors check box (Internet Explorer), 132
Use Default button (Internet Explorer), 133
Use Larger Font button (Internet Explorer), 134
Use Smaller Font buttons (Internet Explorer), 134
UseNet newgroups, *see* newsgroups
users
  e-mail, searching for, 294-295
  IDs, 41-42
  names, 66
    service providers, 63
  unknown, 288
User Preferences command (Options menu), 159
UUDECODING, 226, 323
UUEncode/Decode command (File menu), 225
UUENCODING, 323
  Error 045:Illegal DOS Input filename, 226
  files, 224-225
  Internet Mail services, 263

V

Veronica (Very Easy Rodent-Oriented Net-wide Index to Computerized Archives), 174-176, 323
  -m command, 176
  -t commands, 174-176
videos (MPEG), 318
View menu commands
  Arrange Messages, 217
  Bcc box, 275

Collapse All Conversations, 216
Conversations, 216
Expand All Conversations, 216
Folders, 279
Fonts, 133
Forward, 109
List, 217
Next, 283
Options, 111, 128
Previous, 283
Refresh, 112
Stop, 109
viewing
  codes, 124
  database lists' descriptions, 194
  File view, 217
  FTP sites, 141-142
  List view, 217
  messages, 216
    conversations, 216
  viewers, 323
    adding, 129-131
    defined, 128
viruses, 323
  boot sector, 150
  defined, 150
  downloading files, 151
  file, 150
  terminology, 150
  Trojan Horse, 322
vmsnet (alternative newsgroup), 209
VRML viewer, 129
VT 100 arrows (VT-100 setting), 182
VT-100 setting (Telnet), 181-182

W

W3, *see* World Wide Web
WAIS, 5
  connecting to, 190-191
  defined, 190
  documents
    reading, 201-202
    saving, 201-202
  running, 190-202
  saving documents, 195
  searching, 191-195
    database lists, 193
    Gopher, 195-196
    keywords, 192-194

341

troubleshooting, 201
URL, 192
using directory of
    servers, 199-201
viewing database lists,
    194-195
servers, 197
    finding, 199-201
standard, 191
telnetting to UNIX-based
    clients, 198
Windows programs,
    196-197
    finding, 196
WAIS (Wide Area Information
    Server), 189-190, 324
.WAV files, downloading, 128
Welcome to Microsoft
    Network dialog box, 55
whatis command (Archie), 162
White Pages, 295-296, 323
Wide Area Information Server,
    see WAIS
wild-card searches, 172
Windows
    WAIS programs, 196-197
        finding, 196
windows
    Exchange, 279-280
        messages, 280
        New Message window, 284
        Remote Mail window, 282
Windows 95
    computer requirement, 38
    menu system, starting
        Telnet, 179
    troubleshooting, 59
WinVN newsreader, 227
wizards
    defined, 66
    Install New Modem
        Wizard, 81
World Wide Web (WWW),
    4, 96
    Archie gateway, 155
    browsers, 4, 96-97
        cache, 310
        defined, 102, 310
        Enhanced NCSA
            Mosaic, 312
        Gopher, 168-169
        Internet Explorer, 96,
            101-102
        Netscape, 96, 101-102
        starting Telnet sessions,
            179
        cache, 106

CERN (European Particle
    Physics Laboratory), 310
chats, 311
contents, 103
dedicated lines, 311
defined, 324
directories, 180
displaying, 108
documents
    backgrounds, copying,
        123-124
    displaying, 133-134
    downloading, 125-128
    hypertext links, 132
    saving, 123
    searching, 110
forms, 313
gateways (WAIS), 191
Gopher, 314
    Gopherspace, 314
    history, 166-167
graphics (JPEG), 316
history lists, 114-116, 314
home pages, 108, 314
    defined, 106
    navigating, 109
    saving to hard disks, 114
HTML (HyperText Markup
    Language), 102
    defined, 315
HTTP (HyperText Transfer
    Protocol), 315
hypertext, 96
Internet Explorer
    cache, 110-112
    opening, 106
links, 317
moving around, 109
    backspacing, 109-110
pictures (inline images),
    315
servers, 323
    defined, 101
sites, 323
    *Complete Idiot's Guide to
    the World Wide Web*,
    123
    finding, 121-123
    JumpCity, 122
    viewers, 128-129
    Yahoo, 122
surfing, 108
URL (Uniform Resource
    Locators), 108, 113
viewers, 323
webspace, 323
White Pages, 295-296, 323
Yahoo, 295-296

worms (defined), 150
writing
    e-mail, 275
    scripts (Notepad), 302-304
writing, *see also* composing
WS_Archie, 159-160
    finding, 159
    searching, 159-160
    setting default options,
        159-160
WS_FTP command (Start
    menu), 147
WS_FTP program, 139,
    147-149
    downloading files, 149

X-Y-Z

XBM (X Bitmap graphics
    format), 324

Yahoo, 295-296
    site (URL), 122
    White Pages, 323
Ytalk, 324

zeros (e-mail), 289
ZIP files, 146

GET CONNECTED
to the ultimate source of computer information!

The MCP Forum on CompuServe

Go online with the world's leading computer book publisher! Macmillan Computer Publishing offers everything you need for computer success!

Find the books that are right for you!
A complete online catalog, plus sample chapters and tables of contents give you an in-depth look at all our books. The best way to shop or browse!

➤ Get fast answers and technical support for MCP books and software

➤ Join discussion groups on major computer subjects

➤ Interact with our expert authors via e-mail and conferences

➤ Download software from our immense library:
  ▷ Source code from books
  ▷ Demos of hot software
  ▷ The best shareware and freeware
  ▷ Graphics files

Join now and get a free CompuServe Starter Kit!

To receive your free CompuServe Introductory Membership, call **1-800-848-8199** and ask for representative #597.

The Starter Kit includes:
➤ Personal ID number and password
➤ $15 credit on the system
➤ Subscription to *CompuServe Magazine*

Once on the CompuServe System, type:

GO MACMILLAN

for the most computer information anywhere!

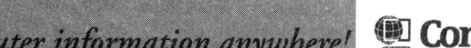

MACMILLAN COMPUTER PUBLISHING

CompuServe

PLUG YOURSELF INTO...

The Macmillan USA Information SuperLibrary (tm)

See the new SuperLibrary Newsletter

sams.net · SAMS PUBLISHING · Hayden Books · que · New Riders · BradyGAMES · Adobe Press · que E&T

THE MACMILLAN INFORMATION SUPERLIBRARY™

Free information and vast computer resources from the world's leading computer book publisher—online!

FIND THE BOOKS THAT ARE RIGHT FOR YOU!
A complete online catalog, plus sample chapters and tables of contents!

- **STAY INFORMED** with the latest computer industry news through our online newsletter, press releases, and customized Information SuperLibrary Reports.
- **GET FAST ANSWERS** to your questions about QUE books.
- **VISIT** our online bookstore for the latest information and editions!
- **COMMUNICATE** with our expert authors through e-mail and conferences.
- **DOWNLOAD SOFTWARE** from the immense Macmillan Computer Publishing library:
    - Source code, shareware, freeware, and demos
- **DISCOVER HOT SPOTS** on other parts of the Internet.
- **WIN BOOKS** in ongoing contests and giveaways!

TO PLUG INTO QUE:

WORLD WIDE WEB: **http://www.mcp.com/que**

FTP: ftp.mcp.com

Complete and Return this Card for a *FREE* Computer Book Catalog

Thank you for purchasing this book! You have purchased a superior computer book written expressly for your needs. To continue to provide the kind of up-to-date, pertinent coverage you've come to expect from us, we need to hear from you. Please take a minute to complete and return this self-addressed, postage-paid form. In return, we'll send you a free catalog of all our computer books on topics ranging from word processing to programming and the internet.

Mr. ☐   Mrs. ☐   Ms. ☐   Dr. ☐

Name (first) [____] (M.I.) [_] (last) [____]
Address [____]
[____]
City [____] State [__] Zip [____]
Phone [____] Fax [____]
Company Name [____]
E-mail address [____]

1. Please check at least (3) influencing factors for purchasing this book.

Front or back cover information on book .... ☐
Special approach to the content .... ☐
Completeness of content .... ☐
Author's reputation .... ☐
Publisher's reputation .... ☐
Book cover design or layout .... ☐
Index or table of contents of book .... ☐
Price of book .... ☐
Special effects, graphics, illustrations .... ☐
Other (Please specify): _____ ☐

2. How did you first learn about this book?

Saw in Macmillan Computer Publishing catalog .... ☐
Recommended by store personnel .... ☐
Saw the book on bookshelf at store .... ☐
Recommended by a friend .... ☐
Received advertisement in the mail .... ☐
Saw an advertisement in: _____ ☐
Read book review in: _____ ☐
Other (Please specify): _____ ☐

3. How many computer books have you purchased in the last six months?

This book only .... ☐   3 to 5 books .... ☐
2 books .... ☐   More than 5 .... ☐

4. Where did you purchase this book?

Bookstore .... ☐
Computer Store .... ☐
Consumer Electronics Store .... ☐
Department Store .... ☐
Office Club .... ☐
Warehouse Club .... ☐
Mail Order .... ☐
Direct from Publisher .... ☐
Internet site .... ☐
Other (Please specify): _____ ☐

5. How long have you been using a computer?

☐ Less than 6 months   ☐ 6 months to a year
☐ 1 to 3 years   ☐ More than 3 years

6. What is your level of experience with personal computers and with the subject of this book?

	With PCs	With subject of book
New	☐	☐
Casual	☐	☐
Accomplished	☐	☐
Expert	☐	☐

Source Code ISBN: 0-7897-0629-6

Which of the following best describes your job title?
- Administrative Assistant ☐
- Coordinator ☐
- Manager/Supervisor ☐
- Director ☐
- Vice President ☐
- President/CEO/COO ☐
- Lawyer/Doctor/Medical Professional ☐
- Teacher/Educator/Trainer ☐
- Engineer/Technician ☐
- Consultant ☐
- Not employed/Student/Retired ☐
- Other (Please specify): _____ ☐

8. Which of the following best describes the area of the company your job title falls under?
- Accounting ☐
- Engineering ☐
- Manufacturing ☐
- Operations ☐
- Marketing ☐
- Sales ☐
- Other (Please specify): _____ ☐

9. What is your age?
- Under 20 ☐
- 21-29 ☐
- 30-39 ☐
- 40-49 ☐
- 50-59 ☐
- 60-over ☐

10. Are you:
- Male ☐
- Female ☐

11. Which computer publications do you read regularly? (Please list)

Comments: _____

Fold here and scotch-tape to mail.

BUSINESS REPLY MAIL
FIRST-CLASS MAIL PERMIT NO. 9918 INDIANAPOLIS IN

POSTAGE WILL BE PAID BY THE ADDRESSEE

ATTN MARKETING
MACMILLAN COMPUTER PUBLISHING
MACMILLAN PUBLISHING USA
201 W 103RD ST
INDIANAPOLIS IN 46290-9042

NO POSTAGE NECESSARY IF MAILED IN THE UNITED STATES